The Recording Industry

Second Edition

by

Geoffrey P. Hull

Routledge
New York & London

Published in 2004 by
Routledge
29 West 35th Street
New York, NY 10001

Published in Great Britain by
Routledge
11 New Fetter Lane
London EC4P 4EE

10 9 8 7 6 5 4 3 2 1

Library of Congress Cataloging-in-Publication Data

Hull, Geoffrey P.
    The recording industry / by Geoffrey P. Hull. — 2nd ed.
        p. cm.
    Includes bibliographical references (p.   ) and index.
    ISBN 0-415-96802-X (alk. paper) — ISBN 0-415-96803-8 (pbk. : alk. paper)
    1.   Sound recording industry.   2.   Music trade.   I.   Title.
ML3790 .H84 2004
338.4'778149'0973 — dc22

                                                                2003024594

Table of Contents

Introduction

It is to no one's surprise that the recording industry has changed substantially in the more than one hundred years it has been in existence. Edison's "talking machine" was invented in 1877 and first sold to the public in 1889. The Victor Talking Machine Company introduced the world to disc recordings in 1901. In the early days, the record companies made recordings primarily so that people would have a reason to buy the playback machines. As the popularity of the machines and recordings grew into the 1920s, the player manufacturers and others began to sell the recordings as commercial products in and of themselves. The Depression of the 1930s brought about the near collapse of the industry. After World War II those firms that had survived began to experience a new prosperity. Entertainment media in general began to flourish. The marriage of necessity between radio and records of the 1930s became a marriage of convenience in the 1940s and 1950s.

The rock and roll explosion of the mid-1950s energized the industry. Markets expanded. More artists, recordings, and labels appeared overnight. Retail began to grow with distribution through mass merchants at first taking the lead. Then retail chains grew with the growth of shopping malls and the movement toward a service economy in general. FM stereo broadcasting meant more radio stations needed recordings to play, and those recordings being played sounded better than on their AM competitors. The compact disc gave the sound recorded another quantum leap in quality. Sales of recordings continued to reach new heights. Retail stores grew in size and number. More recordings were accessible to more people in more places.

The growth of the industry influenced its structure. Large entertainment conglomerates, operating on an international scale, began to control the bulk of the industry. They acquired different branches of the entertainment industry, including film, television, recordings, consumer electronics, music publishing, and record labels, and in some instances even record retail chains. Broadcasting also began a consolidation as first the Federal Communications Commission, then Congress, relaxed ownership rules allowing more stations to be owned by one entity. In what was generally known as the music business, the influence of recordings became dominant. The sale and marketing of hit and non-hit recordings dominated the music publishing and live entertainment businesses. By the end of the twentieth century, sheet music sales dwindled to about 15 percent of publishing revenues and royalties from the sale of recordings and airplay of those recordings made up the bulk of music publishing earnings. Large tours of major recording artists contributed the bulk of the live entertainment earnings.

Technology has always played a central role in the development of the industry. Developments since the invention of recording have enlarged and enhanced the market for recordings, making higher-quality recordings more accessible to more people. Technological advances on the production end of the process meant that recordings could sound better. Diffusion of high-quality, low-cost recording technology into the semiprofessional market meant that musicians could create recordings and market them without having to have access to the capital and facilities of a major record company. More artists could create and market more recordings. With the advent of the Internet it is now possible for those musicians to market those recordings on a worldwide basis without access to the distribution systems of the major labels. Diffusion of high-quality, low-cost, portable playback equipment meant people could enjoy more music in more places.

By the turn of the twenty-first century, the industry again faced a new technological challenge: the control of its recordings and compositions in a digital era. In 1999 Napster woke the industry from its dream about digital distribution of recordings for pay into the nightmare of digital distribution of millions of illegal copies for free. The industry began legal and technological battles to protect its works. Others began to predict the demise of the industry.

Within a year of publication of the first edition of *The Recording Industry*, two significant events altered the landscape of the music business. First, two of the major labels, PolyGram and Universal, merged. That reduced the number of major labels to five and created the largest recording company in the world, Universal Music Group. Second, Congress passed the Digital Millennium Copyright Act and the Copyright Term Extension Act. These two pieces of legislation, prompted by the growth of the Internet and the increasing importance of copyrights in the international marketplace, marked a new era in the way music and recordings are distributed to consumers. Even as the major record companies and most other segments of the recording industry sought to consolidate to increase market share, there was an explosion of distribution of recordings, both authorized and unauthorized, via the Internet. The amount and diversity of music available to consumers grew rapidly.

The industry is clearly entering a new phase. This new postindustrial phase is characterized by decentralization of the means of recording, reproduction, and distribution. Yet at the same time, there is increasing consolidation in the recording industry itself and in the other media. This book examines the recording industry on the brink of something; exactly what that something is remains to be seen. The examination is from an economic perspective because the most significant changes have been what would be generally described as economic. With due respect to those who prefer a cultural or social perspective, there are other publications that take that approach, and such a perspective is not particularly helpful in understanding how and why the industry functions the way it does. Economics is the key to the importance of the recording industry as an entertainment medium of mass communication. Economics is the key to understanding how the three income streams in the industry—the sale of recordings, music publishing, and live appearances—have become dominated by the recording interests and how those streams are interrelated.

The book begins with an examination of the industry overall, the copyrights on which it relies, and its three primary parts or income streams. Following that it launches into an in-depth discussion of the industry functions of production, marketing, retail, its relation to other media, and its good news/bad news relationship with the Internet. In summary, there are several themes that wind their way through these pages:

- The recording industry is now the dominant force in the music business.
- Technological advances have enhanced the industry's ability to make profits from recordings and songs and made those recordings and songs more accessible to more people.
- Although highly concentrated in four large multinational firms, the industry continues to serve the public through the development and dissemination of more recordings by more artists than ever before. The public is the beneficiary of this diversity.
- The industry continues to change, with even the legal underpinnings of copyright being driven by largely economic considerations, now on a global scale.

A final point: the recording industry would be of paltry significance, indeed, were it not for the ability of music to speak to and excite people through recordings. The creative people who combine words and music into songs, create recorded performances, and perform those songs live speak to us in many ways. Our pleasurable task is to listen to, watch, appreciate, and enjoy their creations.

Acknowledgments

A number of people, places, and organizations have provided invaluable support in the preparation of this book. Industry organizations providing a wealth of information include the National Association of Recording Merchandisers (NARM), the Recording Industry Association of America (RIAA), The National Music Publishers Association (NMPA), the American Federation of Musicians (AFM) Local 257, and the National Association of Music Merchandisers (NAMM). The greatest industry source is *Billboard.* Thanks for reporting over one hundred years of recording and entertainment industry news and events. One must also include more recent publications such as *Pollstar*, and *R&R (Radio & Records)* as important sources of information.

I found a great deal of research support and resources on the campus of Middle Tennessee State University (MTSU). Probably the greatest resource was the Center for Popular Music. Thanks especially to director Paul Wells, and Bruce Nemerov, as well as the rest of the staff of the center. How else could I have found a copy of "Payola Blues" or hundreds of other publications about the recording industry without the center's collection? I don't want to think about it. The Walker Library's *Billboard* and *Variety* collection and its online databases, especially Infotrac, and Lexis–Nexis Academic Universe proved most helpful. MTSU's commitment to fiber optics and computers made surfing the World Wide Web a breeze and brought a wealth of information right to my desktop. Administrative thanks to my department chair, Chris Haseleu, for letting me "do my thing," and to the dean of the College of Mass Communication, Anantha Babbili. Thanks to all my colleagues in the Recording Industry Department for being, well, collegial. My student assistant for the past three years, Lindsay Gum, provided research help, photocopying, a cheerful disposition, and relieved me of some tedious duties so I could focus more on writing. Thanks to Jim Progris, now at the University of Miami, Coral Gables, for deciding that I just might make a college teacher and hiring me as an adjunct faculty member for the Commercial Music/Recording program at Georgia State University back in 1974. Thanks to Ed Kimbrell at MTSU for deciding I just might be able to build a recording industry program at Middle Tennessee State back in 1977.

Just as most recording artists would not be very successful without record companies, most authors would not be very successful without publishers. Al Greco of Fordham University took a chance on asking a not very well-known writer to tackle the recording industry book for Allyn & Bacon. Thanks to Allyn & Bacon for letting me move the second edition to Routledge. Thanks to the Routledge folks, especially Richard Carlin, Executive Editor, Music, for picking up on what I hope will be a good thing for both of us.

Thanks especially to my wife, Patty, for all her support and for putting up with my long hours.

1
Understanding the Recording Industry

Introduction

This chapter describes the recording industry's economic and social place in the United States and the world. It explores the nature of the recording industry as it entered the twenty-first century, including its products and markets, relation to the external environment, and place as a medium of mass communication. The industry can best be understood by examining its three primary income streams: the sale and use of recordings; the sale and use of songs (primarily the music publishing industry); and live entertainment.

> Change is the law of life. And those who look only to the past or the present are certain to miss the future.
>
> — John F. Kennedy[1]

Ch-Ch-Changes

As the recording industry entered the twenty-first century, it appeared to be undergoing another one of the dramatic changes in direction that occur in the industry about every twenty years. A general downturn in the economy affected the recording industry more than at any time since the Great Depression of the 1930s. Downloading of digital recordings via the Internet, both authorized and unauthorized, clearly curtailed sales of the all-important hit recordings. Record stores, buoyed by the apparently insatiable appetite for recordings that occurred in the 1980s and 1990s, had overbuilt and were closing by the scores. Sales of recordings dropped from a high of $14.6 billion in 1999 back to 1996 levels of $12.6 billion and appeared to be heading even lower. The major labels laid off employees, cut rosters, downsized, and even closed divisions at a frantic pace. By 2003 the labels were trying desperately to come up with a business model for successfully distributing recordings via the Internet.

As difficult as the times appeared to be, change was really nothing new to the recording industry. The initial period of introduction and growth began in 1889 with the first commercial musical recordings. The 1909 Copyright Act ushered in the next era by creating the mechanical right for music publishers, setting a statutory limit to royalties paid by labels to publishers, and not providing a sound recording copyright. By 1929 the industry had evolved to a consumer business with sales of about 100 million units ($75 million) of primarily disks. The next period saw the near demise of the industry in the Great Depression of the 1930s and its rebirth in the 1940s and early 1950s. Pent-up postwar consumer demand spurred the sale of playback equipment and recordings. The LP (long playing) and 45-rpm single were introduced. Sales grew back from a mere $5.5 million in 1933 to $189 million in 1950. The next phase began with the mid-1950s with the birth of rock and roll. Younger consumers had more money to spend on recordings that addressed their lifestyles. New labels and new sounds emerged. Sales tripled to about $600 million by 1960. Stereo recording was introduced and the 78-rpm single finally died in 1957. Stereo and the Beatles convinced young consumers that they should buy albums instead of singles. Profits rose and the major distribution system emerged. This phase, a transition to a mass market with heavy concentration lasted until the early 1980s. The introduction of the compact disc (CD) in 1982 drove the industry to new heights for almost twenty more years. Sales grew to $14.6 billion (1.2 billion units) by the end of the century (1999). Labels consolidated and the major recording and entertainment conglomerates of today emerged. Record retail, especially chains, saw unparalleled growth. But twenty years had come and gone and the industry appeared headed into a new era.

The recording industry had experienced dramatic change through the 1980s and 1990s. Significant changes in technology, markets, and organizations made the industry function in a substantially different way than it had during the 1960s and 1970s. To understand how twenty-first-century changes might affect the industry, we will examine both its internal and external structure and function as it existed at the end of the 1990s, and how it began to change in the early 2000s. This chapter and those that follow gather evidence of the changes, explore the reasons for them, and examine their impact on the recording industry.

Rapid Growth of a Major Media Player

The recording industry primarily serves the market for prerecorded musical performances through the sale of compact discs (CDs) and tapes.

However, it is also a significant force in the broadcasting industry, because the majority of the programming content of commercial radio is playback of those same musical sound recordings. Music videos and performances by popular recording acts provide significant content for cable and broadcast television. Hit motion pictures are often enhanced or even propelled by the presence of recordings by major recording artists. Even in the consumer magazine industry the presence of the recording industry is felt through popular publications such as *Rolling Stone, Blender, Spin*, and *Vibe*, which focus on popular music artists and recordings. The music performed by artists made popular through the sales of their recordings is largely responsible for the concert and live music industry. And these are only some of the direct effects. The desire of people to make popular music and become part of the recording industry is the driving force behind the sales of millions of dollars worth of musical instruments every year. The National Association of Music Merchants (NAMM) reports musical products' sales for 2002 of $6.97 billion, out of which less than $1 billion was the school musical instrument market.[2] A Gallup survey conducted for NAMM found that there are about 62 million amateur musicians in the United States (age 5 or over) and that 81 percent of survey respondents felt that music participation was an important part of life.[3] Fifty-four percent of American households have at least one member who plays a musical instrument.[4] Without the recordings produced by the recording industry, consumers certainly would not have purchased an estimated $12.3 billion worth of audio playback hardware in 2001.[5]

Even considering just the sale of prerecorded tapes and discs, the recording industry is a major player in the entertainment and media industries. From 1985 to 2000, recorded music moved from fifth to fourth place in consumer media expenditures, surpassing consumer magazines and daily newspapers, and extending the margin over theatrical motion pictures to nearly two to one. Americans spend an estimated 15.2 percent of their media dollars on recorded music, up from 10.3 percent in 1985 (see Table 1.1).

Adjusting for increases in the consumer price index, the data is still impressive. Americans have been on an entertainment spending binge, and the recording industry, more than any other consumer media except cable, satellite, and home video, is reaping the rewards. Whether the Internet will drain away consumers' media dollars from other media or simply increase them, and the extent to which the use of the Internet for unauthorized downloading will impact the other media, remains to be seen.

More significant, for its cultural impact, is the fact that Americans are now spending more time listening to recorded music. Out of the estimated 3,472 hours per year that the average person spends consuming media, 263 hours (7.6 percent) were spent listening to recordings, more time than on any other media except broadcast television (24.8 percent), cable and

TABLE 1.1 Consumer Spending for Media 1985–2000
Per Person Expenditures (dollars)

Media	1985 Expenditures ($)	2000 Expenditures ($)	1985 in 1984 Dollars *	2000 in 1984 Dollars*	Percent Increase	Percent Increase Constant $
Cable and Satellite	45.43	192.82	42.22	111.97	327.7	165.2
Recorded Music	22.39	62.80	21.31	36.47	180.5	71.1
Daily Newspapers	41.84	53.32	38.88	30.96	27.4	-20.4
Consumer Magazines	25.6	39.5	23.79	22.94	54.3	-3.6
Consumer Books	43.39	77.64	40.32	45.09	78.9	11.8
Home Video[1]	20.43	109.22	18.99	63.43	434.6	234.0
Consumer Internet	—	50.63	—	29.40	—	—
Movies in Theaters	19.13	32.49	17.78	18.87	69.8	6.1
Total	218.22	412.85	202.80	239.29	89.2	18.0

*Consumer Price Index adjustment: 1984 = 100; 1985 = 107.6; 2000 = 172.2.
Source: United States Department of Commerce, Bureau of Statistics. *Statistical Abstract of the United States 2002*: 698.

satellite (22.2 percent), and radio (27.7 percent).[6] And, the content of radio is primarily recorded music.

What Are People Buying?

For the first half of the 1990s the recording industry saw rapid sales growth in terms of number of units shipped and dollar volume of those units. Although the number of units shipped leveled off in the mid-1990s, the dollar volume of those shipments continued to climb, thanks mainly to the continued increase in shipments of the higher-priced compact disc albums and singles relative to the declining shipments of lower-priced cassette albums and singles (see Tables 1.2 and 1.3). The flat sales in total units caused Recording Industry Association of America (RIAA) chairman, Jay Berman, to comment, "It's safe to say that, with rare exceptions, we've pretty much exhausted the catalog-replacement business. What's selling now is what's being released now."[7] (Initially, CD sales were driven by buyers replacing their old LPs with CD reissues; these sales were known as *catalog replacement sales*, as opposed to sales driven by new material.) In 2001 and 2002 sales took a dramatic downturn. A slow economy, the terrorist attacks on September 11, 2001, war in Afghanistan and Iraq, lack of interesting new recordings or stars, and illegal downloading were all blamed. The RIAA saw the main culprit as illegal downloads. "Computer

TABLE 1.2 Sales of Recordings by Configuration, 1990–2002
(Unit Shipments in Millions of Units, Net after Returns)

	1990	1992	1994	1996	1998	2000	2002
Cassette	442.2	366.4	345.4	225.3	158.5	76	31.1
CD	286.5	407.5	662.1	778.9	847	942.5	803.3
LP	11.7	2.3	1.9	2.9	3.4	2.2	1.7
Cass. Single	87.4	84.6	81.1	59.9	26.4	1.3	-0.5
Vinyl Single	27.6	19.8	11.7	10.1	5.4	4.8	4.4
CD Single	1.1	7.3	9.3	43.2	56	34.2	4.5
Music Video (incl. DVD)	9.2	7.6	11.2	16.9	27.2	18.2	14.7
DVD audio	—	—	—	—	—	—	0.4
Total	865.7	895.5	1122.7	1137.2	1124.3	1079.3	859.7

Source: Recording Industry Association of America. www.riaa.com/news/marketingdata/pdf/year_end_2002.pdf. Accessed 1 March 2004.

TABLE 1.3 Dollar Volume of Sales by Configuration
(Based on Manufacturers Suggested List Prices, in $ Millions)

	1990	1992	1994	1996	1998	2000	2002
Cassette	3,472.4	3,116.3	2,976.4	1,905.3	1,419.9	626.0	209.8
CD	3,451.6	5,326.5	8,464.5	9,934.7	11,416.0	13,214.5	12,044.1
LP	86.5	13.5	17.8	36.8	34.0	27.7	20.5
Cass. Single	257.9	298.8	274.9	189.3	94.4	4.6	-1.6
Vinyl Single	94.4	66.4	47.2	47.5	25.7	4.8	24.9
CD Single	6.0	45.1	56.1	184.1	213.2	142.7	19.6
Video	172.3	157.4	231.1	236.1	508.0	281.9	288.4
Total	7,541.1	9,024.0	12,068.0	12,533.8	13,723.5	14,323.0	12,614.2

Source: Recording Industry Association of America. www.riaa.com/news/marketingdata/pdf/year_end_2002.pdf. Accessed 1 March 2004.

users illegally download more than 2.6 billion copyrighted files (mostly songs) every month. At any given moment, approximately four to five million users are online offering an estimated 800 million files for copying through various peer-to-peer networks."[8] Whatever the cause, the dollar volume of sales dropped back to 1996 levels and the unit volume of sales fell back to 1990 levels.

Diverse Musical Tastes

The eclectic nature of the public's taste was reflected in the overall trends in the genres of music purchased. No longer was rock music dominating the sales of recordings as it was in the mid-1980s with nearly 50 percent of all shipments. By 2000 rock had dropped to a share of less than 25 percent, with rap/urban steadily increasing to a close second with just over 21 percent (Figure 1.1). Rap had clearly moved out of urban "hoods" and into American mainstream music.

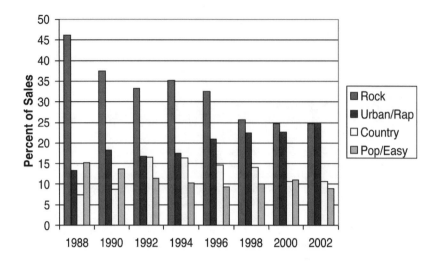

Fig. 1.1 Sales of major genres. Data from the Recording Industry Association of America. www.riaa.com/news/marketingdata/pdf/2002consumerprofile.pdf. Accessed 1 March 2004.

SoundScan (a service that tracks sales of albums through actual purchases) reported that 88 albums sold more than one million copies each in 2000; eighteen of those artists sold more than three million each. The list revealed a wide spectrum of musical genres and Americans' musical tastes. In some instances the recordings sold strongly in select markets. In others they crossed over into the general mainstream market and were purchased by a truly diverse group of people. The list includes teen pop artists, black and white rappers, rock bands, and country crossover sensations (including an all-female group). Urban, dance, and Latin influences also appeared on the list.

In 2000 SoundScan reported that the top 200 albums sold more than 275 million units; all of those top 200 sold more than 500,000 units, about 27 percent of the total album sales for that year. Whereas the albums that sold more than 3 million each accounted for about 26 percent of Sound-Scan's top 200 album sales, they only accounted for about 7 percent of total album sales. That might indicate a trend toward a market that still has some blockbuster albums, but where there are also more albums selling solid numbers of copies to a diverse audience.

Sales by Place of Purchase

Americans became more eclectic in where they purchased their recordings. In the mid-1980s the record store was by far the dominant place where recordings were purchased. By 1995 alternative places for purchasing recordings accounted for nearly as many sales as record stores. By 2000 the record store share had fallen below 50 percent, and in 2002 was surpassed by the "other" category (Figure 1.2). The "other" category includes

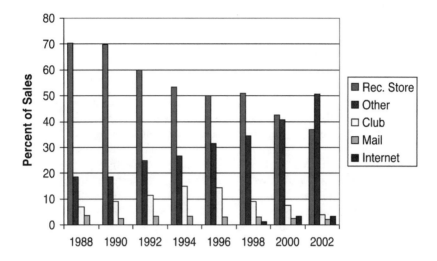

Fig. 1.2 Sales by place of purchase. Data from the Recording Industry Association of America. www.riaa.com/news/marketingdata/pdf/2002consumerprofile.pdf. Accessed 1 March 2004.

department stores, mass merchant discount stores such as Wal-Mart and Kmart, as well as audio and appliance specialty stores such as Best Buy and Circuit City. Meanwhile, the Internet appeared to be taking part of the share of record club and mail order sales.

Record retailing changed. The big chains did not wipe out the independents as predicted. In the mid-1970s, as much as two-thirds of all record sales were through rack locations. (Metal stands or *racks* were used to display records in small retail stores; the people who supplied the records to fill them were known as *rack jobbers*). The typical rack location would handle 500 to 1,000 titles. No wonder the majority of sales were accounted for by only 200 titles. The rapid growth of record store chains in the late 1970s and 1980s meant more recordings could be available to more consumers. The typical store of the times would stock 8,000 to 10,000 titles. In the 1990s the chains discovered they were overbuilt and some major chains, including Wherehouse and Camelot, went into bankruptcy proceedings. The trend had shifted to even larger *megastores* with Tower, HMV, Virgin, and Media Play opening locations with five to ten times the space and inventory of the typical mall retail chain location. The additional space meant that a wider variety of recordings could be carried. Even the rack jobbers began to put in larger locations. The *big box* electronic stores such as Best Buy and Circuit City heavily discounted prices, but also carried larger inventories than rack locations in mass merchandisers. A greater diversity of recordings was available to more people in more places.

Who Buys Recordings?

> A popular music fan is generally wedded to a specific style current
> in the idiom in ... adolescence.
>
> — R. Serge Denisoff, 1975[9]

A 1977 prediction, based on Denisoff's observation and other research at
the time, was that the popular music of the year 2000 would most likely
resemble what could generally be included under the rubric of pop-con-
temporary music of 1977.[10] That music included all categories of rock, but
not middle-of-the-road (MOR), country, or rhythm and blues (R&B). In
1976, 23 percent of adult buyers (ages 25 to 45) preferred country music,[11]
which at that time sounded much less like other pop and rock music than
it did by 1995. The baby boomers entered the over-50 group in significant
numbers in 1996. That group probably grew up liking rock or some music
with a similar feel, and they continued to buy rock in large numbers. However, the music of all races of the next generation became urban and rap,
which suggests its continued presence until some different sound catches
the ear of the next generation. Then we would expect to see urban and rap
decline slowly in market share, just as pop/MOR and rock did for the gen-
erations before.

Consumers of American popular music and recordings are getting
older as a group, and they are still consuming. Figure 1.3 illustrates the
dramatic shift in the percentage of recordings purchased by consumers of
various age brackets over the years from 1990 to 2002. In 1990, over 42
percent of the consumers were under age 25, and just under 20 percent
over the age of 40. By 1995 the under-25 group had dropped to 40 percent
and the 40-and-over group had grown to 24.4 percent. By 2002 the change
was even more dramatic, with the under-25 group only consuming 33.7
percent of recordings sold while the 40-and-over group had surpassed
them with 35.4 percent of sales. The data in Table 1.4 show that this trend,
especially in the 45-and-over group, had been consistent for some time.
Fortunately for the recording industry, the dire predictions made in 1977
that the baby boomers would quit buying music as they aged proved to be incor-
rect. As a result, the industry was no longer a youth or teen-dominated market.
In order to be effective, the recording companies had to appeal to a wider range
of age groups. Even though the groups with the highest per capita expenditures
for recordings continued to be the teen (13 to 17) and college (18 to 25) age
groups, purchasing an average of 6.6 and 5.6 units per year respectively, the older
buyers represented a much larger percentage of the population than the younger
buyers. And, the younger buyers were the heaviest downloaders, so they made
fewer purchases than in the past. A survey done for NARM in 2002 found that
over 70 percent of heavy downloaders were under 25 and that two-thirds of
them were male; this had traditionally been the heaviest music buying
audience.[12]

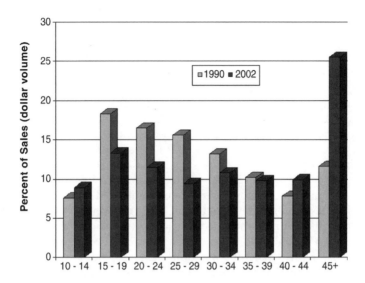

Fig. 1.3 Shift in age of record buyers, 1990–2002. Data from Recording Industry Association of America.

TABLE 1.4 Sales by Age of Consumers (Percent of Dollar Volume)

Age	1990	1992	1994	1996	1998	2000	2002
10–14	7.6	8.6	7.9	7.9	9.1	8.5	8.9
15–19	18.3	18.2	16.8	17.2	15.8	12.9	13.3
20–24	16.5	16.1	15.4	15.0	12.2	12.5	11.5
25–29	14.6	13.8	12.6	12.5	11.4	10.6	9.4
30–34	13.2	12.2	11.8	11.4	11.4	9.8	10.8
35–39	10.2	10.9	11.5	11.1	12.6	10.6	9.8
40–44	7.8	7.4	7.9	9.1	8.3	9.6	9.9
45+	11.6	12.9	16.1	15.1	18.1	23.8	25.5

Source: Recording Industry Association of America. There is an inexplicable conflict in the RIAA reported data in consumer profiles 1993 and earlier and 1994 and later. The data in the table are the figures reported in 1994 and 1995.

International Aspects of the Recording Industry

It's probably fair to say that music is the most universal means of communication we now have, instantly traversing language and other cultural barriers in a way that academics rarely understand. ... [P]opular music is certainly the most global aspect of our "global village."

— Robert Burnett, The Global Jukebox[13]

The recording industry does not exist in isolation in the United States. Of the four major labels/distribution companies, none is based in the United States. Though the United States accounted for almost 40 percent of the dollar volume of worldwide sales in 2001, it accounted for a smaller share, about 30 percent, of the unit sales volume that same year. Sales of the five major companies accounted for about 72 percent of worldwide sales for 1999 through 2001, but that did mean that independent labels accounted for about 28 percent of worldwide sales during that time period. That's a stronger showing by independents on a worldwide basis than in the United States where independent labels account for only about 15 percent share over the same period.[14]

The International Federation of Phonographic Industries (IFPI) reported significant worldwide trends that mirrored many of those in the United States. In many music markets, older consumers were accounting for increasingly larger shares of music consumption. This was seen as being due to several factors: (1) replacement of old vinyl and tape collections with CDs, (2) general population demographics in many developed nations have shifted to older age groups, and (3) the fact that downloading and burning are more prevalent in younger demographics.

While the majors accounted for about 70 percent of worldwide sales, significant portions of those sales were domestic products in many countries. That is important because it indicates that the United States is not necessarily engaged in culturally dominating the world's music industry. The mix of sales varied by region, as indicated in Table 1.5, and even more dramatically by country. India, Pakistan, and the United States all reported sales of domestic products exceeded 90 percent of sales revenues in 2001. Many nations—for example China, France, South Korea, and Argentina—reported strong sales of local repertoire in the neighborhood of 40 to 60 percent of sales revenues.[15]

Finally, technological developments at the end of the twentieth century had a negative impact on the global market for recordings. The IFPI estimated that worldwide piracy had increased from a dollar value of about $2.1 billion in 1995 to over $4.2 billion in 2000. That meant that more than one-third of all sales of recorded music were pirate copies. That total included an estimated 1.2 billion cassettes, 475 million pressed CDs, and 165 million CD-Rs. As in the United States, the market for pirate cassettes is declining. However, the increased presence of CD-Rs in computers all over the world did not bode well for the efforts of the recording industry to stem the tide of pirate copies. By 2002 the breakdown of pirate sales was roughly 40 percent cassette, 32 percent pressed CD, and 28 percent CD-R.[16] The nations with the highest percentage of pirate sales were China and Russia. China's sales of pirate recordings accounted for 90 percent of all sales ($600 million), while 65 percent of all sales in Russia were pirate recordings ($240 million). The IFPI noted that there were twenty-one nations with piracy rates of over 50 percent in the year 2000.[17]

TABLE 1.5 Domestic Repertoire Sales Percentages (Five-Year Average, 1997–2001)

	Domestic	International	Classical
North America	86.9	9.7	3.4
Western Europe	40.7	51.9	7.4
Eastern Europe	54.8	40.8	4.4
Asia	74.1	25	0.9
Latin America	54.6	43.2	2.2
Australasia	19.7	75.4	4.9
Africa	23.8	71.7	4.5
Total Worldwide	66.7	29.2	4.1

Source: International Federation of Phonographic Industries.

In addition to pirate sales, the IFPI reported that downloading of "free" music was having a negative impact on legitimate sales worldwide. A survey in Sweden reported that younger consumers were spending less on CDs, and that downloading, burning, and having less money to spend were the primary reasons. A Canadian survey revealed that those spending less on music most often cited downloading and CD burning (30 percent) or less money to spend (27 percent) as the reasons. The IFPI estimated that there were some 500 million music files available for unauthorized downloading on the three main peer-to-peer networks, KaZaA, iMesh, and Gnutella, in 2002.[18]

Ways of Understanding the Recording Industry

There are several useful models for examining the recording industry. *Systems theory* is useful for exploring the industry on a macro scale, its relations to the business environment, and overall processes. *Cultural theory* is of some use in examining the relationship of the outputs of the industry, recordings and popular music, to society. *Economics*, and the *three-income stream model*, is most useful in examining the inner workings of the industry and its components.

A Systems Approach

Systems theory is a business management tool used to develop an understanding of how an enterprise must function. Systems theory stresses that there are five components of any business system: (1) inputs, (2) some transformation process, (3) outputs (the products which are the results of the transformation process), (4) a feedback process that will influence the selection of inputs into the next round of processing, and (5) an external environment within which the organization carries out its processes.[19] Viewing the recording industry in this manner, one would conclude that the inputs are songs, musicians, engineers, producers, studios, plastic, paper, performances, and technology. The transformation processes are

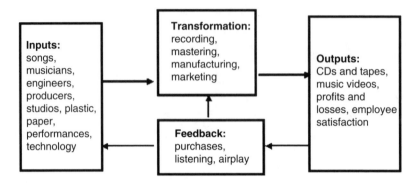

Fig. 1.4. A systems view of the recording industry.

the recording of masters, duplicating of the masters into CDs and tapes, and marketing. Outputs of the recording industry are CDs and other recorded configurations as products and as cultural artifacts, profits and losses for the owners, and employee (including the artists and writers) satisfaction. Feedback occurs primarily through purchases by consumers of recordings and live performances, and listening to or viewing the broadcast media. The external environment contains the social, political, legal, and economic forces that exist outside of the organization (see Figure 1.4). Another key concept in systems analysis is that of the *closed* or *open system*. A closed system does not need to interact with the environment to survive, an open system must. From that perspective, the recording industry is an open system because of its dependence on popular tastes and culture for its market. A final systems concept, *entropy*, refers to the tendency of any organized system to eventually decay into disorganization. If a business does not receive new energy from its environment and inputs, it will cease to exist. The recording industry must constantly seek new creative inputs from the artists and songwriters or it will stagnate. The entropy concept has been used to explain that more product diversity is associated with more entropy in the music industry.[20] Which is to suggest that a less highly structured industry with more independent labels and alternative distribution means is more likely to be accompanied with a greater diversity of recorded product for consumers. This is not, however, saying that a highly structured industry causes a lack of diversity.

The External Environment

The external environment is extremely important to the recording industry. Its products are largely consumed on the basis of taste preferences. As the tastes and desires of the consumers change the record company must be aware and alter its products. The history of the industry is full of examples where a particular label or even the entire industry failed to keep in touch with consumer tastes. Probably the most famous example is the birth and growth of the popularity of rock and roll when the major labels of the day either did not even know it existed, or chose to ignore it. Keeping up with consumer tastes and new trends in music is one job of the artist and repertoire (A&R) department of a label. The A&R department is also charged with finding new creative inputs in terms of songs and performers. If the A&R department has too many failures, the label will be in serious danger of dying. Chapter 7 discusses the A&R function in detail.

Society

Popular music, the mainstay of the recording industry, clearly interfaces with society. It both influences society and is influenced by it. The depth of that influence is highly debatable. Certainly it influences fashion of dress when recording artists appear on stage or in videos in certain attire, such as when pre- and early-teen girls imitated Madonna's style of dress.[21] Social themes are often mirrored in the music, either because that makes the music more acceptable to people or because the recording artist wants to convey a viewpoint on those themes. Did Ozzy Osbourne's recording "Suicide Solution" *cause* some teens to commit suicide or did it *reflect* the despair that some teens felt drove them to commit suicide?[22] Recording artists attempt to engage in social dialog with consumers through their songs and recordings, and sometimes cause social controversies. However, most researchers have concluded that the relationships between popular music, its performers, and consumers, are complex and not easily reduced to simple statements.[23] For instance, was Madonna in the mid- and late 1980s suggesting that girls should become "Boy Toys" or was she instilling a new sense of liberation for young women?[24] Popular music researcher Simon Frith concludes, "The political meaning of *all* popular music … is a matter of negotiation."[25]

Prerecorded music has become a significant component of nearly everyone's life. Half or more of the adult population purchases recorded music every year; that is a much higher percentage than those who vote in elections. Americans spend more time listening to recordings than they do consuming any other medium except television (broadcast, cable, and home video). Recorded music provides opportunities and frameworks for social interchange and expression through dance and karaoke. Respondents in one national survey rated the importance of music in their lives as

6.96 on a ten-point scale; music buyers rated it a 7.89 and classical music buyers a 10.00.[26]

International trade agreements such as North American Free Trade Agreement (NAFTA) and the World Trade Organization (WTO) take into consideration the free exchange of cultural products such as recordings and movies. They cause nations to discuss and debate the cultural impact of outside cultural products on the local culture. They provide protection for the copyrights embodied in these cultural products on a global basis so that the very same nations that complain of cultural imperialism cannot steal the work of artists, writers, and producers and sell it as pirate merchandise around the world.

Political Environment

Usually the political environment is not as important to the recording industry as other external factors. However, every now and then it becomes extremely important. The political/social reactions against rock and roll in the late 1950s brought about the payola scandal and caused serious economic losses for a number of industry figures at the time, most notably Alan Freed and Dick Clark. Many elements of the peace movement during the late 1960s found expression in popular music. The political establishment reacted by attacking popular music that had drug-related lyrics.

In the late 1980s there was a political reaction to violence and profanity in lyrics and music videos. This led to the formation of the Parents Music Resource Center backed by Tipper Gore (the wife of then-Senator Al Gore).[27] Congressional hearings ultimately led the industry to self-regulate and begin identifying some recordings with a warning label that said "Parental Advisory Explicit Content." Prior to the labeling program, some states passed laws forbidding the sale of material "harmful to persons under eighteen" and some sales clerks in retail stores were even arrested. [28] Later some states sought to prohibit the sale of recordings with parental advisory labels to minors. Some stores stopped carrying recordings by artists such as rap act 2 Live Crew and others. One retailer said, "We're not trying to play God, promote censorship, or anything like that. We're just looking out for our image."[29] As late as 2003 the National Association of Recording Merchandisers (NARM) and the RIAA were still promoting awareness of the parental advisory labeling program.[30] At the same time, these two organizations successfully lobbied against passage of some state obscenity laws designed to prohibit sale of "parental advisory" albums to minors.[31]

Similar concerns were raised about Death Metal acts such as Judas Priest, which successfully fought a lawsuit claiming that a subliminal message of "do it, do it" in one of their songs caused two men (eighteen and twenty years old) to commit suicide after listening to the album.[32] The overall significance of these attacks on popular music is debatable. Communication researchers DeFleur and Dennis conclude, "A number of popular music forms have been charged with being the cause of moral collapse when they came on the scene, yet our society has somehow held together. Undoubtedly it will survive whatever is in store."[33]

Legal Environment

The legal environment of the recording industry is similar to that of most businesses in terms of labor laws, environmental regulations, and tax laws. Copyright law, however, is a special legal environment that conveys significant benefits for the industry. It enables the industry to protect its main outputs, songs and recordings, from unauthorized duplication, thereby helping to insure profitability. Copyright (or at least a related right) enables performers to protect their live performances from unauthorized recording, distribution, or unauthorized broadcast. Payola laws limit the extent of control that the labels have over a very important avenue of promotion: radio airplay. Antitrust laws and regulations limit the industry's attempts to control prices and may limit consolidation. International trade treaties protect audio and video recordings throughout the world. Chapters 2 and 3 discuss the copyright environment of the recording industry in detail.

Economic Environment

The overall economy is also important to the recording industry. It is a leisure-time industry, relying on the use of discretionary income from consumers for the purchases of recordings and live performance tickets. In times of serious economic downturn, when people have less discretionary income, the sale of recordings declines. The National Music Publishers' Association (NMPA) observed the importance of the overall economy to the recording industry internationally. In the NMPA's first International Survey of Music Publishing Revenues, a statistical analysis of the data indicated that music publishing revenues were probably more sensitive to per capita GNP than to age or population.[34] During the depression in the 1930s in the United States, the record industry survived, barely, on performance revenues from radio airplay and on the sale of recordings to jukeboxes. At the end of the twentieth century an economic downturn, combined with rampant downloading, spelled hard times for many of the labels and artists.

The world economy is moving in many areas from international to *transnational*. There is not just a market in France and a market in Brazil and a market in China; there is a global market and individual submarkets. Management guru and futurist Peter Drucker tells us, "[T]he goal of management in a transnational enterprise that operates in one world market is *maximization of market share*, not the traditional short-term 'profit maximization' of the old-style corporation."[35] What we used to call the "majors," those record labels that owned their own distribution systems, have realized this. Five international entertainment powerhouses are rapidly dividing up the world recording market. The IFPI estimated 2001 market shares as follows: Universal, 23.5 percent; Sony, 14.7 percent; EMI 13 percent; Warner, 11.8 percent; and BMG 8.2 percent.[36] As noted earlier, independent labels garnered about 29 percent of the world's market for recordings. However, the *big five* were buying out independent labels in countries all over the world, and were creating partnerships in manufacturing and distribution on a global basis.

Media economist Harold Vogel attributes this need for large distribution systems to high wastage (many products will not succeed) and short life cycles of hit recordings (usually less than a year). He says, "[B]ecause efficiency in this area requires that retailers located over a wide geographic swath have their inventories quickly replenished, most records are distributed by large organizations with sufficient capital to stock and ship hundreds of thousands of units at a moments notice."[37] The major entertainment conglomerates are selling recordings from their different labels and from the local labels all over the world. They were integrating horizontally and vertically, controlling more music publishing, film production, television production, audio and video hardware manufacturing, and radio, television, and cable broadcasting. They had learned that there is money to be made in many small successes, not just blockbuster hits. There is good reason to own a label that sells gospel music or new age music even though those recordings may sell less than 100 thousand units because they can be profitable sales. They were willing to let people who know the markets for that kind of music make the creative and production decisions while they (the big five) handled the distribution.

Even from a micro perspective, examining only recording industry organizations and structures, one cannot help but be struck by the fact that the industry's functioning is influenced by other industries and society. The most notable such interface is with broadcasting—particularly radio, and to a lesser extent, television. These are the two primary means that the recording industry uses to promote its products to potential consumers. Because the industry produces a cultural product, it is particularly susceptible to influences from the rest of society, and in turn influences the rest of society.

Radio changed. No longer does Top 40 airplay dominate the promotion and sale of all recordings. From 1986 to 1995, the number of radio stations reporting predominantly music formats increased by more than 2,000, and the number of different formats reported nearly doubled, going from 12 to 23.[38] The two major radio tip sheets, *Radio & Records* (*R&R*) and *Gavin*, more than doubled the number of airplay charts reported over that same period: *Gavin* went from five charts in 1986 to thirteen in 1996, and *R&R* went from six in 1986 to fifteen in 1996 to twenty by 2003. (*Gavin* ceased publication in 2002.) Even as concentration of radio station ownership increased in 1990s at a mind-numbing rate after the deregulation of ownership rules with the Communications Act of 1996, broadcasting executives were predicting further diversity in radio formats. (Chapter 10 examines the relationship of the recording and broadcast industries in detail.) There were conflicting studies as to whether all these changes resulted in a greater diversity of music available to be heard by more people.

Technology and the Recording Industry System

The recording industry owes its existence to technology. Refinements and advances in technology have affected all parts of the system. On the input side, it is easier for more musicians and writers to make high-quality recordings. In the transformation process, sophisticated control over recording and advances in reproduction have made more product available at lower production costs and enabled more sophisticated and lower cost distribution of that product. More methods of exposure are available thanks to cable and satellite television, home video, and the Internet. On the output side, the availability of high-quality and lower-cost playback systems has stimulated demand. The feedback loop has improved with more accurate and faster data-gathering mechanisms.

What Thomas Edison did not know is that his "talking machine" invention in 1877 would lay the groundwork for a "music machine." Emile Berliner's disc recording system made this even more likely because the original recordings were easier to replicate into copies, thereby opening up much greater possibility for a mass-produced item for the general population. Advances in player and recording technology through the 1940s made the music reproduced even more lifelike. Stereo proved that consumers wanted their music to sound even better and more like a real performance. Cassette tapes made music even more portable so that it could go with Americans in their ubiquitous automobiles, even without playing it on the radio. Smaller amplifiers and players soon meant that prerecorded music could go with the listener to the beach, for a jog, for a walk in the park, or to the gymnasium for a workout. The compact disc and digital recording propelled the quality of sound available and the ease of use and durability to higher levels. Digital transmission and the Internet made new delivery systems possible so that people have an almost bewildering diversity of recordings to choose from. Reductions in the costs of manufacturing recordings and in the playback systems led to further market penetration for the players and the recordings. High-quality, inexpensive recordings and playback systems were within the reach of nearly everybody. The subsequent increase in demand for recordings infused the industry with more revenues and made an even greater diversity of product available. Large labels could afford to take more chances on a wider variety of artists. Small labels could find new artists with niche or emerging markets, make smaller investments, and still earn a profit on a relatively small sales base.

The same digital technology that created the CD and the Internet delivery systems also proved a curse for the industry. Every hour of every day hundreds of thousands of music fans illegally downloaded copies of their favorite recordings from a variety of peer-to-peer networks. While the labels struggled to make paid downloads a profitable venture, they fought the free, unauthorized downloads with a barrage of lawsuits (see Chapter 11 for details).

The electronic revolution also had a significant impact on the creative inputs for the industry. As the sophistication of home recording equipment improved, it became possible for creative musicians and writers to have more control over the process of recording. Digital quality recordings could be made in small studios. MIDI (Musical Instrument Digital Interface) and synthesis gave musicians and writers nearly total control over the creation of complex musical arrangements and works. Lower production costs meant that more people could make music and market it. With digital delivery, any musician capable of making a recording could at least get that recording out on the World Wide Web for people to hear if they want to. Stand-alone and computer CD burners made the replication of very small numbers of CD copies practical for almost any musician—or pirate.

Electronic data-gathering mechanisms improved market research for record companies, broadcasters, music publishers, record distributors, and retailers. The Universal Product Code led to better inventory management systems for retailers and distributors. Ultimately, the SoundScan system of gathering sales information on a national basis allowed the development of sophisticated marketing plans and test marketing. Broadcast Data Systems' electronic monitoring of radio and television stations led to more accurate airplay information for labels and performing rights organizations.

The Recording Industry as a Mass Medium

Popular music, the primary content of the recording media, can be partially understood as communication and the recording industry as a mass medium. The main activity of the recording industry is the production and distribution of symbolic content to widely dispersed heterogeneous audiences. It uses several technologies to do this, including digital recording and reproduction, analog recording and reproduction, video recording and reproduction, and the Internet. Media theorist Dennis McQuail characterized the recording industry as a medium having:

- multiple technologies of recording and dissemination: there are digital and analog recording technologies from home recording to professional recording and dissemination means including mail, record stores, and downloads, with thousands of locations where recordings may be obtained.
- low degree of regulation: the Federal Trade Commission regulates this industry the same as any other industry. There is no licensing like there is for broadcasting.
- high degree of internationalization: the five major recording companies reside in different countries and local companies reside in virtually every nation.
- younger audience: the heaviest consumers have traditionally been fifteen to twenty-four years old.
- subversive potential: the industry and artists are frequent subjects of attack for perceived contribution to delinquency, encouragement of drug use, "un-American" activities, and more.
- organizational fragmentation: although distribution is controlled by five major firms, there are hundreds (if not thousands) of individual labels that appear to function autonomously.
- diversity of reception possibilities: recordings may be heard through radio, broadcast television, cable, the Internet, and satellite.[39]

This would appear to be a fair characterization except, as noted earlier, the nature of the audience, at least those who purchase recordings, appears to be growing older.

Popular music communicates in many ways—some intended by the artist and songwriter, some not. Consumers form social groups based on their likes and dislikes of certain genres or artists. Some music is consumed privately to soothe ravaged psyches or to excite them. Music may be used for social activities such as dancing. Music communicates through physical activities, cognitive activities, and emotion. Popular culture analysts continue to comment on its power; James Lull writes, "Music promotes experiences of the extreme for its makers and listeners, turning the perilous emotional edges, vulnerabilities, triumphs, celebrations, and antagonisms of life into hypnotic, reflective tempos that can be experienced privately or shared with others."[40] Similarly, Richard Campbell comments, "The music that helps to shape our identities and comfort us during the transition from childhood to adulthood resonates throughout our lives."[41]

It is clear that music and recordings fit a model of communication that allows for different meanings to be constructed by the message sender(s) and receiver(s). This model also includes gatekeepers: individuals through whom the intended message must pass on its way to the receiver. The gatekeeper "determines what information is passed and how faithfully it is reproduced."[42] An early application of this model focused on radio programmers as gatekeepers.[43] Some consider gatekeepers to be only those who mediate between the industry and its consumers. From a broader perspective, if the sender is the artist and the receiver is the listener or consumer, then there are other gatekeepers as well. If the artist is not also the songwriter, then the writer must get through the music publisher's gate; the publisher must get through the producer's gate; the producer must get through the label A&R department's gate; and the recording must get through the radio and video gates, unless those gates can be held open with payola or through agreements that the programmer will play certain cuts. The retailer keeps gates as well, deciding what recordings to stock, how many to stock, and whether to feature a particular recording. The rack jobber keeps a relatively small gate, only letting through the hits that could sell in large quantity through fairly small record departments in mass-merchandise chains.

Gatekeeper theory is useful in explaining the desire of the various players to use any device they can to keep the gates open so their communication can pass. The problem with this approach is that it tends to assume that the gatekeepers care *which* recordings pass through the gates. A given label does not care which of its recordings become hits, unless they have invested substantial amounts in some superstar artist. It takes *some* hits to sustain a large label, but not usually any particular hit. A small label that has a small roster of artists who make recordings on small budgets may not need hits as much as it needs consistent sales in order to survive. Dedication to the music and sufficient sales may be enough.[44] Radio stations program recordings they think their listeners will like, or at least not dislike, but that is usually without regard to the artist or label. Retailers care that they sell recordings, but as long as the profit on any two given albums is equal, it does not really matter which one a customer purchases. If one considers the artist or songwriter as the communicator, then they are so far removed from most of the gatekeepers that they have little contact or influence.

The Three Income Streams Model

While all of these viewpoints shed some light on the functions of the recording industry, it can best be understood in terms of an economic model. Media economist Alan Albarran notes that, "[T]he study of media economics is the most important [method], in that the ability to attract revenues (and ultimately profits) enables different producers to continue to operate in media markets."[45] At the heart of that economic model are three streams of income, generated through the utilization of a song, a particular recorded performance of that song, and live performances of that song (see Figure 1.5). At the head of each income stream is a creative act: a song is written, a recording is produced, a live performance given. These creative acts give rise to legal rights associated with them. The songwriter's creative act results in copyright in a musical composition. The record label's, producer's, and recording artist's creative acts result in copyrights in the sound recording. Performers have a right to keep others from recording or broadcasting a performance. Three distinct legal rights, three distinct creative acts, and three distinct treatments of a song produce three distinct income streams. While one might argue that "the song is the thing" because it is included in all three streams, it is really the recording that provides most of the drive for the cash flows in all three streams.

Focusing on these three streams is more inclusive than following three streams of royalties—one from the sale of recordings, one from the sale of music, and one from the performance of music—because it includes the live performance of the artist. That live performance is a revenue-generating act for the artist aside from whether it generates any royalties for the music publisher.[46] Including live performance as an income stream also brings it under the general rubric of the recording industry, which is certainly correct because the existence of popular recording artists and their performances accounts for most of the revenues generated in that stream. Finally, including the live performance stream accounts for more points of interconnection between the various streams and leads to the development of a more complete model. It is the presence of the cash flow that drives the major players in the industry to seek control over and participate in all three income streams: not a conscious or unconscious desire to foist any particular kind or quality of music on the consuming public.

Who's Who in the Recording Industry

Before making a model, one is always advised by the instructions to check the parts list to be sure that everything is included. Understanding each component is crucial before attempting to assemble the finished product. For that reason, the basic function of all of the players in each of the three income streams is defined below. The order is that in which they appear in the income stream in Figure 1.5. The simplicity of some of these definitions belies the complex relationships often established by some individuals wearing more than one functional hat in the industry.

The Recordings Stream

- *Recording artists:* Sometimes referred to as *royalty artists,* these are the people who perform for recordings by playing instruments and/ or singing a particular performance that is recorded. The recording artist may or may not be a live performing artist, and may or may not be a songwriter. Most recording artists make money from the income stream by getting a royalty payment based on the sales of copies of the recordings that they make.

- *Record labels*: These organizations employ artists to make recordings that they hope to market in some way to the public. They usually sign the artist to a recording contract promising to pay the artist a royalty for recordings sold in return for the artist's promise to record exclusively for that particular label.
- *Record producers*: These individuals are in charge of the process of creating the recording. They assist the artists by helping select material, studios, and assistants, and by helping the artists give their best performance. They assist the labels by taking care of the business aspects of the recording process and by delivering a marketable product.
- *Side musicians/vocalists:* These performers usually work on a per-job basis for the artist or producer to help create the desired recording. They are to be distinguished from the recording artists because side musicians do not generally receive royalties from the sale of recordings.
- *Recording engineers*: These individuals assist the producer and artist by running the equipment necessary first to capture the performance on tape (or some other medium), and then to shape the final sound that the artist and producer ultimately want on the recording.
- *Record manufacturers*: Often (but not necessarily) the same as the label, manufacturers make copies of the recordings suitable for sale in some manner to the ultimate consumers.
- *Distributors*: This segment of the industry handles copies of the recordings so that they can be conveyed to the end-user for purchase. For the most part, distributors wholesale the copies of the recordings made by the manufacturers to the retailers.
- *Merchandisers*: Retailers that sell copies of the recordings to the consuming public.
- *The public*: In this income stream, this is the record-buying public. This may be a different segment of the public than those who buy tickets to live performances or listen to broadcasts.

The Songwriting Stream

- *Songwriters* (including composers and lyricists): These people write songs.
- *Music publishers*: Publishers acquire rights to songs from songwriters and then license the uses of those songs. Most music publishers sign songwriters to contracts agreeing to pay the writer a share of the royalties that the publisher makes from licensing the uses of the song.
- *Performing rights organizations*: Such organizations license broadcasters and others to perform songs, either live or from recordings.
- *Broadcasters*: These media play recordings of the songs or broadcast live performances of the songs. This term includes regular television

and radio broadcasters as well as cable, satellite, and Internet transmitters.

- *The public (for the broadcasters)*: People listen and watch, usually with no charge other than serving as an audience for the broadcaster's advertising messages.
- *Other media*: They create movies, print sheet music and song books, make recordings, and utilize the songs in other ways that create royalties for the publisher and songwriter.
- *The public (for the other media)*: People watch and buy these other uses of the songs.

The Live Appearances Stream

- *Musicians and singers*: These artists perform live primarily in concerts, in nightclubs, on television, and on radio. Not all live performers are recording artists, though most aspire to be, and not all recording artists are live performers, though most need to be.
- *Personal managers*: These people assist artists in the development and coordination of their careers as performing artists and as recording artists. They are located in this income stream because most of their day-to-day functions revolve around live appearances, not around recordings.
- *Talent agents* (also known as booking agents): Agents book live appearances for performers.
- *Promoters*: They put on live appearances by performers by arranging for the performer, the venue, the date, the production, and the marketing of the performance.
- *Venues*: These are the places for live appearances by artists, including clubs, concert halls, arenas, and stadiums.
- *The public*: These consumers purchase tickets to, or otherwise attend, live artist performances.

The existence of the music publishing and live performance streams is important to the recording industry because the labels often have an economic stake in these other two streams. All of the major record industry conglomerates, and many individual labels, producers, and artists, have publishing interests. Live performance is the crucible in which many new acts are formed. It may be an important medium to expose the public to the artists and their sound in order to promote the sale of recordings. Live performance may keep an artist's catalog of recordings selling long after the artist's recording career has peaked.

Figure 1.5 illustrates the most simplistic depiction of these three income streams. Each stream has its own creative input from an initial source: a recording artist, a songwriter, or a performing artist. Each stream ultimately ends up with the public consuming the output of the stream:

Live Appearances   Recordings   Songwriters

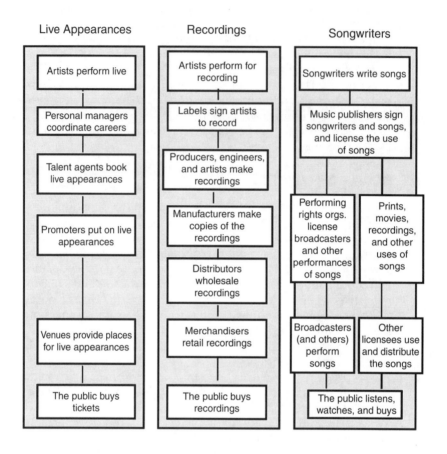

Fig. 1.5 Three income streams model of the recording industry.

the recording, the song, or the live appearance. Each stream has a primary control point through which the creative input is channeled; the record label, the music publisher, and the personal manager. Each stream has a place (a record store, a favorite broadcast station, or a concert hall) where the public has the opportunity to interface with the stream and cast an economic vote for their favorite music with their purchases or attention. Each stream has other parties between the creative person and the public who seek to profit from the income generated in the particular stream by performing some function useful to completion of the flow of that stream.

Perhaps most significantly, it is the public participation in each stream that generates the income. Unless the public buys concert tickets or attends clubs and purchases food and drink, there is no source of revenue for the live appearance stream. Unless the public buys copies of recordings

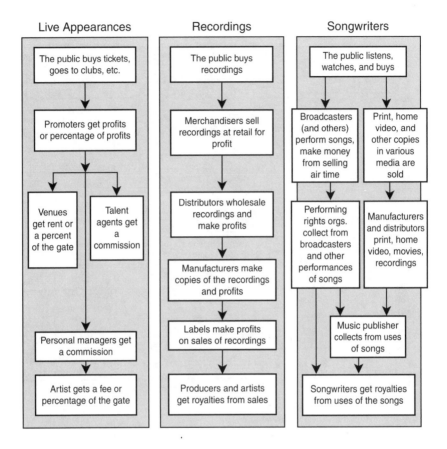

Fig. 1.6 Three income streams—cash flow model.

there is little revenue generated in the recordings stream. Unless the public either consumes the actual products (such as sheet music or recordings), or attends movies, or provides an audience for the advertisers on radio or television, there is little or no money in the songwriting stream. It is also the public that is the target in the communications model discussed earlier. Figure 1.6 illustrates the income flow down in each stream.

Three Income Streams the Hard Way

In order for a player in any stream to maximize security and profitability, participation in the other two streams is necessary. Figure 1.7 illustrates some of the many additional monetary and legal connections that exist between the various streams. The relationships between the three streams are examined in detail in Chapters 4, 5, and 6.

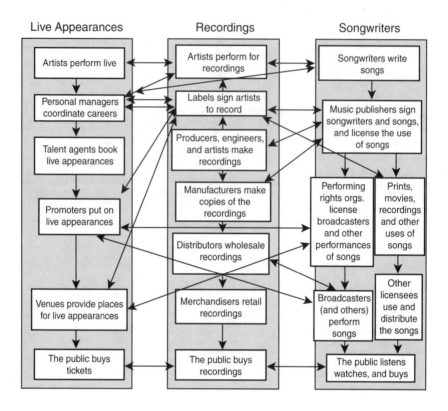

Fig. 1.7 Three income streams—connected.

Summary

The recording industry has become an important player in the mass media in the United States and around the world. It creates and markets recordings that become significant parts of popular culture and that form important parts of the content of radio, television, motion pictures, and live entertainment, as well as being cultural artifacts of their own. Considered from an economic standpoint, the industry consists of three main revenue streams generated by the recordings and those who perform them: music publishing, live entertainment, and the record companies themselves. Each of these components and its relationships to the other components is best understood when examined from an economic and historical context. How each stream operates and why are the questions examined in the next five chapters: one for each stream, and two to lay the groundwork in copyright law, without which the publishing and recording streams—and arguably the live entertainment stream—would be in jeopardy.

2
Copyright Basics in the Recording Industry

Copyrights are very important to the recording industry and to the economy of the United States as a whole. The *copyright industries* (theatrical films, TV programs, home video, DVDs, business and entertainment software, books, music and sound recordings) account for over 5 percent of the total U.S. economy (Gross Domestic Product), employ nearly 5 million workers, and comprise one of the nations largest exports.[1] Chapters 2 and 3, though not intended to be a complete summary of copyright law, address its basics as they apply to the recording industry and a number of specific copyright law provisions and issues of great importance to the recording industry.

Introduction

The recording industry runs on its copyrights. Songwriters create copyrightable songs to be performed by recording artists. Recording artists perform for recording sessions and for live events. Record companies capture the performances of artists and producers in copyrightable sound recordings. All of these products are rather ephemeral and difficult to control. An unauthorized performance of a song takes place in a club in Wyoming; a peer-to-peer file sharer posts an MP3 copy of a recording on the network; a pirate makes CD copies on a bank of twenty CD burners in his or her garage and sells them at flea markets.

Historically, the recording industry has been particularly prone to utilizing legal methods in attempts to gain control over the production, supply, distribution, and income generated by its products in each of the three streams. A performing rights organization attempts to license the club in Wyoming; if the club does not buy a license, it is sued for copyright infringement. Record labels attempt to shut down illegal peer-to-peer networks and even individual users. The record labels or music publishers may ask the Justice Department to indict the pirate for criminal copyright infringement. Without the protection against unauthorized use of recordings and songs, two of the three income streams (sound recordings and music publishing) would be mere shadows of their current size.

The Purpose of Copyright Law

Copyright law exists in the United States as a vehicle to encourage the creation of more literary and artistic works for the general benefit of society. By providing certain rights in their works the law makes it possible for the authors of those works to make a living, and thereby encourages them to create more works for the benefit of society at large. As the U.S. Supreme Court put it:

> The copyright law, like the patent statutes, makes reward to the owner a secondary consideration. However, it is "intended definitely to grant valuable, enforceable rights to authors, publishers, etc., without burdensome requirements; 'to afford greater encouragement to the production of literary [or artistic] works of lasting benefit to the world.' The economic philosophy behind the clause empowering Congress to grant patents and copyrights is the conviction that encouragement of individual effort by personal gain is the best way to advance public welfare through the talents of authors and inventors in 'Science and useful Arts.' Sacrificial days devoted to such creative activities deserve rewards commensurate with the services rendered." [citations omitted][2]

This passage recognizes that there are really three interest groups, or communities, that are concerned with and potentially benefit from copyright laws: the authors who create the works; the publishers who make copies and distribute the works to the public; and the members of the public who read, watch, listen to, and otherwise benefit from the existence of the works. Copyright laws passed by Congress reflect attempts to balance the interests of all three communities. The communities themselves also seek to balance the interests through contractual negotiations and other actions. The need to achieve a balance and to adjust that balance as times change is a fact to bear in mind when trying to understand the ins and outs of copyright law.

Duration of Copyrights

Copyrights in musical compositions and sound recordings last as long as those in any other works. The basic provisions currently allow for copyright protection for the life of the author plus seventy years. If there are multiple authors then the seventy years does not start to run until the death of the last surviving author. Most commercially released sound recordings are created as "works made for hire" for the record companies. In that case the label is considered to be the author for copyright purposes. Because businesses do not have a "life" that will meet a certain natural end, the duration of copyrights for works made for hire is stated as ninety-five years from the year of first publication, or one hundred-twenty years from creation, whichever ends earlier.[3] That means that sound recordings are protected in the United States for longer than most other nations protect them. The standard for World Trade Organization (WTO) members is fifty years, and some countries protect sound recordings for only twenty-five years.[4]

When copyrights expire, the work protected goes into the public domain—that is it becomes available for anyone to use without permission of the previous copyright owner. One of the ways copyright law benefits the public is that the monopoly, given to copyright authors so they can make money and be encouraged to create more works, only lasts for a limited time. At the end of that time the public is served by the work becoming available to anyone, without need for a license, and therefore at a lower price. Thus, more of the arts are available to more people when the work goes into the public domain (PD).

PD or not PD?

The public domain status of sound recordings is a complex matter. Prior to 1972, federal copyright law did not protect sound recordings. They were protected under a patchwork of state laws. Theoretically, pre-1972 recordings will never be in public domain in the strict sense of the word. Most of the state laws do not contain a time when their protection ends. Recordings created after February 15, 1972 (the effective date of the sound recording amendment) are subject to federal protection, and that federal protection preempted any state laws. For those recordings the duration of copyright would be a twenty-eight year original term, and a sixty-seven year renewal term—a total of ninety-five years.[5] None of the sound recording copyrights would have expired before renewal was made automatic in 1992, so they will all get the full ninety-five years. Therefore, none of the copyrights for recordings made between 1972 and 1978 will expire before the end of 2067. (Copyrights expire at the end of the calendar year in which they would otherwise expire.[6]) The duration of copyright was changed to the life of the author plus seventy years in 1998 (life plus fifty in 1978). If most sound recordings are works made for hire, their duration is ninety-five years from first publication, so the total term is the same as for works created between 1972 and 1978.

Even when copyrights in the sound recordings do begin to enter the public domain in 2068, that does not mean that the copyrights in the musical compositions recorded will necessarily be expired. Because one could not make a copy of a sound recording without also copying the musical composition, there are two copyrights to be considered. Most musical compositions, and any other literary or dramatic works likely to be recorded, operate under the "life plus seventy" rules. It is necessary to know who the authors and songwriters were and exactly when they died in order to know whether it is safe to copy a particular recording, even if the sound recording is known to be in the public domain.

Formalities: Notice and Registration

The current copyright laws recognize the existence of copyrights in works from the moment they are "created," (*i.e.*, first fixed in some tangible medium of expression). Formalities, such as publication of the work with the appropriate copyright notice, and registration, are no longer necessary to secure basic copyright protection. That is the same standard used in most other nations, particularly those that have joined the Berne Convention for the Protection of Literary Property or the World Trade Organization (WTO). The WTO requires its members to apply Berne Convention standards in their copyright laws. There are, however, reasons why some formalities are still of importance to the recording industry, particularly in the United States.

Notice

The copyright notice for sound recordings is different from that for other works. For most works, including musical compositions, that notice consists of: (1) the symbol ©, or the word *Copyright*, or the abbreviation *Copr.*; and (2) the year of first publication; and (3) the name of the copyright owner. For sound recordings the notice requirement is (1) the symbol ℗ (often referred to as the *circle P* notice); and (2) the year of first publication of the sound recording (not the work recorded); and (3) the name of the sound recording copyright owner (usually a record label). The circle P notice is required by the Rome Convention[7] for protection of sound recording copyrights on an international basis. One typically sees notices on albums, whatever format, that have both the © and ℗ notices because the labels are claiming copyright in both the recording and the supplemental artwork, liner notes, and so forth that is part of the packaging of the recording.

The Case of "Boogie, Chillen"

A 1995 court decision regarding formality requirements for recordings of some pre-1978 works came close to casting a substantial number of songs into the public domain. The 1909 copyright law required a copyright notice to be placed on copies of published works.[8] Prior to publication, works were protected by common law copyright and some kinds of works, including musical compositions and dramatic works, could be protected by federal copyright registration even if unpublished. When a work was published, it lost common law protection. If the publication was without the required notice, it lost federal protection. Without common law or federal protection the work then became public domain. The 1908 case of *White-Smith Music Pub. Co. v. Apollo Co.*[9] held that a piano roll, and by implication a phonorecord, was not a copy of a work because the work could not be visually perceived from that kind of device. Music publishers had therefore assumed that copyright notice for songs was not, therefore, required on phonorecords of the songs. In 1973 a federal district court in New York upheld that view.[10] However the Ninth Circuit Court of Appeals declined to follow that precedent. In *La Cienega Music Company v. Z.Z. Top,*[11] that court held that distribution of recordings of John Lee Hooker's "Boogie Chillen" was a publication of the song, and if the records did not contain a proper copyright notice for the song, the song would become public domain. The U.S. Supreme Court refused to hear the case.

Because literally thousands of recordings had been released without copyright notices for the songs recorded on them, the music publishing companies were in an uproar at the prospect of thousands of songs suddenly being in the public domain. Congress came to the rescue in 1997 with an amendment to the Copyright Act that states, "The distribution before January 1, 1978, of a phonorecord shall not for any purpose constitute a publication of the musical work embodied therein."[12] The notice dilemma is not a problem for recordings released between January 1, 1978 and March 1, 1989, because the copyright law at that time only required notice on "publicly distributed copies from which the work can be visually perceived."[13] For the most part, then, there was no need for a notice for the song copyrights on the recordings unless the lyrics were reprinted on the sleeve, liner notes, or booklet. Even then, that notice would usually accompany the lyrics and still would not be on the label of the recording itself. Beginning March 1, 1989 notice was no longer required. That change was made in order for U.S. copyright law to comply with the Berne Convention.

Registration

The statute specifically states, "Registration is not a condition of copyright protection."[14] However, registration is necessary in order to sue for infringement of works where the United States is the country of origin.[15] The owner can register at any time, including after the discovery of an infringement, it is just that the suit cannot commence until there is a registration.

Registration soon after the creation of the work is desirable for a number of reasons. If the work is registered within five years of first publication, the registration is considered as *prima facie* evidence of the validity of the copyright and the information contained on the registration form.[16] That means the burden of proof shifts to the other party to prove that the registrant was not the owner of the work—a tactical advantage.

Perhaps more importantly, the copyright owner cannot get certain remedies for the infringement unless the work was registered *prior* to the time infringement began. Awards of statutory damages (see below) or attorney's fees cannot be made for published works unless registration is made within three months of publication or prior to the infringement if the infringement is later than three months after first publication.[17]

Registration of musical compositions is accomplished on form PA (for works of performing arts) and registration of sound recordings is on a form SR; both can be obtained from the U.S. Copyright Office directly by mail, via the "forms hotline" telephone number, or on the Internet.[18] Electronic registration is only available for some publishing companies on a test basis, but is under development for the general public. The basic registration fee was $30.00 per form in 2003.

Although record companies fought a long battle for recognition of sound recording copyrights, they often do not take full advantage of the protection provided through registration. Independents in particular, but even the majors on non-hit products, often fail to register their recordings. The lack of registration within five years of publication means that the registration, which is still required in order to sue for infringement, is not considered *prima facie* evidence establishing the validity of the copyright. Nor is the label able to collect court costs and attorney's fees, or statutory damages if the recording was not registered within three months of publication/release. The labels would have to prove their exact losses and the infringer's exact profits, and pay their own costs and attorney's fees. In addition, deposit with the Library of Congress is required for all works published in the United States, even if the works are not registered. However, a spot check of deposits in 1993 revealed at least a 15 percent noncompliance with the deposit requirements.[19]

Registration of copyrights in sound recordings may be proving a bigger benefit to bands and musicians without label deals than it is to the labels. In 1971 the Librarian of Congress estimated that there would be 15,000 sound recording registrations per year.[20] As Figure 2.1 indicates, the registration of published sound recordings, presumably mainly from the major labels, has been slow to reach that 15,000 per year pace. On the other hand, the registration of unpublished recordings, more likely from unsigned bands

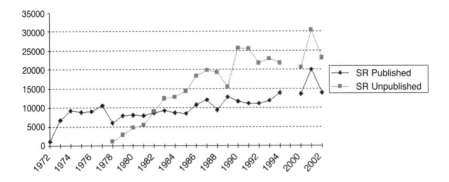

Fig. 2.1 Sound recording copyright registrations. Data from the Register of Copyrights, Annual Reports of the Register of Copyrights 1975–2003, Washington, D.C., and the Librarian of Congress.

and artists, exceeds that of published recordings. Given the growth of home, project, and other small professional *demo* studios this trend is likely to continue.

Registration Tips for Unsigned Bands and Songwriters

A special feature of the sound recording registration form, SR, allows the owner to register both the recording and the underlying musical composition (or other work) recorded. The only catch is that the same person(s) must be the owners of the copyrights of both works. This is particularly useful to unsigned bands or songwriters who either publish their works on their own labels or who simply wish the comfort of a registration. The only caveat is that in a band it is likely that all the members of the band, and additional persons including any audio engineers or producers, are all probably considered to be authors and owners of the copyright in the sound recording, whereas those same people probably are not the writers of all the individual songs on the album or demo recording.

A feature of both sound-recording and musical composition registration (as well as other classes of works) is the registration of collective works. This feature can be turned to the advantage of the performing artist or songwriter who does not have a recording or publishing contract, and hence a label, producer, or publisher, to look out for their copyrights. Provided that the copyright owners of all the works are the same, multiple works can be submitted in one registration as an unpublished collection, such as "The Songs of Geoff Hull, 2004." Whether on a demo CD, tape, or in some sort of folio, the single registration would protect all of the individual compositions or recordings in the collection.[21]

They would not be indexed by their individual titles in the Copyright Office records, but even that could be accomplished by later filing a Supplemental Registration (form CA), which lists the individual titles and refers back to the previous collection registration. Even though the CA registration fee is substantially higher ($100 in 2004) than a basic registration fee, the typical unsigned band or songwriter could register, say, ten songs for the price of the two registrations instead of ten: $130 instead of $300. In fact, the Copyright Office recommends this practice.

The Fair Use Limitation and Parody

All works are limited by a section of the copyright act generally referred to as *fair use*,[22] which permits "criticism, comment, news reporting, teaching (including multiple copies for classroom use), scholarship or research" as fair uses and not infringements, provided they meet certain criteria. Although an extended discussion of fair use is beyond the scope of this book, it is important to understand fair use in trying to answer questions of sampling and parody in musical works and sound recordings.

Fair Use Factors

There are four factors to be considered in determining whether a particular use is a fair use, and all of them must be considered in any given case. Just because a use is for educational or nonprofit purposes, for example, does not necessarily mean it is a fair use. How the use weighs on the other tests may tip the scales of justice toward infringement. Here is the statutory language of each part of the test and a brief commentary:

1. "The purpose and character of the use, including whether such use is of a commercial nature or is for nonprofit educational purposes." Here the uses listed in the first part of the fair use section—criticism, comment, news reporting, teaching (including multiple copies for classroom use), scholarship, or research, plus satire or parody—and general private noncommercial use, are more likely to be considered as fair uses. Uses that change, alter, or make the work into a new work or somehow transform the work are more likely to be considered fair.

2. "The nature of the copyrighted work." Generally, factual works are less likely to receive protection than entirely creative works. Presumably, the reason one creates a factual work is to spread information; facts themselves are not protected by copyright.

3. "The amount and substantiality of the portion used in relation to the copyrighted work as a whole." This test has both a qualitative and a quantitative aspect. Taking the *hook* out of a song, even if only as short as eight notes, may be a significant use. Taking only a few

hundred words out of thousands may be significant if the words taken were a crucial part of a book.

4. "The effect of the use upon the potential market for or value of the copyrighted work." Fair use tries to balance the possible benefit to society (as opposed to the user of the protected work) that results from the use versus the potential harm to the copyright owner. Generally, harm is measured in economic terms, such as lost sales, lost licensing revenues, and even lost opportunities. The more the work created by the claimed fair use provides a substitute for the original work, the less likely the use is to be deemed fair.

The Case of "Oh, Pretty Woman!"

Although there are certainly conceivable fair uses of sound recordings, there have not been any cases that have specifically addressed that issue. However, there are significant cases involving questions of fair use of musical compositions, most notably in the areas of satire and parody. In 1994 the U.S. Supreme Court decided that parody of musical compositions could be a fair use in *Campbell v. Acuff-Rose Music, Inc.*[23] Luther Campbell's group 2 Live Crew had made a parody rap version of the Roy Orbison/William Dees song, "Oh, Pretty Woman." Campbell's version used the famous guitar riff that introduces and is used throughout the song, portions of the melody, and a few lines of the lyrics of the original. Although the Court did not definitively say Campbell's version was a fair use, they said, "2 Live Crew's song reasonably could be perceived as commenting on the original or criticizing it, to some degree. 2 Live Crew juxtaposes the romantic musings of a man whose fantasy comes true, with degrading taunts, a bawdy demand for sex, and a sigh of relief from parental responsibility. The later words can be taken as a comment on the naiveté of the original of an earlier day, as a rejection of its sentiment that ignores the ugliness of street life and the debasement that it signifies. It is this joinder of reference and ridicule that marks off the author's choice of parody from other types of comment and criticism that traditionally have had a claim to fair use protection as transformative works."[24] The Court cautioned, "[T]his is not to say that anyone who calls himself a parodist can skim the cream and get away scot free." The Court sent the case back to the district court to determine whether the repeated use of the bass/introductory riff was excessive and whether the parody version damaged the market for a straight rap version of the song. The parties ultimately settled the case at the district court without further judicial decisions being rendered.

Joint Authorship/Joint Works

It is common practice in the recording industry for people to collaborate on the songs they write or the recordings they create. The songwriting teams of Rogers and Hart, Lennon and McCartney, Ashford and Simpson, and many more are legendary. Popular groups work together to create the recordings they make. This is all well and good, but the copyright law creates some presumptions about people who create works together that might not be what the authors have in mind. If two or more authors create a work with the intention that their contributions be merged into a single unitary work, even if the work contains separate but interdependent parts (such as melody and lyrics), then their work is deemed to be a *joint work*.[25] If a work is a joint work, then each author owns an equal, undivided share unless there is some agreement among the authors that otherwise spells out the ownership shares. So if one person writes a melody and another writes lyrics with the intention of creating a single song, then each owns half of the entire work (i.e., an undivided share) instead of one owning the rights to the lyrics and the other owning rights to the melody. Each author may authorize the use of the work, but is under a duty to account to the other authors for their fair shares of any royalties or revenues received. These things are fine if they are what the authors intended. If they intend otherwise, they would have to have a written agreement spelling out their arrangement.

The situation with bands becomes even more complicated. Suppose one band member comes up with the idea for a song, creates a verse, chorus, and basic melody. That member then presents the unfinished song to the other members of the band. Together they find a "groove" and work out an arrangement suitable for their musical style. Perhaps some of the other band members contribute a lyric line or make some suggestion to modify the melody. The bass player comes up with a bass part. The drummer works out a drum part to anchor the song rhythmically. How many authors are there of the song? How many authors are there of the sound recording that the band later makes as a demo? If the person who had the original idea and wrote some of the basic parts of the song intends all contributors to be equal authors, and if the other contributors intend to be equal authors, then they have a joint work. Notice this has to be what *all* the parties intend, not just the people who later added small parts to the song.

There are also court decisions that hold that each person's contribution, in order to be deemed a joint author, must be *significant*. What is *significant*? Some courts say that contributions must be copyrightable to count as acceptable for the creation of a joint work. Generally, the *head* arrangement that a group of musicians makes for a popular song is not considered as copyrightable. So unless the members of the group have made significant contributions to the melody and lyrics then they are not considered to be authors of the song. Presumably they could have a written agreement that any songs created by the group were to be deemed joint works. Problems are likely to arise when there is no agreement and someone who thinks he/she is an author, such as the drummer, attempts to claim his or her share of the song after the group has split up (as it almost surely will).

Joint authorship in the sound recording is a bit clearer. Under most circumstances, all group members will have made a significant contribution to the recording. They are, therefore, all joint authors of the recording because it is pretty clear that they fully intended to create a recording in which all participated. If the recording is made for a label under a standard recording artist contract, the label will assert that the recording is a *work made for hire* and that it is the author for copyright purposes and copyright owner.

Works Made for Hire

A significant issue for both record labels and music publishers, and the artists (and producers) and songwriters, respectively, who create the works for the labels and publishers, is whether the works created are works made for hire. Generally, works made for hire are works created by employees within the scope of their employment, and certain kinds of commissioned works where the parties have agreed in writing that the work is a work for hire. There are two significant results of considering a work as being made for hire. First, the employer, not the person who created the work, is deemed to be the author for purposes of copyright. That means no further transfer of rights is necessary; it happens automatically. More importantly, the person who created the work does not have any termination rights in the work. Thus, in works for hire, the creator of the work does not have a right to *recapture* the copyrights after a period of time (thirty-five to forty years). The employers can thus be totally sure that they will own the copyrights for their entire duration (95 years from first publication or 120 years from creation, whichever ends earlier). (See discussion below on termination rights.)

While that might seem simple enough on its face, the application has proven quite troublesome to the courts. The statute defines work made for hire as:

(1) a work prepared by an employee within the scope of his or her employment; or

(2) a work specially ordered or commissioned for use as a contribution to a collective work, as a part of a motion picture or other audiovisual work, as a translation, as a supplementary work, as a compilation, as an instructional text, as a test, as answer material for a test, or as an atlas, if the parties expressly agree in a written instrument signed by them that the work shall be considered a work made for hire.[26]

The Case of the Homeless Statue

Sculptor James Earl Reid was contacted by the Community for Creative Non-Violence (CCNV), an activist organization that promoted awareness of homelessness, to create a sculpture. The sculpture was for its December, 1985 Christmastime Pageant of Peace to dramatize the plight of the homeless in Washington, D.C. Reid created the statue using materials paid for by CCNV, at his own studio. After the rally CCNV wanted to take the sculpture on tour. Reid objected saying that the inexpensive material used for the original casting would not withstand a road trip. CCNV asked Reid to return the statue, but Reid refused. Who did the sculpture and the copyrights in it belong to, Reid or CCNV? Was Reid CCNV's employee?

After reviewing the language and legislative history of the work made for hire provision of the Copyright Act, a unanimous Supreme Court in *Community for Creative Non-Violence v. Reid*[27] concluded, "Congress intended to provide two mutually exclusive ways for works to acquire work for hire status: one for employees and the other for independent contractors. Second, the legislative history underscores the clear import of the statutory language: only enumerated categories of commissioned works may be accorded work for hire status."[28] The Supreme Court concluded that the appropriate tests of whether someone was an employee or not were "principles of general common law agency."[29] The Court then referred to a "non-exhaustive" list of factors to be used in determining whether a worker is an employee or an independent contractor. The Court specifically listed thirteen factors, including:

> the hiring party's right to control the manner and means by which the product is accomplished ... the skill required; the source of the instrumentalities and tools; the location of the work; the duration of the relationship between the parties; whether the hiring party has the right to assign additional projects to the hired party; the extent of the hired party's discretion over when and how long to work; the method of payment; the hired party's role in hiring and paying assistants; whether the work is part of the regular business of the hiring party; whether the hiring party is in business; the provision of employee benefits; and the tax treatment of the hired party. [citations omitted][30]

The Court then cautioned, "No one of these factors is determinative."[31]

Analyze the typical contractual and other working conditions of a recording artist (Chapter 7) and a staff songwriter (Chapter 5). You will probably conclude that in most instances it is probable that a recording artist, particularly one who is given freedom to create and even produce their own recordings, is not an employee of the record company. On the other hand, a songwriter who uses staff writing rooms, demo rooms, and recording facilities at the music publisher's place of business may very well be creating works for hire as an employee, without meaning to do so. Both of the situations have recently raised work-for-hire questions in the legal literature, but neither one has been litigated. Nor has a court determined the validity of the record labels' claim that the recordings are contributions to collective works and therefore may be work for hire by agreement, as their recording contracts say they are.

Termination Rights

In an effort to correct the many problems that had developed with copyright renewals under the 1909 copyright law, Congress created a new right for authors in the 1976 revision—the right of termination of transfers. This right is designed (as was the earlier renewal right) to give authors or their heirs a right to recapture the copyrights after a period of time. The theory is that when authors initially bargain away their copyrights for long periods of time, the value of the copyrights is not known because they have not stood the test of the marketplace, and for that reason beginner authors are not in a very good bargaining position with publishers and labels. That certainly holds true for new recording artists, as discussed in Chapter 7. The statute, therefore, allows the authors to recapture their copyrights after a period of time during which the initial transferee, usually a publisher or label, has had ample time to exploit the work.

The *termination window* begins thirty-five years after the transfer and runs for a five-year period. (If the transfer includes the right to publish, the termination window begins after forty years after transfer, or thirty-five years after first publication, whichever begins earlier.) During this time the termination may be effected by written notice to the transferee (owner) signed by a majority of the owners of the termination interest. The termination interest owners are the author(s) themselves; or if an author has died prior to serving the termination notice, the author's surviving spouse and children; or if a child has died, that child's children (the author's grandchildren of the deceased child). If an author has no surviving spouse, children, or grandchildren, then the author's estate or heirs at law own the interest. The people owning a majority of the termination interest must agree to end the transfer. The surviving spouse owns 50 percent and the children the other 50 percent. They must notify the transferee no more than ten and no less than two years before the effective date of termination that they are exercising their right to end the transfer and recapture the copyrights. If notice, number of people, and date of termination all meet the requirements of the statute, then the authors or their heirs regain control of the copyrights. There is nothing that the transferee can do to prevent this. The statute even states that a termination may take place even if the author has contracted not to do it![32]

Termination Problems

For the record companies, the difficulty of establishing that recordings are works made for hire and the existence of termination rights may mean that recording artists and/or producers can end the labels' rights to own the copyrights in the master recordings after thirty-five years. The value of masters that are thirty-five years old was illustrated in 1995 with the release of a collection of Beatles recordings from the 1960s. Capitol Records shipped more than four million units of the *Anthology* collection in late 1995. The album debuted at number one in the *Billboard* album chart the next week with reported sales in the United States alone of more than 800,000 copies in one week.[33] In 2002 valuable old masters resurfaced again in the chart-topping Elvis Presley *Elvis: 30 #1 Hits*, and the Rolling Stones's greatest hits *Forty Licks* albums.[34] Needless to say, the labels would not be pleased to lose the rights to such valuable products. Termination rights proceedings between recording artists and their labels for control over the copyrights in their master recordings made and transferred in 1978 began in 2003. That was the first year in which the artists could send notices of termination for rights in sound recordings. This litigation will likely take a substantial time to resolve.

The record companies are putting lots of effort and language in their recording agreements to try to prevent the artists from recapturing, or more correctly terminating the transfers, of the sound recording copyrights. Particularly, the labels claim that the recordings are "contributions to collective works" under the second part of the previously stated work for hire definition. The labels require artists to agree to that fact and state that the recordings are works made for hire. Again, while this may seem logical on its face, the statutory definition of collective works, the legislative history of the statute, and court decisions interpreting the work for hire and other provisions cast doubt on the labels' claim. On the music publisher and songwriter side of the question, the litigation is likely to occur when some unsuspecting songwriter attempts to terminate the transfer of copyrights to a music publisher only to find that the publisher counterclaims that the work was made for hire because the songwriter was really an employee of the publisher.[35]

The Manufacturing Clause and Parallel Imports

The recording industry is a particular beneficiary of a provision of the copyright laws that is little known outside the publishing and recording industries. It is known as the manufacturing clause because it originally required that English language books or periodicals be manufactured in the United States in order to achieve full copyright protection. From its birth in 1891 it was quite simply a trade barrier designed to protect U.S. publishers and bookbinders from foreign competition.[36] The part of the clause requiring manufacture in the United States to enjoy full copyright protection was abolished when the United States joined the Berne Convention in 1989, but part of the clause continues to this day.

The surviving language prohibits the importation, without the U.S. copyright owner's permission, of copies of works that have been acquired outside of the United States. Such an unauthorized importation is an infringement of the distribution right. The clause is particularly effective in stopping the importation of *gray market* goods—those that have been legally manufactured outside of the United States for distribution *outside* of the United States. Although the copyright law says nothing about goods themselves, it does speak to copyrightable materials that may be part of the goods (such as labels) or boxed with the goods (such as instruction manuals). In some respects the manufacturing clause is a better deterrent to gray market goods than trademark law.[37] For the recording and music industry it prevents the distribution of what are referred to as *parallel imports*.

Domestic Problems

Parallel imports are a problem for the U.S. industry for several reasons. These goods, which are lawfully manufactured outside of the United States for sale outside of the United States, return a lower profit per copy than copies made in the United States and sold in the United States by the U.S. label. Often in foreign manufacturing arrangements the U.S. label gets only a royalty similar to that of a recording artist, based on the retail list price in the foreign country. This is far less profit than the label would make if the records were made and sold in the United States.[38] And when the dollar is particularly strong relative to the foreign currency, these imports can be purchased by a retailer or distributor at a substantially lower price than the domestic product. If they can be sold alongside the U.S. product at the same or slightly lower price, then the distributor and/ or retailer can make more money selling the import than they can by selling the domestic product.

Not only does the U.S. record company lose money when copies of parallel imports are sold instead of domestic copies, so does the recording artist who is often paid at a one-half royalty rate for copies made outside the United States. So also do the music publisher and songwriter because they, too, are usually paid at a one-half or other reduced royalty for copies made outside of the United States.

Poor Man's Copyright

It is not unusual to hear people, particularly musicians and songwriters, refer to *poor man's copyright*, which prior to 1978, was a common law copyright concept. The notion of common law copyright is that the author of a work ought to be the first to be able to decide whether to disclose the work to the public. Until such time as a work was published, the rights in the work belonged to the author. Hence, common law copyright generally became known as the *right of first publication*. On publication, the work was eligible for statutory copyright protection if published with the copyright notice and/or registered (for dramatic and musical works whether published or not). Because registration costs money ($30.00 in 2004), some people chose not to register their unpublished works (and some unpublished works could not be registered), but rather attempted to establish some kind of evidence of ownership and creation of the work by sending it to themselves by registered mail, depositing copies with some writers' protective organization, and so forth. These non-statutory devices became known as poor man's copyright. Whether *poor* should be taken to refer to the typical author's impoverished state or to the quality of evidence resulting from these practices is open to question.

Under the 1976 Act, copyright in any work exists upon the first fixation of the work in a tangible medium of expression. Because common-law protection is specifically preempted upon first fixation, the only thing left for common law to protect is a work until it is first fixed. There would not be many works that would not be *fixed*—perhaps a musical performance by some jazz musicians or a poem or song written and kept "in the head" of the author. Furthermore, registration is no longer a requirement for federal protection. If an impecunious author chooses not to register to save the registration fee, then the "poor man's" alternatives still exist as a means to attempt to create evidence of authorship and ownership. However, registration is *prima facie* evidence of the existence of the copyright and its validity as stated on the registration form.[39] Registration prior to the infringing acts is necessary to get statutory damages and court costs and attorneys fees. Registration is required prior to any court action for infringement for U.S. works or foreign works that are not from Berne-member countries.

In deciding whether to register, a good rule of thumb to follow is that if the author or copyright owner is going to distribute copies to the public, place the work where it is likely to be accessible to members of the public, or where the owner does not really know who will have access to the work, then registration is the best approach. Relying on poor man's copyright is a bit risky in those circumstances.

Summary

This chapter has dealt with general aspects of the copyright law as they apply to sound recordings and musical compositions. The purpose of copyright law is the encouragement of the creation of new artistic works, in order to benefit society. The mechanisms of the law that deal with copyright ownership, formalities, and the duration of copyrights contribute to that purpose. For the most part, those general aspects apply to works in the recording industry in the same way as they apply to all works, regardless of their nature. However, there are some particular twists of the copyright law specifically written to deal with some aspects of sound recordings and musical compositions that must be explored in some detail in order to understand how the recording industry attempts to mold the copyright laws to its advantage. They are discussed in Chapter 3.

3

Copyright in Sound Recordings and Songs

Sound Recordings
Pre-1972: A Recording Is Not a Song

Phonorecords, the objects on which sounds are recorded, have been around in some form or another, cylinder or platter, since before the turn of the twentieth century. They had become a significant enough commercial commodity that by 1899 an estimated 3,750,000 copies were being sold each year. That number reached 27,500,000 per year by 1909, the year of the copyright law revision that gave music publishers the mechanical right (the right to reproduce a song mechanically, such as on a phonorecord).[1] At that time the estimated number of phonographs in the United States was put at 1,310,000 and total sales of phonograph recordings since 1889 was estimated at 97,845,000. During the decade between 1899 and 1909 recordings had become big enough business, and the means of manufacturing had become widespread enough, that the labels began to feel the effects of unauthorized copying of their recordings. The labels sought relief from Congress in the form of legislation amending the copyright law that would allow copyrights in their recordings. At the same time, the music publishers were complaining that the copies of their songs embodied in the phonorecords should not be sold without some compensation to the owners of the copyrights in the musical compositions —a proposition the labels would have preferred to reject. The labels maintained, and the decision of the United States Supreme Court in

White-Smith Music Publishing Co. v. Apollo Co.[2] backed up their position, that a recording that utilized some mechanical device such as a piano roll or cylinder or disc recording to reproduce the song, was not a copy of that song because it could not be visually perceived from the mechanical reproduction. The difficulty with that position was that the labels could not very well maintain that this non-copy of the song should be entitled to some copyright protection of its own. The labels became much more concerned over the prospect of having to negotiate a license for every song they recorded and abandoned the argument that sound recordings should be copyrightable. Then they could maintain, with straight faces, that recordings were not copies of songs and that, therefore, the music publishers and songwriters were not entitled to any right to object to those copies being sold. The labels said that unfair trade laws adequately protected their own rights in the recordings.

The state of the piano roll and player piano manufacturing industry posed an additional complication. In 1899 the Aeolian Organ Company, the largest manufacturer of player pianos, sold 75,000 mechanical pianos and pianolas. By 1921, near their peak of popularity, an estimated 342,000 such devices were sold. The Aeolian company was not only a manufacturer of the pianos, but also of the rolls of music needed to make them perform. As it became clear in 1908 that Congress was going to give music publishers a right to control mechanical reproductions of their songs, it was reported that the Aeolian company had begun to enter into arrangements with many of the largest music publishers to be the exclusive manufacturer of piano rolls of their compositions. Fearing that they might create an Aeolian piano roll monopoly, Congress responded to pleas of the other piano roll manufacturers to make the mechanical right subject to a compulsory license. The effect of the license would be that once a musical composition copyright owner had allowed one party to make a mechanical reproduction of their song, then anyone else might do the same thing provided the publisher was compensated. At the urging of Congress, the record companies, pianola manufacturers, music publishing companies, and authors' groups arrived at a compromise that became the compulsory mechanical licensing provision of the 1909 Copyright Act. Although the labels complained that the statutory rate of two cents per copy was too high, they were pleased to have a guaranteed way to be able to reproduce recordings of popular songs without having to negotiate over a royalty rate.

The labels, and the songwriters and publishers, continued to be at odds over the creation of a copyright in sound recordings through the 1920s. A series of bills introduced in 1912, 1925, 1926, 1928, and 1930 all contained provisions for copyright for sound recordings. All were met with opposition on the grounds it was not fair to require a compulsory license from the writers and publishers for their songs and give the labels an unfettered right in their recordings. None of the proposals were met with much enthusiasm by Congress.

In 1932 a new player, the broadcast industry, emerged as an important force in the discussions. For the first time the National Association of Broadcasters came forward to oppose the creation of copyrights in sound recordings, contending that small broadcasters would be hurt if record companies were given a public performance right. Better, said the broadcasters, to limit the sound recording rights to *dubbing* or duplication. With the record companies, music publishers, and broadcasters all at odds over a copyright for sound recordings, no further progress was made through the 1950s.

Enter: The Pirates The introduction of the 8-track tape cartridge player in the early 1960s meant that there was a convenient way for people to take and play prerecorded music virtually anywhere. Recordings could now be played in automobiles or at a picnic with simple equipment that could reproduce reasonable sound quality. The tape cartridge caught on rapidly and by 1974 there were 6.7 million 8-track tape players (including auto and home) shipped in the United States by the hardware manufacturers.[3] The volume of tape sales had risen to 112 million units that same year. At the same time the volume of sales of vinyl records had risen to 480 million units (including singles and albums).[4]

The popularity of the tape players enticed others into the market. Tape duplicating equipment was much less costly than record pressing equipment, easier to use, and the product much easier to handle. Without the technological barriers to entry into the market, significant numbers of unauthorized duplicators began manufacturing cartridge tapes. By 1971 the volume of unauthorized tape sales had risen to an estimated 100 million units per year—about one-third the sales volume of legitimate tape recordings.[5]

The record companies were nearly powerless to stop it. A 1955 case[6] had determined that recordings were not directly copyrightable under the 1909 copyright law. Although music publishers had rights in the songs being copied on the pirate recordings, they did not have an effective remedy for several reasons. The mechanical royalties for music publishing rights on any one album amounted to only about twenty cents (ten songs at the then two-cent-per-copy statutory mechanical royalty rate). Furthermore, those royalties were often divided between different publishers because the copyrights in the songs recorded did not always belong to the same publisher. So, the publishers' interest per copy was not as high as that of the labels who were losing about $1.80 gross margin per copy. Additionally, some of the pirates claimed that they could make the copies legitimately under the provisions of the compulsory mechanical license. Once the copyright owner of the song had allowed a recording of the song to be made and distributed any one else was allowed to make a "similar use" of the song if they paid the two cents per copy royalty.[7] The federal courts were divided as to whether a "similar use" meant that a new recording had to be made with new musicians or whether that phrase meant that a total duplication could be made. So, even if the publishers might desire to stop the piracy they could sometimes be kept from any remedies by payment of the compulsory mechanical license. Many pirates included labels on their recordings with statements such as "All royalties required by law have been paid." Sometimes that was true; more often it was not. Finally, the penalties available for criminal copyright infringement were only at the misdemeanor level—a small fine and up to one year in prison. Some pirates simply considered these "inconveniences" part of the cost of doing their business.

There was a push for legislative relief at both the state and federal level. For their part, the labels had been actively lobbying the individual states to pass antipiracy legislation. However, by 1971 only eight states had done so. Congress had been considering a total revision of the copyright law since 1962 but appeared unable to reconcile all competing interests. A provision protecting sound recordings was included in the 1966 version of the new law passed by the House of Representatives, but that bill failed to pass the Senate before a new House was elected so Congress had to start over the following year.

1972 to 1977: A Sound Recording Is Still Not a Song

In late 1970 the labels convinced Congress to consider an amendment that would separate the issue of sound recording copyrights from the rest of the revision process. After some compromises on the extent of rights afforded to the owners of the new sound recording copyrights, the legislation passed in 1971 and became effective February 15, 1972. The primary compromise was that there be no right of public performance associated with the sound recording. The broadcasters, particularly radio broadcasters, whose programming consisted primarily of playing recordings on the air, objected to the possible requirement that they pay a royalty to the record companies. Their main arguments were that they already paid the music publishers through the performing rights organizations of ASCAP, BMI, and SESAC, and that their airplay of the recordings was the primary vehicle by which the labels gained the promotional exposure necessary to get consumers interested in buying the records. If the broadcasters had to pay it would be unfair, said the broadcasters, to allow the labels to profit twice from the airplay, once from the sale of the records that the airplay promoted, and once from the payment of a performance royalty by the broadcasters to the labels. Congress also specifically noted in the legislative history, but not in the language of the statute itself, that the new copyrights were not meant to stop private noncommercial home recording from broadcasts or from copying other recordings. The state antipiracy laws, which the labels had worked so hard to get, would be allowed to remain in effect until 2067.[8]

The legislative history also noted that the new rights in recordings were specifically subject to the *First Sale Doctrine*,[9] which states that once the copyright owner has unconditionally parted with a legitimately manufactured copy of the work, the disposition of that particular copy can no longer be controlled. Future disposition could include resale or rental. Due to the fact that vinyl records were easily damaged and worn out and that there was not a very large installed base of home-recording equipment, the record rental business was not a significant threat to the recording industry in the early 1970s. A decade later the situation had changed, so Congress passed the Record Rental Amendment of 1984 (see below).

The music publishers joined with the labels to gain protection for sound recordings. Piracy was hurting their royalties from the sale of legitimate copies of the recordings, and Congress added that the unauthorized reproduction of a sound recording was also unauthorized reproduction of the recorded work. The publishers now also had a remedy to fight record piracy, having discovered that both income streams were negatively impacted by the sale of pirate copies.

1978 to the Present: A Sound Recording Is Still Not a Song

Exclusive Rights. Congress finished the copyright law revision in 1976 and it took effect January 1, 1978. That act listed the rights of copyright owners as the right to:

- reproduce the work in copies or phonorecords;
- prepare derivative works based upon the copyrighted work;
- distribute copies or phonorecords of the copyrighted work to the public by sale or other transfer of ownership, or by rental lease or lending;
- and in the case of literary, musical, dramatic, and choreographic works, pantomimes and motion pictures and other audiovisual works, to perform the copyrighted work publicly; and
- in the case of literary, musical, dramatic, and choreographic works, pantomimes, and pictorial, graphic, or sculptural works, including the individual images of a motion picture or other audiovisual work, to display the copyrighted work publicly.[10]

While these rights are stated rather broadly, they are subject to a number of limitations by way of specific exemptions and the overall fair use exemption as explained in Chapter 2.

Limitations of Rights Rights in sound recordings are not as broad as rights in other kinds of works. A simple perusal of the rights listed above indicates that sound recordings are not in the lists of works having rights of public performance or public display. Although a 1995 amendment gives sound recording copyright owners a limited right of public performance for digital audio transmissions (see below), that right is quite narrow. In fact, a section of the Copyright Act specifically limits sound recording copyrights to those of reproduction, distribution, and the creation of derivative works.[11] It is clear that the rights apply only to the actual sounds captured on the original recording. Thus, one could make another recording that imitated or attempted to sound just like the original recording as long as the new one was made by hiring new musicians, singers, engineers, and so on, and making an entirely independent recording. Unless the makers of the "sound alike" recordings failed to secure mechanical licenses to make recordings of the songs or marketed the recordings in some way that misled consumers to think that they were the original recordings by the original artists, in violation of unfair competition laws, the "sound alike" would be perfectly legitimate. The narrow definition of the rights in sound recordings has led various members of the recording industry, particularly the labels, to frequently ask Congress for changes in the laws to shore up their rather limited protection.

Record Rental

With the Record Rental Amendment of 1984[12] the record labels and music publishers in the United States avoided the significant losses of revenues that had occurred in Japan when record rental became big business there. By the early 1980s cassette decks had become relatively popular in the United States, having been introduced and become very widespread in Japan some years earlier. In 1983, for instance, cassette sales reached 237 million units, surpassing LP sales (210 million) for the first time. Although not as large an enterprise in the United States as it had become in Japan, record rental loomed as a significant threat to the sale of LPs and cassettes by the labels. In 1981 what had been a mom-and-pop kind of business took on alarming proportions for the labels when the first major record retail chain conducted a trial run.[13] A customer could rent an LP for about $0.99 to $2.50, purchasing a blank cassette from the same place, take the disk home, tape it, and return the rented disk to the store the next day having copied the album onto tape. The only copy sold by the label was the one originally sold to the rental store. Even assuming some wear and tear on the rental disk, it could be taped many times before becoming unrentable, thereby supplanting sales by the label. In 1983 there were an estimated 200 rental shops in the United States. Although there was a coalition of rental store owners, blank tape manufacturers, tape deck manufacturers, and some consumers established to lobby against the legislation, Congress ultimately decided that the potential threat to the labels, music publishers, recording artists, and songwriters was great enough to require action. The pending introduction of the compact disc, a more readily rentable and recordable format, into the U.S. market brought added urgency to the situation. In Japan, sales of prerecorded albums had dropped precipitously as the rental business mushroomed.[14]

At the present time the practice of record rental exists in only two developed nations, Japan and Switzerland. It is forbidden in nations that are members of the Word Trade Organization unless there was a system of remuneration for the labels, publishers, artists, and writers in the particular country already in existence in 1994.[15] The U.S. labels (and those of other nations) and Japan agreed to a payment of $6.24 million to compensate for rentals occurring in 1992 through 1994. A per-copy royalty of about $3.10 is to be paid for each copy delivered to rental outlets for 1995 through 1996.[16] Similar agreements paid royalty artists and background vocalists and musicians $2.3 million in royalties for 1996 and 1997. Rental royalties in Japan declined in the late 1990s. Recording artists received $2.3 million in royalties for 1996 and 1997, compared to nearly $18 million for the previous year.[17] The amount received by individual artists ranged from a few dollars to as much as $31,000.[18] Foreign recordings can be rented in Japan, but only after they have been released for one year.[19]

The Record Rental Amendment of 1984 changed the Copyright Act to create an exception to the first sale doctrine by allowing owners of sound recording copyrights to prohibit rental of phonograms. It prohibits, "for purposes of direct or indirect commercial advantage ... the rental, lease, or lending, or ... any other act or practice in the nature of rental, lease, or lending."[20] There is an exemption for nonprofit lending by nonprofit libraries or educational institutions. If a label does decide to allow rental, they are required to compensate the music publishers with a percentage of the rental revenues.

Home Recording

The growth of the cassette hardware market also brought another problem for the recording industry: home taping. The issue had been raised in Congress during the hearings surrounding the creation of sound recording copyrights in 1971, but the legislative history indicated that the new copyrights in the sound recordings were not intended to prohibit home taping for noncommercial purposes. However, there was no similar language in the legislative history of the 1976 Copyright Revision Act on the same sound recording provision, so it became unclear to some whether Congress had meant to prohibit home taping. In 1977 a survey commissioned by Warner Communications found that 21 percent of the

U.S. population over the age of ten taped recordings either off the air from radio broadcasts or from prerecorded albums and tapes. What concerned the industry the most at that time was the fact that those who taped were also those who spent the most money on prerecorded music. The survey concluded, "It is abundantly clear that people who use tape recorders for recording music are more likely to be buyers of prerecorded music, and on average, spend more money for prerecorded music than people who don't have access to a tape recorder, or have the recorders but don't use them to tape music. This, however, does not imply that 'home tapers' would not spend even more money on prerecorded music if tape recorders did not exist."[21]

By 1980 the International Federation of the Phonographic Industry (IFPI) added its voice, stating that home taping was becoming as big a concern as piracy, estimating losses due to the combination as "in the millions." The IFPI urged a legislative fix to the problem, but saw that as a "long and tortuous path."[22] In 1982 home taping losses were set at $2.85 billion per year, with $1.13 billion coming from taping of recordings already owned by the taper and the rest coming from taping recordings borrowed from others, from broadcasts, or from live events. Forty-five percent of the tapers said they taped to avoid buying the product. And, although the lower quality of prerecorded tapes was thought to be an incentive to make home tapes, only 10 percent of tapers said they taped to get a better quality recording. The reasons most often cited for taping were convenience (40 percent) and to use in car or office (35 percent). Tape recorder penetration had increased almost 25 percent in the three years from 1977 to 1980 with almost half of the population over the age of ten having recorders in their homes.[23]

The path to the legislative fix sought by the industry was long and tortuous, indeed. Formidable opposition from the tape recorder and blank tape manufacturers, and a "right to tape" citizens group repeatedly fought the labels to a standstill. In a decision not directly on audio home taping, the U.S. Supreme Court held (in *Sony Corp. v. Universal City Studios, Inc.*) that taping broadcast television programs off the air for private, noncommercial, time-shifting purposes constituted "fair use" in *Sony Corp. v. Universal City Studios, Inc.*[24] This decision weakened the labels' arguments on the applicability of the existing law to prevent home taping.

In the meantime, digital recordings on compact discs had become extremely popular. By 1987 sales of CDs reached about 100 million units, nearly equaling those of vinyl albums. That same year digital audio tape recorders (DAT recorders) were introduced in Japan and in professional markets, and the prospect loomed of generation after generation of near-perfect tape reproduction of CDs. The tape manufacturers wanted to introduce their machines into the U.S. consumer market. The labels threatened potentially long and costly litigation against the manufacturers of the machines as *contributory* copyright infringers. By June 1991 the parties had come to an agreement that they took to Congress.[25] The proposal became the Audio Home Recording Act of 1992, as passed September 22 of that year.[26]

Audio Home Recording Act of 1992 The act represents a compromise between the parties in interest. It provides that:

1. Analog and digital home taping for private noncommercial purposes is exempt from liability for copyright infringement.
2. The manufacture and sale of analog and digital home recording devices is exempt from liability for infringement, but the manufacture and distribution of digital recording devices and blank digital recording media is subject to a compulsory license issued by the Copyright Office.
3. All home-type digital recorders must contain some sort of anti-copying system that prohibits the user from making more than single generation copies.
4. A compulsory license is used to generate royalties for the owners of the sound recording copyrights and the musical composition copyrights. The royalties are collected from the distributors of recorders and blank media based on wholesale prices and the number of units sold. For recorders the royalty is 2 percent of the wholesale price. For blank media it is 3 percent of the wholesale price. The royalties are collected by the Copyright Office quarterly and distributed according to a specific statutory scheme by the Librarian of Congress.
5. Royalty Distribution is to be as follows: The total available for distribution is divided into two funds, a sound recording fund (two-thirds of the total) and a musical works fund (one-third of the total). The labels get 60 percent of the sound recording fund and the artists, including provisions for background musicians and vocalists, get the remaining 40 percent. The music publishers and songwriters each receive one-half of the fund. When all is said and done the shares of the total fund are indicated in Table 3.1.

Collections of royalties under the Audio Home Recording Act, called Digital Audio Recording Technology (DART) royalties by the Copyright Office, were slow to develop. Figure 3.1 indicates a peak of nearly $5.5 million in 2000, then a drop-off. This was due largely to the rapidly falling prices of audio CD recorders and blank CD-Rs. Home recording may eventually become all digital, but the royalties should keep pace with the amount of recording. One proposed solution is for the royalty rates to be adjustable by a Copyright Arbitration Royalty Panel instead of being set

TABLE 3.1 Distribution of Audio Home Recording Act Royalties

	(Percentages Slightly Rounded)
Labels	38.4 %
Featured Artists	25.6 %
AFM Members	1.75 %
AFTRA Members	0.9 %
Music Publishers	16.7 %
Songwriters	16.7 %

Source: 17 U.S.C. § 1006.

so "in stone" in the statute itself. That way the royalty rate could be adjusted that the royalty income bears a closer relationship to the amount of home copying that was actually going on.[27] The Alliance of Artists and Recording Companies (AARC) handles distribution of these royalties to the artists and labels. The AARC also handles distribution of rental royalties from Japan.

Digital Audio Performance Rights

As noted before, the record labels had been attempting to get a performance right for their recordings since the 1909 law. They did not succeed until they got the regular broadcasters, television and radio, to drop opposition to the legislation by exempting traditional broadcast performances, even if the broadcasters later developed digital broadcast systems.[28] Congress ultimately passed the Digital Performance Right in Sound Recordings Act of 1995.[29] It was amended in 1998 as part of the Digital Millennium Copyright Act to clarify the application to Webcasting.[30]

The new public performance right in sound recordings applies only to digital transmissions that are not over the air by over-the-air broadcasters. Streaming by Webcasters, interactive music services, and background music services are subject to licensing. Noninteractive services, such as most Webcasters, is subject to a compulsory license, but interactive services must negotiate directly with the record companies for rights.[31] The compulsory license rate was initially set at 6.5 percent of gross revenues attributable to digital transmissions. In the course of convening a Copyright Arbitration Royalty Panel to adjust the rate, the Copyright Office ruled that radio stations that stream their broadcast signals over the Internet were subject to the compulsory license. That ruling was challenged by the broadcasters, but they ultimately lost.[32] The Librarian of Congress adopted most of the recommendations by the Copyright Arbitration Royalty Panel and set basic rates at 0.07 cents per performance, per listener.[33]

Compulsory license royalties are collected through an RIAA affiliate, SoundExchange, "a modern performance rights organization (PRO) created to collect and distribute performance royalties for sound recording copyright owners, featured and non-featured artists."[34] The distribution of

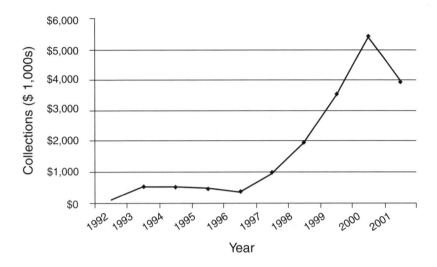

Fig. 3.1 Audio Home Recording Act royalties. Data from U.S. Copyright Office, Licensing Division, Report of Receipts, October 19, 2003.

royalties from negotiated licenses is determined by the recording artists' agreements with the labels.

Whether the licenses are negotiated or compulsory, the division of the sound recording performance royalties between the labels and performers is dictated by the statute as follows: [35]

50 percent to the labels
45 percent to the recording artist(s) featured on the performance
2.5 percent to the American Federation of Musicians (AFM) to be distributed to non-featured musicians, and
2.5 percent to the American Federation of Television and Radio Artists (AFTRA) for distribution to non-featured vocalists.

Infringement and Remedies: Civil(?) Infringement—You Stole My Song!

Civil infringement suits (as opposed to criminal prosecutions) are rare for sound recording copyrights because the statute specifically allows imitation of sounds. So, "sound alike" recordings are not infringements. The most common civil copyright infringement action for sound recordings is for sampling, which is discussed later. The general civil remedies are discussed later in this chapter in the section dealing with musical composition infringement.

Musical Compositions

Initial Copyright Ownership: A Song Is a Song
Copyrights in musical compositions, or songs, usually belong to music publishers. The publishers acquire the rights from songwriters with a transfer of copyright ownership. Copyright initially belongs to the person who creates the work (the author), and that copyright begins from the moment the work is "fixed in a tangible medium of expression." That is to say, as soon as the song is written down, recorded, taped, or otherwise put into some medium from which it can later be perceived or reproduced, the federal copyrights and protection for them spring into existence. Only if the work is never "fixed" would it be protected under state or common law.

Copyright in Musical Arrangements

Although it is quite clear that musical arrangements of musical works are generally copyrightable as derivative works, the situation is not as clear with the arrangements of songs that are often found on popular recordings. The compulsory mechanical license (see below) gives the licensee (the record company), the right to create an arrangement "to the extent necessary to conform it to the style or manner of interpretation of the performance involved," but that arrangement cannot alter the basic melody or character of the song and is not copyrightable as a derivative work.[36] Because the typical negotiated mechanical license often tracks or incorporates by reference the statutory language for the compulsory license, most recorded arrangements of pop songs would not be copyrightable.

The case of "Satin Doll". A court case testing that proposition involved the copyrights in the famous jazz composition and recording "Satin Doll" by Duke Ellington. Ellington originally wrote "Satin Doll" as an instrumental in 1953. That year a *lead sheet* showing the melody was registered with the Copyright Office. A version with harmony and revised melody was recorded by Ellington and released in 1953 on Capitol Records. Billy Strayhorn (actually his estate) claimed copyright in the arrangement as recorded. The court stopped short of holding that there could never be copyrightable arrangements of harmony. Instead the court sent on to trial the question of whether the particular harmony was sufficiently original to qualify for protection. [37]

The case of "Red, Red Robin". A case that *did* decide that the usual piano-vocal arrangements made by publishers and the usual arrangements made by musicians in a recording were not copyrightable involved the 1926 song, "When the Red, Red Robin Comes Bob-Bob-Bobbin' Along." The court concluded that even when the publisher worked from a simple lyric and melody lead sheet from the songwriter, there was not enough creativity in a stock piano-vocal arrangement to qualify it for copyright as a derivative work. "There must be more than cocktail pianist variations of the piece that are standard fare in the music trade by any competent musician. There must be such things as unusual vocal treatment, additional lyrics of consequence, unusual altered harmonies, novel sequential uses of themes—something of substance added making the piece to some extent a new work with the old song embedded in it but from which the new has developed. It is not merely a stylized version of the original song where a major artist may take liberties with the lyrics or tempo, the listener hearing basically the original tune."[38] This is not the sort of thing that members of bands who do not write the basic melody or lyrics of a song like to hear. It is, however, something that they, and the band members who *do* write the lyrics and melodies, should be aware of.

Compulsory Mechanical License

Even though the vast majority of mechanical licenses issued by music publishers in the United States are negotiated and not compulsory, it is important to understand the workings of the *compulsory* (also known as *statutory*) *license*. Many mechanical licenses are pegged to the statutory rate. The existence of certain features of the statutory license establishes the parameters around which many of the terms of a negotiated license are set.

Availability of the Compulsory Mechanical License. The compulsory mechanical license is available for the manufacturing and distribution of *phonorecords* of nondramatic musical works to the public. (A license to do the same thing, but not for public distribution, would usually be referred to as a *transcription license*.) The phonorecord is the material object, be it compact disc, cassette tape, or other device, in which both the sound recording copyright and the musical composition copyright are fixed when a recording of a song is made and distributed. Though not specifically defined as such, the term also includes digital delivery of copies (i.e., a "digital phonorecord delivery").[39] In the United States, licenses for reproduction of songs in videos (motion pictures or music videos) are referred to as *synchronization licenses*. In many other places in the world, video or *videogram licenses* would also be called *mechanical licenses*—a source of some confusion.

A record company could obtain a compulsory mechanical license for a song once the music publisher had allowed a recording of the song to be made and distributed to the public. So while a music publisher could control who could make the first recording of a song, after that any record company or artist could make a recording of the same song by using the compulsory license.[40] Even when the compulsory license is available, its terms are not viewed favorably by record companies. They would prefer to negotiate a lower rate, less frequent payments, and different accounting for returns. So because first-time recordings of songs require negotiated licenses, and because the labels desire to have terms more favorable than the compulsory license, there are not many compulsory licenses used.

Statutory Rate. When the compulsory mechanical license was created in the 1909 revision of the copyright law, the rate was set in the statute as two cents per copy. It remained that way until 1978. Since 1978 the rate has been changed numerous times through procedures set up in the Copyright Act (see Table 3.2). Even though the rate is now determined by Copyright Arbitration Royalty Panels, it is still referred to in the industry as the *statutory rate*. Labels often get a rate below the statutory rate, most often 75 percent of the statutory rate.

Other Compulsory Mechanical Provisions. The statute also requires that the compulsory licensee (the record label) file a notice of intention to obtain a compulsory license with the copyright owner. It requires that payment be made for each record distributed, meaning the label has "voluntarily and permanently parted with its possession." To account for the fact that recordings are usually sold subject to return by the purchaser, the Copyright Office has made regulations further defining the term *distributed* to mean when revenue is recognized by the label from the sale of the record, or when nine months has passed from the date of shipment, whichever is earlier.[41] The labels would prefer to be able to withhold some payments as a reserve against anticipated returns for a longer period and to make payments quarterly instead of monthly.

Performing Rights and Music

Public performance rights are particularly important in the recording industry. Income from public performances is the largest source of revenue for music publishing (as discussed in Chapter 5). Public performance rights in musical compositions were first added to the copyright laws in 1897 but did not take on particular significance until the 1909 copyright revision, in part because minimum damages established by the

TABLE 3.2 Compulsory Mechanical License Rate Changes

Date(s)	Rate	Authority
1909 to 1977	2 cents per copy	Copyright Act of 1909, § 1(e)
January 1, 1978	2.5 cents per copy or 0.5 cents per minute, whichever is greater	1976 Copyright Act, § 115
January 1, 1981	4 cents per copy or 0.75 cents per minute, whichever is greater	1980 Copyright Royalty Tribunal rate adjustment proceeding
January 1, 1983	4.25 cents per copy or 0.8 cents per minute, whichever is greater	1980 Copyright Royalty Tribunal rate adjustment proceeding
July 1, 1984	4.5 cents per copy or 0.8 cents per minute, whichever is greater	1980 Copyright Royalty Tribunal rate adjustment proceeding
January 1, 1986	5 cents per copy or 0.85 cents per minute, whichever is greater	1980 Copyright Royalty Tribunal rate adjustment proceeding
January 1, 1988 to December 31, 1989	5.25 cents per copy or 1 cent per minute, whichever is greater	1980 Copyright Royalty Tribunal rate adjustment proceeding, based on consumer price index, Dec. 1985 to Sept. 1987.
January 1, 1990 to December 31, 1991	5.7 cents per copy or 1.1 cents per minute, whichever is greater	Adjustment based on consumer price index, Oct. 1987 to Oct. 1989.
January 1, 1992 to December 31, 1993	6.25 cents per copy or 1.2 cents per minute, whichever is greater	Adjustment based on consumer price index, Oct. 1989 to Oct. 1991.
January 1, 1994 to December 31, 1995	6.6 cents per copy or 1.25 cents per minute, whichever is greater	Adjustment based on consumer price index, Oct. 1991 to Oct. 1993.
January 1, 1996 to December 31, 1997	6.95 cents per copy or 1.3 cents per minute, whichever is greater	Adjustment based on consumer price index, Sept. 1993 to Oct. 1995.
January 1, 1998 to December 31, 1999	7.1 cents per copy or 1.35 cents per minute, whichever is greater	1997 mechanical rate adjustment proceeding
January 1, 2000 to December 31, 2001	7.55 cents per copy or 1.45 cents per minute, whichever is greater	1997 mechanical rate adjustment proceeding
January 1, 2002 to December 31, 2003	8.0 cents per copy or 1.55 cents per minute, whichever is greater	1997 mechanical rate adjustment proceeding
January 1, 2004 to December 31, 2005	8.5 cents per copy or 1.65 cents per minute, whichever is greater	1997 mechanical rate adjustment proceeding
January 1, 2006 to December 31, 2007	9.1 cents per copy or 1.75 cents per minute, whichever is greater	1997 mechanical rate adjustment proceeding

Source: Copyright Office, Licensing Division. www.copyright.gov/carp/m200a.html. Accessed 9 March 2004.

statute began at $100 for the first performance and went to $50 dollars for subsequent unauthorized performances or "as to the court shall appear to be just."[42] During the 1909 revision process the provision for civil liability for public performance was amended to apply to public performances for profit, the idea being to not have liability for church groups, school children, and other such groups. ASCAP was formed in 1914 to begin a systematic way for publishers and writers to collect for public performance and by 1917 had landed a test case in the U.S. Supreme Court on the issue of just what constituted a for-profit public performance.

The Case of Sweethearts. Composer Victor Herbert, one of the ASCAP founders, found his songs from the operetta *Sweethearts* being performed in Shanley's restaurant, a fancy New York City eatery, by professional singers and musicians for the enjoyment of the diners. Shanley argued that he was not charging the patrons to hear the music, so the music was not for profit within the meaning of the statute. In a brief opinion, Justice Holmes explained that the public performance right did, indeed, apply to such situations because the music really was being performed for the profit of the restaurant, regardless of whether an admission fee was charged. "The defendant's performances are not eleemosynary," said Justice Holmes. "They are part of a total for which the public pays, and the fact that the price of the whole is attributed to a particular item which those present are expected to order, is not important. ... If music did not pay it would be given up. If it pays it is out of the public's pocket. Whether it pays or not the purpose of employing it is profit and that is enough."[43]

Public Performances and Exemptions. The current copyright law defines public performances broadly. To perform a work publicly means, "(1) at a place open to the public or at any place where a substantial number of persons outside of a normal circle of a family and its social acquaintances is gathered; or (2) to transmit or otherwise communicate a performance ... to a place specified in clause (1) or to the public."[44] So, private clubs and most broadcast, closed circuit, or cable transmissions are covered. Although the words "for profit" were dropped from the public performance right in the 1976 revision to broaden the application of the right, a number of specific exemptions were added, generally at the behest of groups representing the special interests that wanted exemptions. All of these exemptions apply at least to nondramatic works—that is, those where the songs are not used in some manner to accompany a dramatic presentation or to tell a story, such as an opera or Broadway musical. The list below paraphrases the statute and covers, out of the ten specific exemptions in the statute, those most interesting or most significant to the recording industry. For details on these and the other exemptions, refer to the statute.[45]

- Performances by instructors or pupils in the course of face-to-face teaching at nonprofit educational institutions, or in distance learning courses (applies to all works).

- Performances in transmissions for educational broadcasting from government or nonprofit educational institutions.
- Performances in the course of religious services at a place or religious worship or assembly (applies to dramatic musical works of religious nature also).
- Noncommercial performances other than in transmissions where there is no payment to musicians or promoters, and either no admission charge, or the proceeds are used for charitable, religious, or educational purposes.
- Public reception of transmissions on single sets of the kinds of receiving devices commonly found in the home if there is no admission charge and no further transmission.
- Performances in stores selling recordings and musical works where the purpose is to promote sale of recordings, or the hardware used to view or listen to the recordings, and there is no admission charge and no transmission.

In 1998 Congress bowed to the interests of restaurants and other merchants when it passed the "Fairness in Musical Licensing Act." That act expanded the exemption for the public reception of a broadcast transmission to cover most eating and drinking establishments of less than 3,750 square feet and most other establishments of less than 2,000 square feet.[46] In 2000, the World Trade Organization (WTO) ruled that the amendment was inconsistent with United States' treaty obligations under the Berne Convention and WTO treaties because it exempted too many establishments.[47] Later, a WTO arbitrator ruled that the United States should bring its statutes into compliance by July 2001.[48] Failure to bring its laws into compliance could allow other members of the WTO to impose trade sanctions against the United States. By 2004, Congress had still not acted.

There are frequently amendments proposed to the law to exempt other performances, usually by special interests that simply do not want to have to pay for performance licenses. Congress then finds it must balance the economic and political interests of the copyright owners with these other groups.

Sampling: Thou Shalt Not Steal

Sampling, sometimes also called *digital sampling*, is the process whereby a recording artist or producer takes a small piece from a previous recording, digitizes it (the actual sampling process) so that it can be manipulated by computer sequencers and MIDI instruments, and puts it in a new recording or song. Sampling is commonplace in most genres of music, particularly in rap and urban dance music. Everything from James Brown's famous yells to the rare congas as heard in the *Miami Vice* theme have been sampled and used by other musicians and producers to make new recordings, that do not imitate the original, but build the actual originally recorded sounds into what is often a new and very different work. There is no question that the use of samples in the creation of new works can be, and often is, quite creative. The problem is that unless the sampling and new use is done with the permission of the owners of the copyrights in the sampled works, copyright infringement is the likely result.

The Case of "Alone Again Naturally." The very first sampling case to proceed all the way through to a court decision was in 1991. It set the tone for future sampling discussions and set into motion a flurry of label, artist, producer, and publisher sampling agreements and clauses. Rap artist Marcel Hall (aka Biz Markie) used three words from a Gilbert O'Sullivan recording and song, "Alone Again (Naturally)." Hall, his attorneys, and Warner Brothers Records (the distributing label for Hall's Cold Chillin' Records) knew they should obtain a sampling *clearance* (license) for the use of the three words in the song and their accompanying music, but for reasons not clear from the court record, they released the Biz Markie recording anyway, even though Gilbert O'Sullivan's publishing company, Grand Upright Music, Ltd., had refused the license. Federal District Court judge Duffy's curt opinion quoted the Bible's commandment, "Thou shalt not steal," and chided the defendants for their "callous disregard for the law and for the rights of others."[49] The settlement caused Warner Brothers Records to physically remove all of the offending recordings from the marketplace, pay heavy damages, and brought a rather abrupt end to Hall's career.

Sample Once, Infringe Twice. Sampling exposes the labels to copyright infringement charges on two possible fronts: the sound recording copyright owners and the song copyright owners. First, whenever *any* sound is taken from a recording made after February 15, 1972, the likelihood is that there is a violation of the sound recording copyright. Whether the sound is an artist's moan or yell, a drummer's kick-drum sound, or a hot guitar lick, there is no doubt that the previous sounds are taken. The copyrights in the recordings of those sounds usually belong to the label that did the original release. So, one label will have to ask another label for permission to use the sample. Permission can usually be had unless there is some problem with the artist not wanting to allow sampling. Permission, however, comes at a price. A typical sampling license from a label can cost anywhere from a one-time flat fee of $1,000 to $5,000 (typically) up to more than $25,000, to a share of up to 50 percent of the new sound recording copyrights. This depends greatly on the significance of the sample taken and the extent to which it is used in the new recording. If the sample also takes any of the words or melody of the song, a second sampling license must be obtained from the copyright owner (usually the music publisher) of the original song. The price there is about the same as for the sound recording sample.

These days, labels and music publishers not only have departments dedicated to tracking down copyright owners and obtaining sampling licenses for their artists who do lots of sampling, but also to chasing down other labels who may have used a sample of one of their recordings or songs. The cost of the sampling licenses is usually deducted from the artist's royalties. The licenses can add up to large sums of money or losses of significant percentages of copyright ownership. Artists who do heavy sampling are frequently quite creative, but they end up costing themselves considerable sums of money. The potential high costs of sampling and loss of ownership of rights have made some labels a bit gun-shy of artists who use lots of sampling. But, judging from the number of recordings that use sampling, the necessity for licenses did not stop uses of samples, creative and otherwise.

The Case of "Get Off Your Ass and Dance!" Those who use samples in making recordings often say that they should not have to pay for the uses because they often do not use much of the previous recording and that it is often manipulated in such a way that the original sound is not even recognizable. Until 2002 there had not been a case decided where the defendant had made that argument. In one of the many cases involving sampling from the songs and recordings of the popular funk group Parliament, and their leader/songwriter George Clinton, the recording of "Get off Your Ass and Jam!" owned by Westbound Records was sampled and used in a recording of the song "100 Miles and Runnin'." What was taken was a three-note arpeggiated chord that played for about two seconds in the original recording. This was slowed down, looped, and used several times in the new recording for a total of about 40 seconds.

In a ground-breaking decision, the district court held that such a use was de minimis (so small as not to be protected by copyright). Even recognizing that there had been "blatant copying," the court said, "No reasonable jury, even one familiar with the works of George Clinton (the author of "Get Off"), would recognize the source of the sample without having been told of its source. This fact, combined with the minimal qualitative copying and the lack of qualitative similarity between the works, warrants dismissal of Westbound's claim. ... If even an aficionado of George Clinton's music might not readily ascertain that his music has been borrowed, the purposes of copyright law would not be served by punishing the borrower for his creative use."[50]

Infringement and Remedies: "You stole my song!" Every Songwriter's Nightmare.

"Get a hit, get an infringement suit" is a not uncommon saying in the music business. Instances of alleged infringement are common for a number of reasons: (1) There are some charlatans who think they can make a

quick buck off of someone else's success. There is not really an infringement, but they figure if they claim that there was and sue, they might get a
settlement and a few thousand dollars. (2) Lots of popular songs do sound
alike. There are form and style constraints in much of popular music, and
there are only so many ways to arrange notes in a melody. Given those two
factors, it is quite possible that two composers could create works that did,
indeed, have similarities, even without ever having seen or heard the other's
work. In that case one is likely to think that the other has infringed them.

Fortunately for music publishers and record companies, it is rather difficult to prove infringement in court. The person claiming infringement
must be able to prove:

1. That they are the author or owner of the copyrights in the work that
   is claimed to have been infringed. That is usually not too difficult
   because a copyright registration form is *prima facie* evidence of the
   validity and ownership of the copyright.
2. That the other party copied their work. To show this the plaintiff
   must prove that the other party somehow had access to their work
   and that the two works are substantially similar. The access is fairly
   easy to prove if the original work enjoyed widespread public distribution or performance but can be quite difficult if the plaintiff's
   work was unpublished.

Substantial similarity means they must be similar in more ways than
simply style or an occasional few notes. There is an old saying that one can
copy up to four bars of music and not be infringing. NOT SO! In the case
of Saturday Night Live's parody of the "I Love New York" song and advertising campaign, the copying of four notes of the original composition was
held to be an infringement. NBC and Saturday Night Live were ultimately
allowed to use the song because their use was deemed to be a fair use
because it was a parody of the original.[51]

The Case of "How Deep Is Your Love." Substantially similarity by itself is
not enough to prove infringement. A fellow named Ronald Selle sued
Barry Gibb and the other Bee Gee brothers for an alleged infringement of
the song "How Deep Is Your Love." The songs were so similar that Barry
played the plaintiff's song on a piano in the courtroom and thought it was
his own. But the court ruled that because the plaintiff's song had not been
published or performed publicly anywhere that the Gibb brothers could
have heard it, there was no reasonable possibility of access so there could
be no infringement.[52]

The Case of "My Sweet Lord." The infringing songwriter does not have to
have done the dirty work intentionally. George Harrison apparently fell

victim to being familiar with the hit song "He's So Fine" as performed by the Chiffons. He wrote his song, "My Sweet Lord," that was similar in structure, much of the melody, and some of the lyrics. Similarities even existed down to accidental grace notes in the two songs. Harrison testified that he did not deliberately copy "He's So Fine." Said the judge, "[Harrison], in seeking musical materials to clothe his thoughts, was working with various possibilities. As he tried this possibility and that, there came to the surface of his mind a particular combination that pleased him as being one he felt would be appealing to a prospective listener; in other words, that this combination of sounds would work. Why? Because his subconscious knew it already had worked in a song his conscious mind did not remember."[53] Even though convinced that Harrison did not deliberately copy "He's So Fine" the judge ordered him to pay $1.6 million in damages. Through rather protracted litigation and a complex settlement, the rights to "He's So Fine" in the United States, United Kingdom, and Canada ultimately ended up with Harrison for the sum of $270,020,[54] but the principle of subconscious infringement, every songwriter's nightmare, had ended up a permanent part of copyright law.

New Directions for Copyright?

Much has been written about whether the existing copyright system can serve effectively into the twenty-first century. New media, new methods of creating works, and new delivery systems are certain to stretch the existing notions of copyright, authorship, and fair use. Copyright law has always changed in response to new technology. It was a new technology, the invention of moveable type by Johannes Gutenberg in 1456,[55] which made possible the mass reproduction of copies of a work. One must remember that the notion of controlling the right to reproduce copies of works began as a method of censorship in England in the late 1400s and 1500s. The crown wished to control who could print books and other materials in order to control the content of those books. Only certain printers were granted licenses or "patents" to print. And only those printers who produced publications to the king or queen's liking were likely to get a license.

By the early 1700s it was not political turmoil that resulted in the passage of the first copyright act, the Statute of Anne of 1710, but rather the needs of commerce. By the early 1700s there were enough competing printing presses in England so that when any printer began to publish a book, it was soon pirated in England (and the colonies). To get some protection from piracy the printers went to Parliament and requested a statutory privilege in the name of themselves and the authors of the works. Parliament noted, "Printers, Booksellers, and other Persons have of late frequently taken the Liberty of Printing, Reprinting, and Publishing, or causing to be Printed, Reprinted, and Published Books, and other Writings, without the Consent of the Authors or Proprietors of such Books and

Writings, to their very great Detriment, and too often to the Ruin of them and their families."[56] The right to make copies (copy, right?) was extended to authors and those who took their rights from those authors for the purposes of preventing piracy and "for the Encouragement of Learned Men to Compose and Write useful Books." These twofold purposes, protecting commercial interests and protecting authors so that they will be encouraged to create more works, have been the significant driving forces for copyright law ever since.[57]

In the United States, those purposes are written into the constitutional authority for Congress to make copyright laws. Article I, Section 8, Clause 8 empowers Congress to make laws "To promote the Progress of Science and the useful Arts, by securing for limited Times to authors and Inventors the exclusive Right to their respective Writings and Discoveries." Even considering only revisions to copyright law that directly affected the recording industry as listed in Table 3.3, it is clear that many changes have been effected in reaction to new technologies, new media, and new methods of utilizing works.

Everyone Is a Manufacturer It is no longer necessary to have a printing press to reproduce a book, a film studio to copy a motion picture, or a record pressing plant to make a copy of a phonorecord. The photocopiers, VCRs, and CD and DVD burners that are in the homes of many have moved manufacturing out of the hands of the capitalists and into the hands of the consumers.

TABLE 3.3 Copyright Law Changes and the Recording Industry

1790	First U.S. Copyright law protects books, charts, and maps
1831	Musical works first protected
1856	Dramatic works first protected, including public performance rights
1897	Public performance rights for musical works protected
1909	Mechanical rights for musical works added; unpublished musical works could be protected by registration.
1912	Motion pictures first protected
1972	Sound Recordings first protected
1978	All works created, whether published or not, are protected. Jukebox performance rights protected. Compulsory mechanical license rate subject to change by the Copyright Royalty Tribunal (later the Librarian of Congress)
1982	Piracy of recordings and motion pictures made a felony with increased fines and jail terms.
1984	Record rental prohibited
1992	Audio Home Recording Act exempts home copying and places a royalty on digital recorders and blank digital media
1994	Anti-bootlegging rights for performers of live musical events
1995	Digital public performance rights for sound recordings, digital delivery rights for sound recordings and the musical works embodied in the phonorecords.
1998	Digital Millennium Copyright Act, Fairness in Musical Licensing Act, and Copyright Term Extension Act.

Source: Various statutory provisions of Title 17 U.S. Code; and R. Gorman and J. Ginsburg, *Copyright Cases and Materials*, 6th ed. (New York: Foundation Press, 2002).

Mass production allowed copyright owners to control their works at the point of production or distribution. One license issued to one producer was sufficient. Where there are thousands of users and thousands of copyright owners, as is the case in musical performance rights, an intermediate agency is needed to keep track of all of the users and to distribute appropriate royalties to all of the many copyright owners. When the number of users and manufacturers reaches into the millions, as is the case with photocopiers and CD burners, the copyright owners are faced with a dilemma. They must either prohibit the users from making copies or using the works in unauthorized ways, find another control and licensing point in the distribution, manufacture, or some other part of the process, or allow the uses and hope to make their profits through more easily controlled ones. Motion picture copyright owners require that digital video disc systems have a system in the playback hardware that prohibits copying—either single or serial copies.

The recording industry has tried the approach of allowing analog and digital home taping by placing a royalty on the devices that allow digital recording, thus finding a different point in the manufacturing process where the control is easier to accomplish. Instead of attempting to license the manufacture of the copy of the recording, which occurs in the private homes of millions of consumers, the industry licenses the manufacture of the recorders and blank media, which still requires mass production technology and only involves a few producers. For the individual consumer, the barrier to entry into the market of being a manufacturer of high quality copies of recordings is low: the cost of a CD burner, a CD player, and a blank disc. The consumer is not concerned with being able to make thousands of copies per hour or per day. One or two copies are probably all the consumer wants.

The other method is to control delivery of the work itself—that is what the digital delivery of phonorecords provision passed in 1995 does. The provider of the soft copy (which the consumer converts into a hard copy) purchases the license and keeps track of how many digital deliveries have been made so that the copyright owners can be appropriately compensated. Whatever approach is used, the trick is to find a point in the manufacturing or distribution chain where the copyright owner can exert some control (licensing) over the process that ultimately leads to the consumers making their own copies. The trials and tribulations of the recording industry as it attempted to cope with rampant Internet theft of recordings, Internet distribution of hard and digital copies, and Internet promotion and marketing are explored in Chapters 8 and 11.

Everyone Is an Author With a computer and a laser printer, anyone can produce books that would have made Gutenberg proud. With a computer and MIDI setup anyone can produce high-quality orchestral recordings that would have made Beethoven proud. Of course, these people can also

author new works. They may not possess the creative writing or compos-
ing talent to produce great works, but they can easily produce copyrightable works. They can even distribute copies of these works electronically
without the need to secure the services of a production plant. To John Pavlik's framework for media analysis, which concentrates on the way media
content is "gathered, processed and produced; transmitted; stored; and
retrieved and displayed,"[58] we need to add "created."

Where Is the Editor? There is one problem with a world where "everyone"
is an author or composer and self-distributor via the Internet. With the
publisher, who had access to the means of mass production through investment of the necessary capital, serving as a filter or gatekeeper, only those
works that the publishers thought worthy would reach the public. The merits and benefits of having a filter or censor in the information stream are
debatable. On the one hand some voices and meritorious works may never
be heard or seen. On the other hand we did not have to open millions of
oysters in order to find a pearl. With so many avenues of free expression
open to the public at large we might like to have an editor or publisher do
some filtering for us—to select which oysters are likely to contain pearls
before we begin opening, or even to present us with a nicely strung set of
pearls. Of course we do have to compensate the publisher or record company for all of the work of opening all of those non-pearl-bearing oysters. If
everyone with a computer can produce a book and everyone with a fairly
simple MIDI setup can produce a sound recording, and then make it available for the rest of the public (distribute it) through the Internet, we are still
going to need music publishers, record companies, and patrons of the arts
to help us decide which works are deserving of our attention because of
their artistic merit or simply because of their mass appeal.

Summary
Sound recordings and the musical compositions that are usually part of
those recordings are two separate copyrightable works. The rights associated with each of those two works are similar, but also differ in several
regards. The economic interests in the music publishing and recording
streams often attempt to mold the copyright law to their advantage and
have succeeded in doing so in a number of instances. This has created a
complex legal environment for the use of recordings and songs that per-
meates current questions of performances, sampling, downloading, and
more. With an understanding of how copyright laws work to the benefit,
and sometimes detriment, of each income stream, it is now time to explore
each stream in some detail in the next three chapters.

4

Music Publishing: The First Stream

It All Begins with a Song

— Slogan of the Nashville Songwriters Association International

Without a song, there would be nothing to perform or record, so it is logical to begin a closer examination of the three income streams with music publishing. This income stream is referred to as the music-publishing stream and not the songwriting stream because very few people ever made any money from simply writing a song. The money was made from the publication (uses) of that song. Even when songwriters "own their own" songs, the songs are almost always actually owned, in the copyright sense, by a music publisher, even if it is the songwriter's music publishing company. Therefore the primary focus of this chapter is music publishing instead of songwriting. However, there are so many aspiring songwriters in bands and as "just plain" songwriters that the development of writers deserves some mention here. The same has been done for aspiring recording artists throughout the book.

The Music Business Three-Income-Stream Model—Revisited

The three income streams in the music business discussed in Chapter 1, recordings, music publishing, and live performances, are interrelated. The common gene in the relationship is recordings. There would be very little music-publishing revenue without popular recordings. The sale of the recordings provides mechanical royalties for the publishers of the songs on those recordings—about 35 percent of music publishing income (see Figure 4.1). Another 15 percent of publishing revenues are derived from radio airplay of recordings. The majority of print music

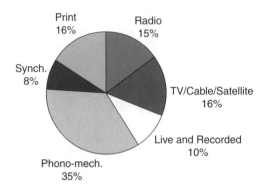

Fig. 4.1 Worldwide publishing revenues (2000). National Music Publishers' Association. *International Survey of Music Publishing Revenues*, 2002.

sales are of piano-vocal editions of popular singles and folios of popular albums or recording artists. Based on the amount of popular music in motion pictures and television, it is reasonable to estimate that one-half (or more) of television performance and film synchronization royalties are the result of songs and recordings by popular recording artists. Finally, the vast majority of live and recorded performances (12 percent of publishing revenues) are of songs made popular by recordings. Totaling these up, *over 75 percent of music publishing royalties are the result of popular recordings.*

Music Publishing: Then and Now

Copyrights Don't Talk Back.

— Attributed to Lou Levy, longtime president of MCA

The music publishing business is not what it used to be. In the 1890s music publishers sold millions of copies of sheet music. In 1893, *After the Ball* became the first song to sell one million copies of sheet music, hit songs sold as many as two million copies in print by 1909. Even though sound recordings were catching on in 1920 and accounted for about $3 million dollars of publishing revenue, sheet music sales still accounted for more than $16 million, about 88 percent, of publishing income. Sheet music sales plummeted during the Depression to a low of about $2 million dollars in 1933. During that same time performance revenues, largely from radio, grew and sustained the music publishing industry through World War II.[1] Print sales failed to make a significant recovery after the war. *Billboard* reported in 1955 that publishers had to find new income because sales of even the most popular songs in sheet music were usually less than

TABLE 4.1 Music Publishing Income Sources: U.S. Details 1992–2000 (U.S. Dollars in Millions)

Source	1992	1994	1996	1998	2000
Radio Performance	147	184	213	242	291
TV/Cable/Satellite	258	242	252	275	317
Live and Recorded	97	150	163	181	203
Phono/Mechanical	305	427	493	530	691
Synchronization	51	52	80	112	157
Print	172	187	198	234	316
TOTAL	1,048	1,242	1,424	1,595	1,975

Source: Data from National Music Publishers' Association, Inc. *International Survey of Music Publishing Revenues* (1994–2002).

300,000 units. The reliable source of income was performance royalties.[2] That, however, was before rock and roll jolted record sales into ever higher gear and pushed mechanical royalties into a close second place behind performance royalties. Even though revenue from print music recovered and accounted for about 38 percent of the publishers' estimated $283 million share of revenues by 1978, the music business had been forever changed.[3] By the twenty-first century, the recording industry dwarfed music publishing. In 2000, domestic revenue from the sale of recordings in the United States was $14.3 billion—nearly ten times the $1.98 billion reported by the National Music Publishers' Association for that same year.[4] Revenues from the sale of recordings and from performances accounted for 77 percent of music-publishing income, while distribution of print music was reduced to a share of about 16 percent (see Table 4.1). A century of technological innovation and evolution and the concomitant change in copyright laws (see Chapters 2 and 3) turned an industry that once created and marketed products into a copyright industry that primarily licenses others to utilize its properties.

Overall Structure

Music publishing is now an integral part of the recording industry. Every major label owns publishing interests, as do many smaller labels, independent producers, and recording artists. Despite the existence of literally thousands of small music publishers, most of the rights are administered through a handful of publishing giants. The small songwriter, artist, and producer-owned publishing companies simply do not have the expertise or personnel to deal with the complexities of music publishing. They usually enter into agreements with some of the giants to copublish or to administer their catalogs.

The large publishing companies are getting larger by acquisition of smaller companies or by entering into administration or copublishing agreements that allow the "Goliaths" to share in the revenues generated by the "Davids." The willingness of the larger companies to use this approach makes it possible for smaller companies to exist and be profitable. It also removes one of the mediators between the songwriters and their audiences. No longer is the publisher trying to second guess what an artist or producer will want to record and therefore accepting only safe songs. *Safe songs* in the twenty-first century are songs that are written by songwriter/artists who are already under contract or who have good possibilities of obtaining recording contracts.

The three largest music publishers in the world, EMI Music, Warner/Chappell Music, and Universal Music, are owned by three of the largest recording conglomerates. From the late 1980s and into the twenty-first century, record conglomerates actively built their music publishing interests. All of them have engaged in major publishing acquisitions. Sony Music had no publishing when it started in 1989 with the acquisition of the CBS, Inc. record labels; CBS had earlier divested itself of its music publishing with the sale of CBS Songs to SBK Entertainment in 1986. At that time CBS Songs was one of the five largest music publishers in the world. By 1993 Sony Music had emerged as a top ten music publisher in the United States through acquisitions such as the Tree catalog (Tree was the most successful country music publisher at that time) in 1989. In 1994 Sony Music entered a co-venture deal with Michael Jackson, who owns many Beatles tunes in his ATV Music catalog. Sony reportedly paid Jackson $100 million for that deal and continues to expand.[5] PolyGram International Music Publishing went from a major player to minor league when it sold Chappell Music to Warner Brothers in 1984 for about $200 million. PolyGram immediately reentered the publishing fray with the acquisition of Dick James Music (early Elton John/Bernie Taupin catalog) in early 1985, Cedarwood (a Nashville firm), and others.[6] MCA Music Publishing (now Universal Music Publishing) also announced its intention to compete globally through catalog acquisition. MCA mentioned no specific catalogs except to say a seven-figure deal was pending for a Nashville company.[7] When PolyGram and Universal merged in 1998, the new company (Universal Music), became the third largest music publisher. Universal made a major addition to its status in 2000 with the acquisition of Rondor Music for a reported $400 million. BMG Music Publishing began in 1987 and went on a building spree after the acquisition of RCA's labels and music interests, buying 73 catalogs in a five-year period from 1988 to 1993. BMG acquired foreign licensing from Famous Music (Viacom's music publishing division of Paramount) in 1995 when Famous's previous deal with Warner/Chappell expired.[8] BMG acquired the entirety of Zomba Music Group, including music publishing and labels, in 2002 for $2.7 billion. That deal may have pulled BMG into third place among the music publishers of the world. EMI Music Publishing (the largest), also continued to acquire song copyrights with the 2003 acquisition of 80 percent of the Jobette catalog—the songs from Berry Gordy's Motown Records.[9]

The competitiveness of the conglomerate-owned publishing companies is evident in their success at having their songs on hit recordings. As Tables 4.2 through 4.4 indicate, the top two popular music publishers in terms of chart share across all three most popular genres—pop, R&B, and country—are EMI and Warner/Chappell. Universal was a clear third with

TABLE 4.2 Top Pop Publishers, 1998–2002
(By Number of Singles in Top 100)

Publisher	Average Rank	Years in Top 5	Average Number of Singles
EMI Music	1	5	162
Warner/Chappell	2	5	128
Universal Music	3	4	82
Sony/ATV Music	4.6	5	56
Zomba	4.3	3	44
Famous Music	4	2	28
Realsongs	4	1	8

Source: Data compiled from *Billboard*, Year-End Issues, 1998–2002.

Zomba probably fourth, but that was prior to the BMG purchase of Zomba. The first year of combined figures will not be out until 2003 or 2004. Sony, BMG, and Almo/Irving round out the top spots. A proposed merger between BMG and Warner Music Group (WMG) in 2003 threatened to upset the hierarchy by merging the music publishing interests of the two firms. WMG was reportedly considering selling Warner/Chappell or some of the Warner/Chappell catalog in order to allow the other parts of the two firms to merge.[10] A similar situation developed with the proposed Sony-BMG merger in late 2003.[11] At the end of 2003 there were no major independent music publishers capable of challenging the power of the big five music/media conglomerates in the music-publishing income stream.

    Why the sudden attention to music publishing by the recording conglomerates? For one thing, the mechanical royalties paid by record companies to music publishers for the right to make recordings of songs are expenses to the labels. If labels owned publishing in the songs their artists recorded, they could take their mechanical royalty expenses out of their record company pockets and put them as revenues into their publishing company pockets. Most recording artists in the 1990s and beyond were entirely self-contained; they wrote and performed their own compositions. It was no longer necessary to obtain songs from a music publisher who had songwriters creating songs for other people to record. The record companies marketed the recordings that created the hit songs. Why,

TABLE 4.3 Top R & B Publishers, 1998–2002
(By Number of Singles in Top 100)

Publisher	Average Rank	Years in Top 5	Average Number of Singles
EMI Music	1	5	197
Warner/Chappell	2	5	134
Universal Music	3.3	4	83
Zomba	3.8	4	58
Sony/ATV Music	5.2	5	46

Source: Data compiled from *Billboard*, Year-End Issues, 1998–2002. (See Table 4.2)

TABLE 4.4 Top Country Publishers, 1998–2002
(By Number of Singles in Top 100)

Publisher	Average Rank	Years in Top 5	Average Number of Singles
Warner/Chappell	1.8	5	67
EMI Music	2.2	5	68
Sony Music	2.6	5	65
Universal Music	3.3	4	56
Almo	4.5	2	26
BMG Music	5	2	25
PolyGram Music	5	1	37
Realsongs	5	1	4

Source: Data from *Billboard*, Year End Issues, 1998–2002. (See Table 4.2)

reasoned the labels, should some other party get all the benefit from the label's promotion of the recordings?

Finally, the income stream from music publishing is more stable and longer term than the income stream from the hit recording that produced the hit song. A label will probably get only three or four shots at earning income on a hit record: the original recording, a greatest hits collection, perhaps a boxed set if the artist really has a long career, and later reissues as historical or collector's items. Every one of these also makes money for the publisher. In addition, the publisher gets royalties every time the original record gets played on the radio as an oldie, whenever the artist may perform it on television, when it is turned into background music for use in hotels, restaurants, and other businesses or organizations (sometimes referred to as in a tongue-in-cheek manner as "elevator music"), when sheet music is sold, and most importantly, when someone else records it. The potential to earn royalties even without recordings is limited, but clearly illustrated by the song "Happy Birthday." Very few recordings are made of "Happy Birthday" any more, but the asking price for the copyright to that song, which is *not* in the public domain, was $12 million in 1988. "Happy Birthday" reportedly earns one million dollars every year in royalties.[12]

Cover versions (recordings made by an artist different from the one who originally recorded the song) can generate publishing profits for years. For example, the song "Who's Sorry Now," originally written in 1923 and a number two hit for Connie Francis in 1958, had been recorded more than four hundred times by artists all over the world ranging from the Glenn Miller Orchestra, to Willie Nelson, to Nat "King" Cole by 1985.[13] That is what publishers call an *evergreen*, a song that keeps on earning royalties long after the popularity of the original recording has faded. Country songwriter/artist Dolly Parton wrote her song, "I Will Always Love You," for her 1974 *Jolene* album. It was a number one country single that year. Then in 1982 it was included in the film version of *The Best Little Whorehouse In Texas* and again hit the top of the country charts. But the greatest success came from the smash hit performance by R&B/Pop artist Whitney Houston in the soundtrack for the movie *The Bodyguard* more than a decade later.[14] Even songs written and originally recorded by rock artists may turn into hits by other artists years later. In 1977 the rock group Aerosmith had a number two hit with "Walk This Way." Nine years later, Run-DMC had a number one hit with a version of it in a genre (rap) that did not even exist when Aerosmith's first version was recorded.[15]

Copyrights generally last for the life of the songwriter plus seventy years (or for ninety-five years for works first published between 1923 and 1978; see Chapter 2 for details), long after most people have lost any interest in purchasing the original recording of a song. The value of the copyrights in the master recording is likely to have a much shorter life. The record company can therefore extend the earning potential of the hit recording they originally created by having an interest in the song which that recording made popular as well as in the original recording.

Music Publishing Functions

Basic Functions

Music publishers perform much the same functions with songs that labels perform with recordings. The primary difference is that the publisher deals with an intangible property right, the copyright, and the label, although it will acquire copyrights in the sound recordings (masters), is much more concerned about selling copies of those masters in the forms of CDs, tapes, and downloads. The primary functions of a music publisher are the acquisition of copyrights and the exploitation (in a positive, business sense) of those copyrights.

Publishing Company Structure

A music publishing company's internal structure and functioning very much mirror the two primary functions of acquisition and exploitation of copyrights. Those functions are usually split between creative and administrative divisions. The creative division is in charge of signing songs and songwriters to contracts with the company, promoting the company's catalog of songs to prospective users (*song plugging*), and possibly developing potential songwriter/artists in a role not unlike that of A&R people at record labels. Usually the people undertaking these roles are known as *professional managers*. (Do not confuse professional managers at music publishing companies with personal managers for artists discussed in Chapter 5.) The professional manager is frequently a song doctor, working with songwriters to help them create the most marketable songs. Professional managers must know producers, artists, A&R people, movie producers, and as many other potential users of their songs as they can in order to fulfill the role of song plugger. Because they become familiar with what makes the best recording for a song and often produce the demos used to promote the song to producers and the like, it is not uncommon for professional managers to become record producers as well.[16]

The administrative side of the music publishing company is the paperwork side of the business. It will usually include copyright administration, licensing, accounting, and perhaps business/legal affairs units. The copyright administration unit takes care of registering the publisher's songs with the Copyright Office, recording other information with the Copyright Office, such as notices of death or transfers of ownership, and renewal of copyrights for songs published prior to 1978. The licensing unit works with the Harry Fox Agency (the primary agency that deals with mechanical licensing; though some companies may work with other agencies) and the publisher's performing rights organization affiliate for the clearance of new compositions and recordings, and directly issues other licenses, including print licensing and advertising uses. Because the music publishing business depends on the pennies earned from royalties as a result of the various uses of the songs, the accounting unit is very important. With thousands of uses for thousands of songs by hundreds of different songwriters, it is a major task to insure that everyone receives their proper payments for their songs. If there is a separate business/legal affairs department, it will be in charge of contract negotiation with songwriters, complex license negotiations, and catalog acquisitions.

Copyright Acquisition

The Traditional Way

The classic model for copyright acquisition goes like this. Songwriters, either on their own or under contract to music publishers, are moved to write songs about something. Melody and lyrics are created and woven together. The songs are presented in some manner (*pitched*), perhaps by a live performance, perhaps by a demonstration recording (*demo*) sent to publishers. The publisher tries to assess the potential that the song has for becoming recorded by other people. If the publisher believes a song is likely to be recorded, the publisher signs a contract with the songwriter in which the songwriter assigns the copyright to the publisher in exchange for roughly half of any royalties that may be generated by the exploitation of the song. The publisher and songwriter enter into a kind of partnership, with the songwriter creating a product that the publisher will then attempt to market. The publisher will probably have a high-quality demo made of the song to present the song to people likely to record it. The publisher will then pitch the song to recording artists, producers, and A&R people at record labels with the hope of attracting someone to record it. Once it is recorded and released, the publisher will then (perhaps) help promote it to radio stations. If the song is successful enough, the publisher might cause sheet music to be printed and sold. The publisher will also try to get other artists to cover the song. The publisher may try to get it used in motion pictures. Meanwhile, the publisher will sit back and collect royalties from the sale of copies of the recording and from the performances of the song on radio and television.

For a long time, beginning before the invention of phonograph recordings, that is the way it worked. In the late 1800s and early 1900s, songwriters wrote tunes and publishers' employees called *song pluggers* pitched them to minstrel show and vaudeville performers. The song pluggers got their name from the fact that a performance before an audience was called a *plug* for the song. People would not buy sheet music for the songs until they had heard the song in performance. The more plugs a song got, the more exposure it got; the more exposure it got, the more sheet music it sold. In those days it was common for a songwriter to receive a flat fee for a song instead of a royalty. Songwriters wrote tunes that went into their own or others' theatrical productions. With the advent and increasing popularity of recordings in the early 1900s, the song pluggers pitched tunes to recording artists and A&R people at record companies to get them recorded. In the 1920s, 1930s, and 1940s, song pluggers pitched tunes to bandleaders to get them performed on network or local radio. For many of these plugs the publisher would often pay a "gratuity" to the performer. This widespread practice later turned into *payola* in the record industry (see Chapter 9).

The "Modern" Model

There are fewer and fewer artists who are just singers. I mean, Bing Crosby's gone.

— John Titta, Creative Vice President, Warner/Chappel Music[17]

The emergence of rock and roll transformed the music publishing business just as it transformed radio and the recording industry in general. In rock it was much more common for the songwriter who wrote the song and the artist who recorded the song to be the same person. Some say it was this genuineness of message from the songwriter interpreting his/her own composition that created much of the appeal of rock music. For performers who understood the business, it may have been an attempt to gain some economic rewards from their performance of a song, in addition to its sales in recordings. Because there was no performance right in a recording, the only way to share in the income generated by radio and television performances was to be a songwriter or copyright owner of the musical composition.[18] Although there were great pop songwriters who did not record their own material in the 1960s and 1970s (Bert Bacharach; Carole King and Gerry Goffin; Brian Holland, Lamont Dozier, and Eddie Holland [the Holland-Dozier-Holland team who wrote many of Motown's great hits] to name just a few), the trend was, and still is, toward the artist/writer dominating the popular music field, particularly rock. Even in country music, the last bastion of the traditional songwriter-publisher relationship, the artist/writer has become the dominant model.

Many of the songwriters whose names appear in *Billboard's* top ten songwriters lists defy categorization. Kenneth Edmonds (aka "Babyface") is one of the most successful songwriters of the 1990s. He is a recording artist with hit records of his own, plus he has produced other artist's hits, plus he has his songs recorded by artists whom he does not produce. A significant number of the songwriter/artists in the top ten list not only write for themselves but for other artists as well. It is extremely rare to find a songwriter in the pop top 10 list who is a songwriter only. The other trend of the 1990s and beyond is co-writing. Two-thirds of the songwriters in the top ten lists for 1991 through 1995 wrote songs with other songwriters, producers, or artists.

How does a publisher proceed to acquire copyrights under the new model? Many publishers have taken on an A&R function. They actively seek songwriters who are, or have the potential to become, recording artists as well. They attempt to sign these songwriters to publishing deals before they are signed by record companies. The publisher may pay the songwriter/artists an advance in a form that allows them to develop their writing, arranging, and performing talents without having to keep a "day job." The publisher also helps the songwriter/artist seek recording and management contracts, or may even go so far as to use the publishing company's studios to create a master that can be released on an independent label in the hopes of selling even 20,000 to 30,000 copies. Songwriters/producers are also a target for this kind of development by publishers, particularly in the R&B and urban field. In exchange for that developmental advance and the possibility of future royalties, the songwriter/artists pledge their output of songs for several years to the publisher.[19] Perhaps the most successful example of this tactic is Alanis Morissette, whose *Jagged Little Pill* album became the best-selling debut album by a female artist to that time when it passed the eight million copies mark in 1996.[20] She had been signed to a publishing deal with MCA Music Publishing in Canada for seven years before her 1995 album debut.[21] Even in such developmental deals, the publishers often have to content themselves with a smaller share of the total publishing income by entering copublishing deals with the songwriter/artist's publishing company.[22]

Publishers also bid for the publishing rights to the songs of new songwriter/artists who have just signed with labels. If the songwriter/artist does not sign with the label's affiliated publishing company at the same time they sign a recording agreement, then the publishing is particularly attractive because there is a high probability that the songs will be earning royalties as soon as the songwriter/artist and label complete and market their first album.

Finally, publishers still sign individual songwriters to agreements even when the songwriter is not likely to develop into a recording artist. In such instances the song material has to be particularly strong, because the publisher will have to find a market for it instead of having a ready-made market with a songwriter/artist's own recordings. It is also still possible for songwriters to have individual songs accepted by a music publisher even though the songwriter is not under any long-term agreement with the publisher. This is, however, becoming much less common in all genres.

Songwriter Agreements
Single-Song Contracts
The most basic agreement between a publisher and songwriter is the single-song agreement. It is signed whenever a publisher acquires the copyrights to a song, whether it is from an unknown songwriter for one song only, or from a songwriter under a long-term exclusive songwriter agreement (see below). Most of the terms in a single-song agreement, like most of those in an exclusive agreement, are negotiable. What appears below are the terms likely to be in a typical agreement. [23] If the songwriter is of sufficient stature, has their own publishing company already set up, or already has a recording agreement, then the share of the publishing revenues may be increased by negotiating a different kind of deal such as copublishing or administration. One observer commented, "Fading into distant memory is the era when, by and large, a publisher took a song and held 100 percent of the publishing."[24]

Typical single-song agreement terms include:

- Grant of rights: The songwriter assigns (sells) all of the copyrights in the song to the publisher for the life of the copyrights, throughout the world. International rights are somewhat negotiable, especially if the publisher is not large enough to have the ability to market the song on a worldwide basis.
- Reversion: Any grant of copyright is subject to the Copyright Act's termination right. The songwriter has the statutory authority to end a transfer of ownership or nonexclusive license after a period of thirty-five to forty years (see Chapter 2 for details). A songwriter with some leverage may also be able to negotiate a contractual right to have the publisher transfer the copyrights back to the songwriter if the publisher fails to have the songs recorded or published within some set period of time, usually one to two years with five years as a maximum. The publisher will be willing to do this if there are no unrecouped advances outstanding at the time.

- Advances: Advances are prepayments of royalties that the publisher will seek to recoup out of royalties earned. In a single-song agreement the advance is usually a small lump sum ranging from nothing to typically several hundred dollars. Publishers usually will not pay advances unless the songwriter has some track record of success or the near assurance that the song will be recorded by some popular artist or by the songwriter/artists themselves. Major advances occur only in exclusive songwriter agreements.
- Royalties:
  1. Mechanical royalties are usually divided 50/50 after any collection fee from the Harry Fox Agency or other mechanical collection organization is deducted.
  2. Performance royalties are usually split by the collecting performing rights organization (ASCAP, BMI, SESAC, and a few smaller agencies) and paid separately to the publisher and songwriter. Therefore, the songwriter does not usually get any percentage of what the publisher collects. *If* the performance income were paid 100 percent to the publisher, then the songwriter would expect to get 50 percent of the publisher's net.
  3. Print royalties may simply be split 50/50 out of the publisher's net receipts. More often, the publisher pays a percentage royalty based on the wholesale or retail price of the music being sold, or even a *penny* rate (a flat rate of so many cents per copy sold). If a percentage of a price is used, the songwriter typically gets 10 to 15 percent of wholesale for folios (song books), and 10 percent of wholesale for other print (not including sheet music). For sheet music (also known as piano-vocal editions) publishers often pay a penny rate of 7 to 10 cents per copy. This approach to sheet music does not come close to a 50/50 split because the publisher is paid a percentage of the retail price approximating 70 to 80 cents per copy. The per-copy sheet music rate is not often negotiable. One songwriter refers to it as a "sacred cow."[25]
  4. Other royalties and fees covering a wide range of uses, specified and unspecified, are usually split 50/50 based on the publisher's net receipts.
- Cross-collateralization: The publisher will usually ask that any advances be recouped out of any royalties due to the songwriter under "this or any other agreement" between the two parties. For example, royalties earned in one year can be used to recoup advances paid in an earlier year. Royalties earned from one song can be used to recoup advances paid for a different song. The worst scenario is that publishing advances can be recouped from any recording royalties or advances, although it would be more common for recording

advances to be recouped out of publishing advances if the songwriter/artist had signed recording and publishing agreements with the same company. A songwriter can usually at least limit the cross-collateralization in a publishing agreement to publishing royalties. On the other hand, a publisher would have no right to cross-collateralize against a songwriter/artist's income earned from a concert performance because that agreement would not be between the songwriter/artist and the publisher, but rather between the songwriter/artist and a concert promoter.

- Demo costs: Publishers try to recoup demo costs by deeming them to be advances in their agreements with the songwriters. A new songwriter could expect 50 percent of demo costs to be recoupable, with as little as none recoupable for a songwriter with a good track record. Other publisher expenses are generally not recoupable at all.

Exclusive Songwriter Agreements

Under these contracts the songwriter agrees to deliver all of the songs written for a certain period of time to the publisher in exchange for a usually substantial advance against royalties. Previously written songs may also be covered if their copyrights have not already been transferred to some other publisher.

Typical exclusive songwriter agreement terms:

- Royalties: The base rates and splits are typically structured as in single-song agreements.
- Exclusivity: These contracts are *exclusive,* that is the songwriter agrees that no other publisher can have claim to the songs written during the agreement. To put it another way, the publisher says, "Thou shalt have no other publisher before me."
- Duration: The term of the agreement is usually for one year with up to four one-year options to extend the agreement for another year. These options are the publisher's. If the publisher wants to keep the songwriter under contract and keep paying the advances, then the publisher may elect to do so after the end of each year. If not, the contract simply ends. Another variation is for the term of the exclusive songwriter agreement to run coterminously with the recording contract if the songwriter is also a recording artist. If the recording contract ended, then the publisher would have the option of ending the songwriting contract. Of course, the publisher usually is able to keep all copyrights in all songs written during the term of the agreement. The obligation to pay royalties on those songs would also continue after the end of the agreement, because

each individual song is transferred for the life of the copyright under a single song agreement as outlined above.

- Advances: The primary reason for a songwriter to enter an exclusive agreement is the promise of the publisher to pay a substantial advance against royalties. These advances (sometimes known as a *draw*) usually range from several hundred dollars a week for a new songwriter to thousands of dollars a week for an established song-writer, or a songwriter/artist who is successful. Even songwriter/art-ists without a recording agreement may get substantial advances if the publisher believes enough in the material and the ability of the songwriter/artist to get a recording contract. Publishing advances for writer/artists tend to be in the neighborhood of $100,000, and per-haps up to $500,000 if there is a bidding war going on between pub-lishers.[26] Publishers may even go so far as to purchase substantial amounts of recording equipment for songwriter/artists to perfect their craft.
- Output requirements: The publisher may require the songwriter to complete a certain minimum number of songs per year, typi-cally twelve to twenty. The songs will usually have to be accepted by the publisher. The minimum may even be stated in terms of commercially recorded songs, especially if the songwriter is also an artist.
- Collaboration: Writing with other songwriters is especially impor-tant to a songwriter's creative processes and to getting material recorded. Some songwriters take half-finished songs to recording artists and suggest that they finish them together. The result is that the songwriter now is a half-writer of the song with the artist. Half a loaf is better than none, but it is important to make sure that the half-loaf counts toward the minimum number of songs commit-ment if there is one. It is also important to the songwriter that other collaborators, such as producers or artists who did not really create any of the composition, cannot be added to a song as songwriters without the original songwriter's permission.

Songwriter Royalty Example

Assume an artist has a number one hit. How much money would the songwriter of that song make? As with many such questions in the recording industry, the answer is, "It depends." Several assumptions have to be made before one can even begin to calculate.

- First, it is likely that this song is licensed for mechanical royalties at ¾ of the statutory mechanical royalty rate, even if the songwriter is not the artist, because of restrictions on total mechanical royalties in many artist agreements (see Chapter 7 for details). At the 2004 statutory mechanical rate of 8.5 cents per copy that would equal 6.375 cents per copy. Also assume that the mechanicals are collected through the Harry Fox Agency. It is uncommon for a hit single to sell "gold" (500,000 units), so let's assume successful single sales of 200,000 units. Let's also assume that the album containing the song has sold 500,000 units and is also licensed at a ¾ rate.

- Assume that performance royalties are collected and divided by the performing rights organization (PRO; see "Performance Licensing" later in this chapter) and paid 50 percent to the publisher and 50 percent to the songwriter separately. Performance royalties for one year vary greatly depending upon the genre of the music, how long it is a hit, and whether it receives television airplay. One report had performance royalties for a country hit varying by as much as $80,000 or more depending upon how much airplay even a number one song receives and on what stations. An average figure that is close for all three PROs would be about $140,000 for one year for either the publisher or songwriter share.[27] Another estimate placed royalties for a "major across-the-board chart song" at as much as $650,000 for a pop song with significant television airplay.[28]
- Assume a ten-cent, per-copy rate for sheet music and that the song has sold 80,000 pieces. This assumption may be a bit high, because many singles do not have sheet music printed.
- Finally, assume the songwriter is under an exclusive agreement and has been receiving an advance for the past year of $350 per week, a total of $18,200.

The advance is added back in to show that it is money that the songwriter actually had received during the year and probably used to live on. That looks like a respectable sum, but most songs are not number one hits. In fact, estimates are that only about 2 to 5 percent of songwriters make $10,000 per year.[29] Also, if the song was co-written with just one other person, then our songwriter would only receive half of the above amount from the various royalties.

Other Copyright Acquisition Methods

Because so many songwriters, producers, and recording artists have their own publishing companies, there are lots of small catalogs of songs (all the songs owned by a publisher constitute its *catalog*) available for possible purchase. Larger publishers often buy these small publishers' catalogs. Larger catalogs of independent publishers are also purchased, typically by the major publishers. In a catalog purchase the

Songwriter Royalties Example

Mechanical Royalties:

Single sales: 200,000 units @ 6.375 cents	$ 12,750.00
Album sales: 500,000 units @ 6.375 cents	31,875.00
Total:	44,625.00
Less: HFA collection fee 5.75%	2,565.94
Net Mechanicals collections	42,069.06
Writer's share @ 50%	$21,029.53
Print sales: 80,000 copies @ 0.10 per copy	8,000.00
Gross earnings from publisher	$29,029.53
Less: recoupable advance 52 weeks @ $300	$18,200.00
Net due from publisher	$10,829.53
Performance royalties (writer's share paid directly to songwriter)	$140,000.00
Writer's earnings	$150,829.53
Plus advance	18,200.00
Writer's net earnings	$169,029.53

buying publisher usually obtains copyrights to all of the songs in the catalog as well as demos of those songs. The amount paid for the catalog varies greatly and depends on the number and value of the songs included.

Sharing the Publishing

Songwriters or songwriter/artists may be able to keep part of the publishing in their own publishing company and agree to split the ownership of the copyrights with a larger publisher. This is called *copublishing*. The songwriters still get their 50 percent share, and the two publishers split the remaining 50 percent in a negotiated share, often 50/50. The net result of such a deal is that the songwriter gets 50 percent of the revenues, the songwriter's publishing company gets another 25 percent of the revenues (half of the publisher share) and the co-publisher gets the other 25 percent of the revenues. At a minimum, the co-publisher then takes care of administrative duties associated with the songs, such as collection of royalties, licensing, and copyright administration. In addition the co-publisher may actively engage in plugging the song.

Instead of owning a share of the copyright, the larger publisher may be content to make a deal just for a percentage share of the revenues earned in exchange for providing the administrative support for the catalog. These copyright administration deals usually involve catalogs from successful artists and producers and from smaller independent publishing companies. Administration fees charged by the administrative publisher are typically 10 percent to 25 percent of gross publishing revenues. Gross publishing revenues would include the share of songwriter income that flows through the publisher, as well as the publisher share. Administrative deals usually do not last for the duration of the copyrights, but rather for a period of three to five years, including renewals.

Exploiting Copyrights

Income Sources

Most publishers make all of their revenue from licensing (permitting others to use) their copyrights. Unlike record companies, which make most of their money from the sale of copies of their masters, music publishers (with a few notable exceptions) do not directly sell copies of anything. They license other people to do that. To develop an understanding of the various income sources for music publishers it is necessary to understand the various licensing arrangements that lead to these income sources. As Figure 4.1 indicates, music publishers earn most of their revenues from three sources: public performances, sale of recordings, and sheet music sales. Another significant source of revenue for some publishers is synchronization fees: licensing songs for use in motion pictures, television, and home video. So, how does one get permission to use a song in any of these fashions? As any publisher would probably say, "No problem, just bring money."

Performance Licensing

Copyrights in songs include the right of public performance. Note that this is not limited to for-profit performances because many nonprofit performances are not exempt by the copyright act (see Chapter 3 for more details). There are tens of thousands of nightclubs, retail stores, radio stations, television stations, and other places where music is performed publicly. The practical difficulties inherent in any single publisher attempting to license all of these outlets has led to the creation of performing rights organizations (PROs) which act as clearing houses for the publishers to license large numbers of performance places and for the performance places to access the thousands of songs of thousands of publishers. There are three major PROs in the United States; ASCAP (The American Society of Composers, Authors and Publishers), BMI (Broadcast Music, Inc.), and SESAC (SESAC, Inc. SESAC is no longer an abbreviation of anything in particular).[30] A comparison of the three organizations on various points follows the description of basic performance licensing.

How Performance Licensing Works

The three PROs function in very similar manners. They all acquire non-exclusive rights to license public performances from the songwriters and music publishers that belong to their organizations. The rights are

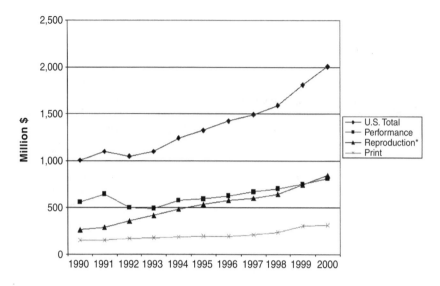

Fig. 4.2 U.S. music publishing revenues (1990–2000). National Music Publishers' Association. *International Survey of Music Publishing Revenues*, 1992–2003.

nonexclusive because the publishers retain the right to license the works directly themselves. The PROs obtain only *nondramatic* performance rights. Dramatic performances, those that involve the performance of more than one composition from an opera or musical theatrical production or that involve the use of the composition to tell a story in some dramatic manner (as on stage or screen),[31] are licensed directly by the publisher or by a theatrical licensing agency that represents the publisher. Dramatic performance rights are known as *grand rights* and nondramatic performing rights are known as *small rights*. Both the publisher and the songwriter of the composition must belong to the same performing rights organization. Most music publishers of any size operate at least two separate companies, affiliated with different PROs, so that any songwriter that the publisher may sign can be accommodated, whichever PRO the songwriter prefers.

The PROs then issue licenses to anyone and anywhere their music might be performed publicly. (See Chapter 3 for a definition of public performance under the Copyright Act.) Figure 4.3 indicates the flow of the licenses from the initial copyright owners to the licensees, and of the royalties/license fees collected from the licensees back to the songwriters and publishers. For most places where music is performed, the most economical way to obtain permission to use a vast number of songs is to obtain a *blanket license*. The blanket license from a performing rights organization allows the licensee to perform, or have performed under its roof, any of

Rights Owners   Performing Rights Organizations   Licensees/Users

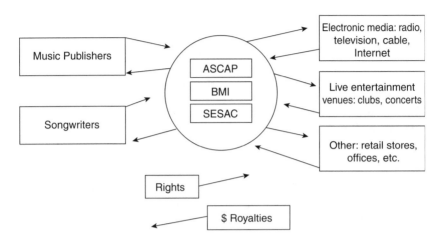

Fig. 4.3 Performance rights licensing.

the compositions that the PRO represents, as many times as desired. Such a license is particularly valuable to radio stations and night clubs where thousands of different songs may be performed, some of them hundreds of times. Keeping track of individual performances would be a real nightmare. The Supreme Court of the United States has even recognized the value of the blanket license. In an anti-trust suit brought against BMI by Columbia Broadcasting System, the Court upheld the validity of the blanket license, saying,

> [T]he blanket license developed … out of the practical situation in the marketplace: thousands of users, thousands of copyright owners, and millions of compositions. Most users want unplanned, rapid, and indemnified access to any and all of the repertory of the compositions, and the owners want a reliable method of collecting for the use of their copyrights. Individual sales transactions in this industry are quite expensive, as would be individual monitoring and enforcement, especially in light of the resources of single composers. … A middleman with a blanket license was an obvious necessity if the thousands of individual negotiations, a virtual impossibility, were to be avoided.[32]

The PROs must also offer a per-use or per-program license to those users who wish to take advantage of it. Per-use or per-program licenses are more costly on a per-song basis, but may be less expensive overall than a blanket license if a broadcaster, particularly a television broadcaster, only needs access to a very limited number of clearly identified compositions on a regular basis.

Who Obtains the License?

Although technically speaking the actual musician performing a song live in a club would be liable for the public performance, it is the operator/ owner of the venue who is obtaining the benefit of the performances and is also liable for copyright infringement if there is an unlicensed performance. As a practical matter, it is much easier to license the premises than to license a bunch of traveling musicians. Therefore, owners of nightclubs, radio and television stations, retail outlets where background music is being played, and concert venues (or the concert promoter if the venue does not have much music performed during a typical year) all must have performance licenses to cover the compositions performed in their establishments. An exception to the public performance right allows many retail stores and food and beverage establishments to play radio programs over speakers in their establishments without having to obtain a license. (see Chapter 3 for more detail).

How Much Is the License?

The cost of the license depends upon a number of factors. Background music licenses cost less than live entertainment licenses. Live entertainment licenses cost less than broadcast performance licenses. The bigger the operation in terms of physical size, number of seats, amount of music being performed, power of transmitter, and other factors, the more the license costs. A small retail store playing recorded music might obtain background licenses for a few hundred dollars per year. A major nightspot, such a casino in Las Vegas, spends tens of thousands of dollars per year. A television network spends millions of dollars per year for broadcast performance licenses. All three PROs deduct their operating expenses from the available pot of money; SESAC takes an additional profit for their owners.

Who Gets the Money?

The PRO collects the license fees from all of the various users then attempts to determine how much money each song in the PRO's repertoire is entitled to receive. This daunting task is accomplished somewhat differently by each PRO (see below). Suffice it to say, however, that the best any of the PROs can do is get an exact count of performances from some licensees, such as the television networks; get a sample or actual *spin count* of a larger group, such as local radio stations; and use those as an estimate of what songs were performed live in clubs, discotheques, and as background music. The various methodologies are the subject of great debate among the three organizations as to who does the best job of accurately paying their publishers and songwriters. The methodologies all have their merits and shortcomings and no one is perfect, or will ever be perfect because of the virtual impossibility of monitoring all songs played live in clubs. Nightclubs and other live performances account for about 26 percent of performance license fee collections (see Table 4.1).

Once the amount to pay for each song is determined, the PRO divides the payment in half and sends half to the songwriter and half to the publisher. If there are multiple songwriters or multiple publishers then the PRO divides the money according to the directions supplied by the songwriters and publishers. If a songwriter specifically instructs the PRO to pay the songwriter's share to the publisher, perhaps because the songwriter is a staff songwriter who has a significant advance to be recouped, the PRO will do so.

Comparing ASCAP, BMI, and SESAC

- *Organization*: ASCAP is a non-profit organization run by its members—the publishers and songwriters. BMI is a corporation owned by broadcasters but which operates on a non-profit basis. SESAC is a privately held corporation that operates on a profit-making basis for its owners (who are not the songwriter or publisher affiliates).
- *Size*: BMI claims to represent 300,000 songwriters, composers, arrangers, and publishers; ASCAP boasts 145,000 members. SESAC, though clearly the smaller organization with 2,700 affiliates, has become much more aggressive in acquisition of songwriter catalog in recent years, notably with acquisition of licensing rights to Bob Dylan's and Neil Diamond's catalogs.[33] ASCAP reported receipts of $560 million in 1999 and distributed $435 million to its songwriter and publisher members.[34] BMI states its 1999 collections as $450 million. SESAC does not publicly report its annual receipts but they were estimated at about $8 million before their significant rights acquisitions of the Dylan and Diamond catalogs.[35]
- *Kinds of music licensed*: Initially SESAC had a stronger hold in Latin and Gospel music, ASCAP in "standards" because they were the oldest organization, and BMI in country, R&B, and rock. Now all three organizations compete well in all genres.
- *Online clearances and licensing*: All three organizations have online listings of their repertoire. All three have some performance licenses available online; some are click-through, and some are simply downloadable. They also allow online clearance of songs by users and listing of new songs by their affiliates using their pages on the World Wide Web.[36]

- *Logging methodology*: *Logging* is the method used by PROs to determine which songs are being played most frequently, and becomes the basis of how the license income is split among composers. A detailed discussion of logging is beyond the scope of this text, but important recent changes in methodology for all three PROs indicate that more music from more diverse sources and voices is being logged and paid royalties. All three organizations have been expanding the scope of their sample and improving its accuracy in recent years. For example, ASCAP began actual monitoring of live performance venues and getting song logs from the top 100 touring acts.[37] BMI added college radio stations to its list of stations completing logs. SESAC increased the number of radio formats for which it receives actual airplay information from BDS (Nielsen Broadcast Data Systems) and moved to a "watermarking" system to identify radio airplay in 2001.[38] BDS monitored more than 1,200 stations in the United States and Canada in 2003, including some in nearly every format. ASCAP used BDS and then partnered with a similar system in 2003.[39] All of these changes mean that more songs will be logged and paid for their performances. This means that not only mainstream hits will be logged, but also songs by artists who either do not receive much airplay or who receive airplay on small stations, or less popular formats. This in turn increases the prospect for non-mainstream songwriter/artists to collect performance royalties for their songs and increases the possibility that they can sustain a career.

  Broadly speaking, all three PROs get actual program logs from television and radio networks that provide a numerical census of airplay. ASCAP *samples* most local TV and radio by actually recording broadcasts and deciphering which songs have been played. BMI *samples* by requiring all of its broadcast licensees to complete an actual log, accounting for every song played, once per year for one week. SESAC was the first to use the BDS to obtain actual counts of which songs were performed on stations monitored by BDS and combines that with other information to make their best estimate of performances. Because BDS does not monitor all radio stations (about 10 percent of the more than 13,000 stations in the United States) this too is a sample. All of these methods still only provide an estimate of the total number of actual performances for any given song. Some song performances will never be logged. Other songs may have their performances overrepresented in the sample because they are mainstream hits and are performed in all markets. The PROs attempt to adjust for these shortcomings in their methodologies, but none of the systems is perfect.

- *Age*: ASCAP was founded in 1914 to begin to develop a way for U.S. composers to collect for live performances of their songs. SESAC was founded in 1930 primarily to license European composers' music in the United States. BMI was founded in 1940 to provide broadcasters with music to play when they refused to agree to pay the fees demanded by ASCAP in the 1940 license negotiations. If they refused the ASCAP license they could not play any of the popular songs licensed by ASCAP. That sent the broadcasters scrambling to get performance rights for country, blues, and anything else that they could play to fill their programming.

· *Payments*: The three organizations debate long and hard about which will pay the most money. There are situations in which either might pay more for a given song than the other two depending on where and how often it was performed. A comparison of average payments on hit songs revealed that the three were within about a seven thousand dollar range of each other out of an average song-writer share of about $140,000. However the PROs reported a range from a low of $114,000 to a high of $194,000 for recent hits (country).[40] These three organizations compete to sign songwriters and publishers and aggressively pursued previously unlicensed users into the twenty-first century, but the share of publishing income from performance licensing increased only 62 percent, compared to the 127 percent increase in mechanical royalties between 1992 and 2000 (see Table 4.1).

Mechanical Licensing

Although the Copyright Act allows a record company to procure a statutory (compulsory) license to record a musical composition (see discussion in Chapter 3), most labels prefer to obtain negotiated licenses from the publishers. The National Music Publishers' Association (then the Music Publisher's Protective Association) established the Harry Fox Agency (HFA) in 1927 to provide a clearinghouse for mechanical rights for the rapidly growing sales of recordings and piano rolls in the 1920s. Now the HFA issues and collects for about three fourths of the mechanical licenses in the United States.[41] By 2003 the HFA represented the catalogs of more than 27,000 music publishers and has annual collections of more than $500 million. The agency charges the member publishers collection fees of 5.75 percent of mechanical royalties collected. In addition to collecting the fees from the record labels and distributing them to the appropriate publishers the agency conducts audits of its licensees on behalf of the members. The HFA reported audit recoveries of $12 million in 1994.[42] As indicated by Figure 4.4, these collections are distributed to the publishers, who then divide them with the songwriters according to their contractual agreement, usually 50/50. The HFA allows potential licensees to obtain licenses electronically via their World Wide Web site, especially for productions of less than 2,500 copies.[43]

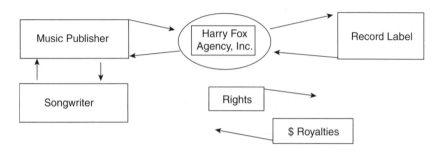

Fig. 4.4 Mechanical rights licensing.

Mechanical Rates

Although most mechanical licensing is not through the statutory compulsory license, the rates tend to follow the compulsory amount. Because a large amount of the compositions licensed are by songwriter/artists and because these people tend to have controlled composition clauses in their recording agreements (see discussion in Chapter 6), most licenses are for ¾ of the statutory rate. The HFA states that it will not issue mechanical licenses at a rate below the statutory rate without instructions from the publisher, but publishers are often willing to do so, especially when songwriter/artists are involved. The net result is that typical mechanical license rates in 2002 ranged from 6.0 cents per side to the full statutory rate of 8.0 cents per side. The increase in statutory mechanical rates beginning in 1978 from 2.75 cents (it had been 2.0 cents since 1909) to 8.0 cents in 2002 represented a 191 percent increase, somewhat ahead of the 175 percent increase in the consumer price index for the same period.[44] Total mechanical royalties collections for the same period increased from $148.5 million to $691.5 million, a 366 percent increase. The growth of total mechanical royalties at a rate greater than inflation is accounted for by the real growth in sales of recordings during that time period as indicated in Chapter 1. Figure 4.2 indicates the rapid growth of mechanical royalties compared to others between 1990 and 2000. Performance income increased from an estimated $238 million in 1978 to $812 million in 2000, a 241 percent increase, also ahead of the inflation rate.[45]

Print Publishing

Structure

Total print music publishing sales worldwide amounted to about $770 million in 2000. About $350 to $400 million of that is sold through record stores according to the American Music Conference.[46] Most music publishers, even some of the largest, do not manufacture and distribute print editions of their own songs. Some do not even license print editions of their songs at all. Nearly 25 percent of the top 100 hits do not even appear in print editions.[47] Economies of scale in manufacturing and distribution have collapsed print music publishing into a highly concentrated industry with only four major players. They are the Hal Leonard Corporation (an independent), Warner Brothers Publications (the print division of Warner/Chappell Music, which is owned by the Warner Music Group), Cherry Lane Music (an independent), and Music Sales Group (a U.S. company with publishing and retail interests in the United Kingdom). A fifth player, CPP-Belwin (formerly owned by Columbia Pictures), was purchased in 1994 by Warner Brothers Publications after Warner lost the EMI Music print rights to Hal Leonard.[48] EMI Music, arguably the world's largest music publisher, has its print publishing done through Hal Leonard as do Paramount's Famous Music, Disney, Universal, and BMG. The print music oligopoly is even tighter when the songs considered are current hits. The two giant print publishers, Hal Leonard and Warner Brothers Music (individually and in some cases jointly) control roughly equal shares of the sheet music for hit songs.[49] It is unusual to see any other print publisher with sheet music rights to more than one or two songs in the top 100.

Print Licensing

Print publishing income amounts to only about 16 percent of total publishing income (Figure 4.1), but the United States has a significantly higher percentage of worldwide print income (over 40 percent) than it does of other publishing revenues (see Table 4.5). The print publisher typically agrees to pay the music publisher as follows: 35 to 50 cents per copy for sheet music (piano/vocal) if a penny rate and 20 percent of the suggested retail list price (SRLP) if a percentage royalty; and 10 to 15 percent of SRLP for folios (pro-rated based on the number of songs the

TABLE 4.5 U.S. Share of Worldwide Publishing Revenues, 2000 (U.S. Dollars in Millions)

Source	Worldwide ($)	U.S.A. ($)	U.S.A. (%)
Performance	3,076	812	26.4
Phono/Mechanical	1,995	691	34.6
Synchronization	670	157	23.4
Print	769	316	41.1
Other*	367	31	8.4
Total	6,877	2,007	29.2

* "Other" includes broadcast mechanicals, private copy, reprint, rental, interest investment, and misc.
Source: National Music Publishers' Association, Inc. *International Survey of Music Publishing Revenues* (2003).

particular music publisher has in the folio). The print publisher may have to pay an additional 2 ½ to 5 percent for the right to use the recording artist's name on a personality folio that is keyed to a particular artist or album. Print rights are usually granted on a non-exclusive basis to the print publisher with the duration of the license being three to five years.[50]

Synchronization rights

Synchronization rights refer to the right to use music, as the contracts often put it, "in timed relation to visual images." In the early days of attempts to accompany motion pictures with sound, recordings were played while the motion picture was being played and elaborate devices attempted to keep the sound synchronized with the screen action. When the sound became integrated on the film on a separate track, it still had to be synchronized because the sound had to precede the image with which it was associated in order for the viewer to perceive the sound as originating at the correct time from the screen. Synchronization rights must be obtained for film, television, and videogram (home video) uses. Licenses are highly individualized depending upon the nature of the use of the song in the film (is it a theme, or featured as in a performance, or simply background), the amount of the song that is used (a few seconds or entirely), and the stature of the song (is it a recognizable hit or a new song that might benefit from exposure in the film). For example, synch license fees for a major studio film would be anywhere from $25,000 to $50,000 up to $150,000 if the song is the main title song for the film. Uses in commercials may run anywhere from $75,000 to $500,000 for a one-year use. Television program synch licenses will run from $1,500 to $10,000 per episode, all depending upon the nature of the use and the popularity of the song.

Songwriting

> Great songs are about people's hopes, dreams, and aspirations.
>
> —Bill Lowery, owner Lowery Music Group[51]

Because, as some people say, "It all begins with a song," why consider songwriters last in this chapter? Because all of the issues already discussed have implications for people who want to write songs. With rare exception, the songwriters of pop, rock, and R&B hits tend to be the people who perform or produce them. Even in country music, being a "just plain songwriter" is becoming increasingly difficult; a connection with an artist or producer is extremely important. A connection with a music publisher is also extremely important; most publishers will not accept unsolicited demos of songs. To get that contact at the publisher, songwriters can perform in showcases, perform in clubs, work through a performing rights organization, or just plain knock on doors. A songwriter will have to do these things someplace where a publisher is likely to hear them. Writing with a songwriter who already has songs placed with a publisher is also a quick track to the inside.

As to song content, we have all heard songs on the radio that we think are not very good. Perhaps they just do not communicate with us personally. Perhaps they do not communicate very well with *anyone*. Those songs may not be well crafted in terms of lyrics and structure. The craft of songwriting can be learned. There are numerous books on the subject.[52] The songwriters' organizations in major cities often have songwriters' workshops, as do the performing rights organizations. Two important organizations for developing professional songwriters are the Songwriters Guild of America, and the Nashville Songwriters Association International.[53]

The important thing is to write often and to get feedback from somebody who has some background or experience that qualifies them to judge songs. It is difficult for many songwriters to accept even constructive criticism because the very nature of the early stages of songwriting is that the songs become highly personal statements. There is not much point to complain, "Well, they are *my* songs and I don't care if anybody else will understand them." If that is the songwriter's real perspective, then they need not be trying to get a publisher or label interested in the songs. If, however, the songwriter would like to use the songs to communicate or share ideas or feelings with a broader audience, then the use of popular music as a communication medium is appropriate. If a songwriter or artist asks others to invest time and money in their message, then the investors need some reasonable assurance that the song or recording stands a chance of recouping the initial investment (i.e., that it is reasonably commercial).

Songwriting is both art and craft. While it is easy to write a song, it is difficult to come up with a song that is well crafted and has enough appeal to get an artist to feel that it could be a hit. Country songwriter Will Rambeaux put it this way: "It takes years to develop that craft to the point where you're writing songs that are good enough for the radio. I know that sounds simple and shallow, but it's not easy to do that, to write songs that have universal appeal."[54] Few songwriters have ever managed to accomplish that as well in modern times as Diane Warren. She is not a recording artist, or a producer, yet she has songs recorded by artists in nearly every genre, in motion pictures, and television. She says a good song is "Something that touches you, makes you feel something."[55]

Summary

The music publishing stream begins with the acquisition of songs, and the copyrights in those songs, from songwriters—whether independent writers, or recording artists who create their own material. The labels have become prominent players in this stream because recordings generate the lion's share of revenues from reproduction (mechanical rights) and public performances of these songs. Important licensing agencies are the Harry Fox Agency for mechanical rights, and the performing rights organizations, ASCAP, BMI, and SESAC. Even though the roughly $2 billion music publishing stream is not as large monetarily as the live entertainment or recordings streams, without songs to perform and record the other two income streams simply would not exist.

5

Live Entertainment: The Second Stream

The Rolling Stones are ... showing us all you can be in your 60s and still rock 'n' roll.

—Artist's Group International President, Dennis Arfa[1]

The power of popular recordings is overwhelmingly evident in the live-entertainment business. Popular artists performing the songs they have recorded create the vast majority of the income generated in the live-performance stream. For example, in 1995, *Performance Magazine* reported that only three nonmusical acts, the Mighty Morphin Power Rangers (East and West editions), magician David Copperfield, and Walt Disney's World on Ice, were among the top fifty acts, and these three accounted for only 5.7 percent of the reported $635.3 million gross ticket sales.[2] *Pollstar* estimated that ticket sales revenue for major concerts amounted to $2.1 billion in 2002 and their top fifty artists (who only included two nonmusical acts, comedians Jerry Seinfeld and Robin Williams) accounted for 62.8 percent of ticket sales revenue. The top ten tours accounted for nearly 28 percent of ticket sales revenues. As with recording sales, the majority of the revenues are generated by a small number of the artists.

The turn of the twenty-first century continued the trend of recording artists dominating the performance charts, but saw an aging of both the top performers and their audiences. Of the top ten grossing touring artists for 2002, all but two, Dave Matthews Band and Creed, were artists in their fifties and sixties. Top grossing act Paul McCartney (b. 1942) celebrated his sixtieth birthday. The Rolling Stones range in age from 55 to 66. Other top ten acts with half a century or more under their belts were Cher (b. 1946), Billy Joel (b. 1949), Elton John (b. 1947), Bruce Springsteen (b. 1949),

Aerosmith's Steven Tyler (b. 1948), Neil Diamond (b. 1941), and The Eagles, who were all born in 1947 or 1948. Apparently the baby boomers had lots of money to spend on tickets to see these acts. Average ticket prices ranged from a low of $55.31 for Neil Diamond to $129.92 for McCartney. Two other acts, the Rolling Stones ($119.20) and Billy Joel/ Elton John tour ($107.88), had average ticket prices above $100.[3] *Billboard* wondered, "Who will take their place in years to come?"[4]

How big is a big tour? In 2002, top-grossing Paul McCartney brought in an estimated $103.3 million by doing 53 shows and selling nearly 800,000 tickets. The Dave Mattthews Band reached the most fans, selling more than 1.5 million tickets at 77 shows. A number of hard-working rock bands played more than 80 shows, including Creed, Tool, and Incubus; Tool performed 86 shows in 86 different cities. Country acts Toby Keith, Kenny Chesney, and Alan Jackson gave 70 to 80 shows each and grossed about $21 million each. Rap acts did not fare as well, with the top tour being Eminem's, with 30 shows earning gross sales of $15 million. Classical act Andrea Bocelli brought in more than $17 million and sold 9,400 tickets at only 13 shows; he had the highest average ticket price, $138.61, of any of the top 100 tours.[5]

The live performance income generated by major acts topped $2 billion for the first time in 2002. By comparison, it averaged about $1.1 billion per year between 1991 and 1995. Figure 5.1 indicates that major tour income was not very consistent and maintained only a slight upward trend during the 1990 to 1995 period, but began a steady growth in 1995, increasing 121 percent by 2002. Although some of the increase can be accounted for by

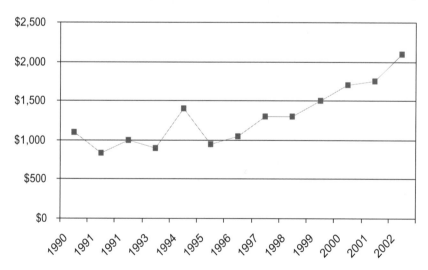

Fig. 5.1 Touring grosses, 1990–2002 (U.S. $ in Millions). "Concert Industry Ticket Sales," *Pollstar*, 13 January 2003, 10.

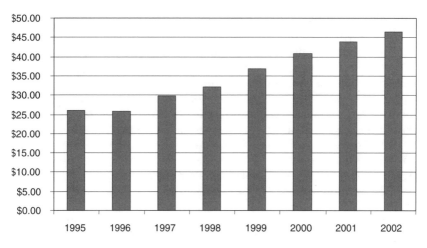

Fig. 5.2 Average ticket prices. "Top 100 Tours Average Ticket Price," *Pollstar*, 13 January 2003, 8.

increases in average ticket prices (Figure 5.2), ticket prices only climbed about 79 percent over the same period. The presence or absence of a couple of major stadium tours in a given year can change the gross receipts by as much as 55 percent. In 1994, stadium shows, including two huge tours by the Rolling Stones and Pink Floyd, accounted for $143.9 million in ticket sales, 10.3 percent of the gross that year compared to 3.9 percent in 1995. Although not all live entertainment is before large audiences, it is the large tours that account for the lion's share of the live-performance revenues. As Table 5.1 indicates, forty venues with capacities larger than 10,000 accounted for over 19 percent of total concert income in 2002. *Pollstar* listed nearly 1,500 venues in its 1995 *Concert Venue Directory* and more than 1,700 in the 2003 directory. Even those 1,700 do not account for the thousands of small bars and clubs where aspiring musicians play for the door receipts (aka the *door*), tips, their supper, or even for free just for the experience and exposure.

TABLE 5.1 Venue Size and Share of Performance Revenues
Share of 2002 Ticket Sales by Top 10 Venues in Each Size Range

Venue Size	Top 10 Venues' Sales ($ millions)	Percent of Total Sales
Stadiums	77.7	3.7
Amphitheaters	169.2	8.1
Indoor, 15,001 or more	71.5	3.4
Indoor, 10,001 – 15,000	84.1	4
Indoor, 5,001 – 10,000	133.8	6.4
Indoor, 5,000 or less	156.5	7.4
Total	692.8	33

Source: "Touring Charts," *Billboard*, 28 December 2002, YE-46, YE-66, YE-70.

The Major Players

There are five key roles in the live-entertainment stream: performer, personal manager, talent agent, promoter, and venue operator (see Figure 5.3).[6] The role of the record label is discussed later in this chapter, but it is not a *must* role. In an idealized situation, the performer decides, usually in conjunction with the personal manager, that it is time to do a tour. The manager and performer decide when the tour should be, often to promote the release of a new album. Other details such as what parts of the country to play, what cities, what size venues, and how many dates are roughed out. The manager then contacts the talent agent (aka booking agent) who has contracted to arrange performances for the artist.

The agent and manager, in consultation with the artist, arrive at a minimum price for the show and some basic terms of a performance agreement. The agent then begins contacting promoters to line up potential dates. The promoters contact venues to see what dates are open for what prices and probably put holds on dates that would fit the tour. The promoters then call the agent back and say what dates and venues are available and present the agent with the basics of a deal. As the agent begins putting together pieces of the tour, the promoters are notified of any definite dates or at least which holds from the venue operators can be released for some other artist. Finally, when a tour itinerary is fairly firm, the agent approaches the manager (and perhaps artist) for approval.

If the artist and manager approve, the agent begins to issue contracts to the promoters. The promoters then sign contracts with the venue operators. Then the promoters develop plans for advertising and promoting the shows and begin arranging whatever details are called for by the performer's agreement. With luck, the performer shows up for the show, the tickets have all been sold, the performance happens without a hitch, and the promoter and artist's representative divide the receipts according to their agreement.

That is the ideal world. In the real world things seldom go precisely that way or that smoothly. A closer examination of the roles of the major players will help explain why.

Personal Managers

> An artist's career represents a lot of investment in terms not just of money but of time, energy, sweat and disappointment.
>
> —Ed Bicknell, personal manager for Dire Straits[7]

Structure of the Personal Management Business

The business of personal management is run by a large number of firms and managers, who generally manage only three or four acts—very few handle more than a dozen. There is no concentration of market share in the management business. There are easily a thousand or more personal

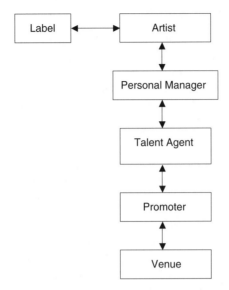

Fig. 5.3 Concert promotion: The Players.

managers in the United States alone.[8] Some manage major artists, some are just beginners who hope to build a local band into an international superstar. Whatever the stature of their artists, their roles are surprisingly similar.

What Does a Personal Manager Do?

It is difficult, if not impossible, to be a recording artist who performs live without someone at least performing the functions of a personal manager.[9] Personal managers are in charge of developing all aspects of a performer's career. To that end they must possess good people skills to be able to work closely with the artist and others in this income stream. They must also possess significant knowledge of the industry and contacts within it to be able to create the kinds of opportunities that the artist needs to develop a significant career.

In the early stages, the personal manager will work with the artist to develop a good live act and performance, giving the performer feedback and constructive criticism. Based on the manager's assessment of the artist's talent and potential, the manager will probably develop a career plan that will at least take the artist through the first recording. The career plan will undoubtedly be altered later if the artist achieves substantial success and as other opportunities present themselves. If the performer writes original material, the manager will help the performer become a better songwriter by providing feedback on songs or finding or hiring people who can. The manager will attempt to secure the artist a publishing agreement if that is a good possibility. The manager will find an appropriate talent agent for the artist at the early stages of the artist's career if the artist does not already have an agent.

Managers do not generally procure personal appearances for the artist, except as ancillary to their job; that is the agent's job. In fact, in California it is illegal for managers to procure employment beyond a recording contract unless they are licensed talent agents; most managers are not. The manager's most important task in the early stages is to get the artist to the point where they are ready to sign a recording contract, then help them get such a contract.

Once the artist has a recording contract, the manager works to see that the recording is released and is successful. The task probably begins with encouraging the artist in the successful completion of his or her first master recording. Usually the manager will watch closely the development of the label's marketing and promotion plans and may even assist by hiring independent promotion services or making sure the artist performs the necessary promotional engagements. The manager will work with the label and the music video director to be sure that the marketing and promotion plans of the label and the video fit the artist's image and music. If the artist got the label deal without a publishing or agency agreement, the manager will actively seek those deals for the artist as well. Once touring begins, the manager will work to assure that everything goes as smoothly for the artist as possible. If the recording and tour are successful enough, the manager repeats these functions for a second album and tour.

As the artist's career progresses, the manager must begin to expose the artist to an ever-widening audience. The manager will probably attempt to get talk show and variety show appearances for the artist, and perhaps, if the artist has any acting talent, motion picture and dramatic television appearances. Career growth will require more work from the manager, so the manager will probably expand by outsourcing some functions that he or she had performed at the early stages of the artist's career. Somewhere in this development, the manager will probably need to engage the services of a public relations specialist unless the management company is large enough to provide that service itself. In addition, the manager will probably need to engage the services of a business manager to handle the artist's money to assure that the income from the artist's peak earning years is invested in ways to provide for long-term financial security.

Finally, the manager will attempt to sustain the artist's career for as long as possible if the artist is willing. Long after most artists have stopped having hit records, they are still able to have successful performing careers. During the 1990s and 2000s, the revival or reunion tour and the farewell (maybe) tour were common. Major artists from the 1960s, 1970s, and 1980s such as the Eagles, Jimmy Page and Robert Plant (Led Zeppelin), the Allman Brothers Band, and the Beach Boys (to name just a few) had top 50 tours in 1995.[10] In 2002 the list included Cher, Paul McCartney, Neil

Diamond, Bob Dylan, Santana, and John Mellencamp.[11] The personal side of the manager's role is that of caretaker, confidant, and surrogate mother. Says Bill Curbishley, at one time the personal manager of Jimmy Page, Robert Plant, The Who, and Judas Priest (and others), "To be a personal manager, you're involved in their marriages, divorces, births, deaths, traumas, dramas, happiness, sadness—all of it."[12] In order to do these things the manager must believe in the artist's abilities and desire to succeed. The artist must trust the manager implicitly with the details of the artist's career and the manager must be deserving of that trust.

When the trust breaks down, the relationship rapidly deteriorates. For many artists at a lower echelon of success, the breakup simply results in frustration for the manager and a "What have you ever done for me?" from the artist. When the artist has achieved substantial levels of success, the breakup can cost the manager literally millions of dollars, especially if the legal and moral trust that the manager holds has been breached. Writer/artist Billy Joel was awarded sums totaling more than $2.6 million in separate suits against his former business manager for conversion of Joel's investments in a real estate partnership.[13] Former Beatle George Harrison won an $11.6 million recovery of half of the debt of his film company because his business manager had never made his initial 50 percent investment in the company.[14]

Sometimes the relationship between manager and artist can produce a series of strange events once that relationship is severed. Harrison won a suit against his former personal manager, Alan Klein, whom Harrison had fired in 1973. Klein later purchased the Brite Tunes Music catalog that contained the song, "He's So Fine." Brite Tunes then sued Harrison, claiming that Harrison's "My Sweet Lord" was a copyright infringement of "He's So Fine." A court ruled against Harrison on the infringement issue. Later, Harrison won a judgment against Klein that held that a personal manager could not buy the song in order to sue his former client. Harrison wound up owning both songs.[15]

Management Agreements

Although some attorneys refer to a personal management agreement as "air"—because the manager usually just promises to exercise "best efforts" to promote the artist's career, and so these agreements are notoriously difficult to enforce—there are some typical terms.[16] As with most entertainment industry agreements, these tend to be highly negotiated, especially if the artist has much stature. While some managers may be willing to work on an oral "handshake" agreement, most attorneys cringe at the thought of their client, either the artist or the manager, working under such nebulous terms.

- Compensation. Personal managers are typically compensated on the basis of a percentage of the artist's gross earnings. That percentage ranges from 10 percent to as high as 25 percent in some instances. The norm is 15 to 20 percent. Allegedly, Colonel Tom Parker, who managed Elvis Presley, received a 50-percent commission. That commission is usually on the artist's gross earnings, but may be restricted to entertainment earnings, further restricted to live appearances, or restricted to earnings from appearances and agreements that the manager helped obtain. Advances for which the artist does not receive actual cash in hand, such as recording costs, video production costs, and tour support should not be commissionable. Some attorney's recommend fewer restrictions in order to keep the manager more motivated.
- Duration. Most agreements are for an initial term of one or two years with option years adding up to three to five years. The options are usually the manager's, but the artist may be able to limit the manager's right to exercise the options unless the artist has reached some plateau of earnings, say $100,000 in year one, $200,000 in year two, for example.
- Key person (a term slowly evolving from the former sexist moniker *key man*). Personal managers are usually *very* personal to the artist. Even if the artist signs an agreement with a management company, it is usually a particular person who is handling the affairs of the artist and in whom the artist has placed his or her trust. For that reason artists often ask that if the key person leaves the firm then the agreement is ended.
- Power of attorney. The manager will usually ask for power to enter into agreements on behalf of the artist. While it may be easier for the manager to be able to sign anything for the artist, it is usually advisable for the artist to attempt to limit the power of attorney to routine matters such as short engagements. *Routine matters* should be carefully defined, and the manager should seek the artist's approval on all but these very routine matters. Whether such detail is necessary in the agreement is a matter of trust.

Talent Agents

The Agent's Role

The primary function of a talent agent is to find employment opportunities for the artist in live entertainment. The agent is the ultimate middleperson, between the artist and the venue operator or promoter, with an almost purely sales function. Although the agent strictly speaking represents the artist and must make the artist's interest paramount, there is also pressure to please the promoter or venue operator. If an agent arranges many deals that displease one or the other, the agent will soon either have no artists to book or nowhere to book them. The agent has knowledge of the kinds of performers booked in what venues by what promoters or venue operators. Putting the wrong act in the wrong venue is a double disaster. Agents often know promoters and venue operators personally, at least over the phone "personally" (most of an agent's work is done over the telephone). Agents usually represent a substantial number of artists, although there may be a particular individual at an agency who is in charge of bookings for a particular artist.

Agency Structure

Talent agents tend to exist in three varieties, depending upon the size of the geographic area in which they book talent. Local agents work just in a particular city or small group of cities. They tend to book acts into smaller clubs, parties, and local events. Because the acts they book do not command large talent fees, they have to work fast to keep lots of acts working throughout the year in order to survive. It is most likely that an aspiring artist or group will encounter a local agency first on their rise to stardom. That agent will be one of the first people to pass judgment on the performer and have concluded that they are of substantial enough talent to perform in local venues without embarrassing the venue operator, the agent, or themselves. All a local agent needs to be in business is a telephone, an act to represent, a list of clubs to start calling, and perhaps a license (see below for a discussion of agency licensing requirements).

Regional agents can book artists in several, usually adjoining, states. They book some larger clubs and shows and may have the ability to get an act on as an opening act for a larger artist if they have good connections with the promoter. The dream of the regional agent is to hook up with some rising artist who becomes a star and who will take the agent along. Regional agents can book an act into a small tour. The number of artists represented by regional agents may be just as many as by local agents, but they are usually of higher caliber and have more experience. Regional agencies tend to have several agents in the office.

Finally, national agencies are those that can book an act anywhere in the country and perhaps abroad. They usually will not represent an artist unless that artist already has a recording contract, or perhaps a substantial development agreement with a publisher. They may represent more than one hundred artists and have a substantial number of actual agents working at the agency. These national agencies are the ones that work out tours for established recording artists.

The talent agency business continues to expand, at least in terms of the number of agents. In 1996 *Pollstar's Agency Roster* listed nearly 600 talent agencies in the United States; by 2003 that listing had grown to about 620 agents. They are not owned by media conglomerates but are independent businesses. That is not to say that they are not dependent upon artists who have recording contracts, and other artists who dream of having recording contracts, for their talent. Just like other aspects of the industry, the big money is concentrated in the hands of a few players. The William Morris Agency is by far the largest talent agency in the United States, representing more than six hundred artists. On a plateau below that are several agencies representing two hundred or more artists each. In roughly descending order they are The Agency Group Limited, Universal Attractions, Creative Artists Agency, Columbia Artists Management, International Creative Management Artists, Ltd., Monterey Peninsula Artists, and Steve Feldman and Associates. Another dozen or so represent one to two hundred acts.[17]

The number of artists an agency represents is not the only measure of their success. Their gross bookings in terms of dollars are another good measure. *Pollstar* listed the top ten agencies of 1995 as booking $712.2 million worth of shows. That is about three-fourths of the estimated $950 million in major concert ticket sales in 1995. The top five agencies generated over 50 percent of the concert gross. One could fairly describe the agency industry as approaching a tight oligopoly (the top four firms control 60 percent of the market), but because the top four firms vary from year to year depending upon whose artists happen to be making a major tour,[18] the industry is really better characterized as an effective competition that is "somewhat concentrated." Seven years later, in 2002, the industry could still be characterized as "somewhat concentrated" as indicated by Table 5.2 below. The top five agencies controlled about 56 percent of the $1.2 billion in tour income generated by the top fifty acts that year. Coincidentally, those same agencies also controlled 56 percent of the top 100 acts that year. For the 2002 season, no single agency represented more than eleven of the top 50 touring acts.[19]

Unlike personal managers who sometimes do business on a handshake, talent agents almost never do business in this way, either with the artists they represent or with the venues and talent buyers to whom they sell. That is partially because they are usually dealing at a distance, over the telephone, by fax, or by e-mail, with their clients. It is also because they are often subject to specific licensing requirements from the states and/or the unions.

TABLE 5.2 Top Ten Talent Agencies 2002 (Based on Share of Top 100 Tours)

Agency	Number of Tours
1. Creative Artists Agency	28
2. William Morris Agency	17
3. Monterey Peninsula Artists	10
4. Artist Group International	4
5. Evolution Talent	6
6. United Talent Agency	3
7–10. Twelve agencies had only two shows.	2

Source: "Top 100 Tours," *Pollstar,* 13 January 2003, 4–6.

Agency Licensing

Talent agencies, because they are employment agencies, are usually regulated as such by state laws. Some states, among them California, Florida, New York, Minnesota, Texas, and Illinois, require specific licenses to be a talent agent; most do not. California and New York laws are particularly important because many agencies have their main offices in one of these states. Talent agents are known as "theatrical employment agencies" in these codes.[20] The two main labor unions concerned with recording artists, the American Federation of Musicians (AFM) and the American Federation of Television and Radio Artists (AFTRA), also regulate agents in their dealings with the union's members. Generally speaking, a talent agent must be licensed by both the state in which the agency is located, and by the union that represents the musicians or vocalists booked by the agent.

Agency Agreements[21]

The licensing requirements mean that agency agreements with performers are somewhat limited in their terms:

- Commissions and fees. These are usually 10 to 20 percent of the gross payable to the performer. The AFM limits the amount according to the duration of the performance, with 20 percent the limit for one-niters. Most agencies will agree to limit their commissions to a "standard" 10 percent. The commissions should only be applicable to engagements procured by the agency.
- Duration. The AFM limits talent agents to three-year agreements. If the agent is a *general agent* (one who also books film, television, theater, literary, etc.) the duration is limited to seven years. As a general rule, the lower the level of agency, the shorter the term of the agreement should be so that when/if an artist gets a recording agreement they can switch to an agency that is capable of booking them nationwide.
- Exclusivity. Agents often ask for exclusive rights (i.e., no other agent can book the artist during the term of the agreement). While this is certainly understandable and usual when an artist has reached the national agency level, it is more questionable at the regional level, and quite undesirable for the artist at the local level.

Promoters

This is a business for manic depressives.

—Regional promoter Philip Lashinsky[22]

The Role of the Concert Promoter

Promoters present live entertainment events. To do that, the promoter must obtain some talent to present, presumably from an agency, and must have some place to present it—a club or other venue. Like the agent, the promoter is a middle-person in between the artist and the audience. But unlike the agent, the promoter takes on a substantial managerial role in the ultimate presentation of the event. Promoters used to be a highly independent entrepreneurial group, working only in one or a few cities, willing to risk large losses in order to make substantial profits. They would hear about the availability of an artist from an agent, publication, or the grapevine, contact the agent and the venues for available dates, make a match, then try to sell tickets. A good show that sold out could reap substantial profits for the promoter and the performer; a show that did poorly in terms of ticket sales could spell disaster, especially for the promoter. The pressure on all parties involved became to reduce their risk of loss but still to share in the high profits that were available for successful shows. The person least able to reduce risk was the local or regional promoter, who did not have the resources to spread the risk over a larger number of shows.

Structure of the Promotion Business

During the 1960s it was common for a local or regional promoter to have a virtual lock on any significant shows happening in "their" towns. They did this by getting *buy back agreements* with agents and managers. The buy back allowed the promoter to be the first to bid on a date for an act's next tour date when they had just finished promoting the current date. The promoters could therefore assure themselves of being able to promote shows most likely to be successful in the future. If they had a profitable show with an artist, they would pick up the date for the next tour. If not, they could pass and let someone else do the show. The promoters also worked closely with the venues securing large numbers of holds (a nonbinding agreement to tentatively keep a date open for the promoter and not let someone else book the venue), which effectively kept other promoters from booking that venue.

Beginning in the late 1960s the grip of local and regional promoters on cities began to slip as national promoters, particularly Concerts West, came on the scene.[23] The national promoter could book a large number of dates for a particular tour and spread the risk of a loss from any one or two shows through a larger number of shows. By spreading the risk and being efficient in their operations, the national promoters could offer the artists and venues higher percentages and fees and still make profits themselves. Even when the national promoters would use a local or regional promoter to work out the details for a particular show, the local promoter might only be given a flat fee instead of any percentage of potential profits.[24] National promoters expanded their use of holds to the point where they had exclusive agreements with some venues so that no show could be promoted in the venue unless that promoter arranged it.

The other pressure on local and regional promoters' profits and losses came from the artists. Major artists and their managers became aware of the high profitability of promoting a successful act. A sellout became a given with some big artists. They reasoned that they should get a higher percentage of the profits from such sell-outs. The promoters, however, needed the high profits from the sell-outs to cover the big losses from the flops. At the same time, the major artists began to put on larger and larger shows. The acts went from requiring the promoter to supply staging, sound, and lights to carrying a self-contained show that only needed a place to play. The artists' expenses skyrocketed. Instead of a van-sized truck for the show and a bus for the artist, fleets of tractor-trailers and several buses were necessary to move a show from one venue to the next. The higher cost to the artist of all this personnel and equipment meant that the artists had to demand a larger guarantee (the minimum amount that the promoter had to pay for the artist's performance) for each show in order to meet their daily operating expenses and payroll. By asking for a higher guarantee and a higher percentage of the profits, the artists reduced the profitability for the promoters on successful shows and increased the risk of loss on shows that did not do well. Guarantees for a *shed* or arena show were typically $100,000 to $150,000 by 1996, having increased about 10 percent over the previous few years.[25]

Higher costs, higher guarantees, and bigger shows meant that the shows had to have larger audiences. Shows went from local gymnasiums to basketball arenas to football and baseball stadiums. With larger audiences and the partylike atmosphere that often accompanied the concerts came other headaches for the promoters: potential liability for injury to the fans or the artists, or damage to the facilities. Law suits for injuries or deaths occurring at concerts became more common with the heavy metal acts of the 1980s.[26] Injuries at rap concerts of the late 1980s and 1990s caused some promoters to cancel shows instead of facing the liability.[27] By the mid-1990s the violent behavior of fans in *mosh pits* and *stage diving* by fans (and even artists on some occasions) raised the specter of even greater liability.[28] The promoter's cost of liability insurance went from pennies per ticket to dollars per ticket over the course of about five years. Increased security measures became necessary. Those factors raised the price of the tickets even higher and decreased the profitability of the shows further.

The net result of all of these pressures was the concentration of the promotion business into large regional and national promotion companies. Table 5.3 indicates that the top ten grossing promoters of 1995 accounted for about 44 percent ($510.5 million) of the $950 million in concert sales that year. Looking at concentration ratios for the top four and top eight

TABLE 5.3 Top 10 Grossing Promoters 1995

Promoter	Shows Reported	Gross Sales ($)
1. Cellar Door Productions	481	83,855,748
2. PACE USA	529	81,280,559
3. MCA Concerts	682	75,579,846
4. Bill Graham Presents	217	46,162,652
5. Delsener/Slater Enterprises	245	40,197,652
6. Metropolitan Entertainment	318	39,880,235
7. Jam Productions	489	37,743,942
8. Belkin Productions	243	35,394,829
9. Haymon Entertainment, Inc.	120	35,370,528
10. Contemporary Presentations	403	35,178,547

Source: *Performance*, 29 December 1995.

promoters finds a concentration of 30.2 percent and 46.2 percent, respectively. The entire top twenty promoters accounted for 73.5 percent of concert sales. These ratios indicate a healthy competition among the major promoters.

Which promoters were the most successful in a given year varied substantially, just as it did with the most successful agents, depending on who was on tour and which promoter had the major tours of a given year. However, there was some stability among the top promoters. Three major promoters, Cellar Door Productions, CPI USA, and Metropolitan Entertainment, held the top spot for all but one of the ten years between 1986 and 1995.

By 2000 the picture had changed radically. Pollstar's list of top 10 promoters by ticket sales had a new leader that had not even been in the concert business in 1995. SFX (SFX Broadcasting, Inc.)—which had sold nearly 57 percent of all tickets offered by the top 10 promoters in 2000—was a broadcaster when it purchased Delsener-Slater Enterprises and Sunshine Promotions in 1996; in 1997 it sold its radio stations to Capstar. (Capstar later became a part of the major radio conglomerate, Clear Channel). In 1997 SFX acquired PACE Concerts, Bill Graham Presents, Contemporary Group, and Concert/Southern Promotions, Cellar Door, and others.[29] Then, in 2000, SFX merged with its former broadcast competitor, Clear Channel Communications, to bring together the largest concert promotion company with the largest radio conglomerate in the United States. Clear Channel purchased SFX for $3.3 billion.

All the implications of the Clear Channel/SFX merger/purchase were still unclear by the end of 2000. Clear Channel owned radio and outdoor advertising in nearly every market where SFX owned venues. In all, SFX owned or operated 120 live entertainment venues in the top 50 markets, including 16 amphitheaters in the top 10 markets; Clear Channel owned 867 radio stations and 19 television stations in the United States. Various commentators speculated as to whether Clear Channel stations would be interested in

TABLE 5.4   Top 10 Grossing Promoters 2002

Promoter	Tickets Sold (millions)
1. Clear Channel Entertainment	30.0
2. House of Blues Concerts	4.5
3. Concerts West/Goldenvoice	2.2
4. Palace Sports and Entertainment	1.6
5. Jack Utsick Presents	1.5
6. Jam Productions	1.5
7. Metropolitan Entertainment	1.3
8. CIE Events/OCESA/R.A.C/Hauser	1.1
9. Nederlander Concerts	1.1
10. Radio City Entertainment	0.9

Source: Pollstar, 13 January 2003.

promoting concerts from other promoters. The nearest competitor, House of Blues (which had earlier bought out Universal Concerts), was a distant second. A House of Blues officer commented, "This business that used to be a bunch of wildcatters has been turned into a big business."[30]

The impact of the Clear Channel purchase on the promotion business was, however, abundantly clear by 2003. The degree of concentration in the promotion business had changed markedly. Clear Channel Entertainment sold over 50 percent of the tickets sold by the top 50 promoters in 2002. Although far behind in ticket sales, the rest of the top five combined with Clear Channel to sell 70 percent of the tickets of the top 50 promoters (compare Tables 5.3 and 5.4). Clear Channel continued to expand their share of the promotion business with the purchased of Metropolitan Entertainment Group for an estimated $10 to $12 million in 2002.[31]

Clear Channel's hold over the promotion business was largely because of their ownership of more than 1,200 radio stations and more than one hundred of the top venues in the nation. In 2001, a Denver, Colorado, promoter, Nobody In Particular Productions, sued Clear Channel claiming violation of antitrust laws. The suit claimed that Clear Channel Entertainment unfairly competes by threatening musical acts with limited airtime for their recordings on Clear Channel radio stations if they don't promote their concerts with Clear Channel Entertainment. Clear Channel also allegedly used its size to force smaller promoters out of business. For example, House of Blues promoter Barry Fey reported that Clear Channel offered Neil Diamond *all* of the net profits from a show and half of their concession money to prevent House of Blues from getting the show. Clear Channel denied any strong arm or anticompetitive practices.[32] As of September 2003 a trial date had yet to be set.

Promoter-Artist Agreements

Performance agreements for concerts and club appearances typically contain two parts. The first part simply sets the fee structure, date and

time of appearance, and a few other basics. The other part is the *rider.*
This contains the requirements that the artist must have in order to put
on the show. For a major act, the rider will contain details of how much
parking must be available for the artist's trucks and buses, how much
weight the venue rafters must be able to support so the sound and lights
can be "flown," how much and what kind of food needs to be provided
for the traveling crew and artist, how much power (A/C) needs to be
available and where it needs to be, what local personnel such as musicians, security, follow spot operators, electricians, plumbers, and so on
must be provided, how backstage security is to be handled, and more.
The larger the show, the more details the rider is likely to contain. The
promoter needs to have the rider far enough in advance to be sure there
are no problems that cannot be overcome. For example, if a show has a
large piece of stage set that cannot be disassembled and must have doors
of a certain size to be able to get it into the building, the venue may have
to enlarge an entrance or cancel the show. If the roof cannot support the
load of the sound and lights, it may have to be reinforced or the show
canceled.

The payment part of the contract typically calls for the artist to get a
guarantee of some amount of money and often a percentage of the *gate*
(ticket sales revenue). There are several ways of structuring the deal. Artists playing small clubs or opening for other major acts usually just get a
flat fee for the show. Typically half of the guarantee or flat fee is paid in
advance. It is out of this payment that the talent agency takes their commission. The amount of the guarantee can go from a few thousand dollars
for an opening act to as much as a million dollars for a superstar act on a
major tour. The amount is determined by the artist and manager to be
enough to cover their expenses plus make what they consider to be a fair
profit no matter how many people actually buy tickets. In theory, the artist
will get this guarantee even if no tickets are sold. In practice, if sales are
going very badly, the artist and promoter will try to work out a compromise. It is not good for the artist's reputation to require the promoters to
take huge losses if the artist is not able to attract a good-sized audience to
the show. Major acts also get a percentage of the profits, which usually
kicks in after the promoter reaches a *breakeven point* (where ticket sales
revenues equal the promoter's expenses, including the artist's guarantee).
The percentage is highly negotiable, ranging from 50 percent to as high as
90 percent.

The Venue
Venue Agreements
The promoter must also enter into an agreement with the venue. The
details of that agreement include the venue's rental fee and what other services are to be provided by the venue to the promoter. Arrangements run

from the venue providing the facility and nothing more, called a *four walls deal*, to the venue providing significant services in terms of cleanup, ushers, ticket takers, electricians, stagehands, and so forth. Halls may also want either a flat fee, a flat fee against a percentage of the gate (meaning the venue will get whichever is greater, the guarantee or the percentage of the gate), or a guarantee plus a percentage of profits after the promoter's breakeven point. Services provided by the venue are usually billed separately but may be included in the flat fee.

Accounting for Performance Dollars

Ticket sales 8,900@ $45.00		$400,500
Less: ticket sales commission	$8,010	
Less: venue rental and services	$30,000	
Promoter's gross receipts		$362,490
Less: opening act	$10,000	
Less: artist guarantee	$95,000	
Less: promotion expenses	$70,000	
Available after breakeven		$187,490.00
Less: artist's 50 percent		$93,745.00
Producer's net profit		$93,745.00
Artist's income		
Guarantee	$95,000.00	
Plus % after breakeven	$93,745.00	
Artist gross		$188,745.00
Less: agency commission	$18,874.50	
Less: manager's commission	$37,749.00	
Less: tour expenses	$50,000.00	
Artist's net		$82,121.50

In addition to rental fees, the venues can also make money from other things. Venues often charge the artist a percentage of sales from artist concessions such as T-shirts, hats, and so forth that are sold at the shows. These percentages can range from nothing to as high as 50 percent. The promoter or artist usually does not receive a percentage of any ancillary income for the venue from things such as food and drink sales and parking.

The following example shows the basic flow of dollars from a show to the venue, promoter, agent, manager, and artist. The figures are based on a number of different specific examples to create a generic kind of concert that does not reflect any particular artist, promoter, venue, or concert. Assume a 12,000-seat arena with potential sales of 10,000 tickets (the show production and stage takes up 2,000 seats worth of space). Sales are 89 percent of the available seats. The venue fee is a flat fee and includes the venue rental plus ushers, security, technicians, and other services provided by the venue. The ticket price is an average; some seats sold for more than $45.00, some for less. The artist has a guarantee of $95,000 plus 50 percent after the promoter breaks even. The agent has a 10 percent commission. The artist's personal manager has a 20 percent commission. An opening act gets a $10,000 flat fee.

This example illustrates a successful show. On the other hand, it is not uncommon for shows to sell less than 60 percent of the available seats.[33] If the promoter only planned to sell 60 percent, perhaps because the only available venue did not really match the demand for the artist in that market, then all would be well. But the likelihood is that somebody is losing money at 60 percent. That somebody is undoubtedly the promoter.

In-house Promotion

The existence of national promotion of tours and the possibility of ancillary income led many venues to promote concerts in-house. In such an arrangement, it is really the venue that is promoting the show instead of an independent local or regional promoter. If the venue knows it is going to make a significant amount of money from the ancillary revenues, then it can afford to give the artist a higher percentage above the breakeven. The venue may even provide that if ticket sales have not hit a certain plateau by a week or two before the show, then the venue may give away the rest of the tickets (known as *papering the house*). Attendees with the papered tickets pay nothing to see the artist, but do pay for parking and concessions so the venue can make money even if the artist does not, or only makes the minimum guarantee. Venue owners also sell advertising and naming rights. These changes mean that the venue is no longer really in the concert-promotion business, but in the "attract-a-large-crowd business."

Major artist tours are so self-contained that there is little that a local promoter has to provide that is not usually available from the venue. Chain ownership of venues, especially of outdoor amphitheaters, makes it possible for the venue owner to book several dates at large venues in significant markets. Clear Channel could promote a major tour, playing in thirty-four of the top fifty markets in the country, and never leave Clear Channel facilities. Again, the local or regional promoter is left out. The majority of club shows are also promoted in-house. This practice, coupled with the increasing use of national promoters, has led to fewer shows available for local or regional promoters. Sometimes, though, a club will simply rent the facility for a new promoter wanting to break in with a small show.

Ticket Selling

Economic pressures on promoters and venues and the development of online sales technology in the 1980s and 1990s changed the way tickets to events are sold. It used to be that if someone wanted tickets to a show they had to go to or call the box office or go to some other ticket outlet, such as a record store, that sold *hard tickets*. The selling agent for the tickets printed them, distributed them, and perhaps ran the box office to sell them, for a small commission. Beginning in about 1982, the firm

Ticketmaster started selling *soft tickets*—tickets that did not exist at all until printed out by the selling agent's computer when a customer ordered them and paid for them by charge card over a telephone line. The service was much more convenient for the customers than having to go to a location to purchase tickets. Efficiencies in the telephone operations meant that Ticketmaster could sell tickets to many shows at the same time from many locations using networked computers. By the early 1990s, Ticketmaster had purchased Ticketron, its primary competitor.

In addition to efficient operations, Ticketmaster began to use exclusive selling agreements with venues and some promoters as a means to secure business. The venues and promoters sometimes received a percentage of the service charge added on to the ticket price in exchange for the exclusive arrangements.[34] Because the service charge was not part of the gross ticket sales on which the promoter had to pay the artist, it was not subject to the artist's percentage requirements. It was, therefore, a revenue source that did not have to be shared. Independent promoters, in-house promoters, and venues all moved to take advantage of these arrangements. It soon became virtually impossible to play a concert tour without having tickets sold by Ticketmaster. Ticketmaster's service charges increased from $3.50 to $5.50 per ticket.

Some consumers and artists began to complain. In 1994 the popular group Pearl Jam announced that it wanted ticket service charges held to $1.80 on an $18.00 ticket. Promoters and venue operators complained that their exclusive agreements with Ticketmaster would not allow them to use alternative ticket sellers, and Ticketmaster would continue to charge its higher fees. Pearl Jam canceled their summer 1994 tour and complained to the U.S. Justice Department that Ticketmaster had a monopoly. At least one legal writer concluded that Ticketmaster's practices did violate federal and California antitrust laws.[35] The Justice Department began an investigation and members of Pearl Jam testified before a congressional committee. By the summer of 1995, however, the Justice Department had dropped its probe of Ticketmaster's practices without further comment.[36] Ticketmaster reported ticket sales revenue of $1.6 billion for 1995. For its part, Ticketmaster had expanded its operations into promotional partnerships with credit card companies and even a record label: Capitol Records began a promotion to give away sampler albums to people who used the Ticketmaster or Capitol World Wide Web sites.[37] Ticketmaster became part of a label in late 2001 when Vivendi Universal purchased U.S.A. Networks' entertainment properties, including Ticketmaster.[38]

New England concert promoter Don Law went for a share of the ticket revenues in a direct way, starting his own ticket-selling company in 1996. Because he had exclusive booking arrangements with a number of venues, he had guaranteed ticket sales and commissions. Service charges for Law's company, "Next Ticketing," were no lower than Ticketmaster's.[39]

The Labels in the Concert Business

Live appearances by a recording artist help sell albums. The shows them-selves may even be the outlet where the albums are sold. In addition to T-shirts and hats, many artists are now offering their albums for sale at their concerts. One survey reported that 65 percent of the consumers who attended a concert in the last half of 1995 reported seeing the artist's album for sale at the show. Ten percent said they bought the album at the show, while another 25 percent bought the album prior to the show. About one-fourth of those who did not see the album at the show said they would probably have bought it if they had seen it.[40]

For new artists who need to build an audience through performance, or for an artist who is just beginning to break, the labels may provide tour support in the form of extra advertising and promotional dollars when an artist plays a market or in the form of *shortfall*. In the case of shortfall, the label guarantees that the artist will make a certain amount of money per appearance; if not, the label will make up the difference. The label is not attempting to make money in the concert business, but is hoping that the exposure of the artist through live performances will enhance sales of recordings. Tour support dollars spent by the label are usually treated as an advance and are recoupable out of artist royalties earned from the sale of recordings.

At various times, some of the major record labels have entered the waters of the second income stream associated with their recording artists. Consider the following examples of horizontal integration across income streams. In 1990 PolyGram (before it merged with Universal) established the PolyGram Diversification Division to become involved in local and national concert promotion, artist management, venue ownership and development, and merchandising of artist-related materials such as cloth-ing. PolyGram initially bought a minority interest in promoter Jim Scher's Metropolitan Entertainment.[41] PolyGram later sold its share to Ogden Corp., a firm with substantial venue management interests. The new firm planned a total integration of record label, music publishing, artist man-agement, concert promotion, and venue management, thereby combining all three income streams.[42] MCA also had a concert promotion division, MCA Concerts, as well as venue management and concert merchandising operations. CBS Records, prior to its sale to Sony, had a deal with Pace Group (which owned amphitheaters) to develop more venues and pro-mote tours.[43] As these examples indicate, there was already vertical inte-gration in the live music stream, with promoters owning and operating venues and venues doing in-house promotion.

One of the most successful promoters who owned his own venues was Bill Graham, who owned the famous Fillmore East and West ballrooms. Although Graham was killed in a plane crash in 1991, his production com-pany, Bill Graham Presents, was the third top grossing promotion com-pany in 1995 (see Table 5.3).[44] Clear Channel took the example and ran with it, eventually purchasing 39 amphitheaters, 51 theaters, 9 clubs, and 3 arenas. Clear Channel annual reports indicated that $2.4 billion of its $8.4 billion revenue in 2002 was generated by its entertainment division.[45]

Sponsored Tours

Other businesses with products to sell to people likely to attend concerts have entered the concert business by sponsoring tours for major or even relatively new artists. The sponsor usually provides some underwriting for the entire tour in the form of lump sum or per-show payments for the artist and significant promotional money to be spent on radio and television advertising nationally and in markets where the artist is appearing. In return, the artist allows the association with the tour, the use of the artist's name and likeness in advertising, probably agrees to some time for making ads for the sponsor, probably agrees to allow the sponsor to have a presence at concerts in terms of signs or other product placement, and may agree to "meet and greets" backstage where local employees of the sponsor and local buyers of the sponsor's products can meet the artist personally. Companies who sponsor musical events and other shows report sales increases of from 50 to 1,000 percent in markets where the sponsored show appears.[46]

A new wrinkle? As revenues from the sales of recordings dwindle in the early 2000s, the labels began to look to the live performance stream as a source of income. In 2002, EMI advanced European superstar, Robbie Williams, a reported $20 million for a 25 percent share of all his non-recording income. While most artists strongly resist such deals, there was speculation that the label pressure to participate in the live entertainment stream might increase.[47] Some artists also discovered the value of mentioning specific products by brand name in their songs.[48] Advertisers and manufacturers typically pay motion pictures for product placement of recognizable brands in movies. While such deals had not become widespread in the recording industry by the end of 2003, it was reasonable to speculate that the labels might want a piece of that action, too.

The Unions

There is substantial involvement of labor unions in the presentation of live entertainment. The performers themselves are likely to be members of either The American Federation of Musicians (AFM) or the American Guild of Variety Artists (AGVA). In addition, the International Alliance of Theatrical Stage Employees (IATSE) members will undoubtedly be involved in lighting, sound, and stage crews. Finally, the electricians, plumbers, and other craft unions are likely to be involved with the venue as support personnel, particularly in states such as New York and California where unions are quite strong.

The AFM

The American Federation of Musicians of the United States and Canada is the official name of the AFM. It represents musicians, conductors, arrangers, orchestrators, copyists, and others involved in the preparation and presentation of live music (but not composers). The union has a national organization, which is primarily responsible for the negotiation of national agreements with the major labels (see Chapter 7) and national television and radio networks, and local chapters. The performing musician will be a member of both the national and a particular local. The locals set wage scales for live performances in their areas. The scales vary considerably from local to local depending upon the strength of the union in a particular city. The strongest locals are in cities and states where it is legal to have a *union shop,* a venue that has agreed with the union to allow only union members to perform there. Because these are primarily in the northeastern and north central states and because most musicians will ultimately want to perform there, they will ultimately have to join the union. Even in *right to work states,* where state laws prohibit establishments from agreeing to hire only union members, nonunion musicians may have difficulty playing at significant concerts because union musicians have agreed not to perform with nonunion musicians.

The locals and the national organization finance their activities through initiation fees and work dues. When someone first becomes a member, they pay national and local initiation fees. The national fee was $65.00 in 2003 and the local fees vary from local to local, but tend to be around $100.00.[49] Most of that one-time fee goes to the national organization. Locals may have annual dues as well. Members also pay work dues based on the wages they earn as musicians. The amount varies from local to local but ranges from about one to five percent of scale wages. This may be paid by the employer directly to the union or by the musician.

In addition to setting scale wages, the union provides other benefits for its members. Because musicians are independent contractors, they usually have no corporate health insurance, life insurance, or retirement benefits unless they arrange for them on their own. The union is able to provide group insurance and retirement plans for its members through its own health and welfare fund, and retirement pension fund to which the members as well as the record labels (see Chapter 7) contribute. The union also protects members from employers who do not pay on time. A "defaulters" list names conductors, promoters, and record producers who do not pay.

AGVA

The American Guild of Variety Artists represents singers, dancers, comediennes, and others who perform live. It is one of the "4 As" unions, a group of unions also including the Actors' Equity Association, the American Guild of Musical Artists, the Screen Actors Guild (SAG), the Screen Extras

Guild, and the American Federation of Television and Radio Artists (AFTRA). The "4 As" nickname comes from the name of the parent union, the Associated Actors and Artists of America. AFTRA is not as important a force in the live performance area, but its impact in record production is discussed in Chapter 7. In 2003 AFTRA and SAG attempted to merge into the Alliance of International Media Artists, but the merger had to be approved by both unions and the SAG members rejected the deal.[50]

IATSE

The International Alliance of Theatrical Stage Employees represents non-performers in theater, television, and film. Its members include stage-hands, camera operators, gaffers, lighting technicians, wardrobe people, and others. Most major performance venues have agreements with IATSE to employ union members. Artist performance contract riders often specify the employment of IATSE members.

The Management Team

It is usually necessary for an artist to have more than one person taking care of business for them. That is partly because there is need of expertise that is often not available in a single person, and partly because it may not be wise to engage a single person, even if they did have all the expertise. Certainly an artist who has, or is to enjoy, much success must have a personal manager. They will have to have an agent representing them, securing employment and performances. From the artist's perspective, the recording industry is a business of providing their personal services to everyone from record companies to concert promoters. Most of the arrangements under which the artist will be performing will be under contract. As has been noted in previous chapters and as will be discussed further in Chapter 7, these contractual relationships are often complex and require the services of an attorney familiar with entertainment industry contracts. Finally, the artist will invariably want/need to audit the accounts of various people with whom he or she has financial dealings, such as record labels, music publishers, agents, and personal managers, the services of an accountant should be retained. These four people, the personal manager, the agent, the attorney, and the accountant, make up the basis of a management team.

It is important for the members of the management team to be independent of each other. For one thing, four independent opinions, each founded on the best interests of the artist, are more likely to generate the course of action most appropriate for the artist to take. This is not to say that all four team members would be consulted on every decision. Attorneys and accountants are legally and ethically bound to represent their client's best interests. Managers also have duties to their clients but they are not as clear cut and well enforced as those of accountants and attorneys. Managers generally cannot be talent agents by law in some states and by union agreements generally.

Conflicts of Interest

Suppose the manager is negotiating the recording contract for the artist. That manager may get a 20 percent commission on all of the artist's income. Suppose that manager needs cash now for the management company. Do you suppose that manager would rather go for a large advance for the artist or for higher royalty percentages? The higher percentages may be in the better long-term interest of the artist, but the manager finds a conflict between his or her own interest and that of the artist. The best way to avoid such conflicts is simply not to be in a position where they are likely to arise. The manager should let the attorney negotiate the agreement, within some agreed-upon parameters. Certainly the manager and accountant have to be different people if the accountant may be called upon to audit the manager's books.

Summary

The live entertainment income stream is the least consolidated of the three streams. That is not to say that there is not significant consolidation, particularly in the concert promotion business, or that the trend is not toward consolidation. Although the roughly $2 billion in annual revenues from concert ticket sales is only about one-sixth of the revenues from recording sales, it is the stars of the recording industry who are the stars of the live performance stage. Furthermore, the $2 billion in annual sales does not account for the thousands of lounges, bars, restaurants, and clubs that have live entertainment and pay their bands without selling tickets. Live performance is an important part of the career of most recording artists in that it provides a stable, more long-term income than recordings and is an important source of income while waiting for the sale of recordings to reach the point where advances have been recouped (see Chapter 7).

6
Recordings: The Main Stream

Basic Functions

In order to produce income in this stream, a record company, usually referred to as a *label*, gains control over a master recording of a performance by an artist and then sells copies to consumers. Usually this takes the form of signing the artist to an exclusive recording agreement with the label, producing a recording, then manufacturing and marketing copies of that recording for ultimate purchase by consumers. The label therefore has two basic functions that it must perform: acquire masters and market those masters. The acquisition of masters is discussed in detail in Chapter 7 on the production and A&R function; marketing is discussed in detail in Chapter 8. This chapter examines the overall market structure of the recordings stream and the structure of a typical individual label within that stream.

Oligopoly

From almost every perspective, the recording industry is in an oligopolistic state. *Oligopoly* is usually defined as a "few" sellers occupying the market, with "few" being everything between one firm (monopoly) and many firms (pure competition). A more useful definition, which takes into account the concentration of the market in the number of sellers, defines three levels of oligopoly. In a dominant firm oligopoly, one firm holds 50 to 90 percent of the market. In a *tight oligopoly*, a concentration of four firms holds more than 60 percent of the market. If it takes more than four firms to reach sixty percent of the market, but less than "many," that type of oligopoly is called *effective competition*. [1]

It should be noted that oligopoly is not a "four-letter word," either literally or figuratively. There is nothing inherently bad about an oligopoly existing in any given market. Oligopoly is simply a word that describes a market in which there are certain kinds of conditions. Generally, markets are described by four significant factors: the number of firms, the seller concentration, the product differentiation, and the barriers to entry.[2] The number of firms involved in the distribution of recordings is relatively small, but the number of individual labels is large. Looking at the market share of the individual labels (Table 6.1), one can see a market that is fairly well spread. Even the top 15 labels do not control more than 40 percent of the top 200 market. If one considers label ownership on the theory that the individual labels do not operate autonomously within their corporate organizations, then there is much higher concentration of sellers. Although all labels sell the same basic products—recordings—there is usually very high differentiation among those recordings. That is why some recordings find favor with consumers and are hits and others are not. That is why some recordings are the toast of the critics and others are panned. That is why consumers have favorite artists and favorite recordings.

On the label side, the barriers to entry are not as great as they used to be. There are many acts wanting to record, costs of recording are lower than they used to be, and the label does not have to manufacture its own recordings (most of these factors are discussed in more detail in Chapter 7). From the perspective of the distribution of hard copies of recordings, there are high barriers to entry. Setting up a nationwide distribution system entails building warehouses, stocking inventory, and hiring personnel, all creating high barriers to entry. On the other hand, if recordings are distributed through cyberspace on the Internet, then barriers to entry are very low.

TABLE 6.1 Top 200 Album Labels and Distributors
(By Number of Albums in Billboard's Top 200 Albums Chart)

	1998		2000		2002	
	Number	%	Number	%	Number	%
Controlled by top 15 labels	220	26.9	268	25	364	36.5
Controlled by major distributors	732	89.4	960	89.5	882	88
Controlled by Independents	87	10.6	113	10.5	120	12
Total Albums in Top 200	819	100	1073	100	1002	100

Source: Data from *Billboard* Year End Issues, 30 December 2002; 26 December 2000; 26 December 1998.

Oligopoly from Birth to the 1950s

For most of its existence, the recording industry has been in a state of tight oligopoly. Thomas Edison's patent monopoly lasted only nine years from the invention of the "talking machine" in 1877. The founding of his Edison Speaking Phonograph Company in 1878 led Alexander Graham Bell to create a better cylinder and player and form the American Graphophone Company in 1887. Edison first started offering cylinders for sale to the public in 1889. Shortly thereafter, Columbia was formed and started offering cylinders for sale for coin-operated players. By 1901 the Victor Talking Machine Company was formed and began offering Emile Berliner's (the German who invented disk recording) disk players and recordings. Columbia began to market both cylinders and disks under patent licenses. By 1909 the three companies with patent monopolies (or licenses) controlled the market: Edison, Columbia, and Victor. A three-firm tight oligopoly continued until the 1950s, although the firms comprising the top three changed over time. Edison folded in the market crash of 1929, but Decca emerged in the 1930s.[3] By 1950 RCA Victor and Decca claimed 67 percent of *Billboard's* Top Pop Records chart. Mercury and Capitol were emerging as significant labels with a 10-percent share each and Columbia had dropped to less than a 4-percent share.[4] The popularity charts of *Billboard* magazine are a convenient and reasonably accurate way to measure a record's or label's success before the days of SoundScan. Although the methodologies used in compiling the charts have changed somewhat over time, they have always included a significant sales component.

During the early 1950s more labels and artists began to emerge, but the tight oligopoly remained. Phonograph players became more plentiful in the home market, and jukeboxes spread in commercial establishments such as bars and restaurants. As late as 1953 the top four firms, Columbia (reenergized by Broadway cast albums, MOR hits, and Mitch Miller recordings), Capitol, Mercury, and RCA Victor, controlled 78 percent of the charted records.[5] Only seven labels had any chart action at all. As R&B, country, and folk became more popular, more labels appeared in the year-end chart summary. In 1954 fourteen labels reported top 30 chart activity but there was still a tight oligopoly with RCA Victor, Capitol, Mercury, and Columbia controlling 62 percent of chart activity.[6]

Mom and Pop, and Rock 'n' Roll

The birth of rock and roll in 1955 ended the tight oligopoly and brought effective competition with the emergence of many independent labels, especially R&B, into the top charts. In 1955 the top six labels held a 60-percent share; this dropped to 53 percent the next year. *Billboard* reported 25 R&B hits on the charts and 20 rock hits (many of them cover versions of R&B songs by pop artists such as Perry Como).[7] The public's demand for the new music drove sales of recordings up with a 44 percent increase in sales volume from 1955 to 1956. The new artists came from everywhere, on dozens of new labels, and the chart share of the independents skyrocketed to 76 percent in 1958.[8] Even as albums began to replace singles as the dominant selling product in the early 1960s, it was clear that the oligopoly was broken. The 1962 *Billboard* album chart summary showed forty-two labels with at least one charted album, and the top six firms controlled less than 50 percent of those records.[9]

Back to Oligopoly

Over the next twenty years the major corporations began to assert more control through branch distribution (see Chapter 8) and mergers. By 1972 the top five labels controlled only 31.4 percent of the album charts, but the top five *corporations* controlled 58.2 percent of those charts. The industry was returning to a tight oligopoly (four firms controlling more than 60 percent) with the top four corporations controlling 52.6 percent of the album chart (WEA 26.2 percent, CBS 13.1 percent, A&M 7.7 percent, Capitol and RCA tied at 5.6 percent).[10] As the 1970s wore on into the 1980s the oligopoly became more pronounced. The most significant independent labels abandoned independent distribution and agreed to become distributed through the majors' distribution systems. In 1979 A&M joined RCA distribution, followed by Arista and Ariola in 1983. United Artists merged with Capitol in 1979. In 1983 Chrysalis went to CBS distribution and Motown went to MCA. In the flurry of consolidation and merger of the late 1980s and 1990s, *ownership* became the key factor. Large labels bought out smaller labels. The identity of the smaller label may have been retained, but ownership was usually in the hands of a large entertainment conglomerate.

Into the Twenty-first Century

By 2000 the structure of the industry had returned to a tight oligopoly. The top four distributing firms controlled about 62 percent of the market in the United States for the first half of the 1990s. WEA averaged about 21.5 percent, Sony about 15.5 percent, and PolyGram (PGD) and BMG about 12.8 percent each. Independent labels had been increasing their share of the market, from 14.6 percent in 1993 to 21.2 percent in 1996.[11] Following the merger of PolyGram and Universal in 1998, the top four firms—Universal, Warner, BMG, and Sony—controlled almost 75 percent of the total album market in the United States (see Figure 8.6). The likelihood is that the tight oligopoly will continue. Even if the share of independent labels increased to 20 percent, the remaining 80 percent would still be divided among four major companies. If the big four divided up their 80 percent evenly (one-fourth of 80 is 20)—and there is no indication that would happen—three of them would still control over 75 percent of the market. Once an independent label begins to show significant market share and profitability, it is subject to being purchased by one of the big five. Unlike the situation in the late 1950s, the large companies do not ignore new musical genres or trends.

The Big Four[12]

Four large international conglomerates own and control the bulk of the recording industry in the world—not just the United States. In case there is any doubt that the recording industry operates on an international level, one only has to look at the ownership of these four largest record companies: Warner Music Group is owned by a Canadian company, AOL-Time Warner; Universal Music Group is owned by Vivendi Universal SA of France; Sony-BMG is jointly owned by the Japanese Sony Corporation and Bertelsmann, A.G. in Germany. EMI Ltd. is a U.K. firm. Not every one of the large entertainment conglomerates breaks out the earnings or sales of their music divisions. Where that information is available, it is given in the discussion of the big four that follows. Financial data from 2000 is used for the sake of establishing a benchmark.

Universal Music Group

Universal Music Group is the world's largest record/music company. It was created in 1998 by the merger of Universal Music Group (formerly MCA) and PolyGram. In 2001 it was merged with the French Vivendi SA to create Vivendi Universal SA. Prior to the planned sale of its Vivendi Universal Entertainment unit which included Universal Films, cable TV channels, and theme parks to NBC/General Electric at the end of 2003, Universal was the third largest media group in the world (behind AOL-Time Warner and Walt Disney) with 2000 revenues of $22.6 billion. The original Vivendi-Universal merger combined Vivendi's substantial European and American television, cable, and film interests with those of Universal. The main recording and music components that went into the making of the new media giant were PolyGram and Universal.

PolyGram N.V. was a Dutch (Netherlands) entertainment holding company that in turn was 75 percent owned by Philips Electronics N.V. PolyGram built its recording interests piecemeal. Philips originally purchased Polydor (a German label) in the early 1950s, and Mercury Records in 1961. MGM Records was acquired in 1972. PolyGram was formed in 1972 when parent company Philips merged Polydor with Phonogram International. In 1989 PolyGram acquired the Island Records Group, in 1990 A&M Records, and then R&B powerhouse Motown in 1993 for $300 million. In 1994 PolyGram acquired a 50-percent interest in Def Jam Records.

Prior to 1998, Universal Music Group was composed primarily of the assets of the former MCA Records. The early history of MCA is particularly interesting. It began in New York in 1924 as a talent agency and moved to California in 1937 to add film talent to its operations. Television talent booking was added in 1949. The company moved into the production business in 1959 with the purchase of Universal Studios film facilities. MCA added recordings in 1962 when it purchased U.S. Decca and shortly thereafter the Coral and Kapp labels. The ABC-Dunhill labels were added in 1979. MCA purchased about 20 percent ownership of Motown Records in 1988, but later sold that interest for $60 million in 1993 when Motown was purchased entirely by PolyGram. Ownership of MCA moved to Japan in 1990 when the electronics giant, Matsushita Electric Industrial Co., purchased it for $6.13 billion. MCA added Geffen Records to the label roster in 1991, and the company changed the name of its branch distribution system to Uni Distribution. Another important acquisition was a 50-percent share of the rock and rap label Interscope for a reported $200 million in 1996.[13] Seagram Co., Ltd. of Canada (a beverage company) purchased 80 percent of Matsushita's ownership of MCA in 1995 for $5.7 billion. The new parent, Seagram, earned about 63 percent of its revenues from the sales of beverages, spirits, and wines, and 37 percent from its holdings in MCA.

Universal Music Group labels now include MCA, Geffen, Interscope, DGC, GRP, Mercury, Polydor, London, Vertigo, Verve, Wing, A&M, Island/Def Jam, Motown, Decca, Deutche Grammophon, and Philips Classics. Also under the Universal Music Group umbrella are the record and video distribution system, Uni Distribution, and music publishing interests. Vivendi Universal owns film and television production and distribution, and cable and television networks. In 2001 Universal announced the purchase of Internet Music distributors MP3.com and Emusic.com. Meanwhile, Vivendi was in the process of selling the drink division it acquired in the purchase of Universal's former owner, Seagram, and its real estate division. Vivendi started as a water and waste management company. Prior to the Vivendi merger, Universal Music reported 2000 revenues of $6.24 billion and profits (before interest, tax, and depreciation) of more than $1 billion.[14] The $13 billion sale of the Entertainment Group, which did not include the Music Group, to NBC enabled Vivendi to reduce the substantial debt acquired by the original merger with Universal.[15]

Warner Music Group

Warner Brothers records began as the music division of Warner Brothers film company to control music interests for its film productions in the 1920s. In the Depression of the 1930s Warner sold off its music publishing interests. In 1958 it reformed its music publishing and record labels, primarily to promote and sell its film- and television-related music. Warner Brothers had early 1960s success with the Everly Brothers and Bill Cosby comedy recordings and bought Frank Sinatra's label, Reprise, between 1963 –and 1965 (they purchased the label in halves). In 1967 Warner Brothers purchased Atlantic Records and was in turn purchased by 7 Arts. In 1969 the Kinney Corporation (not the shoe company, but a building services, construction, and parking company) purchased 7 Arts and changed its name to Warner Communications, Inc. With the addition of the Elektra Records label purchased in 1970, Warner/Elektra/Atlantic Distribution (later just WEA Distribution) was formed. Time Warner was formed by the merger of print-publishing giant Time, Inc., and electronic publishing giant Warner Communications, Inc.; after 2000 the name changed to AOL-Time Warner Inc. to reflect the merger with the Internet provider. In late 2003 AOL Time Warner sold the Warner Music Group to a consortium of Canadian investors headed by Edgar Bronfman, the former head of Universal Music when it belonged to Seagram's. The selling price was $2.6 billion.[16]

Warner Music Group consists of the labels and Warner/Chappel Music Publishing. In addition, it owns WEA Inc., which consists of WEA Corporation, the branch distribution system.[17] In 2003 WEA sold its manufacturing division to a Canadian hardware manufacturing company, Cinram, for $1.05 billion. Speculation as to the motive at the time of sale was that the parent AOL-Time Warner simply needed some cash.[18] Warner Music Group labels are: Warner Brothers, Elektra/Asylum, Atlantic, Atco, Reprise, Rhino, and joint ventures with Maverick, Tommy Boy, and Giant records.

Sony Music

Because the proposed Sony-BMG merger was still pending at the time of this writing and because the new entity music group would still be jointly owned by Sony and Bertelsmann, the two parts are considered seperately below. Sony Corporation, the Japanese electronics manufacturing company, saw the importance of developing software industries to complement its hardware manufacturing when it entered into an agreement with CBS Records to create the Digital Audio Disc Corporation, the first manufacturer of compact discs in the United States. The cornerstones of Sony Music are Sony Music Publishing and the venerable label Columbia Records. Columbia, originally the Columbia Graphophone Company of pre-1900, existed as a separate entity until the Depression saw the merger of Columbia Graphophone, Gramophone Company, and Parlophone to create Electric and Musical Industries, Ltd. (EMI) in England. EMI sold its American stock to the American Record Corporation (ARC). Columbia Broadcasting System (CBS) purchased ARC in 1938 and revitalized the Columbia label. Columbia seceded from EMI in England in 1952.

Sony built its music interests primarily through the acquisition of CBS Records group for $2 billion in 1988 from CBS, Inc. Sony's Music Group revenues amounted to about $4.6 billion in 2000 and 2001, which is about

32 percent of Sony's entertainment business revenues (music, games, and film) of $14.2 billion, and about 24 percent of Sony's total revenues for that year.[19] Sony also owns film production and distribution interests Columbia Pictures and Tri-Star Pictures, as well as home video production and distribution, television production companies, and a large consumer electronics division. Sony Music labels are: Columbia, Epic, and Epic Associated Labels. Sony Music owns 7.5 percent of the Columbia House record club; Warner owns a 7.5-percent share as well. Sony also owns a branch distribution system (Sony Distribution) and CD and tape manufacturing facilities in the United States.

BMG

BMG is part of the German corporation, Bertelsmann, A.G. BMG used to stand for Bertelsmann Music Group, but was shortened to BMG. BMG's record business took off in the United States when it acquired Arista Records from its founder Clive Davis in 1979. In 1986 BMG purchased all the RCA Victor interests from General Electric (which had earlier that year acquired RCA Corporation's recording interests for $6.4 billion). Victor was one of the earliest record labels, going all the way back to 1901 in its founding as the Victor Talking Machine Company. It was the first company to market Emile Berliner's lateral cut disk recordings and players. BMG owns or operates more than 200 labels including Ariola, RCA, LaFace/Arista, Zoo Entertainment, Private, Windham Hill, Disques Vogue, Jive/Silvertone, Wired, Mushroom, Deconstruction, American Recordings, Absorbing, Gun, Red Rooster, Goldrush, K&P, Chodwig, MSM, Expressive, Coconut, Nahsa, MCI, Sing Sing, Jupiter, and Lawine. BMG's labels operate under BMG Entertainment. Under that same group are BMG Music Publishing and BMG Music, the distribution and manufacturing operations, and the record club, BMG Music Service. The parent company also owns television and radio stations (outside of the United States), film production and distribution, magazine publishing, book publishing, and newspapers. Bertelsmann owns, in whole or part, more than two hundred entertainment and publishing entities throughout the world and continued to expand throughout the 1990s, acquiring 73 percent of Ricordi (the largest Italian independent record company) and 50 percent of the new age label Private Music in 1994.[20] In 2002 BMG acquired all of Zomba's recording and music publishing interest for a reported $2.7 billion.[21] Bertelsmann's 2000 net revenues were Euros 18.4 billion (about $15.8 billion) with total assets of Euros 14.7 billion (about $12.6 billion). BMG operations accounted for about $2.8 billion.

EMI

EMI began with the merger of three labels in the United Kingdom in 1930. Columbia Graphophone, Gramophone Company (the folks who originated the famous logo of the dog listening to the gramophone player, "His Masters Voice"), and Parlophone joined to create Electric and Musical Industries, Ltd. (later just EMI, Ltd.). EMI remained a primarily European operation until 1956 when it acquired Capitol Records in the United States. Capitol had been formed in the United States in 1942 by Johnny Mercer, Buddy DeSylva, and Glenn Wallichs. In the United States, Capitol-EMI Industries grew into a major label with a branch distribution system. In 1974 EMI acquired the rights to the substantial Decca U.K. catalog. (There were two Decca record companies until 1974; Decca U.K. was formed in 1929 and U.S. Decca in 1934.) Thorn EMI, PLC was formed in 1979 when electrical/electronics company Thorn merged with EMI. The new company began expansion with the acquisition of Chrysalis Records in 1989, SBK Entertainment World in 1990, Filmtrax and Thames Television in 1990, the Virgin Music Group in 1992, Sparrow Corp. (a gospel label) in 1992, and Toshiba-EMI Music Publishing Co. and Star Song publishing in 1994. In 1996 Thorn and EMI demerged.

The resulting EMI Group contained two divisions: EMI Music Group operated the 65 labels and 23 music publishing companies, including Capitol, EMI Records, EMI Music Publishing, Virgin Records Ltd., and Capitol-EMI Music. The Music Group also includes EMD (EMI Music Distribution, formerly Cema Distribution) distribution, and manufacturing facilities. The HMV group operated a retail division consisting of 240 record stores, 144 of which were outside of the United Kingdom. EMI Group reported revenues of 3.3 billion pounds sterling (about U.S. $4.7 billion) with about 2.7 billion pounds sterling (about U.S. $3.9 billion) attributable to its music and recording operations.[22] The demerger fueled speculation that EMI would be purchased by some other conglomerate, at a speculated price of $9+ billion.[23] Indeed, both Time Warner and Bertelsmann expressed interest in EMI. The Time Warner deal fell through in late 2000 as the European Union's Merger Task Force was reportedly ready to block the merger. [24] Later that year and continuing into 2001, EMI and Bertelsmann were reportedly in merger talks.[25] By mid-2003, the merger talks had shifted to BMG and Warner, then back to EMI and Warner again.[26]

The success of the big four at producing hits is illustrated in Table 6.1. The success of the various individual labels tends to vary from year to year. But in the years near the end of the twentieth century, the top 15 labels controlled only 25 percent to 37 percent of *Billboard*'s Top 200 Album Chart. This indicates effective competition between labels, but not between distribution companies. Independent labels only accounted for about 10 to 12 percent of the chart action in each year.

An important point about this table is that it shows significant diversity and lack of concentration when looking at the individual labels and much more concentration when looking at the distributors. The major distributors controlled nearly 90 percent of the Album Chart action in those years.

That represents significant concentration. However, if the individual labels function autonomously in terms of A&R and marketing in finding, developing, and promoting new talent, then there is much less concentration of label power and there should be much more diversity of music to be heard, regardless of who the corporate owner or distributor of any individual label might be.

The Structure of Record Companies

Corporate Structure

The upper-level structure of the big five recording companies is basically the same. As shown in Figure 6.1, each corporate owner usually holds several different businesses in addition to its recording companies. These other businesses range from other entertainment enterprises such as film, television, and magazine publishing, to consumer electronics. The music group usually includes at least music publishing and record companies. The record group usually includes various labels, which tend to operate as freestanding units for purposes of A&R and marketing; the record distribution system, which distributes all labels owned by the company plus others under a variety of agreements; and a manufacturing division (except for WMG), which makes all of the owned labels' CDs and tapes and usually also fills special orders from outside labels.

The conglomerates have significant vertical integration. That means they seek to own and control all aspects in the production of their products from the raw ingredients of recording artists and songs to retail sale of recordings to consumers. Most of these corporations own labels that control the creative inputs from recording artists. They own music publishing companies, controlling the creative inputs from songwriters. They own manufacturing facilities to make the CDs and tapes that will ultimately be sold to the public. They own distribution companies to get the recordings to the retailers. None own brick-and-mortar retail stores since EMI sold its HMV stores in 1998. However, three (BMG, Time Warner, and Sony) have some ownership interests in record clubs, another form of retail selling, and all have some interests in Internet distribution. They also seek horizontal integration, when they buy up competing labels in order to insure a larger total share of the recording market.

Structure at the Label Level

Although the two basic functions of any label are A&R and marketing, any given label may perform those functions in depth, spread across a number of departments and personnel, or simply either not do them or hire an outside organization to provide the service (outsourcing). Figure 6.2 illustrates the divisions likely to be present at a large label. While there is not a

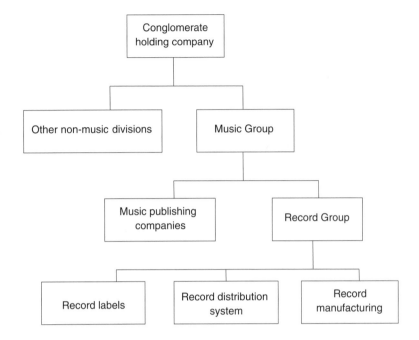

Fig. 6.1 Typical Big Four corporate structure.

great deal of commonality in what a given label may call a particular department, the divisions are typical.

Label president. The label president is usually someone who has experience in A&R, although not necessarily. Sometimes the presidents come from the business affairs departments and are attorneys, less often they are from the marketing departments. Label presidents oversee all operations, but depending upon the depth of their personal involvement in A&R, either as producers or "talent scouts," the other divisions may have additional independence. (Note that the business affairs and accounting divisions are "staff" divisions not directly involved in the production and marketing of the recordings.)

Business affairs. This is usually the legal department of the label. It is in charge of negotiating artist and producer agreements, and other licensing arrangements, including sampling and film use. This department typically finalizes foreign licensing deals, distribution deals with other labels, and soundtrack album deals. An advantage of this split of the negotiating function from the president or A&R people is that it enables the creative people

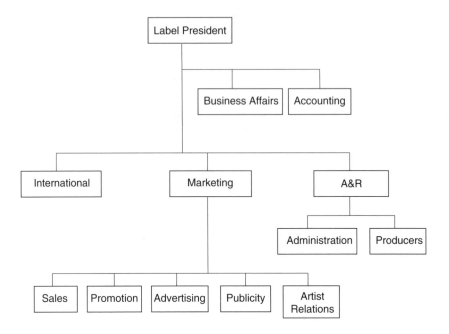

Fig. 6.2 Typical individual label organization.

and the marketing people to be at peace with the artist, while any hard-nosed bargaining is handled by individuals who are not as likely to have to deal with the artist in later production or marketing of the recordings.

Accounting. Accounting is critical to the profitability of the company in any business that depends upon sales of so many different individual units where there are so many people with an interest in each unit. The counting of sales, returns, free goods, and promotional albums and the payment of royalties to at least three (artist, producer, and music publisher) but as many as a dozen or more interests (multiple artists, multiple producers, a different publisher for each song) per recording is a complex task. The accounting departments can rest assured that artists, producers, publishers, and the Harry Fox Agency are all likely to audit the account books for any given album or artist once every year or two.

International division. This unit works out international distribution deals and coordinates marketing plans around the world. It may be responsible for A&R in foreign territories. Some smaller labels hire other labels outside of the United States or a major U.S. label to take care of international marketing and distribution for them.

Marketing. This is usually the largest division of a label. However, a small independent label may rely on a deal with a major label to supply all of these services, while the independent label only provides an A&R function. The term *marketing,* generally said to include product conception and development, manufacturing, promotion, and distribution (see Chapter 8), is significantly broader than most record companies use the term in their internal structure. The A&R department handles conception and development, manufacturing is through a separate subsidiary or entirely outside entity, and actual distribution is through a separate distributing company. The responsibility of the marketing department is limited to getting the recordings to the consumer through retail and rack sales, and to promoting consumer awareness of the records through radio and TV airplay, print publicity, and advertising in any and all media.

Sales. The sales department is responsible for getting orders for records from rack jobbers, major retail chains, and one-stops. There may be merchandising specialists working in sales whose job it is to visit stores and help set up displays. Salespeople may be organized on a national, regional, local basis, or may be set up by account size or type, then regionalized or localized.

Promotion. The primary job of promotion is to get exposure through radio and video airplay. Some labels separate the radio and video promotion arms. Most large labels have their own promotion staffs and hire independent promotion people as well. Promotion people work with radio and TV broadcast outlets, and work with the artist when the artist is on a tour, whether it is a paying tour with concerts or a promotional tour offering showcases for local media people to hear the act. The promotion staff sees to it that the "right" people from the media and record retail area get the opportunity to hear their artists whenever their artist is playing in a given locale. Promotion people may even have to take the artists around to visit local radio and television stations or record stores while the artist is on tour.

Advertising. Advertising personnel create the media plans to go with a given album or single. Because the advertising plan must be carefully designed to promote a unified and consistent image of the artist and album, many labels create the actual advertisements that go to retailers or local radio or television stations. The advertising department will also make national media buys or dispense co-op advertising money to retailers and distributors who come up with additional advertising plans for the label's recordings. Co-op advertising money in the recording industry most often means that the label will pay 100 percent of a retailer's advertising costs for certain kinds of ads. Sometimes a label will go for a true cooperative advertising plan where the expense is shared by the label and the retailer.

Publicity. Publicity consists of nonpaid exposure other than radio airplay or music video airplay. This department contains people who write press releases, create press kits including artist bios (biographies) and photos, and try to get the artist appearances as talk-show guests or performers on radio or TV. Publicity is probably one of the easiest functions for a label to farm out to independent publicists. In fact, an artist's manager will often have an independent publicity firm working alongside the label's public relations people. The publicity people try to see to it that while an artist is touring there is publicity material flowing to the media in towns where the artist will be performing, but ahead of the artist's actual appearance dates. Publicity people will work with promotion people to set up press conferences or "meet and greet" opportunities for local media. The publicity department is also in charge of trying to get album reviews in local and national media.

Artist relations. This department may be designated by a number of other names, including product development and career development. Whatever it is called, its primary task is to coordinate the work of the other departments to be sure that there is a unified marketing plan for every album. People in this department often work with the artist's personal manager to insure that a uniform image is projected. They may work with the artist or producer during the recording of an album to get a better idea of what the album is about and to develop a marketing plan that the artist will support. They will make sure that copies of the recordings for sales and promotion, as well as advertising and publicity, follow the artist whenever the artist is on tour. Artist relations is a function that labels began to add during the late 1970s as they became aware that marketing plans had to be more sophisticated and integrated in order to succeed.

A&R. The A&R (artist and repertoire) department is in charge of finding and recording artists. It may also look for songs for artists who do not write their own compositions. Because the A&R department is in charge of delivery of a completed product, ready to be marketed, it also has to perform administrative duties associated with the finished master.

A&R administration. This is where the coordination takes place for getting mechanical licenses and clearances for sampling. The administrative staff must make sure that all people who played on an album get proper credits. They may help the producers screen material for an artist if asked. They coordinate delivery of the recording, artwork, and liner notes to make sure that all materials necessary to complete production of the discs and tapes are delivered to the manufacturing plants. They make sure that all musicians, artists, and producers get paid when they are supposed to for the initial production of the album.

Producers. These people are in charge of the recording process. They may find the talent and record it, record it after others have found it, or screen talent being pitched to the label. They may be staff producers who work for a salary and royalty, or be entirely independent of the label and just work for a royalty and advances. (See Chapter 7 for an in-depth discussion of producers.)

Profitability in the Recording Industry

In a given year it is likely that less than one percent of records will sell more than 250,000 units (see discussion below). The large record labels are fond of saying that less than 20 percent of the recordings they release ever recoup their costs, but the high profit margins on compact discs must make one a little suspicious of that calculation. As explained in Chapter 7, recording costs and some marketing costs are generally recouped out of artist royalties. Table 6.2 illustrates a typical (and somewhat simplified) situation for pre- and post-recoupment profits. The label does not pay the artists and producers their royalties of $2.25 per copy *until* that royalty equals the total recoupable amounts. Suppose a major label spends $200,000 in recoupable production and marketing costs, and that total production and marketing costs are $300,000. It will take sales of 88,889 units for artist and producer royalties to equal the recoupable amounts. By that time the label's gross margin, after deducting the actual costs of mechanical royalties for the music publisher, distribution charges, and manufacturing, is over $737,000—more than $400,000 in gross profits. Even allowing for the label paying for its overhead, that is a substantial figure for a relatively low-selling album. To reach the *economic* breakeven point, where the total fixed costs (production and marketing) are equal to gross profits, takes sales of only 36,145 units (rounded up). That is calculated by dividing the $300,000 production and marketing costs as fixed by the $8.30 gross margin per disc sold. By the time the artist has hit the recoupment point and the label's gross margin drops to $6.00, the label has sold 52,744 units beyond the breakeven point, making a gross profit of $437,775.20. So, for a lot of artists who never see any royalties on the sale of their albums, the record companies *are* making money.[27] Thus, the labels can afford to try to release more albums, even if sales are relatively low. In effect, the artists are subsidizing them because recoupment of advances at the artist royalty rate is a lot slower than actual recovery of

TABLE 6.2 Pre- and Post-Recoupment Profitability

	Pre-recoupment ($)	Post-recoupment ($)
Wholesale price	11.75	11.75
Less: Manufacturing costs	1.00	1.00
Artist and producer royalties	0.00	2.25
Mechanical royalties	0.75	0.75
Distributor charges	1.75	1.75
Gross margin	8.25	6.00

total fixed costs at the label's gross margin per CD rate. This high profitability, particularly on CD sales, also fuels the independent labels.

The "Indies"

Independent record companies are usually thought of as those not owned
by one of the major labels or conglomerates. Such a definition is rather
broad, covering everything from a small label in a large city with a couple
of artists that just markets recordings on a local or regional level, to Disney
which is part of a major entertainment company (just not one of the big
four), to a label with a significant artist roster and national distribution
through independent distributors, such as Sugar Hill or TVT, or a label
that has its recordings distributed by one of the big four but is not owned
by them. Some people would argue that the latter is not a true indie
because it is not distributed through true independent distributors, but in
a time of consolidation and vertical integration any label that is not *owned*
by a major label is deserving of the title *indie.*

The indies play an important role in the recording industry. They are a
development area for record labels. Several of what might now be called
major labels began life as indies: Warner Brothers, Def Jam, Arista, and
MCA for example. The indies provide consumers with diversity and specialty music that the larger labels often ignore because the small volume of
sales (in the 3,000 to 30,000 units range) is not enough for a large label to
consider. They also provide the larger labels with a source of new talent
and new directions in music. The rock and roll explosion began on independent labels. New Age music began as an independent phenomenon.
Rap began on small inner-city independents, then entered the mainstream, then was bought into by the large labels.

Size of the Indie Labels

SoundScan and RIAA data indicate that the independent labels account for
about 16 percent of the total album sales, yet they release about 66 percent
of the titles. Of more than 35,000 titles released in 2000, over 29,000 were
by independent labels—almost a five-to-one ratio of independent releases
to major label releases. The vast majority (85 percent) of current releases
(not just new, but catalog as well) sell less than 1,000 copies per year. The
number of albums selling more than 250,000 units per year was just 406 in
2000, but those recordings accounted for over 44 percent of the total sales
volume; the major labels released most of those. Of the 29,000 independent
albums released in 2000, only 4,743 sold more than 1,000 units. The average sales of a new release from an independent label were 1,438 units, while
the average sales of a major label release was 8,350 units.[28]

How do the independent labels survive? The growth of the megastores
carrying tens of thousands of titles has provided a place for the independent

labels to sell their products to a larger audience. They have also relied on specialty independent stores in larger cities. They keep production and marketing costs low. Coupled with the high profit margins in CDs, low-cost albums can turn a profit with minimal sales. As Table 6.2 indicates, a low cost CD generates a margin of more than $6 per copy. If that recording can sell 3,000 units, it would earn more than $18,000 in potential profits. If recording and marketing costs are kept low ($10,000 or less), then there is substantial profit. Even an average-selling indie release would generate $8,400 in revenues before recording and marketing costs. With the growth of project studios and inexpensive CD replication, even releases selling at that level could be profitable. There is even profitability in having more low-budget, low-selling albums than having fewer. Because these recordings are not as costly to make or market, more titles can be released toward a very small market. That is the same as it was even back into the 1940s. A *Billboard* article described indie labels in 1949 as having breakeven points on singles of 5,000 units, compared to the majors' breakeven points of 15,000 units.[29] The Association for Independent Music (AFIM) represents more than 350 small labels, mostly in the specialty music areas of bluegrass, reggae, dance, jazz, classical, and others. That figure of 350 does not even count the thousands of custom albums that do not go through independent distribution, but are sold by the artists only in their own locales or at their performances.

Indie Labels and Indie Distribution

Although some independent labels are distributed by the majors, most indie records find their way to the marketplace through independent distributors. Most independent distributors operate on a regional basis and some even on a national basis. A trend of the 1990s was the growth in size of independent distributors and their consolidation into fewer firms. For example, in 1995 Passport Music Distribution, Inc. was formed out of Encore Distribution and Sound Solutions (USA) Inc. (an import and budget distributor). Passport, in turn, was part of the largest independent distributor, Alliance Entertainment, which also owns Independent National Distributors, Inc. and labels Castle Communications, Concord Jazz, and Red Ant Entertainment.[30]

Diversity in Spite of Itself

A particularly popular criticism of the recording industry is that it is run by huge conglomerates that for one reason or another are bent upon shoving much "bad" music down the throats of consumers while "good" music and artists languish without access to the system.[31] To be sure, there is much in popular music at any given time that may not measure up well on some critical scale. The labels are large bureaucratic organizations that tend to be conservative in their releases and follow the patterns of previous successes. At the same time, a large label must be aware that because the majority of releases are not likely to produce much profit, the only way to stabilize revenues is to have a large enough number of releases that enough of them will make enough profits to support the superstructure.

The big four conglomerates must behave like the investor for a retirement fund. Wall Street analysts know that the best way to minimize risk in the stock market is through a diversity of holdings. That way the main risk is just that inherent in stocks as a *kind* of investment instead of a particular company. So the large label will release artists that essentially compete with each other as well as those from other labels instead of risking large sums on a single artist who might not catch the public's fancy.[32] Large numbers of releases make it likely that more consumers will find recordings that they like and will buy. The worst problem for the industry would be a market diminished overall because there were fewer releases.[33] The trend, then, should be toward diversity of music being offered rather than toward homogeneity. That trend has been observed by some as not what would have been predicted by the presence of larger and larger conglomerates controlling more and more of the market.[34] In fact one observer predicts that levels of high product diversity are most associated with moderately concentrated markets and that less diversity is associated with low and high levels of concentration.[35] The question is whether the recording industry is at such a high level of concentration (now a tight oligopoly) that diversity will begin to suffer.

Summary

In any discussion of the basic structure of the recording industry, it is important to remember that there at least three perspectives from which to discuss the labels. First, one can look at the individual names on individual labels. For some purposes that may be the best way because individual labels, even if owned by the same corporate conglomerate, tend to compete with each other for artists and for the consumers' dollars. Labels can also be viewed based on ownership at the corporate level. From that perspective, the four conglomerates control about 85 percent of the industry. Finally, one could look at labels from the perspective of distribution. The number of distribution firms is smaller than the number of individual labels, or the number of label firms, due to the high costs associated with distribution. The concentration of distribution in the five multinationals is about the same as the concentration of market share by corporate owner, but there are significantly fewer competing independent distributors and they too appeared to be going through a phase of concentration of ownership in the 1990s. The individual label perspective focuses on the A&R function. The distribution perspective focuses on the marketing function. The ownership perspective focuses on the profitability of the bottom line. All three perspectives can provide valuable insight into the workings of the recording industry. Each is used at different times throughout this book.

7

Production and the A&R Function

Recording Industry Core Functions

The next three chapters examine in detail the two core record company functions: the acquisition of masters and the marketing of those masters. This chapter explores the ways a label can acquire masters, primarily focusing on the label's efforts in finding recording artists, signing them to contractual obligations to record masters, and producing those masters. Chapter 8 analyzes the ways labels market their recorded products using the "four Ps" approach to focus on *product* lines, *promotion*, *place* of sale and distribution, and *pricing*. Although most labels do not sell their recordings directly to consumers, retail, the final phase of marketing, is critical to the industry. It is especially important because sales of most recordings are through specialty stores or through specialty rack jobbers who provide recordings to mass merchandiser's record/electronics departments. Chapter 9 provides a closer look at record retailing.

In order to be a record company, a label must acquire rights to market copies of master recordings; this is the A&R (artist and repertoire) function. The labels can either create the masters themselves or have somebody else do it for them. A&R is about taking and reducing risks—knowing when to take and when not to take risks, and knowing how to reduce the risk of making a poor choice. Like most things in business, higher risks are usually associated with higher rewards if there is success. The label can engage in the higher risk/greater reward activity of having new masters created for it by acquiring exclusive recording rights from artists and having those artists make master recordings. As an alternative, the label can acquire masters that have already been finished from smaller production companies or labels, thereby reducing risk by knowing what the finished product will sound like, and perhaps by having some marketing track record on a small scale. The label can acquire masters that have already been successfully marketed in some manner and attempt to repackage, remaster, or in some way create a recording that is a new and different assembly of the older masters. There, the initial risk of recording and marketing has already been taken and a market has been established. Greatest hits, essentials, boxed sets, repackages, and digital remasterings of older analog recordings are examples of this method.

Finding and Recording New Talent

New or Used?

It is often said that the lifeblood of a record label is new talent. Without infusions of new recordings that excite consumers to purchase them, a label as an entity or the industry collectively, fails to advance. As noted in Chapter 1, it may even fall into a state of decay moving toward entropy. Strictly speaking, a label does not have to find talent that has never been recorded before or that has never had a record released on a major (or any other) label. A label can acquire talent by "buying" established talent from other labels when the artist's contract with the former label has expired. However, that is an expensive proposition for two reasons. First, the artist is already established and will therefore demand a large advance per album. When Island Records signed Janet Jackson from Columbia in 1995, she was reportedly given an advance of $5 million per album plus $25 million just for signing her new contract.[1] When Clive Davis at Columbia signed a ten-album deal with Neil Diamond for $4 million in 1971 it was a major deal.[2] The reward of such deals is that the label gets an artist who can already sell millions of records without the label having to pour hundreds of thousands of dollars into marketing and a slow development process. The risk is that the label may have acquired the talents of the artist at, or after, their artistic peak—never to be as successful again. In that event, the huge advances may never be recovered. Several 1990s mega deals did not bear as much fruit as the labels might have wished, notably Michael Jackson's $60 million deal with Sony Music, Madonna's $60 million deal with Warner Bros., and ZZ Top's $35 million deal with RCA. One way that the labels hedge their bets with such large deals is to make any per-album advances contingent on sales performance of the prior albums. In some instances the total package might wind up actually costing only about half or less of its initially reported value.[3] In 2001 EMI/Virgin signed Mariah Carey for a deal estimated to be worth $80 million after her Columbia contract expired. Then, less than one year later, they bought her out of the deal for $29 million, taking a $54.3 million loss.[4]

The reasons to sign and develop *new* artists are (1) that their royalty rates and advances will be much lower because they are an unknown quantity in terms of how many records they can sell, and (2) if successful they will be obligated to the label for a significant number of future albums. New artists do not have sufficiently strong bargaining positions based on a track record of sales to negotiate for high royalties and high advances per album. If such an artist is successful, the label will obtain a much higher profit per copy sold because their artist royalties will be substantially less than those for an established artist. A typical new artist contract usually requires a royalty of 60 to 70 percent of what a superstar can command (see discussion of royalties below). If a new artist nets roughly $1.25 per unit sold, then a superstar probably nets $2.50 or as much as $2.80 per unit sold. A label would rather sell a million units of the new artist and take home an extra $1.2 million in profit. The problem is that there is much less certainty that the new artist will sell that million units. In fact, there is a likelihood that the artist will sell substantially less than that, and that the label will probably not sell enough to recoup its advances (that does not necessarily mean the label will not have made a profit on the sales; see discussion in Chapter 8).

The other reason for developing a new artist into a major artist is that they will be obligated to make more records for the label than the already developed superstar. A typical new artist deal will call for six to eight albums over the life of the agreement. A major artist deal will probably be from four to six albums. So if a new artist becomes successful, the label will probably have that artist under contract for the most profitable part of his or her recording career—typically no more than five to seven years.

Finally, because the recording industry runs primarily on popular musical tastes, it is imperative to continue seeking and signing the next new sound; the next hit. A label can only rest on its laurels and current acts for so long. After a while, new faces and new sounds catch the public's attention and purchases. The formerly reliable sales from the established acts begin to drop and the label has no new blood under development to take up the slack. It happened to Columbia about the time that Clive Davis took over in the mid-1960s. They were relying on Broadway cast albums and a few middle-of-the-road artists to make up most of their sales—missing the important new wave of rock artists. It happened to RCA in the mid 1970s—relying too much on John Denver and a couple of other artists who were passing their peak. No label is immune. There has to be attention paid to what is new, on the streets, in the small clubs, and on the local, regional, or custom labels. That is the job of the A&R department.

Who Has "Good Ears?"

How does an A&R person know whether a particular new artist will be a hit? They don't. Industry people say, "You have to have good ears." People with good ears become producers and A&R vice presidents. We know they have good ears because they signed or found the latest hit artist. Of course, that is an after-the-fact test. If that same artist had *stiffed* (done very poorly on their first album sales), the person who found them obviously did not have good ears. Whatever good ears are, they are a product of listening to lots of popular music, not only what is being recorded now, but to what is not being recorded yet. Ear training for A&R people is going to clubs, and listening to demos from bands, personal managers, and publishing companies. It is recognizing social trends. It is knowing some history of popular music, for example, when a sound or artist that has not been heard in a while might be given a new twist that suddenly fits in. And, by the way, it is a little bit of luck. Hearing the next big act and signing them before some other label does may simply be the result of being in the right place at the right time. The solution to improving the odds is to be in lots of places, lots of times. Knowing the timing of the next sound that will capture the public's fancy and what that sound will be is partially a product of hearing lots of music and talking to lots of people. Those are the reasons why being on the street is important to the A&R function.

A good example of someone with good ears is Jason Flom, president of Lava Records, part of the Warner Music Group's Atlantic label. Flom began his career as a merchandiser, creating store displays for the label. While doing that he discovered his first act and got them signed with Atlantic. The success of that act, Zebra, was enough to get Flom moved into the A&R department. From there he signed national and international successes to the label. In 1995 he was given his own label to preside over. In the next seven years Lava proceeded to break new artists responsible for sales of more than 50 million copies in the United States alone. Those acts included Kid Rock, The Corrs, matchbox twenty, Blue Man Group, and more.[5]

Money Matters

A label will usually be able to spend only a limited amount of money recording and promoting its artists. Based on the cash flows predicted, on past experience, and knowledge that there have to be some new artists being signed, most labels set aside a certain amount of money to develop new artists. If they know it will take $150,000 to record an album, and another $150,000 to introduce it to the market, then the number of new artists that can be signed by that label is the number of $300,000 "lumps" the label can afford to spend from its current budget.

The label will want to reduce the risk of spending $300,000 on a new artist whose record turns out to be a stiff. New talent can be drawn from the pool of artists who have proven themselves in live performances. Live performances sell records. An artist with a great live show that really gets an audience excited will probably be able to sell more records than one with a mediocre live show. That is why A&R people want to hear and see an artist perform before signing them,[6] and why artists and managers often set up "showcase" performances where the artist can play for a select crowd of influential record company, radio, and other people. An artist who can make a good visual appearance will also sell more recordings because of the impact that MTV and other video channels have on record sales. That is why A&R people may even want to see some video on an artist they are thinking about signing.

A&R people don't like to sign artists who do not already have a personal manager—someone else who has already invested time and money, is an industry insider, and believes the artist has the talent and drive to become a success. A&R people do like to sign artists who sound like somebody else who has just broken a new sound. The risk is that the label will be trying to get into a market that is already too crowded. A&R people do like to sign artists who have publishing deals where a music publisher has invested substantial amounts of money in the development of the artist's writing abilities. A&R people like to hear a high-quality demo so that they can get a very good idea of what this artist will sound like on a finished master. All of these are ways for the label to minimize the risk that they will invest several hundred thousand dollars and come up with nothing.

Another way to minimize the risk, but still retain an option to record new artists, is to enter a development deal with the artist. These deals are a step short of a full recording contract. A label may feel that the artist has potential but is not quite ready to record, perhaps because they need to work on their songwriting, live performance, or recording techniques. In that case, the label may decide to offer the artist an agreement where the artist promises to remain available to enter an exclusive contract with the label in exchange for working on whatever deficiency the label feels exists. The artist will usually be given an advance to do a demo recording of three or four songs to showcase their abilities. The advances for these recordings are rather small, usually in the $4,000 to $6,000 range. These advances are recoupable from any royalties earned under a recording agreement that may be signed later. (See the discussion and example later in this chapter about advances, royalties, and recoupment.) The label substantially reduces its financial risk compared to a full album contract with the new artist and reduces the risk that someone else may find and sign this potentially hit artist first.

Artists' Recording Contracts

At its most basic level, a recording agreement between an artist and a label is a contractual arrangement between the two parties based on an exchange of promises. The artist promises to make recordings for this label and for no other (an exclusive agreement), in exchange for the label's promise to pay the artist royalties based on the sale of those recordings, when and if those sales occur. What the two parties both want from these agreements is to minimize their risks and maximize their profits. To that end recording agreements are highly negotiated. There are a lot more points of concern to both parties, which is why the agreements are likely to be thirty to sixty pages in length.

Bargaining Position

The critical factor deciding who has the upper hand in the negotiations is the relative bargaining power of the two parties. That boils down to a question of size—the "size" of the artist and the size of the label. A new artist with no track record of sales has very little bargaining power compared to the superstar whose last album sold five million copies. The new artist is all risk to the label—all unknown. On the other hand, from the artist's perspective, the size of the label is a factor. A major label has marketing know-how and money to spend on delivery of an album to the public. A major label also has lots of artists and it is possible to get lost in the shuffle. A smaller, independent label does not have the marketing resources, but the artist will be more important to the small label because the label does not have a large artist roster. In order to minimize their own risks, artists will want to minimize the length of their recording commitment to the label and to maximize profits through high royalties and advances. Labels seek to minimize risk by including as many ways to get out of the recording agreement as they can (i.e., less commitment), and to maximize profits by paying lower royalties and advances. The conflicts are obvious. There is no standard agreement, but there are provisions standard to most contracts .[7]

Commitment: A Two-Way Street

The labels minimize risk through the artist's recording contracts by trying to build in ways to get out of the deal at an early stage.

1. The label will delay signing the contract at all. This gives them more time to make up their minds and to see if anything better comes along.
2. The label may decide not to record the artist once they are signed. The label may make this decision because they found some other artist who really gets them excited, or they are running out of money to invest in new recordings. Perhaps the artist has created some major public relations problem, such as the married Christian music artist who is discovered to be having an affair with a band member, and the label does not want to try to market albums in the face of this negative publicity. The label will therefore try to place in the contract a "play or pay" clause that lets the label not even hold recording sessions at all, just pay the artist a single session union

wage as if the session had been held. That is a lot cheaper than all the costs associated with production.

3. The label may not accept the finished master or refuse to release it. Even if they have paid recording and studio costs, the label may feel they should cut their losses by ceasing to put money into the project rather than market what is going to be an obvious (to them) stiff.

4. The label may release the record but only put a minimum amount of marketing money into it, figuring that if the record begins to make waves on its own strength, then they will invest some money in marketing.

The artist wants the label to guarantee everything instead of allowing the label to have options to quit the project. At a minimum, from the artist's point of view, one is not much of a recording artist if there are no recordings available to the public. Even new artists can usually get a label agreement to *record* a minimum number of *sides* (single songs) or perhaps an entire album. If the label fails to record, then the artist is released from the agreement. Similarly, a guaranteed *release clause*, usually only available to a middle-level/established artist or higher, does not mean that the label must release a recording—only that the artist can get out of the agreement if the label fails to release the album within a certain time. It is even harder for the artist to get the label to commit to spending a certain amount of money on marketing. If the artist can get such a guarantee, the label will try to get the artist to underwrite part of the expense by making the marketing guarantees 50 to 100 percent recoupable from the artist's royalties. Even if an artist could get all of these guarantees in the contract, there can be no guarantee that the label will fulfill these terms with enthusiasm—just as there is no guarantee that the artist will put heart and soul into the recording.

Just as the label will seek to minimize its commitment to the artist, it will try to maximize the artist's commitment. This is usually spelled out in the clause dealing with recording obligation. Typically a new artist will be obligated to record as many as six to eight albums, total. The label has the option to require each successive album or drop the artist. The label gets to decide which to do, usually on a yearly basis or within a certain length of time after release of the previous album. The artist can be required to record the total number of albums. What artists like is being required to record fewer albums so they can get out of the deal and possibly go to a different label for a much more lucrative arrangement after a few years. (Artists, of course, always assume they will be successful; that is the kind of ego it takes to be a recording artist.) In reality, what most often happens is that the initial deal with the new artist gets restructured after (if) the artist has a reasonable amount of success. Then they are established artists and less of a risk to the label because they have a track record of album sales. This renegotiation process will invariably result in a more lucrative contract for the artist with the same label, but also in a commitment of the artist to deliver more albums to the label.

Why would a label be willing to renegotiate? Why not just say, "Hey, you made this agreement, now stick to it!" Simply because an artist who is upset with the label over the fairness of their recording agreement is not likely to produce a very exciting recording for the next album. Two excellent examples of the dilemma were the suits between the Dixie Chicks and Sony Music and the suits between Incubus and Sony Music. After their first album was successful, the Chicks negotiated a new deal with Sony for higher royalties. After the second album's success and total sales for the first two albums of more than 20 million copies, the Chicks sued to get out of their remaining recording commitment. Sony counter-sued for $100 million for the five albums still owed under their second agreement. The Chicks then added another suit, charging Sony with, "continual, intentional and wrongful failure to account for and pay royalties it owes." Ultimately the parties were back in business with the Dixie Chicks getting a reported $20-million advance that was only 75 percent recoupable and a 20-percent royalty rate.[8]

In 2003 Incubus sued Sony to get out of the remaining four-album commitment in its recording contract. The group had previously sold about 7.5 million albums and claimed the financial reward to Sony was unfair compared to how much the artists had made. Sony again counter-sued, claiming the band still owed them four albums and potential losses of millions of dollars if the albums were not delivered. As with the Dixie Chicks, money managed to heal the wounds with Sony and Incubus eventually getting back together. Sony reportedly agreed to pay an $8-million advance for the next album, and $2.5 million for the three after that, and agreed to forego $3 million in unrecouped marketing costs that had been charged against the band's royalties.[9] Keeping the artist happy is about the only way the label has of being sure they can get more good albums. They cannot force the artist to record a good album or even record at all. About all the label can do is come to financial terms with the artist or call it quits, get a "divorce," and maybe prevent the artist from making a new "marriage" with another label until the duration of the original contract is over.

Royalty Rates and Deductions

Paying artists royalties for exclusive recording arrangements goes all the way back to Enrico Caruso's arrangement with Victor records in the early 1900s. His 1904 contract called for a royalty of 40 cents per disk (equivalent to more than $7 per disk in 2002 prices), and an advance of $4,000. Sales of his recordings totaled into the millions and his total lifetime income from recordings is estimated at $2 to $5 million.[10] In 2002 dollars that would be equivalent to total earnings of $36 to $91 million—earnings as good or better than many of today's superstars. In the 1950s typical royalties were 5 percent of retail list, paid on 90 percent of sales. By the 1960s they began to move up, driven by the popularity of rock and roll and the growth of record sales, with *Billboard* reporting nearly a dozen artists with royalties exceeding 5 percent.[11] By the mid-1970s new artist royalties pushed up as high as 8 percent of retail list. If the royalty included the producer's royalty in an *all-in* deal, new artists could expect to start in the 10 to 12 percent range.[12] By the mid-1990s the all-in deal was the norm. Typical royalty rates for new artists signed with major labels now range from 12 to 14 percent, for established artists from 15 to 16 percent, and for major artists from 18 to 20 percent; superstar artists sometimes exceeded 20 percent.[13]

But those royalty rates are not as lucrative for the artist as it might first appear. First, they are paid only on records *sold*. Because most records are sold on a 100-percent return privilege, there is no guarantee that shipment of a million recordings means that a million have been sold. A substantial number may end up being returned to the label by retailers and sub-distributors. Artists receive no royalties for promotional copies and others that are given away to dealers and wholesalers as incentives or discounts. Some labels define sales to be 85 percent of shipments. In a practice that goes back to the days when 78-rpm records were made of shellac and broke easily, some labels pay on only 90 percent of actual sales to account for breakage. Of course CDs seldom break. Both of these practices are just ways for the label to reduce its royalty costs by paying less. Also, virtually all labels deduct from the list price a container charge (typically 25 percent for compact discs, usually less for other formats). This supposedly is to cover the cost of the manufactured product itself. Compact discs do not cost $4.75 (25 percent of the typical $18.98 list price) to manufacture; one dollar for the disc, box, and all inserts is closer. The deduction is just a way to pay the artist less per unit and increase the label's profits.

Advances

Advances are prepayments of royalties; they are highly negotiable. Some artists get paid an advance upon signing the contract. Most get paid an advance upon delivery and acceptance of the master by the label. As the artist earns royalties, these advances are recouped (deducted) from earnings. The advances are nonreturnable, meaning the artist does not owe them to the label, and if no records sell or not enough to recover the advance from the artist's royalties, then the label simply writes off the difference. That is the label's risk. The labels also include things such as recording costs, producer fees, all or half of the video production costs if a music video is made, and even some marketing expenses such as independent promotion or other marketing guarantees demanded by the artist, as advances. Recording and production advances are often included in a lump sum *recording fund*. If the artist does not spend the entire recording fund advance on actual recording costs, then any remainder can be paid to the artist, which in effect will amount to an advance for the delivery of the master.

A Gold Record and a Bounced Check

So how much would an artist really make on an album that went *gold* (sold 500,000 copies)? Suppose this is a recording by a new artist with an all-in rate of 12 percent. The producer has a royalty of 3 percent, which is deducted from the total, making the artist's net rate 9 percent. For the sake of simplicity, suppose that the sales are all CDs with a list price of $19.00. After the 25 percent packaging deduction, the artist is paid 9 percent of $14.25, or $1.28 per disc. (In reality, decimal parts of pennies would *not* be rounded in calculating royalties.) Even if the 500,000 are net sales after deducting returns, this new artist may be paid on only 90 percent of sales. That means the artist gets $1.28 for 450,000 discs or $576,000.

Now, about those recoupable advances. Recording fund advances for a new artist depend upon the genre of the music and the stature of the artist, but suppose this is a new rock/pop artist with a fund of $250,000. A careful artist may have been able to hold on to as much as $50,000 of that fund to actually put into their pockets. Assume the label did two music videos at a cost of $70,000 apiece. (Typical video production costs for new artists run $50,000 to $100,000 per song.)[14] One-half of video production costs are usually recoupable out of record royalties. The label spent $100,000 on marketing, one-half of which also happens to be recoupable. Because this is a new artist, the label will probably withhold payment on 30 to 50 percent of royalties otherwise due (or from the number of records counted as shipped) as a reserve against anticipated returns. The reserve is to protect the label from the possibility of paying out royalties on records that appear to be sold, but are later shipped back as returns from retailers and distributors. For the sake of simplicity, assume this artist's 40-percent reserve is out of royalties otherwise earned. Here are the calculations:

Net sales		450,000
(90 percent of 85 percent of units shipped, minus returns)		$1.28
Times base rate per unit		*
Gross royalties earned		$576,000
Less: reserve (40 percent)		(230,400)
Net earnings after reserve		$345,600
Recoupments:		
Recording fund	$250,000	
Video (50 percent)	70,000	
Promotion (50 percent)	50,000	
Total recoupable		($370,000)
Net due artist		($24,400)

This artist is in an *unrecouped position.* The label doesn't have to be paid back for this amount, but neither have royalties accumulated yet to the point where they cover all of the advances. Furthermore, those unre-couped advances are *cross-collateralized*. They may be recovered from any other income earned by the artist from the label. So, if still not recouped when the next album comes out, they will be deducted from royalties due from sales of the *second* album, in addition to the other recoupables directly attributable to it. The label cannot keep the reserves indefinitely. When the label liquidates (pays out) the reserve, usually over three or four accounting periods (up to two years), the artist will get the $230,400 reserve minus the $24,400 unrecouped amount left over at the end of the first accounting period. Over a two-year period this artist kept $50,000 from the recording fund advance plus $206,000 from royalties, a total of $256,000. Is $128,000 per year a lot of income? Suppose this "artist" is a four-piece band. Each member gets $32,000 per year *before* taxes. Because recording artists are self-employed they have to pay their regular income taxes plus the additional self-employment tax of over 15 percent (their share of social security taxes plus the share normally paid by the employer). This band better hope they make money from their live appearances that have been made more profitable by the exposure from the gold album.

Unfortunately, a new artist is highly unlikely to sell this many albums. SoundScan reported that only 406 of 288,000 titles that the service tracked sold more than 250,000 units in 2000, and that the average new release from a major label sold only 8,350 units in 2000, down somewhat from 9,134 in 1995.[15]

Publishing Rights and Controlled Compositions

Many recording artists write or co-write the songs they record. All labels have affiliated music-publishing companies, and would like to have artists who are also songwriters sign publishing agreements with them. To *require* the artist/writers to do so would probably be a restraint of trade (although this has not been confirmed by a court opinion). However, the label can *encourage* the artist to sign with the label's music-publishing affiliate, and it is possible that an artist who is willing to do so will have more leverage in negotiating the recording or publishing agreement. The label's argument is that the existence of the recording they paid for and will promote gives the artist/writer the chance to record the songs. Further, it is sales and airplay of these recordings that generate most of the publishing income. On the other hand, many established artists who are also writers have their own publishing companies and are able to retain their own publishing rights. In most such cases they would pay a regular music publishing company a fee to either copublish or to administer their songs. That fee ranges from 10 to 25 percent of collections through the administrative company. Of course the administration or co-publishing could be through the label's publishing affiliate.

Since the 1909 Copyright Act, record companies have had to pay the music copyright owner, usually a music publisher, a mechanical license fee for the right to make and sell copies of a recording of the song. From 1909 to 1978 that rate was 2 cents per song, per copy (see Chapter 3 for further discussion). From the label's point of view, mechanical royalties are a per-album expense, just the same as the pressing costs. As would any manufacturer, the label would like to control or reduce these expenses. As early as the mid-1970s the labels, spurred by the probable increase in the statutory rate to 2.75 cents in the new copyright law, began to seek ways to limit their mechanical license fees. What they came up with is a contractual provision that has caused much controversy but is now the norm: the *controlled compositions* clause. Because the recording and music publishing income streams intersect when the artist is a singer/songwriter or a self-contained group, the labels are able to control their expenses at the expense of the publishing stream.

A controlled composition is one written, owned, or controlled in whole or part by the artist (or probably the producer as well, especially in a producer-label agreement). The clause requires the artist/songwriter to license such compositions to the label at a specified rate, typically 75 percent of the statutory rate at the time of release. In addition, the labels often put a limit on the total mechanical royalties payable per album to about ten times the controlled composition rate. Here is the kicker: any mechanical royalties paid in excess of the limit are recoupable out of controlled composition royalties or out of artist recording royalties. It is not unusual for CDs to contain eleven or twelve songs and exceed the limit of total mechanical royalties. So an artist/writer who puts twelve songs on an album would be, in essence, recording two for free. A particular problem arises when the artist co-writes with other songwriters. In such cases the other writers are either forced to take the reduced rate on their shares of the songs, or the artist is forced to allow the label to take any difference between the full rate and the controlled composition rate out of his or her own royalties. Those results caused an uproar among artist/writers and co-writers when country artist Randy Travis released an album full of co-written songs and his label refused to pay the co-writers the full statutory rate, even though Travis initially thought they would get it. He ultimately agreed to pay them the full rate with the differences deducted from his own royalties. The NSAI (Nashville Songwriters Association International) formally petitioned (to no avail) most of the major labels to drop the clauses from their contracts, especially as they applied to co-writers.[16]

How does this all work? Suppose the artist has a controlled composition rate of 75 percent of the statutory rate. That rate in 2002 was 8.00 cents per song or 1.55 cents per minute of playing time, whichever was greater (see Chapter 3, compulsory mechanical license rate table, for future rate changes). For the sake of simplicity (and because the contracts usually limit the rate to the per-song rate) assume that the per-song rate applies.

That means the label will pay only 6 cents per song and a maximum of 60 cents per album. If the artist records 11 of her or his own songs, the eleventh must be licensed for free or the record royalties (or mechanical royalties paid for the other songs) will go down by six cents per copy of the album sold.

If the artist is due *all* of the mechanical royalty, that would not be too bad, in essence being a trade-off of songwriter royalties with recording artist royalties. More likely, the artist as a songwriter will not get 100 percent of the mechanical royalties. If the songs are owned by a music publishing company that is not the artist's company, the writer will usually get 50 percent of mechanicals after the publisher/writer split. Even if the writer owned a publishing company, they would probably be paying someone else to administer the company and still get only 75 to 90 percent of mechanical income after the administration fee. If the artist/writer co-wrote with *other* songwriters, then those other writers would have to be willing to take the reduced rate and limits or the artist would have to pay them a full rate and have the label take the difference out of the artist's own record royalties. All of the percentages, amounts, and limits in the controlled composition clause are highly negotiable if the artist has any stature, and are particularly important points for artist/writers.

New Deals for Artists?

In 2002 and 2003, the major labels came under pressure from the Recording Artists Coalition, California legislators, and other lobbyists to alter some of the significant terms of their recording agreements. Among the significant points reported in the new agreements from some, but not all, major labels were:

- Movement to wholesale price as the royalty basis instead of retail list price. The total dollar amount of the royalty received by the artist would remain the same, but some of the deductions, like packaging, would disappear.
- Some labels eliminated the *new media deduction* that paid artists a lower royalty rate, often 50 to 75 percent of their usual rate, on things dubbed new media by the label. In the 1980s CDs were new media and it took the artists years to get the labels to stop applying the lower rate to CD sales.
- Royalty statements would indicate the number of units manufactured, instead of just the number shipped, to make it easier for the artists to audit their accounts with the labels.
- *Free goods* would be deducted from net sales *after* returns so that free goods will not be deducted twice from an artist's sales, once when shipped out, and once again if returned.[17]

Video Rights

The birth of Music Television (MTV) in 1981 caused labels to add yet more pages to their artists' contracts to deal with the creation and ownership of rights to music videos and other video performances of the artist. Initially many labels paid for all of the video production costs for music videos. But that increasingly expensive proposition, coupled with the fact that the videos themselves were little more than promotional tools— albeit valuable ones—caused a shift to having the artists pay part or all of the production costs as advances. By the mid-1990s it was customary to recoup half of the video production costs from recording royalties with the other half recouped from video royalties. Some labels would allow recoupment of all video production costs from video royalties. But as a practical matter for most artists, video royalties never approached half of the $30,000 to $100,000 production costs for the typical single-song music video. However, for concert-length videos, usually shot live, the production costs per minute were substantially less and a market existed from the cable services such as HBO, Showtime, Cinemax, and others to show the video as programming, as well as a growing DVD consumer market.[18] It is over creation and use of such non-promotional music video productions that most of the difficult negotiations occur.

The labels prefer to view music videos as "recordings" and say that they have exclusive rights to all the artist's "recordings." The artists say those exclusive rights are limited to phonograph recordings or perhaps promotional music videos, but not to concert-length performances. To counter that, the labels often ask a right of first refusal that would allow them to make the concert video on the same or slightly more favorable (to them) terms if they wish. Royalties earned from the sale of a video tend to be about equal on a per-copy basis to the royalties earned for the sale of a phonorecord. If the videos are sold through licensees, then the artist usually gets 50 percent of net label receipts.

Union Agreements: AFM and AFTRA

Two labor unions have significant impact on recordings. The American Federation of Musicians of the United States and Canada (AFM) and the American Federation of Television and Radio Artists (AFTRA) have agreements with all major labels (and most independents) that require certain scale payments to non-royalty performers on all recordings sold by the label. The labels require that all of their artists join the appropriate union. The AFM-required payment to a side musician in a standard three-hour recording session in 2003 was $329.32, up from $236.81 in 1995. A maximum of fifteen minutes of music could be recorded. The rates, set in the Phonograph Record Labor Agreement, include provisions for overdubs, premium hours, and a wide variety of other issues. The union leader on the session and the record producer make sure that all musicians are credited and proper payments made to the union, including a contribution of 10 percent of total wages to the union pension fund and a $19.00 health-and-welfare-fund payment for each musician.

The AFM has two other agreements with the record labels, the Phonograph Record Trust Agreement, and the Phonograph Record Manufacturers' Special Payments Fund Agreement. The first requires that the label pay about 0.3 percent of the suggested retail list price (SRLP; this amount is capped at $8.98 for tapes and $10.98 for discs) of each recording sold to a fund that is used to provide free live musical performances for the public. The Special Payments Fund is a pot of money that is generated by the labels paying another percentage of the SRLP (with the same caps) of records sold, about 0.5 percent. This fund is then distributed to all musicians who performed on master recordings according to how many masters each recorded. The total of both payments is less than one percent. It is important to the recording artist to not allow the label to deduct these charges from the record royalties payable to the artist. Whereas the union scale wages are recording costs, the per-copy charges are not.

Background singers and other vocal performers are covered under the AFTRA agreements with the labels. In 2003 the AFTRA Code of Fair Practice for Phonograph Records required soloists to be paid a scale wage for master sessions of approximately $168 per hour or per song (side) whichever was greater. Group members are paid on a sliding scale depending on how large the group is—the bigger the group, the less each member is paid. AFTRA also requires the labels to make contingent payments of 50 percent of minimum scale for the master session vocalists when certain sales plateaus are reached. There are ten steps that go from 157,500 to 3,000,000 units, and total up to five times the original scale. Like the per-unit AFM payments, these should not be considered recording costs to be charged against the artist's royalties.

Record Production

Q: "How many producers does it take to make a hit record?"

A: "I don't know ... what do you think?"

This inside joke in the record industry reflects the (supposedly) typical response by producers to any question about how good a recording or track or whatever, is.

Whether it takes an actual individual identifiable as a *producer* to produce a hit record or any other record is perhaps debatable. It does require somebody performing the functions that in most instances are relegated to a record producer. The producer may be the artist, or somebody in the A&R department at the label, or an independent person hired by the artist

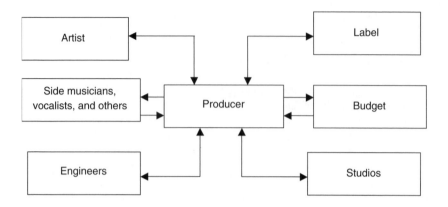

Fig. 7.1 Producer responsibilities.

or label to help deliver the finished album to the label. Sociologist Simon Frith argues that the production of popular music is a process "that fuses (and confuses) capital, technical, and musical arguments."[19] It is the record, *not* a song or music, that is the final product, and it is the producer who is at the center of the creation of that product (Figure 7.1).

Producers have one goal, whoever they are: to complete a finished, marketable recording. The producer must bring together the talent and the physical and monetary resources necessary to create a master recording. To achieve this goal, the producer must serve two masters: the artist and the label. The producer must possess good ears for hearing hit songs and performances; good people skills for getting the best performances out of artists, engineers, musicians, and label personnel; and good creative instincts to add to the chemistry of a recording project.

Producer Functions

Producers provide input into the process of the creation of recordings on three levels:

1. They perform A&R functions by finding talented artists and good material to record, and by matching artists and material.
2. They are managers of the production process—arranging and supervising recording sessions; hiring studios, musicians, and engineers, and getting the best performances out of those people; supervising the creative aspects of the recording and mixing process to get the best sounding recording; supervising and approving the mastering and references—all with the goal of producing a recording that

is marketable and at the same time is a good representation of the artist's abilities and any messages that the artist wishes to convey with the recording.

3. Producers perform business functions such as budgeting the recording sessions, making sure the recording process does not go over budget and that proper tax, withholding, and union forms are completed.

Kinds of Producers

At one time virtually all producers worked directly for record labels. They were A&R men and worked on salaries. They found the perfect songs for the recording artists, most of whom did not write their own songs. They set up recording sessions, hired arrangers to create musical parts for trained musicians to perform, then listened as they and the artists plied their crafts for a few *takes* (tries at recording the song), picking the best one for release. With rock and roll came artists who had great amounts of creativity and energy, but sometimes lacked great musical skills. They needed someone who could nurture their performances in a studio. With multitrack recording came the possibility of taking just a few musicians and turning out a recording that sounded like it had fifty people singing and playing on it, when it really only had four.

All of these developments meant that a producer had to take on a much more creative and managerial role. Rock artists did not want producers who were label employees, even though some of those people were quite talented. It was too "corporate" for the rock image. The independent producer became the norm. Producers began to be paid a royalty on the sales of albums, just like artists. Reportedly this began with Snuff Garrett, a producer in the late 1950s and 1960s, who was the first to ask his label for a royalty—a penny per album.[20] Artists began to produce or coproduce, their own recordings out of ego, a desire to be more in control of the creative aspects of their recordings, and a desire to keep more of the available money. Some successful producers became label executives but retained their production deals. In those instances the producer/executive (not to be confused with an executive producer) would typically be paid a royalty on sales of those artists produced, and a salary in their capacity as executives (usually in the A&R department, but sometimes as label presidents).

Independent producers work under a variety of contractual arrangements with artists and labels. Sometimes an independent producer will find a potential recording talent, sign the talent to a deal to make a demo in the hopes that the producer can then succeed in getting a label to sign the artist—and producer—to a full-blown recording contract. In such instances the producer may even go so far as to release the recording on a personal label, aiming to either start a small record company or create some local sales and excitement to better attract the majors. In both of these instances the independent producer is performing valuable A&R functions: finding and recording new talent that may later get introduced to the public through a small or even major label. Artists or labels may also hire independent producers to produce recordings or artists under contract to the label. In those instances, the label has performed the A&R function of finding the talent, and the producer has to bring the recording to fruition.

Recording artists, particularly after several successful records, may be allowed to produce themselves. In practical terms, that usually means that the artist becomes almost totally in charge of the creative aspects of the production process. But the artist will still need someone, an associate or a coproducer, to handle the business aspects of the process. Artists who successfully produce themselves have usually proven themselves capable of producing marketable recordings and making the creative decisions that go into those recordings. It is also possible that artists who have produced themselves can get recording contracts based on the strength of their demos alone, though this is rare. The label still prefers to have an experienced person in charge of the business aspects of the production process. With the advent of project studios owned by the artists and producers themselves, the 1990s saw a movement to artists and producers being even more in charge of their production, leaving only the marketing to the record companies.

Producer Pay

Through the 1990s advances and royalties for independent producers slowly crept upward, perhaps due to the rising importance of producers in urban music and rap. In those genres, the creative role of the producer is extremely important. By 2001 producer royalties were typically 2 to 6 percent of SRLP and paid on the same terms as artist royalties. Producers are also paid advances per side (song/cut) or per album depending on whether they have agreed to produce certain cuts or an artist's entire album. Per-cut advances run in the range of $2,500 to $15,000, with the latter figure reserved for superstar producers (even higher for some urban/rap producers). Per-album advances begin as low as $25,000 per album and run as high as $150,000 per album (even higher for some urban/rap producers). Because producer advances are not recording or marketing cost advances, producers usually actually end up being able to keep and spend their advances because the advances are not consumed by recording costs as those of artists usually are.

The size of the producer's advance depends primarily on experience, whether the producer has a track record of success in the market, and whether that producer also produces other important artists for the same label. Assuming the artist has an all-in royalty, the producer's royalty is paid out of it. This can lead to a variety of complex situations regarding recoupment of artist and producer advances, when the producer gets paid, and possible *double recoupment* of the producer's advance as a recording cost from artist royalties *and* as an advance under the producer's royalties. These complexities are just more reasons why artists and producers are well advised to have music-industry attorneys negotiate their arrangements with the labels.

Stages of Production

While much production actually takes place in the recording sessions, there is also work to be done in the pre- and postproduction phases of the process. In preproduction, the songs are selected, studios reserved, arrangers hired, session musicians and singers selected, engineers contracted, the concept of the song decided upon by the artist and producer, and (for budget-minded producers and artists) rehearsals held. In the production stage, tracks are recorded, overdubs are completed, and the songs are mixed down to a finished master, ready to be delivered to the label. The postproduction phase is likely to have duties shared between the actual producer and the A&R department for the label. Tasks such as getting correct liner notes, credits, lyric sheets, and licenses/clearances when needed for samples and for the songs themselves are usually carried out after the production is completed. The producer will also oversee or approve creation of master tapes and discs for manufacturing into CDs and other formats. Alternate mixes for clubs, radio, or singles are made. Madonna, for example, often had as many as eight or nine versions of commercial singles available, and even had multiple albums composed entirely of remixes. The producer may consult with the marketing department or product manager over which cut should be the first single released from an album.

Production Budgeting

One of the producer's responsibilities will be to submit to the label a budget for the production of the recording(s). The sizes of the budgets vary from less than $50,000 to hundreds of thousands of dollars. One of the factors contributing to the variation is the genre: jazz is usually recorded live with just a few takes, so studio and musician time is minimal; country can be simple or elaborate with budgets approaching pop or rock in some instances; rap can be very inexpensive, especially if the rappers have their own rhythm tracks already created in a project or MIDI studio; rock can be very expensive, especially if the artist wants to write the songs and work out arrangements in the studio, and/or is not really a very good musician/ vocalist. In some respects, the budgets end up being governed by how many recordings the label thinks it can sell of this particular artist. An artist who can sell 200,000 copies on a good album cannot be allowed to spend as much on production as an artist who can sell 3 million albums. Particularly in rock and pop, album advances are intended to cover production and leave some money left over for the artist. It is usual that after an artist's first album, the per-album recording fund advance increases substantially, so that the artist does have a larger production budget with which to be creative, and will have more money to take home after all production expenses are paid.

If the production costs exceed the budget, the producer has put the label in a difficult situation. If the project is nearly completed and is worth releasing, the label is essentially forced to come up with more money. The label may, however, have a contractual right to demand that any over-budget amount be repaid immediately out of the producer's or artist's album delivery advance, if there is one. It is almost always possible to spend a few more thousand dollars to work on a track or a mix just a little more. One of the producer's jobs is to know when to say "when." Money is not the only factor determining when a production is finished. The label has deadlines for delivery of the master so that the release date can fit into a certain schedule decided to be best not only for this album and artist, but for all of the label's upcoming releases.

Creative Controls

The trend in recording and production contracts is to let the artist and producer make most of the creative decisions, especially if they are experienced and have delivered satisfactory masters in the past. Selection of songs, studios, musicians and vocalists, engineers and assistants, and the producers themselves is usually up to the artist working in concert with the producer. At most, some labels want a right to approve these decisions. In such cases the producers and artists can usually successfully demand that approval cannot be unreasonably withheld.

Master Delivery Requirements

Both producers and artists are contractually obligated to deliver masters that are satisfactory to the label. The difficult problem is what standard of satisfaction is to be applied. The label would like to insist that the masters be "commercially acceptable." After all, the label is in the business of selling records. Artists and producers, on the other hand, do not want the label to be second-guessing their creativity. They would insist that the master merely be "technically satisfactory." The impasse can often be cured with language that says the label will accept an album that is at least as technically and commercially satisfactory as the previous album or other albums by artists of similar stature on the label. Whatever the language in the contract, it would be unusual for a label to reject an album when the artist and producer have made a serious effort. Acceptability standards most often come into play when artists attempt to throw together an album simply to meet their recording obligations, in the hope of getting out of the contract.

Acquisition through Licensing

Instead of going through all the grief of finding artists and producers, and risking the inevitable stiffs, a label could get all or part of its masters by licensing them from other labels. Rhino Records, for example, sells significant numbers of albums that are repackages and remasters of older artists. Rhino does careful research on the artists and songs, careful remastering, and produces Grammy-winning albums. The Musical Heritage Society also does this in the art/classical music field.

The label could also acquire masters that already exist by licensing or purchasing them outright from some smaller label or production company. In the 1990s this was a particularly popular approach in rap music. Some labels such as K-Tel sell albums like *The Greatest Hits of 19xx* that are simply collections of masters licensed from the labels that had the original artists and hits. In those cases the releasing label pays the original label a per-copy royalty per cut, usually three to five cents.

In 1998 in the United States (1983 in the United Kingdom) a consortium of labels launched the *NOW That's What I Call Music* series. The collections of pop, urban, and generally teen-oriented singles were the most successful in the history of the recording industry. The consortium of labels sharing the releases of the various *NOW* albums claimed sales of more than 37 million units in the United States and 53 million worldwide by 2003. Several of the installments debuted at Number 1 in Billboard's album chart.[21]

Studios and Recording Engineers

No discussion of production could be complete without at least an overview of the recording process as it involves studios and recording engineers. The recording gear and the people who operate it have become an integral part of the creative process in the production of master recordings. The diffusion of recording technology through lower costs and greater availability to musicians has created a situation where the production process has become more democratized. More people are able to afford and produce high-quality recordings, and the big five conglomerates enjoy much less control of the production of recordings.

Studios, Then and Now

Studios have not always been studios. In the late 1800s and early 1900s they were often referred to as *labs*. The first professional disc recording studio was set up in Philadelphia in 1897 for recording the Berliner discs.

A lot of early recording was done by taking the recording machines to locations that were convenient to the artists and setting up in some hotel or warehouse. In fact, Caruso's first major recordings were done in a hotel in Milan, Italy, in 1902; he cut ten master cylinders in one day. Prior to 1902, when the making of molds for cylinder mass production was finally a viable procedure, every cylinder was an original or a direct dub of an original. When recording facilities were set up for cylinders, they often involved the performers singing into a set of horns, with each attached to a different cylinder cutter; as many as twenty cylinders could be recorded at once. Of course the performer had to repeat the performance many times. Those who could perform steadily and repeatedly found plentiful work. One source called them "durable citizens with lungs of brass."[22] The number of times a performer had to record was referred to as *rounds*. The studios were small, often barely able to hold more than a dozen musicians and the recording machines.

Until the advent of electrical recordings in 1925, all recordings were acoustic. The sound pressure energy from the performer had to be transferred into mechanical energy that moved a cutting stylus to make a groove in the master disc or cylinder. This was done by singing or playing into a large horn. Isolation from surrounding background noise was not critical because it would not likely be picked up by the recording horns, much less reproduced by the consumer's playback machine. But the electrical process, which captured the sounds in a carbon microphone and converted them to electrical energy that could be amplified to run an electromechanical cutting lathe, meant much greater frequency response. Response improved to from 200 Hz to 9,000 Hz—almost two and one-half octaves greater than the purely mechanical systems. The microphones were also more sensitive than acoustic horns and necessitated more isolation from outside sounds. Studios began to resemble more modern ones.

World War II spurred the development of more high-quality amplifiers, radios, microphones, and most importantly for the recording industry, the practical development of recording tape. Tape could be easily edited and it became possible to "construct" a recording by splicing together bits and pieces of a performance or of several performances. Bing Crosby was the first to utilize this important ability for the creation of his network radio show in 1948. Later, multitrack recording made it possible to break down the construction of the recording into even more components, one track per instrument. Fewer musicians were needed to produce a complex recording and the importance and size of the control room grew. Popular music researcher Steve Jones points out that increasing amount of control over time, timbre, and all the musical and sound elements of the recording became integral to the process.[23]

Audio Engineers

As the importance of the control room grew, so did the importance of the recording engineer, the person who ran all of the machinery that controlled the sound. At one time, for example, the effect of reverberation (the echo effect of sound bouncing around in a room and gradually dying out after the initial sound was made) was only possible to create by actually having a room into which the sound could be fed and allowed to reverberate, or by recording live in such a room with a microphone available to pick up the reverberant effect. With digital processors it is possible to simulate many different rooms and echoes and control many different aspects of how that room sounds with an electronic box no bigger than a ream of paper. More sophisticated devices meant a higher level of technological expertise was required from the engineers. Because of their knowledge of and ability to control all of the technology of recording, the engineers began to take on more of a creative role in the process.

The Industrial Model

Although it had always been possible to do location recordings, the assemblage of a large number of cylinder or disc cutters in the early days, the use of expensive amplifiers and disc cutters not available to the general public, the need for isolation from outside sounds, and the required presence of a significant number of skilled players and vocalists, dictated an industrial model for the recording process. By analogy, the studio was a "factory" where capital and labor were gathered together to complete a product. Not until the 1970s when good quality multitrack recording equipment, known as "semiprofessional," became available to consumers was there significant diffusion of the recording process away from the factory/industrial model. By the mid-1990s high-quality recording was possible with digital multitrack recorders available for the semiprofessional market. The MIDI (Musical Instrument Digital Interface) and sequencing revolution meant that single musicians could create complex sounds and even orchestral arrangements. The diffusion of recording technology does not necessarily create more high-quality recordings, any more than the diffusion of watercolor paints creates more great watercolor paintings, but it does give more creative people ready access to the possibility of creating quality recordings and it has had a significant impact on the studio business and recording processes.

By 1995 seventy percent of professional studios reported at least some degree of competition from home-based private production studios, with 28 percent noting "very much" competition from the home studios.[24] In many instances the artists and producers used these home facilities to create basic synthesis or sampled tracks, or work out arrangements so that when they did go to the higher-end professional studio, they spent less time and money. The label practice of paying advances in the form of a recording fund, where the artist and/or producer keeps what is left after expenses, encourages such cost-cutting procedures. Also, the labels often approved the practice of the artist charging recording time and expenses from the artist's own facilities toward the recording costs. The artist is then in a position to set up their own studio and recover the cost through their own recording budgets. After a few albums, the studio is paid for.

This same practice has led established and superstar artists to build their own top-of-the-line studios to be used in their own productions. These facilities are most commonly known as *project rooms*. Again, 70 percent of studio owners said in 1995 that they felt at least "some degree" of competition from these rooms, with 24 percent reporting "very much" competition from the project studios owned by producers or artists.[25] This trend continues into the twenty-first century. A fairly typical path of development is for a small private studio to develop into a project studio, which then begins to book commercial clients and turns into a part-time commercial studio. Even the major artist-owned studios sometimes book outside clients. A problem with project studios is that they are often built in homes in residential neighborhoods. When they become commercial, they may run afoul of zoning restrictions and tax laws.[26]

Kinds of Studios

While the lines of distinction between professional and semiprofessional, and private, project, and commercial are blurring, the latter classification system still has some usefulness in understanding the studio business.

Private studios tend to be small in size and track capability. They are usually owned by aspiring artists, songwriters, or producers and seldom book any outside time. They most often use top-of-the-line, semiprofessional equipment and may have as much as 24-track digital capability, although more commonly make due with 16 tracks or less.

Commercial studios are those that are primarily used by outside clients and are in the studio business for profit. These studios are primarily 24 track and higher. They may be analog or digital formats, though the majority (about 55 percent as of 1995) have multitrack (at least 24-track) digital recording capabilities.[27] They charge the higher rates, with 24-track analog studios charging from $85 to $120 per hour, and the 24-track digital studios charging from $107 to $165 per hour. These rates are 65 to 100 percent higher than their 16-track or less counterparts.[28] Some world-class studios charge as high as $300 per hour.[29] A fair characterization of the smaller commercial studios is as "demo" studios for music recording or for small advertising clients.

Project studios, as distinguished from private studios, are most often owned by established artists and producers. They have all the capabilities of the commercial studios and some are as well equipped as the best commercial facilities. They tend to be 24-track (or more), digital-format rooms. They are used primarily by the owners for producing their own recordings (projects) but may sometimes be rented to outside clients.

Studio Business Survival

The recording-studio business is centered in five geographic locations: New York City, Los Angeles, Nashville, Chicago, and southeastern Florida (Orlando to the Keys). Any city with a population of more than 100,000 has at least one commercial studio catering primarily to advertising clients. Private studios are as widespread as aspiring artists and writers, but the bulk of the recording for released masters, major client advertising, and film is done in these five areas. In 1994, average annual income for studios in these centers ranged from a high of $425,000 in New York City to $333,000 in southeast Florida. Los Angeles incomes tend to be very near the New York City incomes, which tend to be about $70,000 per year higher than the incomes in Nashville, Chicago, or southeast Florida. A four-year trend analysis, conducted between 1990 and 1994, revealed that the Los Angeles and New York annual incomes tended to fluctuate the most, dependent upon the larger recording budgets in major recording artist and film contracts, ranging from a high of $473,000 to a low of $390,000. The other three centers were more stable, hovering near $350,000 per year over the same period.[30] Nationally, the average for all studios income was reported at $256,000 in 1995.

As sales of recordings began to go flat at the beginning of the twenty-first century, studio owners found themselves in difficult times. One analyst laid most of the blame on the decreasing price of digital recording devices and the increasing ease of starting a project studio. Writing in *Pro Sound News*, Chris Steinwand noted that the price of a 24-track hard-disk recorder was about 1/50 the price of a 24-track tape machine. He said, "Project studios can now afford truly professional quality equipment and can turn out recordings that are every bit as professional as what the major studios are producing."[31] The project studios tended to be more focused on lower-priced gear, and that drove down the impetus for manufacturers to produce top-end equipment for the major studios. The number of major studios was also declining due to competition from project studios. That, said Steinwand, contributed to even less demand for expensive gear that only major studios could afford. The difficult times for the studios thus impacted on the recording hardware manufacturers as well.

By 2003 incomes at nearly all studios, but especially the larger ones, had shrunk. The decline in sales of recordings led to cutbacks in artist rosters and album budgets by the major labels. As one studio owner put it, "The cost of promotion is up, because you've got to buy your way into distribution. The cost of pretty much everything, including talent, has been inflated, whereas the actual studio cost has stayed flat or even gone down a little."[32]

Profile of the Typical Recording Studio

As of 1995, most studios had only one control room (67 percent), were about ten years old, equipped with MIDI (70 percent), used 24 tracks or more (55 percent), earned most of their income (58 percent) from music recording (advertising and broadcast recording revenues were a distant second at 13 percent), and were booked an average of 180 hours per month.[33] Note that this last figure is an average of about 42 hours per week, just in case one is inclined to think that recording engineers do not work long hours.

By the mid-1990s recording studios as businesses were faced with difficult times. A *Pro Sound News* article summed up the problem: "In a nutshell: traditional studios find that they cannot raise their rates to offset the cost of equipment demanded by an increasingly sophisticated clientele that does more and more of its recording outside of those same studios."[34] In response, a number of studios started their own record labels or began manufacturing audio gear in addition to providing other ancillary services, such as tape duplication or postproduction of audio for video.[35]

Recording Engineers

The task of the recording engineer is to operate the equipment that captures, and in some instances creates, the sounds that the artist and producer want on the recording. The recording engineer is more of a technician than an engineer in the sense that the term is used in other professions. In addition to a thorough understanding of the specific equipment that they operate, most engineers find useful a basic level of knowledge in the areas of electronics, acoustics and sound, and music. Recording engineers must also possess the ability to get along with people, some of whom will have quite large egos and can be difficult to work with. Engineers must have good ears capable of discerning often subtle differences in sounds, and an understanding of how those differences will contribute to or detract from the finished master. Engineers must also be capable of making creative decisions. The producer or artist may not be at every recording session for a particular project. The engineer will then have to decide what is the best sound for the purpose. Even when the producer or artist is present, they will often ask the engineer what they think about a particular track or sound. Sometimes they want real advice, sometimes they only want their egos stroked.

Recording engineers are often classified based on their knowledge, experience, and skill, into four groups: senior engineers, assistant engineers, freelance engineers, and maintenance engineers. *Senior engineers* are usually associated with a particular studio. As the name implies, they are the most knowledgeable and experienced engineers available at that facility. Even when an artist or producer brings their own favorite independent engineers to a session, the presence of a senior staff engineer from the studio is usually necessary to help with knowledge of the ins and outs and particular quirks of the studio and its equipment. *Assistant engineers*, also known as second engineers, often work primarily at one studio or with one particular independent engineer. *Freelance engineers* tend to be senior-level engineers who have a track record of recording successful albums with established artists. They work in studios wherever their artists want to work. They may have worked with the artist in the early days of the artist's career or they may have been doing the live sound reinforcement for the artist, but in some way, the artist has become convinced that this particular person is helpful in getting the sound that the artist wants on record. *Maintenance engineers* have the most electronics expertise. They tend to be associated with one particular studio, but some successfully freelance among several smaller studios. Engineers are usually paid on an hourly basis. In 1995 *Pro Sound News* reported that salaries ranged from a low of $6.60 per hour in some cities for assistant engineers to a high of $26.60 per hour for maintenance engineers in the Los Angeles area.[36] By 2003 the entry-level positions had increased to about $10.00 per hour and the upper levels to about $30.00 per hour.

Organizations

Three industry professional organizations are of particular interest to studio owners and audio engineers: the Society of Professional Audio Recording Services (SPARS), the Audio Engineering Society (AES), and the Society of Motion Picture and Television Engineers (SMPTE). SMPTE is the oldest organization, and was formed in 1916 as the Society of Motion Picture Engineers. Its membership consists of engineers involved in the creation of "motion pictures, television, computer imaging, telecommunications, and the related arts and sciences." Among other things, it helps set technical standards and publishes the technical journal, the *SMPTE Journal.* The members of the AES are involved in the creation of audio and recording devices, and recordings and live sound reinforcement. AES, like SMPTE, is an international organization, publishes a technical journal, the *Journal of the Audio Engineering Society,* and helps set technical standards for its industry. AES was founded in the mid-1940s. The newest of these organizations is SPARS. It was founded in the 1970s to represent professional studio owners as a trade organization. For more information on all of these organizations, visit their World Wide Web sites listed in the Internet Appendix.

Going to School

Two factors, the complexity of recording and the popularity of recordings in general, have led to the growth of preparatory programs for recording engineers and the music business. In addition, the increased sales of recordings and a growing interest in popular music in general has led to increased interest of young people in careers in recording and the music business. Those two factors prompted a significant number of institutions to offer programs that aim to provide some of the necessary training.

In the 1960s and 1970s, someone who wanted to learn audio would show up at a studio, convince the owners of their desire to work, and be assigned to help keep the studio clean. After a while they could usually convince the engineer to teach them something about some of the equipment. They learned on the job by doing. However, the equipment has increased in complexity and sophistication to the point where it is very difficult to come in off the street and pick up the necessary knowledge in an apprenticeship situation.

There are well over 200 and perhaps as many as 300 institutions offering some kind of training in audio engineering and/or the music business. The programs range from seminars and short courses, often at studios seeking to sell their down time, to accredited vocational programs, associate degree programs, four-year bachelor's degree programs, master's programs, and even a few Ph.D. programs. The providers range from individual studios, to schools of the arts, to major colleges and universities. At all levels, there are some very good programs and some that are not as good. There is no industry certification or accreditation process for these programs, and students need to investigate carefully the range of alternatives and compare the relative merits of various programs. The two most thorough listings are in the *Mix Master Directory* published by *Mix Magazine*, and the Audio Engineering Society's *Directory of Educational Programs*.[37]

These audio and music business programs began to develop in the early 1970s, and by the mid-1990s a number were quite sophisticated. They, like the studios themselves, have benefited from the diffusion of lower-priced, high-quality recording equipment and technology. While having a degree or certificate is not a requirement of being a recording engineer or a label-promotion person, many of these programs place interns in the slots formerly occupied by apprentice-type learners. They also provide entry-level personnel who do possess the base-level knowledge required of assistant engineers and employees. A study for NARM found that over 65 percent of its affiliates (including labels, retail, wholesale, and distribution firms) would give preference to graduates of a music-business program when hiring new employees.[38] Some studios and recording industry businesses will not hire entry-level employees that have not been through one of the audio or music-business programs, in part simply because there are quite a few students from these programs seeking employment and employed in the recording industry. There is a professional organization of college faculty who teach in such programs called the Music and Entertainment Industry Educators Association (MEIEA), which promotes the development of college audio and music-business programs. During the late 1980s the National Academy of Recording Arts and Sciences (NARAS) launched its Grammy in the Schools program to pique the interest of high-school students in the recording industry.

Who Is Ultimately in Charge of A&R and Production?

Technological advances are making it more possible for musicians and bands to record and distribute their music to wider audiences. On one front, the advances in low-cost, high-quality home recording equipment mean that many bands and musicians can afford their own recording gear or to work in a low-cost demo studio. The equipment available enables them to make high-quality recordings without having to go through any record company or pay studio rentals of hundreds of dollars per hour. Lower costs in manufacturing of compact discs now mean that these same bands can make CDs in small numbers. By 2001 the prices for custom manufactured CDs had dropped to the point where 1,000 CDs could be made complete with boxes, trays, inserts, and shrink wrap for as low as $1,000. One hundred could be had for $200 to $300. Bands with patience and computers with CD burners (CD-RW drives) could make them one at a time and print their own labels and jewel box inserts with inexpensive software for pennies apiece.

The Internet makes possible distribution by individual bands and musicians (or by very small labels) of their recordings to a worldwide audience. This should ultimately mean that more recordings of more music would be available to more people.[39] The difficulty is in sorting through the myriad of available recordings to find those with merit or appeal. That is where the A&R department of the label performs a gatekeeping function by deciding which recordings to promote to the public at large.

8
The Marketing Function

The Four Ps of Marketing

Marketing is a term that encompasses a wide variety of activities. The American Marketing Association defines it as "the process of planning and executing conception, pricing, promotion, and distribution of ideas, goods and services to create exchanges that satisfy individual and organizational objectives."[1] Marketing is said, at a simpler level, to involve four functions, each beginning with the letter "P": *product, pricing, promotion,* and *place* (distribution).[2] The objective of these functions for most firms is usually stated as the *marketing concept*—the creation and delivery of a product (broadly speaking) that will satisfy consumer needs, at a price that will allow a profit to be made for the organization.[3]

Most record labels, even the major labels, think of marketing less broadly. The identification of consumer needs and product creation is basically the A&R and production function. The marketing department focuses primarily on the sales, promotion, and publicity functions. Distribution is also handled separately, either through one of the major's distribution systems or through independent distribution. Which of the basic marketing functions a label may choose to perform within its own organization is a management decision. However, all of the functions must be performed.

At its broadest, the definition of marketing includes retailing because that is the final *place* of delivery of the product to the consumer. Retailing is discussed in Chapter 9; A&R and production was discussed in Chapter 7. A description of the market for recordings, who is buying, what they are buying, and why they buy, was a significant part of Chapter 1. This chapter will discuss the labels' attempts to reach that market, specifically including those aspects of product, price, promotion, and place that are central to this task. In so doing, the discussion will cover a broader range of activities than most labels would refer to as marketing.

Recording industry products—albums, singles, and music videos—are generally what marketing people would call *highly differentiated*. That is, no two products are really alike and each has a built-in uniqueness because of the performances by the artist, input of the producer, engineers, and others, and the compositions that are recorded. Unlike, for example, the cereal industry, which spends millions of dollars to convince us that company Y's brand of corn flake cereal is different from and better than that of competitor X, the record industry does not focus on product differentiation in its marketing. That is the job of the A&R department: to find an artist with a unique/different sound that will appeal to record buyers. The marketing departments either assume or are told that the A&R department has done its job and delivered a highly differentiated product, which the marketing department is then told to sell. The marketing departments of the labels focus their efforts on product awareness; if the consumer is aware of a particular recording and has heard it, then the uniqueness and special appeal of that recording will provide enough product differentiation. The labels do not spend marketing dollars and efforts to convince potential buyers that a particular angst-ridden band is better than that of their competitor, or that one rapper's rhymes are more appealing than another's, or that a particular "hunky," black-hatted, country male singer is better than that of the competition. They simply let the recordings speak for themselves.

The problem with relying primarily on product awareness for a marketing program is that the product must, in fact, be highly differentiated. While no one would argue that any two recordings were not differentiated *somewhat* from each other, the question is whether the consumer perceives that difference and whether it is enough to make the consumer want to purchase the new recording. If the consumer does not perceive significant differences between two recordings, then the consumer will figure, "I already have an album like this, why do I need another one?" That phenomenon explains why, when the labels flood the market with artists that sound, look, and perform too much alike, consumers slow down their overall levels of purchasing.

Product

Product considerations have two dimensions for record labels: the *style and quality* of the artist recorded; and the *packaging* of the final recorded product. Both of these considerations must be keyed to consumer taste and demand, but also need to fit with the other products that the label is offering. There is no intention of offending artistic sensibilities by referring to recordings as *product*. One might argue that such an appellation depersonalizes the artistic performance recorded, but the labels use the term for the sake of simplicity, and that is a good enough reason to use it here as well.

Style of the Music

Recalling Figure 1.1 (Sales by Genre), four genres dominate music sales: rock, urban/rap, country, and pop/easy listening account for about 70 percent of the market. This is the *mainstream market* for recordings. Here the sales potential is the greatest, but so is the competition for those sales.

What happened to country music in the 1990s is a good example of the competitiveness of mainstream markets. The country music market grew rapidly in the early 1990s. In 1993, country music comprised over 18 percent of all sales; by 1996, 30 percent of music buyers reported purchasing country music over a six-month period. White females were noted as most likely to purchase country music. Younger consumers (16 to 17) made nearly twice as many purchases as older buyers.[4] The popularity of country music spurred growth of labels, with more labels and artists competing for a share of the larger market. Country radio also grew with more stations in almost every market competing for listeners who preferred country music. That, of course, led to many more country releases vying for spots on the radio stations' playlists. The country radio stations found themselves in a much more competitive environment for listeners, so they became much more careful about which records, and the number of records, that were added to playlists. "There's just not enough space for all these records,"

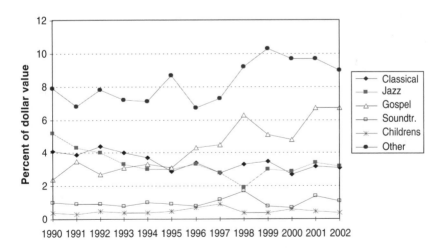

Fig. 8.1 Specialty genre sales 1990–2002. Recording Industry Association of America. www.riaa.com/news/marketingdata/pdf/2002consumerprofile.pdf. Accessed 1 March 2004.

said one country radio station music director.[5] Country promotion and marketing had become just as competitive as pop/rock. Country sales then dropped back to a steady rate of just over 10 percent entering the twenty-first century.

Specialty Markets

With two notable exceptions, the market shares of the genres outside the mainstream have remained fairly stable, as indicated by Figure 8.1. For the most part, sales of the specialty genres indicated have varied by no more than plus or minus one percentage point since 1990.

The decline in the sale of jazz recordings appears to have stopped at about 3.3 percent of total sales. This is partly attributable to the fact that the first year on the chart (1990) was a relatively high year for jazz sales. For most of the previous decade, jazz sales had hovered around 3 percent of the total. It must be pointed out that the RIAA's research data is from a sample, not from SoundScan, and is accurate only within 2 percent according to their statisticians. At these relative low sales levels, a 2-percent variance could make a significant difference. One might be curious, for example, why the multiplatinum hit soundtrack from *The Bodyguard,* which sold about 10 million copies in 1993, did not have some effect on the soundtrack sales numbers. The probable reason is that even sales of 10 million units only represents about 1.2 percent of total shipments that year. It is also quite likely that some consumers in the RIAA interviews simply reported purchases of *The Bodyguard* soundtrack album as pop or urban.

A specialty category not specifically broken out, but which showed some surprising gains during the 1990s, was the Original Broadway Cast album. Some of the big Broadway hits of the 1950s and 1960s saw a resurgence in popularity during that time with more frequent touring casts and local performances. In 1996, 12 percent of consumers in one survey said they had purchased an original cast album during the past year, an increase of four percentage points over previous data from 1990. Original cast albums tended mostly to be purchased by the 45-and-over age group, perhaps because that group is affluent enough to afford the often pricey live performance sets. NARM reported that the SoundData Consumer Panel showed that the age category in second place for the purchase of original cast albums was the 18 to 20 age bracket.[6]

The Christian/Gospel market is a bit puzzling. The RIAA reported Christian sales under the more general Gospel category, until 1999 when they adopted the term *religious music* to include Christian, gospel, religious, and spiritual recordings. While consumers indicate a strong interest in Christian music with just over 25 percent of consumers saying they "strongly like" or "like" it,[7] the data indicate that this is not being translated into sales. Perhaps people are reluctant to say they *dislike* Christian music. Christian artists began appearing on the *Billboard* Top 200 album chart as soon as SoundScan data from Christian bookstores was added to its database because the predominant source of sales for these recordings is not through mainstream record outlets but through these bookstores. A handful of major Christian artists appear in the Top 200 Albums chart, and some even sell as much as 50,000 to 80,000 units during their first week of release. One Christian label executive stated, "Mainstream retail is still driven by mainstream radio, mainstream video, and all the promotional things that happen. ... I think if we've done anything, we've overestimated our core consumers that shop at mainstream stores."[8] One analyst of the Christian and gospel market attributes the lack of sales partly to the fact that, "For other performers, the music comes first and foremost; for the gospel performer, music is secondary to the ministry ... presenting the Christian message to the public."[9] Sales of gospel/religious music rose to new heights in 1998 on the heels of popular hits from several acts generally categorized as Christian. In 1997, Bob Carlisle had a monster single hit on pop and adult formats with "Butterfly Kisses." Similarly, rock/alternative Christian act Jars of Clay had a double-platinum album based on sales between 1995 and 1997. As the decade drew to a close, however, religious music sales had begun to slide back to levels of the mid-1990s. The terrorist attacks of September 11, 2001, apparently had a positive effect on religious sales, according to research and industry insiders, as did the fact that the RIAA and SoundScan reported some of the sales of the phenomenally successful *Oh, Brother Where Are Thou?* soundtrack as religious sales.[10]

The significant increase in the Other category in the late 1990s is probably due to a steady increase in sales of Latin product. While the Other category includes everything from holiday music to humor and big band, Latin is its largest component. *Latin* is defined by the RIAA as product that is 51 percent or more in Spanish language. That seems a strange definition because other categories are defined based on the music (as in jazz, classical, pop, urban, and so forth), or its source (as in soundtracks), or its theme (as in children's or religious). In 2001, Latin music accounted for over 4.5 percent of the total market in terms of unit and dollar volume of sales—more than any other specialty genre except religious.[11] This was accomplished despite the declining sales in other genres and the fact that Latin music apparently is more pirated than mainstream music.[12]

Repackaging

The value of a hit album does not end once it drops off the charts after the first year or so. By that time production and initial promotion and marketing costs are probably already recouped. Older recordings are usually referred to as *catalog product*, and remain available to retailers through the record label's catalog of current products. An accepted industry definition is that current product sales are those taking place within fifteen months of release, and that catalog sales are those occurring thereafter. NARM estimates that catalog product so defined accounts for 43.4 percent of record sales based on dollar volume.[13] Because catalog usually has a lower retail and wholesale price than current *front line product*, this would indicate that in terms of units purchased, catalog product probably accounts for more than half of all recordings sold. If an artist continues to have success, the catalog sales of earlier albums inevitably picks up with subsequent hits.

Continued success also opens up the possibilities for a *greatest hits* package. Greatest hits albums are popular with consumers who have recently discovered an artist who has an extensive catalog. When CDs were introduced, these packages enabled consumers, who had the hits on an older format (say tape or vinyl) to own an artist's key songs in the new format without replacing an entire album collection. The SoundData Consumer Panel information from NARM reports that one-third of music buyers had purchased greatest hits albums during a 90-day period, a figure that was consistent with a prior 90-day period. Nearly three-fourths of those buying the greatest hits albums had at least one other record by that artist.[14]

An elaborate form of the greatest hits package is the *boxed set*. These are usually reserved for artists with long careers or who are historically significant. They frequently include not only greatest hits but some previously unreleased tracks. Usually these include two, three, or more discs, with elaborate packaging featuring biographical material, photos, interviews, and other material not usually accompanying a standard release. In 1996 a reported 20 percent of consumers of recordings had purchased a boxed set compared to 30 percent in 1995. NARM speculates that boxed sets are most popular with older consumers, "probably due to the wide variety of older artists that publish these sets and the[ir] higher cost."[15]

Configuration

Configuration of the recording is yet another variable of the product dimension. Problems associated with changing and multiple configurations have made life difficult for the record labels since discs and cylinders both appeared. First it was, "Cylinder or disc?" Then, "What size of disc?" Later the questions changed to the speed of the discs, to album or single, then mono or stereo, then eight-track or vinyl, then cassette or eight-track or vinyl, then cassette or vinyl or CD, then CD or cassette or enhanced CD or DVD. Ever since the appearance of the true long-playing album on a single disc in 1948, records have existed in at least two formats, single and album. The question for the digital millennium is whether singles may be disappearing as a hard consumer format.

Singles

The decision whether to release a given cut as a single is one of the more difficult for the label. The single is primarily a promotional tool. It is what most radio stations actually play, although many also play cuts from albums. The release of a single signals which cut the label will promote. Finally, it is also a product to sell. Figure 8.2 indicates that the popularity of singles as an item to purchase has declined fairly steadily since 1973. Vinyl singles had all but disappeared by 1995, declining to 10.2 million units shipped—less than one percent of total recordings shipped that year. The cassette single, or *cassingle*, had replaced the vinyl sales to some extent, but the single's popularity continued to decline. NARM research indicated that only 16 percent of buyers had purchased a cassette single within a six-month survey period, and only 11 percent had purchased a CD single.[16] By 2003 the bottom had fallen out of the singles market (Figure 8.2 below), despite the labels efforts at heavy discounting, price reductions, and including multiple cuts on singles. Singles accounted for less than 1 percent of unit volume and less than 0.5 percent of sales dollars in 2002.

The probable reason for the near death of the single was the presence of digital downloading of singles and albums. File swapping of individual songs grew and reached a zenith in the heyday of Napster. In July 2000, just before the trial court issued the temporary injunction to halt Napster use, Napster estimated it had 20 million users, downloading 12 to 30 million recordings per day at the rate of about 14,000 per minute.[17] The ease and accessibility of Napster and the relative price of a download versus a single—free versus $3.50—certainly contributed to the demise of the singles market. Even with Napster shut down, other file-sharing networks took its place, providing those willing to take for free with ample opportunity.

Whether the singles market will shift from hard copies purchased through brick-and-mortar retailers to soft copies at a price of $0.99 downloaded from cyber *e-tailers*, remains to be seen. The labels' legitimate download services, launched in 2001, have not made significant headway against the illegal market; they had an estimated total of only 250,000 subscribers in 2003.[18] Apple's iTunes service—launched in 2003 and compatible only with Mac computers—reported more than 5 million downloads in two months, with 54 percent being singles and 46 percent as albums. These numbers were especially impressive because Apple's operating system accounts for only approximately 3 percent of the global computer market.[19] A PC version was launched later that year. In 2003 *Billboard* introduced the first download singles chart, using SoundScan data. In the first week, Beyonce's "Crazy in Love" generated 1,500 legitimate downloads to earn the top position.[20]

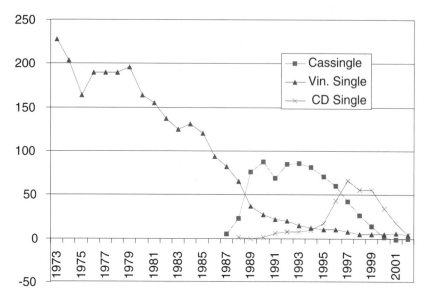

Fig. 8.2 Singles sales (millions of units). Recording Industry Association of America. www.riaa.com/news/marketingdata/pdf/2002consumerprofile.pdf. Accessed 5 March 2004.

Albums

The album replaced the single at the retail level. Single record albums were initially introduced by Columbia in 1948 as 33 ⅓-rpm vinyl recordings. That same year RCA introduced a new single format, the 45-rpm recording. These two formats competed for nearly a decade with the 78-rpm single, finally driving it to extinction in 1957. Even so, it was not until the 1960s that albums became the most significant aspect of the business. By the early 1970s some record labels began describing themselves as *album labels*. The album was almost as easy to ship and handle as a single; it had more room on the cover for eye-catching artwork; its sales represented more profit for the label and the retailer; and it represented a better value for consumers with ten songs for $3 or $4 (as of the early 1970s). Artists have created album projects with themes ever since the Beatle's *Rubber Soul* album. Even so, in 1973, singles accounted for 37 percent of all units sold. However, by 1983 that share had declined to 12 percent, and by 2003 to less than one percent.

Price

Any discussion of price in marketing recordings needs to take account of the fact that there are actually three different prices that are important. Most labels have a stated Suggested Retail List Price (SRLP, or sometimes called Manufacturer's Suggested Retail Price [MSRP]) for several different levels of releases. *Front line product*, new releases by major artists, carries the highest SRLP other than some soundtracks and classical titles. The most common front line CD SRLP was $18.98 in 2003. *Mid-line product* is often catalog product or perhaps recordings by new artists at introductory prices. Mid-line SRLP tended to be $11.98 in 2003. *Budget lines*, in the neighborhood of $8.98 to $9.98 SRLP, were often deep catalog or artists whose popularity had faded significantly but not so significantly that they were discontinued.

The wholesale price of albums is typically keyed to the SRLP. For example, the stated wholesale prices of $18.98 SRLP albums tended to be about $11.75 to $12.00 depending upon manufacturer. However, all labels run a variety of discount programs that can substantially reduce the actual wholesale price paid by a retailer or rack jobber. New releases are often discounted heavily to encourage retailers to buy more product and offer it at sale prices to get an album off to a good sales start. Various other seasonal and quantity discounts were often applied that could reduce the actual price paid by a retailer to $9 to $10.

The price paid by the consumer often bears only slight relationship to either the SRLP or wholesale price. Most retailers regularly price all albums lower than the SRLP. This gives the store an aura of offering the customer a deal. That standard store price is referred to as the *shelf price*. Stores also run special sale prices (often prompted by lower wholesale prices) on new releases, current hot product, and others. Some stores, particularly the electronics stores that also carry recordings, even sell their specials priced below the wholesale cost in an effort to create more traffic in the store. To make the retail situation even more complicated, there appears to be a perceived price that the customer feels they are paying. That is one reason why many products are priced at, for example $12.98, to make the customer think of the price as $12.00 instead of the nearly $13.00 that it is.

SRLP

The suggested retail price of albums is one thing on which the labels did not compete very much prior to 2003. They had behaved as oligopolists in a market where there is high product differentiation and tacit coordination of prices, but no outright cartel or price collusion. In September 2003 Universal Music and Video Distribution (UMVD), which had the largest market share, unilaterally lowered its SRLP of front line products to $12.98 and its concomitant wholesale prices to $9.09. At the time, Universal Music Group Chairman and CEO Doug Morris stated, "We strongly believe that when the prices are dramatically reduced on so many titles, we will drive consumers back to the stores and significantly bolster music sales."[21]

The other majors did not immediately follow suit, but history indicates that pricing moves follow a pattern with one of the majors stepping out as the first to make pricing adjustments and the others following later. For example, in 1993 WEA lowered wholesale prices across the board on its various CD suggested retail list prices, but moved some individual albums up to a higher SRLP, and therefore a higher wholesale price. Their $15.98 and $16.98 list CDs were reduced from $10.30 to $10.18 and $10.88 to $10.67 wholesale price, respectively.[22] In late 1995 PolyGram Distribution (PGD) was the first distributor to lower wholesale prices on CDs in response to retailers' demands for more margin in the price wars that had developed between the retail record chains and the mass merchants. Poly-Gram Distribution's $16.98 list CDs were reduced from $10.65 to $10.50 wholesale and $17.98 CDs list from $11.39 to $11.00 wholesale.[23] Note the similarity of wholesale prices between WEA and PGD for the $16.98 SRLP albums prior to PGD's adjustment.

Wholesale

Wholesale price differentials of a few pennies among the majors have been the norm in the industry for a long time. In 1955, for example, wholesale prices for $3.98 list price vinyl albums varied among the majors by only a few cents from $2.45 to $2.48. Singles prices for $0.89 list singles varied by only 3 cents among the majors from $0.52 to $0.55.[24] In 1979, wholesale prices for the $7.98 vinyl album lines ranged from $4.00 to $4.11.[25] In 1999 Sony stepped out front to increase wholesale prices on $17.98 list CDs to $11.41.[26] By 2002 the $18.98 SRLP was the norm for CDs, with wholesale prices for the majors all running about $11.75 before discounts. Although Universal dropped wholesale prices to $9.09 in its 2003 price cut, that apparent $6.00 drop in SRLP did not translate into as significant a drop in wholesale price because of the practice of discounting. Universal discontinued most discounts and co-op advertising plans for the new price structure and required that buyers at the new price devote at least 25 percent of their bin space to Universal product.

Consumer Price and Demand

One place where price is important is in the mid-line and budget line album categories. Industry estimates placed sales of these lower-priced albums at 16 to 18 percent of total unit sales in 1995 and 1996.[27] Although not all catalog (older than 18 months) and deep catalog (older than 36 months)[28] albums are mid-line or budget priced, SoundScan figures for 2002 revealed that just under 50 percent of all CD sales do not involve current product. SRLP on these products was typically $11.98 for CDs and $6.98 to $7.98 for tapes in the mid-line category, and $8.98 to $9.98 for CDs and $5.98 for tapes in the budget category. Wholesale prices for these products run between $7.00 and $8.00 for CDs and between $4.50 and $5.00 for cassettes on mid-line, and about $6.50 for CD and $3.00 for tapes on budget lines.[29] Solid-selling mid-line albums in 1996 included: Beastie Boys, *Licensed to Ill*; James Taylor, *Greatest Hits*; Tracy Chapman, *Tracy Chapman* (debut album); Patsy Cline, *Twelve Greatest Hits*; Carole King, *Tapestry*; and Guns N' Roses, *Appetite for Destruction*. All of those albums were priced at an SRLP of $11.98 and all are multiplatinum with certified sales ranging from 4 million for Tracy Chapman to 13 million for Guns N' Roses. Typical strong selling budget albums in 1996 included: Janis Joplin, *Greatest Hits* and Hank Williams, Jr., *Greatest Hits, Vol. 1*. Both of those were priced at an SRLP of $9.98 and had certified platinum status with lifetime sales of more than 2 million and 1 million, respectively.[30] Reissues on CD are another important part of the lower-priced catalogs. For example, Patsy Cline's *Twelve Greatest Hits* was a strong 1996 seller with certified sales of over 2 million.[31] Often consumers replaced vinyl discs or tapes or bought CDs for the first time for recordings they may have wished they had purchased before. All major labels report that moving albums to mid- or budget-pricing increases sales significantly. For example, WEA reported shipping more than 90,000 units on a *Best of Jimmy Durante* budget album and PolyGram 500,000 units on mid-line Beastie Boys' *Licensed to Ill*. In addition to the regular labels offering these products, there are several labels that specialize in them. Rhino Records, K-tel, Collectables Records, and Essex Entertainment, for example, frequently package greatest hits compilations either by artist, genre, or year to sell at budget prices. K-tel reports more than 500 titles available at budget prices and Essex more than 800 budget titles.[32]

While the overall prices of various SRLP lines do not vary much from label to label, there is often movement of albums by particular artists from one SRLP category to another. Moving individual albums up or down to a different SRLP suggests that the labels are very aware that there is high product differentiation in the eyes of the consumer based on the particular artist and particular album. In other words, when a consumer goes to purchase a recording, they wish to purchase a particular current recording or a recording by a particular currently popular artist, not just *any* recording.

Two studies bear this out. A study published in 1978 found that "taste" (as measured by the popularity of singles from the album) was the most important factor in the quantity of an artist's album demanded. The second most important factor was exposure of the artist/recording as measured by a combination of radio airplay and live appearances during the time of release. The artist's status (measured by the success of the previous album) was found to be the third most significant factor. A factor measuring submarket appeal (the ability of the record to crossover into or out of a submarket such as country or R&B) was found to be more important than the price of the album, the last factor of significance. "Price," said the author, "does not seem to be a significant detriment to sales, reinforcing the opinion of some in the industry that 'the public will pay for what it wants, even though it may bitch about the higher cost.'"[33]

In another study conducted by a record retail chain in the early 1980s, the price of a popular artist's new record was varied at two outlets of the chain in the same city. At one store the album was placed on sale as is common with new releases. At the other store it was carried at the regular shelf price of other non-sale albums in the store. After a week, the two stores switched their pricing. At the end of the two weeks the store managers compared sales and found that there was essentially no difference in sales of the "hot" new product at the sale or shelf price.[34]

Perceived prices. This is not to say that there is not an overall interest in price by consumers. When vinyl LP list prices were raised across the board from $5.98 to $6.98 in the mid-1970s, the industry estimated a 14-percent drop in unit sales due to the 16.7-percent increase in price.[35] By the 1990s the industry appeared to have found a more workable mechanism to adjust prices and avoid lost sales. They introduced a new price point (usually higher) by setting it for the new release of a hot artist. If the album proves popular, the public is usually willing to pay the higher price. Then other new albums by hot artists can be introduced at the new higher price. Soon the higher price becomes the norm for new albums by major artists. The older price may be maintained as a catalog price for older albums before moving them back to a mid-line price.

Consumers began to balk at higher prices for CDs in the early 2000s. When CDs were first introduced in the early 1980s, suggested retail list prices ran about $19.00 and wholesale prices about $11.75. As volume of production, sales, and demand increased, the labels began to drop their SRLPs and wholesale prices. By mid-1984 SRLPs had fallen to $15.98 and wholesale prices to around $10.00.[36] As more CD manufacturing capacity came online and the volume of sales continued to increase, the cost to manufacture the CDs dropped from nearly $4 dollars per disc when CDs were first introduced to less than $1 per disc by 1995.[37] Wholesale prices, however, did not continue to decline. Wholesale prices crept back up to about $10.65 as the typical SRLP rose to $16.98 by 1995, then to about $11.75 for the typical $18.98 SRLP by 2003.

Although there was some consumer complaining and a lawsuit by an independent record store alleging price collusion by the major labels, the answer to the question of why CDs cost so much was simply, as *Consumer Reports* put it, "Because people are prepared to pay more for compact discs."[38] In mid-1996 two consumers in Knoxville, Tennessee, filed an antitrust suit alleging that the major labels had "coerced and cajoled" stores into keeping prices high.[39] It should also be noted that the average price paid by consumers for CDs fell to a low of about $12.00 in 1990 and remained near $13.00 for the first half of the 1990s. But in the latter portion of the 1990s and into the 2000s, average prices continued to rise back up to about $15.00. Because Figure 8.3 reflects RIAA figures for all CDs, it is likely that part of the reason for the average being lower than $17.98 or

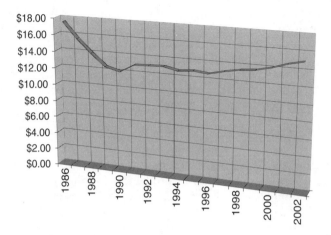

Fig. 8.3 Average prices of CDs. Recording Industry Association of America, based on dollar value of shipments divided by number of units shipped. www.riaa.com/news/ newsletter/pdf/2003yearend.pdf. Accessed 5 March 2004.

$18.98 is that significant numbers of purchases were of lower-priced catalog product at mid-line and budget price points. Shelf prices for these front-line CDs in record stores ran in the $16.00 to $17.00 range, but $9.99 to $11.99 in large "box" stores such as Circuit City or Best Buy. Consumers began to *perceive* the price in the record specialty stores as $20.00 by the time tax was added on. Their complaints were further fueled by the Minimum Advertised Price investigation and litigation discussed below.

In marketing terms, the perceived value of the CD was significantly higher than that of the cassette. There are many components of that perceived value. CDs do have significantly higher quality of sound. They do not get hung up in and destroyed by their players nearly as often as tapes, and they do not wear out as quickly as tapes. CD players allow more flexibility than most tape players, allowing the listener to quickly shuttle back and forth between cuts or even between CDs (on multidisc players). Most CD players allow the listener to program the order of the cuts they hear or to leave out certain cuts when playing the discs; most cassette players do not. The CD technology developed by Phillips and Sony gave consumers a highly desirable product for which they had been willing to pay a higher price.

By the end of 2003, three phenomena contributed to consumer perception that CD prices were too high. Many discounting outlets began selling new CDs at prices ranging from $10.00 to $12.00. With shelf prices in major record retail chains running $16.00 to $18.00 for the same product, consumers began to question the big differences. A $17.00 CD plus tax left consumers with a dollar and some change from a $20.00 bill. That made the price of that CD look like $20.00. Consumers then compared that to the cost of a motion picture DVD at the same price. A DVD provided two hours or more of entertainment, and a CD just over an hour in most cases. Even though consumers would play a CD many more times than they would play a DVD, that distinction did not seem to matter as much. Finally, with the wide availability of free illegal downloads, any product with a price other than free appeared too expensive, especially if the consumer only wanted one or two of the songs from the CD.

Price and Profit

As a result of declining manufacturing costs and increasing wholesale prices, the profit margins of the record labels rose during the 1990s. Consider the example below (Table 8.1). The calculations operate on several assumptions:

- SRLP is $18.98.[40]
- Manufacturing costs of a completed disc with all graphics and inserts, shrink-wrapped, and ready to sell are about $1.00.
- Distribution charges amount to about $1.50.[41]
- Artist and producer royalties (all-in) are 20 percent in the high-cost example and 12 percent in the low-cost example.
- The CD royalty rate is 100 percent of the base rate in both examples.
- Mechanical royalties are for 12 cuts at full statutory rate (8.0 cents per cut for the years 2002 and 2003) in the high-cost example and at 75 percent rate in the low-cost example.

Even in the high-cost example, the label ends up with a gross margin of $5.64 per disc and over $1.30 more, most of which comes out of artist and producer royalties, in the low-cost example. Certainly there is a logic, as far as the label is concerned, to raise prices in order to increase profits. This is especially true given the apparently price inelastic demand (i.e., an increase in price does not bring about an offsetting decrease in demand) for CDs. The concern must be that the labels could price themselves out of the market or create an even greater demand and market for used CDs or free downloads (see Chapter 9).

TABLE 8.1 Low-Margin and High-Margin CD Example

	Low Margin (High Cost)	High Margin (Low Cost)
Wholesale price	$12.00	$12.00
Less: Manufacturing costs	$ 1.00	$ 1.00
Artist and producer royalties	$ 2.70	$ 1.62
Mechanical royalties	$ 0.96	$ 0.72
Distributor charges	$ 1.70	$ 1.70
Gross margin	$ 5.64	$ 6.96

Minimum Advertised Prices

In a move that tied price with promotion, the labels in the 1990s began to threaten retailers with the loss of co-op advertising money if they advertised product for sale at less than a certain minimum price. The Minimum Advertised Price (MAP) policies varied among the major distribution companies, but each distributor set prices for each category or list price of product. If a retailer advertised the product for sale below that price, then the label might go so far as to stop all advertising funds for all product from that distributor for a period of time (WEA's policy), or just cut off funds for that particular record (BMG's policy).[42] Theoretically the store could still sell a recording for less than the MAP, just not advertise that price using money that the label had provided. The labels put the policies in place to help regular record retailers who found themselves in price competition with some retail chains such as Best Buy, Circuit City, Lechmere/Montgomery Ward, and Target, who used the low-balled (priced way below the competition) prices on CDs as loss leaders (priced below cost) to entice people into their stores to purchase electronics and other merchandise. As the price wars intensified in the last quarter of 1995, the labels began enforcing or strengthening their policies. By June 1996 *Billboard* reported, "Thanks to the majors' new-found resolve on MAP, prices of hit CDs at discount chains rose by $2 to $11.99 over the last month."[43] In the meantime, NARM reported that the average price paid by their SoundData Consumer panel during the period of December 1995 through February 1996 was $13.64, up from $12.71 in the previous survey.[44]

The MAP policies spawned an unwanted side effect: an investigation into price fixing by the Federal Trade Commission. In 1993 the commission began investigating advertising price policies of the major labels.[45] By early 2000 it was becoming apparent that the FTC would likely rule against the major distribution companies.[46] They began to consider settlement with the FTC, and in May of 2000 the FTC and the majors entered consent decrees. The majors agreed not to link advertising funds with advertised prices of retail clients for seven years. For an additional thirteen years, the majors could not condition promotional money on the prices contained in advertisements that the majors did not pay for. In its news release on the agreement, the FTC said, "The Commission has unanimously found reason to believe that the arrangements entered into by the five largest distributors of prerecorded music violate the antitrust laws in two respects. First, when considered together, the arrangements constitute practices that facilitate horizontal collusion among the distributors ... Second, when viewed individually, each distributor's arrangement constitutes an unreasonable vertical restraint of trade under the rule of reason."[47]

The FTC settlement did not stop the attorneys general of 42 states from suing all of the major labels and three major retail chains, Tower, Transworld Entertainment, and Musicland, in 2000 alleging that the MAP policies were a form of price fixing. In 2002 the defendants settled with the states for $67.4 million in cash and $75.7 million worth of CDs. The cash was awarded at the rate of about $13 to each consumer who registered at the court's Web site. The recordings were to be distributed to the states on a pro-rata population basis and then distributed to libraries and archives in the states.[48]

The MAP pricing problems were not the first time that the major labels had come under scrutiny for their possibly anticompetitive practices. In 1985 WEA, Capitol, PolyGram, RCA, MCA, CBS, and ABC settled a decade-long price-fixing suit by independent and other distributors. A settlement fund of over $26 million was approved for distribution to distributors who purchased recordings for resale from January 1971 through December 1982.[49] In the mid-1990s, the labels were again the target of suits contending that they had conspired to fix CD prices, and a separate suit claiming that they conspired to keep some wholesalers out of the business of selling cutouts.[50] Finally, in 1996 the Justice Department began an investigation against Time Warner, Sony, EMI, BMG, and PolyGram for price fixing of license fees for music videos. The altercation centered around an alleged attempt by the majors to keep MuchMusic USA from launching a music video channel.[51]

Even different sectors of the industry sometimes engage in antitrust actions. In 2000 the National Association of Recording Merchandisers (NARM), which represents record retailers and distributors, sued Sony Music for antitrust violations. NARM claimed that bundling of services such as computer links to Sony direct retail sites and other merchandise advertising on Sony CDs and other products was an unlawful "tying" arrangement. The suit was finally dropped in late 2001 as NARM decided a better course of action would be to focus "on educating industry executive and government officials about retail concerns relating to digital distribution, copyright law, and antitrust via other channels."[52]

Direct government investigations included looking into the MusicNet and PressPlay Internet distribution companies proposed by the major labels. These Internet distribution systems were funded by consortia of the labels, with MusicNet owned by BMG, EMI, and WEA, and PressPlay by Sony and Universal Music. In mid-2001 it was not apparent how, or if, the two Internet companies would allow a label to sell its products on either or both systems unless it was one of the owner/founder labels. Only EMI had agreements with both of the systems.[53] By 2003 the majors had agreed to cross-license products to both services, probably because they realized that there would be government intervention if they did not.

Promotion

"There is no accounting for taste."

The driving force behind the labels' promotional efforts is the well-founded belief that the consuming public is unlikely to purchase a recording until they have heard the album or a cut from it. The exposure can take the form of radio, record store, or MTV (or other video channel) air play, live performance by the artist, sampler album, Internet streaming or samples, or record-store listening station or kiosk. Advertising, record reviews, and other forms of exposure that do not result in the public being able to hear the record, receive a secondary priority. They promote an awareness of the existence of the album as opposed to knowledge of its content. These secondary promotional methods may help, especially if the artist has had previous success and has a following. Print advertisements have some limited impact. Only 4 percent of the SoundData panel reported purchasing the last recording they saw advertised. A larger percentage (about one-third) reported seeing newspaper ads for individual records at specific stores.[54]

Radio

Radio is still the primary means of promotion for most labels for albums that would be considered popular mainstream. (For a discussion of television and MTV as promotion media, see Chapter 10.) However, radio is no longer almost the *only* means. While only 44 percent of consumers report purchasing their last album because they heard a song on the radio or television,[55] it is important to remember that nearly half of the recordings purchased are catalog product, which is much less likely to be the subject of radio or music-video airplay. Chapter 10 discusses the basic relationship of radio and the recording industry.

The primary job of any record promotion person is to get radio airplay. Except with follow-up albums and singles by hit artists, very few recordings are played "out of the box." Airplay usually has to be built up from stations in smaller markets or smaller stations in large markets. Once the record proves to be popular enough, larger stations will consider playing it. If enough stations play the record and if that begins translating into sales, the label will push to maximize the radio exposure in a concentrated effort to produce the highest possible chart position—an effort that the label hopes will maximize sales. A radio airplay hit that does not translate into sales is referred to as a *turntable hit*.

Promotion people are either label employees or independent. Independent record promoters are often hired when the label promotion department has too many releases to try to promote at once. Also, the artist, manager, or music publisher sometimes hires independent promotion people directly to help the label staff. Expenses of independent promotion are often split between the label and the artist or even 100 percent paid for by the artist as a recoupable expense. How expensive is independent promotion? *Rolling Stone* reported that in the mid-1990s independent promotion people hit upon a new method of promotion: the radio station exclusive.[56] The independent promotion person would pay a significant sum of money to a radio station in exchange for the station promising to talk *only* to that promoter. The cost of such an arrangement to the indie promoter can be up to $50,000 a year. Record labels pay independent promotion people on the basis of records "worked" per week at a cost of $500 to $700 dollars with a bonus for every radio station that adds a record. If an independent promoter has a station as exclusive, then every label that has that promoter under contract will pay the promoter for every record the station plays, whether the promoter had anything to do with it or not. The new breed of independent promoters, concluded *Rolling Stone*, "are essentially lobbyists who cultivate close relationships with key programmers and make money schmoozing them on behalf of the labels."[57] The end result of all of this is that labels may spend $25,000 or more in independent promotion fees to start a modern rock single.

Payola

Today, getting your song on the radio more often is not about your local fan base or the quality of your music. It's about what resources you are able to muster to put the machinery in place that can get your song pushed through.

— Michael Bracey, cofounder and chairman of the Future of Music Coalition.[58]

From the layperson's point of view, payola in the recording industry is paying a bribe to someone to perform or play a certain song or recording in order to increase exposure for that song or recording in the hope that the exposure will lead to increased sales. Using that definition, payola was a common practice in the industry since the turn of the twentieth century.[59] Particularly, music publishers often made payments to performers or orchestra leaders to perform their compositions or to plug the song (see Chapter 4). Industry estimates in those days placed the cost of paying singers for plugs at $200,000 per year. When radio became a significant medium for the exposure of songs, the publishers switched to paying orchestra leaders and directors for exposure on the radio. The practice was dubbed *payola* in 1938 by *Variety*. At that time some publishers had been paying orchestra leaders to influence not only exposure of the song but also ASCAP's logging of songs so they would receive more performance royalties.[60] By 1945 payola payments from publishers had risen to about

$500,000 per year.[61] The practice crept into television broadcasting as well. Eventually some television producers, not content to accept advance payments for songs used in their shows, began to form their own publishing companies to cash in on the lucrative performance royalties that the use of the songs in the shows generated.[62] Record companies got into the act with the rock and roll explosion in the mid-1950s.

The payola and game-show rigging scandals of the late 1950s caused Congress to pass legislation to clean up broadcasting. Broadcasters exist because they sell airtime for money, so Congress reasoned that what had to be done was to make the secret payment for airtime (i.e., payola) illegal. The statute ultimately read, "All matter broadcast by any radio station for which any money, service or other valuable consideration is directly or indirectly paid, or promised to or charged or accepted by, the station so broadcasting, from any person, shall at the time the same is so broadcast, be announced as paid for or furnished, as the case may be, by such person."[63]

The statute excepted such things as identification "reasonably related" to the broadcast, so a station could announce the title of a song and the artist, even if they had received the records for free in order to play them. In order to remove the disc jockeys from the end of the payola stream, the statute made station management responsible if employees failed to disclose payments. Penalties were set at fines up to $10,000 and jail terms up to one year.

The payola statute clearly has some limits. It requires an undisclosed payment to a broadcaster in exchange for airplay. If the station discloses the payment, then there is no wrongdoing. So if a station announced that a "promotional consideration" had been paid for the play of a record, then there would be no violation. Similarly, if payments from independent promotion people, or even the labels directly, were simply "consulting fees" that program directors received without any specific directions or purpose of receiving play for a particular recording then that, too, would not be in violation of the statute. Because an organized plan of bribery (payola) to violate a federal statute (the payola law) would mean that the labels were violating the Racketeering Influenced Corrupt Organizations law (RICO), the labels began paying independent promotion people to insulate themselves from any potential criminal act.[64]

There is some speculation that there might be federal trade law violations if records were added to playlists as though this was the result of some form of consumer demand.[65] This forced programming decisions up to a higher level, giving the disc jockeys very little say in what music was played. The Top 40 format had already removed many programming decisions from the disc jockey, and the payola laws were the coup de grace. The lack of control over airplay apparently had damaging results on air personalities' creativity. While DJs continued to perceive themselves as creative in their announcements and humor, one 1990 study found them no more creative in their on-air patter than the least-creative college students.[66] The payola hearings and scandals of the late 1950s are often characterized as a last-ditch attack on rock and roll by the music business establishment of the time.[67] This attack clearly failed. The power of the new popular music to sell recordings and receive airplay convinced potential artists, songwriters, record producers, and label executives that the future lay in embracing new music and new artists. In his book, *Hit Men*, Fredric Dannen argues that the labels' expenditures of millions of dollars to independent promotion people during the rock era was an attempt to guarantee airplay of their recordings in a high-stakes game that the smaller labels could not play. Estimates are that the labels paid out as much as $60 million to $80 million for independent promotion in 1985.[68] Of course, even if the labels could guarantee airplay, the airplay could not guarantee sales unless the public liked a recording enough to buy it. Because the labels primarily made their money through the sale of recordings, Dannen noted that, by the mid-1980s, independent promotion had become too expensive. Another payola scandal at this time (see the description of the Isgro trial later in this chapter) gave the labels an excuse to cut independent promotion, and they did so with a vengeance in 1986.[69]

As the labels continued to struggle to get airplay, the nature of payola continued to evolve. In 2000, the FCC (Federal Communications Commission) fined Clear Channel Communications—a major radio-station conglomerate—saying that several of their stations, "willfully and repeatedly" violated the law by increasing the airplay of a Bryan Adams song in return for money for commercial time and a guarantee that Adams would perform free at station concert events.[70] The radio stations, meantime, moved to sell an announcement of the name of the artist who had performed the song that a station had just played (a *back announcement*) as advertising,[71] which would not be payola as long as it was apparent that the announcement had been paid for.

The focus on independent promotion budgets for record labels and the links with those budgets to radio airplay was detailed in a *Los Angeles Times* article in 2001. The article explained the practice of independent promoters maintaining "banks" for stations. The promoters put funds into the banks when they were paid by the labels to work for airplay of a particular recording, as much as $4,000 per song. The stations had access to the banks for a variety of expenses including vacations, giveaways, and other promotions. The more a station played the "right" recordings, the larger the bank account on which they could draw. Some stations had accounts with as much as $120,000 per year from the promoters. The promoters and labels claimed that the operations were *not* tied directly to airplay of specific songs and were therefore within the letter of the law.[72]

Direct payola from a label to a radio executive resulted in a $15,000 fine and twenty-four months probation in a case involving Fonovisa records and a Spanish-language radio network in 2001. The program director of Z-Spanish Radio admitted receiving $15,000 per month from Fonovisa in exchange for airplay of Fonovisa records. Senior executives at the label also pleaded guilty in the case.[73]

By 2002 the problems had again come to the attention of Congress. Senators Russell Finegold and John McCain promised hearings and an investigation, and Senator Finegold introduced legislation to ban a variety of play-for-pay schemes. The broadcasters reacted by cutting ties to independent promoters: Cox Communications led the way in 2002, and Clear Channel Communications, the nation's largest radio chain with more than 1,200 stations, followed suit in 2003. This affected the stations with contemporary music formats—about one-third of the Clear Channel stations and 14 of the 79 Cox stations—that previously had contracts with promoters.[74]

Independent Promotion and the Isgro Trial

The most public airing of the connections between independent record promotion and payola was the trial of promoter Joe Isgro. It began on February 23, 1986, when NBC's *Nightly News* broadcast a special report purporting to show that the record industry was making huge payments to independent record promoters and that one of them, Joe Isgro, allegedly had ties to organized crime figures in the New York area. The major record labels quickly moved to stop using independent promoters. Isgro filed suit against twelve labels, alleging that the sudden boycott of independent promotion was an attempt to stifle competition and fix prices and violated antitrust laws. That dispute was ultimately settled by all of the twelve label defendants.[75]

However, a three-year federal investigation ended in charging Isgro and others with fifty-seven counts of racketeering and other crimes.[76] One of the defendants, Ralph Tashjian, pleaded guilty to one count of payola by distribution of cocaine in exchange for a promise of airplay, one count of tax evasion, and one count of obstruction of justice. In exchange for this plea bargain, Tashjian promised to testify against others involved, especially Joe Isgro.[77] During Isgro's trial, the program directors testified that they had received payments ranging from $150 to $750 for adding a song (an *add*) to their playlists. Others testified that the payments totaled from $1,000 to as much as $5,000 per month.[78] The case was ultimately dismissed due to prosecutorial misconduct, but it caused the record labels to become even more careful in their payments to independent record promoters. And, it caused the promoters to make the links between the payments to the stations and the play of any particular recording even more obscure.

Other Promotion Methods

Retail

There is no law that restricts retailers from selling advertising space in their stores, aside from some sign ordinances restricting outdoor advertising. The large chain superstores began by selling outdoor four-by-fours (4' x 4' displays) of album covers to the labels in the 1970s. Soon the practice moved inside the stores with the sale of display space on walls. While the labels had been giving the stores point-of-purchase display materials free, some stores began to limit display spaces and charge the labels for any use of it. The stores soon found that not only would the labels pay for the space, they would send around their own personnel to set up the displays. By the mid-1990s retail record stores had taken cues from their other retail cousins and began charging for positioning of product in stores on special sale displays or *end caps* (displays at the ends of aisles). Because in-store airplay is not "broadcasting," it is not illegal to pay a store to play a recording over the in-house system. More often, however, the labels paid for positioning and other retail promotions with free albums given to the retailers as an incentive. All of these retail promotions are still no guarantee that the public will buy the recording.

Because word of mouth is an important factor in sales of recordings, the labels give away copies of entire albums or *sampler* albums to try to get people interested in purchasing the whole album, or in telling their friends that they had heard an interesting new album by such-and-such an artist. Most labels also hire people to post messages in Internet chat rooms that mention that they like a certain recording or artist. No payola there, either.

Samplers

The use of sampler albums is another method to get more product into the hands of consumers to try to get them interested in particular artists and recordings. Samplers are made available through record stores, magazine offers, radio stations, direct mail, or via the World Wide Web. NARM data revealed that about 30 percent of its SoundData panel of consumers had received music samplers in 1995, and about one-half received these samplers unsolicited through the mail. Most of the consumers (80 percent) who received the free samplers listened to them. The most significant statistic was that 21 percent of those who heard a sampler reported purchasing music as a result. If those percentages were applied to all music consumers, it would amount to about five percent of all music consumers.[79] Many of the labels' home pages on the World Wide Web have short samples of recent releases and product information online. It is also possible to request samplers at many of the home pages. (See the Internet Appendix in this book for URLs of label home pages.)

Listening stations

A related way to get consumers to hear the recording is to place it in some sort of listening station at record stores. Listening stations that could play CD samplers were becoming common by the mid-1990s. Thirty-seven percent of the SoundData respondents said their favorite store had a listening station in late 1995.[80] Ninety percent of those using listening stations reported that it "somewhat" or "very much" influenced their decision to purchase. Other research supports that conclusion and notes that listening station users are more likely to purchase an additional record because of listening station use. Additionally, 70 percent of consumers said it was "somewhat important" to preview music at a listening station before purchasing. Those who did not use listening stations tended to already have their minds made up about what to buy before entering the store.[81]

Place

The place analysis for marketing must include the physical (or cyber) place where the customer purchases the recording, the mechanisms used to distribute the recordings to those places, and the place *in time* that the recordings are purchased. Chapter 9 deals with retailing by independent stores, chain stores, and mass marketers. Distribution place and time are discussed below.

Distribution

Figure 8.4 depicts the basic product flow from a major or independent label to retail store. Each player in the system has distinctive characteristics, but consolidation of functions at some levels makes the actual system much more complex. A description of the players at each level follows:

Independent label: A record company not owned by one of the majors that has its records manufactured and shipped to various independent distributors around the country. The label or the distributor may handle promotion and sales activities. Some independents have distribution deals with majors or are partially owned by majors, in which case their albums go through branch distribution.

Major label: A record company owned by one of the four conglomerates that has its own branch distribution system. Note that even a small label, if it is owned by one of the big four, could be considered a major label for this purpose, to distinguish it from a true independent label. It has records manufactured and shipped to its branch locations for further sale to independent or to chain-owned one-stops (dealers who sell to individual stores; see below). Sometimes a

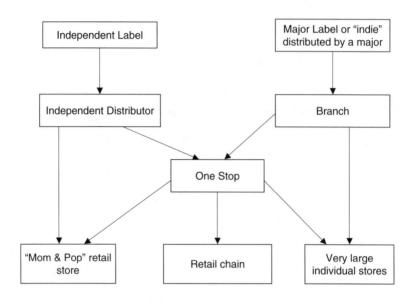

Fig. 8.4 The distribution system for recordings.

very large single retail account or store can buy directly from the branch.

Independent distributor buys records from independent labels, usually several or all, and sells those records to retail stores and to one-stops that handle all lines. Typically independent distributors are also one-stops.

Branch distributor sells only the labels manufactured by its corporate owner or other labels that the parent company has agreed to distribute. The branch distribution companies are: WEA (Warner Music Group), UMVD (Vivendi-Universal), Sony Distribution (Sony Music Entertainment), BMG Distribution (Bertelsmann, AG), and EMD (EMI).

One-stop sells all labels. It purchases records from branch and independent distributors. It sells records to individual stores whether they are independent mom-and-pop stores or individual locations of retail chains. Many chains are serviced by an in-house one-stop. One-stops began by servicing singles to jukebox operators. Because they handled all labels, a natural evolution for them was to begin selling to retailers and to begin their own rack-jobbing operations as well.

Mom-and-Pop stores are single stores or very small chains. The mom-and-pop name comes from the notion that they are sole proprietorships or family owned, though that is not necessarily the case. They usually buy from one-stops for the ease of being able to purchase all records from a single source and because the branch operations will not sell labels distributed by the majors directly to small stores. Because the one-stop must make a profit, the small retailer ends up paying a higher price for the records.

Retail chain: A group of stores with a common owner. Most chains buy from a one-stop that is owned by the same parent company as the chain. Individual stores usually have authority to buy from a local one-stop when "emergency" product shortages occur for a very hot product and the store would not be able to get resupplied fast enough by the company one-stop.

Very large individual stores may sometimes buy directly from branch operations if the branch will allow it. Otherwise, such stores are often part of chains that buy from their chain one-stops.

The recording industry's distribution system has evolved through several phases. Initially, each label was in charge of its own distribution. As the number of releases and labels increased, so did the need for a middleperson who could handle several labels and deal directly with the retailers, which inspired the birth of independent distributors. During the rock and roll explosion of the 1950s and 1960s, independent labels flourished and so did the independent distributors who sold them. By the end of the 1960s, the major labels felt the need to compete more effectively and bolstered their own distribution systems, moving into a stronger branch system. During the 1970s and 1980s, the significant independent labels, such as Motown, Arista, A&M, and Chrysalis, were purchased by the majors. With very little product flow through their own operations, the independent distributors were forced to begin to handle all labels, taking on the functions of a one-stop. As one-stops, they also discovered the profitability of record retailing and many opened their own record-store chains, while the chains that already existed discovered the profitability and other benefits of having their own company-owned one-stop. Because they carried all lines, one-stops also began to service rack locations. The lines of distribution began to crisscross and functions were merged, especially at the ownership level of the one-stops. In the 1990s a resurgence of independent labels brought renewed life to the independent distributors. While branch distribution through the majors still controlled about 80 percent of records sold, Figure 8.5 indicates that the share of the independents grew substantially in the 1990s.

The Universal-PolyGram merger in 1998 greatly altered the distribution landscape. Prior to that time (Figure 8.5), the market had been drifting toward parity. Each of the major distribution companies and the indies controlled between 10 and 20 percent of the market. The brief spurt of independent distribution in the mid-1990s had halted, as many of those indie labels chose to use distribution through the majors in order to improve their marketing clout.

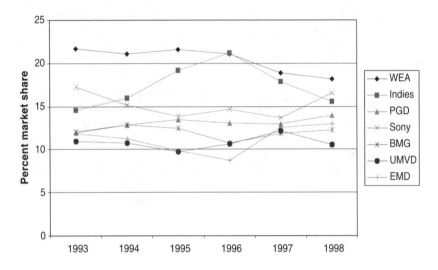

Fig. 8.5 Total U.S. album market share by distributor (pre-1999). *Billboard*, 23 January 1999; 24 January 1998; 20 January 1996; 21 January 1995.

After the merger, Universal Music and Video Distribution (UNI) jumped to controlling over 26 percent of the market (Figure 8.6 below). The other majors, except EMD and the independents, had stabilized at about a 15-percent share each. The proposed Sony-BMG merger would create a second distributor with a nearly 30 percent share.

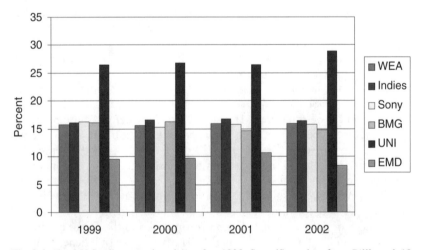

Fig. 8.6 Total U.S. album market share after 1998. SoundScan data from *Billboard*, 18 January 2003; 20 January 2001.

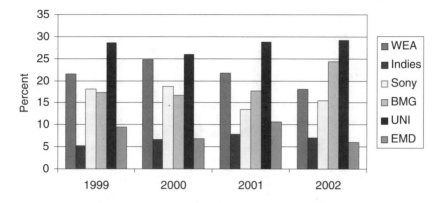

Fig. 8.7 Country album market share after 1998. SoundScan data from *Billboard*, 18 January 2003, 47; 20 January 2001, 71.

Distribution shares of the major specialty markets, country and R&B (which included rap and urban until 2001), followed different paths. Keep in mind that at these levels, the presence or absence of a couple of mega stars on a given label could make an important difference in market share because the market share of country (about 11 percent in 2002) and R&B/ urban (about 11 percent in 2002) and rap/hip-hop (about 14 percent in 2002) were much smaller than the total market. In country (Figure 8.7), independent distribution was a less-significant force (under 10 percent)

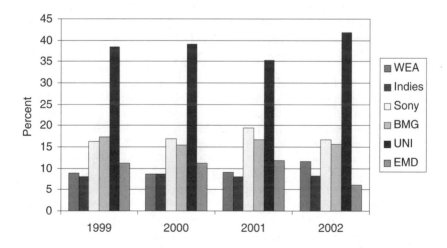

Fig. 8.8 Total R&B album market share after 1998. SoundScan data from *Billboard*, 18 January 2003, 37; 20 January 2001, 71.

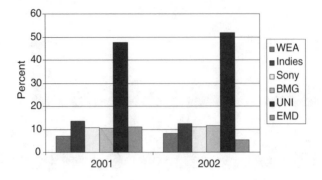

Fig. 8.9   Total rap album market share. SoundScan data from *Billboard*, 18 January 2003, 37.

throughout the 1990s. Though UMVD jumped into the upper 20th percentiles as its market share after the merger, it had strong competition from WEA. In the R&B market, the Universal-PolyGram merger created a very lopsided situation with UMVD controlling more than twice the market share of its closest competitor (Figure 8.8). The most striking graphic (Figure 8.9) shows that Universal controlled over 50 percent of the rap market in 2002. That was due in large part to its ownership of the Interscope and Island/Def Jam labels.

Product Availability

From a marketing perspective, it is important to remember that not all places that sell records sell *all* records. For a record to sell, it has to be available at the place where the consumer is looking for it. That is why if a record is getting airplay in a particular town, the label must make sure that the stores in that town that are likely to carry that particular record have copies of it. NARM SoundData information indicated that 44 percent of record consumers will try to find a record elsewhere if it is not available at the store they first try. That is good news for the label, but bad news for the store. Thirty-seven percent of buyers said they would buy nothing. That is bad news for both the label and the store.[82]

Two industry practices try to keep the lack of product availability from causing a loss of sale. First, the labels will often give free goods to the retailers to encourage them to stock the record. Second, records of new acts are often sold on a 100 percent returnable basis. That is important because the labels do have policies that allow a retailer (or distributor) to return only a limited percentage, typically 15 percent, of orders. Records that are 100-percent returnable are not counted toward the return limits, making these in effect consignment sales. That 100-percent returnable practice was introduced by RCA in 1957.[83]

Product Placement

Place also means placement at a particular location *within* the record store. Most retailers rent the high-visibility and high-traffic spaces in their stores, particularly special sale displays for hot or new products and end caps at the end of aisles, to the labels. These displays are effective in promoting impulse purchases. Fifteen percent of music buyers report making unplanned purchases because of displays. The most effective single type of display is the end cap, influencing 40 percent of those impulse buyers. The least effective in-store means of prompting impulse buys are reportedly posters and artist cutouts.[84]

Place in Time

Labels work hard to plan their release dates. They want to spread out the recordings they release so that their promotion budgets can be spread out. They will attempt to second-guess the competition in order not to release an album that might directly compete with some other label's release by a bigger artist. They try to avoid releasing new acts the same week as a major act, because the major act will demand all of their promotion resources. A label promotion person may have to push a record by a major artist whose record was expensive to produce and who is demanding the label's attention instead of a record by a new artist. Finally, the label will frequently try to have important releases in the fourth quarter of the year in order to capitalize on the Christmas buying season.

The Season to Be Jolly

There is no doubt about it. Sales of recordings, like many other things, soar during the roughly five to six weeks between Thanksgiving at the end of November and early January. Figure 8.10 indicates that sales of albums begin to pick up significantly about the week before Thanksgiving. (The dates in Figure 8.10 are standardized to the weekly 1995 issue dates of *Billboard*. The SoundScan data contained in the issues is about ten days to two weeks old at the time of the issue.) By the week of Christmas, sales are at their peak for the year—about three times their previously weekly average of 11 to 12 million units per week. By the end of the second week in January they are back at their old average, which remains quite consistent during the non-holiday season. As the chart indicates, the pattern is remarkably stable, even through nine years of data.

How much of the total sales are accounted for by the holidays? A tally of SoundScan figures from *Billboard's* "Market Watch" feature for a nine-week

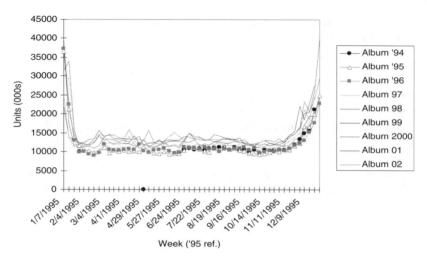

Fig. 8.10   Weekly album sales 1994–2002. SoundScan data from *Billboard*, each week.

period beginning with the week of Thanksgiving and ending with the third week in January 1997 indicated that 195.6 million albums were sold. That accounts for about 27 percent of the total year's sales of 715.2 million albums. That 27 percent was sold in about 17 percent of the year. A similar comparison of 2002 sales data in a shorter seven-week segment of the holiday period indicated that 24 percent of the sales occurred in a time spanning only about 13 percent of the year. Certainly that is an impressive jump in the rate of album sales, but it is not near the 40 percent of total sales that some label executives believe occurs in the Christmas season.[85] A *Billboard* columnist pointed out that a problem with releasing so many major albums in the fourth quarter means that they compete with each other for sales and none has the attention of the buyers for very long. In addition, any albums by new artists that are released in the fourth quarter are competing with releases by the major acts for the discretionary dollars of consumers. Finally, if the "wrong" single is picked to promote a later-year release, then the album will not be able to get a second chance because it will be too late to change marketing directions once the error is discovered.[86]

Entering the Information Age

The recording industry has been accused of having difficulty with marketing. Music critic R. Serge Denisoff notes, "Success in the record industry is basically believed to be a combination of luck, timing, hard work and the great man theory. Only hard work is a controllable force."[87] Labels would often employ the "shotgun" approach, shooting out a lot of releases, hoping that some would be hits. They would try to outdo each other at making the most noise about their current releases. The results were often nothing but hype (short for hyperbole)—exaggerated claims of the quality and value of a particular artist's record. Beginning in the 1970s the labels began to put more effort into marketing plans, creating separate plans for each release, hiring product-development specialists to work with the artist and producer to develop a marketing plan suitable to the particular record. The problem was that they lacked essential information about the extent and nature of their market. Was it limited to teens? Who was really buying recordings? Why did they buy them? Late 1970s studies by NARM, Warner Communications, and CBS Records began to examine the nature of the market.[88] Still, the industry lacked hard information on sales patterns, buying preferences, and trends.

Universal Product Code

In 1979 the labels began to use Universal Product Code (UPC) identification on all of their releases. Each UPC *bar code* uniquely identifies the label (manufacturer), the specific album, and the configuration (tape, CD, cassingle, vinyl single, and so on). The bar code can be read by laser and other light scanners and the data then recorded in a computer. Once all recordings were bar coded, a retailer could know exactly how many pieces of exactly which products had been sold in a given day, month, week, or year. Information such as price could be looked up by computer/cash registers attached to a local database and automatically printed on a receipt. The implications for precision in inventory management at the retail and wholesale levels were not lost on the industry. A NARM report for rack jobbers stated:

> In the broadest terms, UPC offers rack jobbers the benefits of comprehensive, timely and accurate management information with which they can more effectively control their businesses. If well used, a UPC system can improve operational performance, allocate resources more wisely, and enhance the return on investment.[89]

SoundScan

As more retailers and rack jobbers began to use point-of-sale scanning devices that read the UPC and tracked sales, it became possible to gather actual data on sales on a national basis. In 1989 market researcher Mike Shalett began SoundScan, a company that worked out agreements with retailers to gather their point-of-sale (POS) data, compile it, and make national sales reports available to retailers, distributors, record labels, and others in the industry who needed to know actual piece-count data. The data could be broken down by artist and title, market, and retail location. Armed with SoundScan information, a label could know if their purchase of display space in a chain of retail stores was having any noticeable impact on the sales. Retailers could watch sales in other stores or other markets to look for opportunities or trends in consumer purchases. All kinds of data on the effects of test marketing, advertising, and other promotional tools became available.

SoundScan made its biggest splash in 1991 when *Billboard* added SoundScan data to its calculations for determining chart position in the Pop Albums (Top 200 Albums) and Top Country Album charts. By that time SoundScan was gathering data from more than 2,000 retail locations, including many of the major national record store chains and the Handleman Company, the nation's largest rack jobber.[90] The use of SoundScan data had an immediate effect on the charts, moving popular country albums and artists on some independent labels into higher positions, while dropping some new pop/rock acts off the chart entirely. Within a week, the major labels were complaining that the new actual sales data might not be fair to new acts for which the labels desired to have a good chart performance. The sample of retailers, said the labels, was too heavily weighted in favor of artists who sold at major mall chains and rack jobber locations, and did not accurately reflect enough sales through independent stores and smaller chains. Shalett simply replied that other outlets would be added as soon as they had the data-gathering capabilities and could work out arrangements with SoundScan.[91]

Not surprisingly, many independent labels had a more positive reaction. Those that sold pop product, particularly rap and dance, had better chart numbers than in prior years. Tommy Boy Records chief executive officer Tom Silverman commented, "SoundScan is a great thing for indies—we realize we're a bigger part of the industry than we thought we were."[92] Independent labels with specialty product did not chart well in early SoundScan charts because they tended to sell through specialty shops and very large full-line stores that were not well represented in the early SoundScan database. Blues specialty label Alligator Records president, Bruce Iglauer noted, "When more full-line stores that don't do their buying off the charts come on line, it will be a marvelous thing for the industry."[93] The sudden appearance of more independent labels in the charts and the increasing share of the charts belonging to independent labels (see earlier discussion), in the words of a Cheetah Records (primarily an alternative rock label) executive, "Legitimized indie labels, proved we're a factor in the industry. The indies never had the money to market like the larger labels."[94]

As the use of POS technology became more widespread, more sales outlets were indeed added to SoundScan's database. By 1997 SoundScan was gathering data from more than 14,000 retail locations.[95] In addition, the use of actual sales data continued to enter more charts. Eventually SoundScan figured into the computing almost all of *Billboard*'s charts that had a sales component.[96] By 2003 all of *Billboard*'s domestic sales charts and general popularity charts (other than exclusively airplay charts) included SoundScan data. The depth of sales information enabled the creation of additional specialty charts such as Top Kid Audio and Regional Mexican Albums.

SoundScan data is also very useful for developing marketing strategies. Labels (and other users such as personal managers, agents, music publishers, and concert promoters), can access national sales information by region, by specific Designated Market Area (DMA), by store, and more. Summary reports on sales by configuration and store type can be created, in addition to sales charts in most music genres. See SoundScan's Web site for sample reports (www.soundscan.com). Users pay annual fees ranging from about $5,000 per year to more than $80,000 per year, depending upon the size of the client's annual sales.[97] The availability of such detailed information makes more detailed marketing plans possible. All of this was the result of the bar coding that began in 1979.

What kind of sales does a number one album have? It usually takes sales of more than 200,000 units in a week to be at the top of the chart. Some major hits, such as 50 Cent's debut album, sell as many as 800,000 units or more in one week. More often than not, the record in second place is substantially behind that sales pace at about 150,000 units. Sales fall off rapidly as you go down the chart. A number ten seller will have sales around 60,000 to 80,000 units. Albums in the forties tend to sell around 30,000 to 40,000 units per week. During the peak Christmas weeks, sales are much higher, not just for the top album but for all those in the charts, with sales of more than 100,000 units for any album in the top 50 during good year.[98]

Broadcast Data Systems

Data availability through new technology also had a significant impact on a record company's ability to monitor actual radio airplay. Broadcast Data Systems (BDS) was formed as an affiliate of *Billboard's* BPI Communications to create a computer-driven method of monitoring actual radio airplay. Prior to 1990, radio airplay charts had been compiled from information provided by the music and program directors at radio stations, who were contacted by the chart compilers, *R&R* (*Radio & Records*), *Billboard*, *Gavin Report*, and others. The performing rights organizations either sampled airplay by recording (ASCAP) or by having the stations list which songs were performed (BMI), or by using the charts themselves as an indication of airplay (SESAC).

The new BDS system was described by *Billboard* as:

> a proprietary, passive, pattern-recognition technology that monitors broadcast waves and recognizes songs and/or commercials aired by radio and TV stations. Records and commercials must first be played into the system's computer, which in turn creates a digital fingerprint of that

material. The fingerprint is downloaded to BDS monitors in each market. Those monitors can recognize that fingerprint or "pattern," when the song or commercial is broadcast on one of the monitored stations.[99]

The monitors then transmit data back to BDS headquarters for compilation. BDS sells the information to performing rights organizations, the labels, advertisers, and others needing that specific airplay information. In 1994 the system was improved to reduce the number of unrecognized songs. The BDS monitors would capture all airplay on a separate unit. Any song not recognized would be transmitted back to headquarters in Kansas City, Missouri, where it could be compared to a master library containing more "fingerprints." Songs not recognized by the master library (said to contain several million patterns) could then be listened to by actual persons for recognition and counting.[100]

Billboard first began using BDS information in March 1990 for the Hot Country Singles chart. By late 1990, *Billboard* and *R&R*, its major competitor in the radio airplay chart business, were in a war of words over which system provided a more accurate accounting of actual airplay. *R&R*, which still relied on reports from station music managers in the form of playlists, contended that the two systems had discrepancies of as many as thirty plays for a song in some locations, with *R&R* picking up the greater number of plays. BDS countered that discrepancies were accounted for partly due to doctored playlists that radio people were providing *R&R*, some methodology differences with both systems, and some software problems of the early BDS system. BDS undoubtedly has the long-term edge in this battle; the lure of actual data has a very strong appeal to music publishers. "It's obviously a purer system if it really monitors what's really being played," said a BMG music-publishing executive.[101] *Billboard* pressed BDS information into more of its radio airplay charts.[102] By 2003 all of *Billboard*'s charts that used an airplay component relied on BDS information. *R&R*'s airplay charts all reported actual spin counts.

As the BDS monitors were in place in more markets, the labels began to use them to monitor not only airplay, but also the success of their label and independent promotion persons. RCA announced a plan to pay independent promoters for top 40 adds only after the records had appeared in the station's top 35 for a week, as measured by BDS. Other labels began to follow suit.[103]

What is the extent of radio airplay? Table 8.2 reflects the number of spins that a number one hit might have in a given format as reported to *R&R* reporting stations for that particular format/chart. The number of reporting stations varies for each chart, so the fact that there were more spins for the number one country song is due mainly to the fact that there are 159 country reporting stations, compared to 79 alternative stations. Note that the Contemporary Hit Radio (CHR) and urban stations tended to play

TABLE 8.2 Typical Spin Counts of Number 1 Records (Weekly)

R & R Chart	Total Spins	Average per Station	Average Number of Plays per Day per Station	Gross Impressions
CHR/Pop 50	3115	59.9	8.6	88,000
Country 50	5459	36.6	5.2	—
Urban 50	3867	58.6	8.4	624,000
Alternative 50	2893	37.6	5.4	330,000

Source: Sample data from *Radio & Records*, 21 February 2003 (various charts).

their top songs more often each day than the country or alternative stations. "Gross impressions" is the number of times that recording was heard by listeners of those reporting stations based on the spin count and the station's Arbitron ratings.

The information gathering and dissemination systems in the recording industry were not immune from the trend toward consolidation that affected the entire industry as the twentieth century drew to a close. In early 1995 BDS merged with its former competitor, Competitive Media Reporting, to form a new entity under *Mediaweek* parent, VNU.[104] BPI Communications, the parent of *Billboard* and BDS had been purchased by VNU, a Dutch company, in 1994.[105] In 2001 VNU purchased AC Nielsen, the market research company that had previously purchased SoundScan. So, as the twenty-first century began, virtually all hard information on radio airplay and sales of recordings, and the industry's premier trade publication, *Billboard*, were owned by one company, VNU.

Computer technology has also had a direct impact on consumers. As record stores got larger in terms of square feet and number of different albums stocked, it became increasingly difficult for consumers to locate the product they wanted unless it was a mainstream hit. With thousands of titles and artists, it also became impossible for store personnel to know the inventory in detail. As a result, some stores began putting a kiosk in the store where the consumer or clerk could access the store's database of recordings to find out if a particular recording or artist was in stock and where in the store it was located. By 1996 over 40 percent of music buyers were using kiosks as listening or look-up stations.[106]

Market Research

The labels have used other market research methodologies over the years. For example, one survey research company sends out albums to a group of 100 country music buyers, asking each a number of questions about the albums. That data is then assembled into a report for the label buying the service, and is used in helping to decide what singles to release or promote. Focus groups, a less-expensive methodology, often help a label identify a particular appeal or turn-off that some cut might have. These methods sometimes hit and sometimes miss. For example, a focus group told RCA that the group Alabama's *Mountain Music* was too much like rock and roll; the album became one of the group's biggest sellers. Other albums or cuts are projected to be hits but turn out to be stiffs. Most labels want at least some kind of information other than their own marketing department's gut feel. As one researcher put it, "Competition has stiffened and labels need as much ammunition and information as they can get."[107]

Conclusion

Even with additional information, the labels still face a marketing dilemma. They sell products that are highly differentiated and rely on consumer taste preferences for success. It is difficult to predict how consumers will react to a particular album or artist. If labels only follow the current trends, they tend to release more of the "same old, same old," which leads to less than enthusiastic consumer responses. Trying to anticipate trends and "new waves" is risky and still may not receive an enthusiastic consumer response, yet the best consumer response and the most profit can be made from taking the risks. What the marketing information can do for the labels is to help reduce the risk and get the most return from the product that they produce.

9
Retailing: Software on Hard and Soft Copies

Overview

The development of record retailing, its place in the recording industry, state in the beginning of the twenty-first century, and future are best understood by keeping in mind the function(s) that retailers play in any industry. *Retailing* is the selling of goods and services to the ultimate consumer. In particular, record retailing occupies a place in the sale of goods to ultimate consumers for *personal* (as opposed to business or industrial) use. The retailer provides valuable functions for both the manufacturers and distributors, and for the consumers. For the manufacturer, the retailer is the final stop in the distribution chain. Retailers provide one last opportunity to influence consumer purchases at the point of sale. They convey important information on what is selling and what consumers want. And most importantly, they supply the manufacturer with the purchase dollar, without which there would be no multibillion-dollar recording industry.

From a consumer point of view, retailers provide a place to purchase the music. This is generally a physical place such as the corner or mall record store, but can also be a place such as a catalog for direct purchase through a record club or place in cyberspace from an online service selling hard copies or downloads. In 1995 NARM estimated that there were more than 25,000 different places to buy music recordings, with about 16,000 of those being record specialty stores.[1] By 2003 that number had shrunk substantially due to the closings of hundreds of stores by the major chains and hundreds of K-Marts (see discussion below), but there were still many thousands of places to purchase recordings. Retailers also help the customers sort through merchandise, provide a selection of inventory from which the customers can choose, and information to help the consumers get the recordings that they want.

What *do* consumers want from a record store? One survey found 49 percent of record buyers cited selection as the "most liked" feature of buying locations, while price was a second place (16.5 percent), location fourth (9.2 percent), and "other" third (9.8 percent). ("Other" appeared to be factors involving the store atmosphere.)[2] These top four image components accounted for almost 85 percent of the most liked features of record-selling locations. They remain the primary image factors by which record stores seek to differentiate themselves from their competitors.

Record Retail: 1890 to 1950

The Early Years

In the 1890s, cylinder recordings were sold by mail order direct from the manufacturer (label). By 1895 Emile Berliner had established the first store to sell disk recordings in Philadelphia. Columbia opened its first phonorecord *parlor* in Washington, D.C., at about the same time. Most recordings were sold to the parlors, which played the cylinders and disks in *coin-ops*, a kind of predecessor to the modern jukebox. Customers could insert a coin in the machine to play their favorite recordings. Very few recordings were sold for home use because they were just too expensive for most consumers. But as the century turned, the prices of the players fell from around $150.00 each to as little as $35.00 or less. Consumers became owners of phonograph players in significant numbers, and stores that sold the players also sold the recordings. Columbia, Victor, and Edison, the makers of the players, were also the makers of the recordings and sold both through the same outlets. The player manufacturers became labels because they had to provide software (i.e., records) to drive the sales of their hardware (phonographs), much as the radio manufacturers later would establish radio stations and networks to provide programming for the receivers they were attempting to sell. There continued to be a significant mail-order business direct from the labels. The manufacturers thus were in total control of the system. They sold the machines to play the recordings, and made and sold the recordings direct to consumers through mail order and through company-owned retail outlets. This scheme of vertical integration had few rivals before or since.[3]

The End of Monopolies

When the Edison, Victor, and Columbia patent monopolies ended in 1917, a number of other labels sprang up, including Okeh (a 1920 Columbia subsidiary selling primarily blues and minority, and later hillbilly recordings), Brunswick, Pathé, Vocalion, and Emerson. The presence of these other labels created the need for stores that sold recordings of several labels and the independent record store was born.

Depression and Recovery

The 1930s saw the collapse of the recording industry into a few major labels, the establishment of significant connections with broadcasting, and the near death of record retailing. In 1929 Victor Talking Machine had been purchased by RCA, the electronics and broadcasting firm, later to become RCA Victor. Columbia collapsed into American Record Corporation (ARC), along with a number of other labels, and re-emerged in 1938 and 1939 when CBS, the electronics and broadcasting firm, purchased ARC. In England a 1930 merger of Columbia Graphophone with Gramophone (His Master's Voice/HMV) and Parlophone created Electric and Musical Industries, Ltd. (EMI). Decca, a British company founded in 1929, ended up with the U.K. rights to ARC Group; in 1934 U.S. Decca was formed. Eventually Decca was purchased by the talent agency MCA, which also owned Universal Pictures. These labels formed the core of four of the labels that became the "majors" in the United States and internationally: RCA Victor, Columbia, EMI, and MCA.

The broadcasting connection was important because radio stations in the 1930s began to play more and more recordings instead of featuring live orchestras. The recordings were much less expensive to program. Radio became both a market for the recordings (because at that time the stations had to purchase the recordings that they played) and a promotional tool for the exposure of the recordings to the public.

The other savior of the recording industry in the 1930s was the arrival of the jukebox. The first coin-operated machine for playing recordings was introduced in 1927 and by 1930 there were 12,000 in use. In the Depression, most people relied on either radio or jukeboxes for their musical entertainment. The machines became immensely popular. By 1936 there were 150,000 of them, consuming 40 percent of all records sold that year. By 1939, the 300,000 jukeboxes consumed 30 million 78s per year, well over half of all records sold. They continued to be a significant factor right through the war years and the early 1950s. Overall, jukeboxes proved particularly important to the spread of the popularity of country music.

Independent retailers became more important during the 1940s and 1950s. A pent-up demand for recordings during the war years led to sales of 350 million records in 1946, up from 130 million only four years earlier. Important new labels, MGM, Capitol, Mercury, Atlantic, and others, formed during the forties.

The explosion of record sales and record labels brought on by the advent of rock and roll in the mid-1950s also inspired significant developments in record retailing. With so many new labels to keep up with and so much near instantaneous demand for the hits as heard on the local radio station, the mom-and-pop record shops simply could not keep up. Into their places stepped rack jobbers, retail chains, superstores, and megastores.

Rack Jobbers

> What the rack jobber did was they really made it easy for people to buy records.
>
> —Former NARM president Jules Malmud[4]

The first record rack jobber, Music Merchants, began by setting up racks of discount records in drugstores, supermarkets, and variety stores in 1952. They sold the top 15 hits. John and David Handleman, destined to become the nation's largest rack-jobber operation, soon entered the business along with others. The rack jobber was a sub-distributor, like a one-stop, and got a 10 percent discount from the wholesale price paid by retailers. As the public appetite for records expanded, so did the racks' business. They had to provide more than a single 4.5-foot metal rack of the top 15 hits. They either ran entire leased record departments in department stores and mass-merchant discount houses, or provided all of the items necessary for creating a record department: the stock, fixtures, inventory control, pricing, and virtually everything else except sweeping the floors and running the cash register. By selling only the hit records, they were able to sell at a high volume and therefore a lower price than the other retailers. In addition, they had a 100-percent return privilege with the labels. If they overbought or guessed wrong on what would be hot, the label would take it back.

Rack locations accounted for about 18 percent of all sales in 1960, growing to a third of all sales by 1965, and 80 percent of all records sold by a decade later. Racks provided people with lots of places (location convenience) to purchase the most desired recordings. They also provided access to recordings at the kinds of locations—discount mass merchandisers and other large retail stores such as Sears—where people were likely to be. A 1994 poll found that 60 percent of the sample had visited a Kmart or Wal-Mart in the last thirty days.[5] That is the same reason why record store chains flocked to shopping malls in the late 1970s and 1980s. It is not, however, convenient to go to a mall just to buy a record. A freestanding store or strip center is a much more convenient for a single purchase.

Shipped Out Platinum, Came Back Gold

The rack jobbers provided the labels with a way to sell larger quantities of records to a single buyer. Label executives said the racks allowed them to move "tonnage" of product. That was the good news. The bad news was that the racks, with their 100-percent return privilege, often *returned* tonnage of product. Some label executives coined the expression, "shipped out platinum, came back gold." (Translation: orders for 1 million copies, returns of 500,000 copies.) The labels were then left with piles of often unsellable inventory. When this material was not destroyed, labels would "remainder" extra copies to retailers to be sold at heavy discount in so-called cutout bins. Copies of the Bee Gees/Peter Frampton soundtrack album for the film of *Sgt. Pepper's Lonely Hearts Club Band* appeared in cutout bins for years after its ill-fated 1978 release.

The other problem that the rack jobbers presented was that they could not stock a very deep inventory. A typical record store would stock 8,000 to 10,000 titles,[6] while a typical rack location (record department) would have only 500 to 1,000 titles. For the industry in general, the top 200 titles generated the majority of sales—as much as 70 percent.[7] In the early stages of development of a market for a particular recording, the racks would not stock the product. A new recording had to be showing significant signs of consumer acceptance before the racks would stock it unless it was from a well-established artist with a good sales history. On the other hand, because the majority of the business is sales of hit product, one could argue that the rack jobber provided the consumer with a preselection of the music that the consumer was most likely to want.

Handleman Co.

Like most of the recording industry in the 1990s, rack jobbing consolidated with the largest accounts getting larger and one company, Handleman, getting more of the accounts. In 1991 and 1992 Handleman acquired its largest rack competitor, Lieberman Enterprises. By the mid-1990s Handleman was the largest single retail account in the recording industry, followed by the chain retailers, Musicland Group, Blockbuster Music, and Trans World Music.[8] Handleman serviced more than 22,000 rack locations, primarily in Kmart and Wal-Mart stores (those two accounted for about 65 percent of Handleman's sales), with some of the locations being leased departments where the rack jobber supplied everything, including personnel to run the department. Handleman's typical leased departments, called Entertainment Zones, were about 1,400 square feet and included 5,000 SKUs of CDs, 3,500 of cassettes, and 2,000 to 3000 of home video. In these leased departments, the rack jobber owns the product until the ultimate customer buys it. The rack jobber pays a rental based on a fee per square foot plus a percentage of sales. In the more typical rack situation, the retailer buys the product from the rack jobber, but it is the rack jobber who supplies all of the fixtures, keeps track of stock selection, ordering, and replenishment. Like many other recorded music retailers in the 1990s, Handleman expanded its rack sales to include books, home video, and computer software, reporting sales as music (53 percent), video (38 percent), books (5 percent), and computer software (4 percent).[9] With the continued increase in sales through non-record store locations, Handleman's sales through rack accounts at Kmart and Wal-Mart accounted for 77 percent of the company's sales by 2001.[10]

By 2002 Handleman had major competition from another rack jobber, Anderson Merchandisers, and from mass merchandisers that racked their own stores, such as Target and Best Buy, which had bought the Musicland chain and also sold recordings in its "big box" style appliance/electronics stores. Anderson Merchandisers entered the recording rack-jobbing fray in 1994 when it purchased Western Merchandisers. Prior to that Anderson had racked periodicals, books, trading cards, and comics to a number of retailers, most importantly, Wal-Mart.[11] Anderson and Handleman then competed for a share of the record business of the nation's single largest retail account, Wal-Mart.

The Chain Gang
Chain Retail Record Stores
Consumer interest in a larger selection of recordings, the development of the shopping mall, and the overall increase in the demand for recordings (noted in Chapter 1) influenced the growth of the record retail chains. That growth was dramatic from the mid-1970s into the early 1990s. As Table 9.1 indicates, the number of record stores (which does not include rack locations) more than doubled in a fifteen-year span from 1977 to 1992. By 1997 the increase was nearly 125 percent over a twenty-year period. This was at a time when other related stores such as musical instrument and radio/TV/Electronics stores were decreasing in number. By 2000 the growth of record-store locations had stopped while sales through non-record store locations continued to increase; overall sales of recordings decreased and a number of chains went into Chapter 11 reorganization and began closing unprofitable locations.

Once the chain retailers began to grow, they grew both in number of firms and locations, and in power. In 1977 the largest firm, the only chain

TABLE 9.1 Record Store Growth

Census Year	Record Stores	Musical Instruments	Radio/TV/Electronics
1977	3,655	5,748	24,752
1987	6,272	4,690	18,892
1992	7,924	4,149	17,324
1997	8,158	4,477	16,870

Source: U.S. Department of Commerce, Census of Retail Trade (1977–1992); Economic Census (1997). (Note that the Census of Retail Trade is compiled every five years and that results are typically not available until two years after it is completed.)

TABLE 9.2 The Growth of Record Retail Chains (Units per Firm)

Census Year	Mom-and-Pop (1 Unit)	25 or More Units	100 or More Units
1977	2,026	8 firms account for 580 establishments	1 firm accounts for 218 establishments
1987	2,635	22 firms account for 2,562 establishments	6 firms account for 1,656 establishments
1992	2,923	20 firms account for 4,064 establishments	12 firms account for 3,648 establishments
1997	3,189	18 firms account for 4,141 establishments	10 firms account for 3,819 establishments

Source: U.S. Department of Commerce, Census of Retail Trade (1977–1997). (Note that the Census of Retail Trade is compiled every five years and that results are typically not available until two years after it is completed.)

with more than 100 units, accounted for fewer than 10 percent of the locations (see Table 9.2.) By 1992 the large chains (100 plus units) accounted for 46 percent of the stores. Chains with at least 25 locations accounted for more than half of the nearly 8,000 locations. Even though the number of mom-and-pop, single-store locations grew, their share of the stores had dropped from 60 percent in 1977 to 37 percent in 1992—still a significant factor but not a dominant force in the industry. By 1997 as the major chains began to close unprofitable units and the number of mom-and-pop stores continued to grow slightly. The share of total record stores that was accounted for by sole proprietorships (mom-and-pops) rose back to 39 percent.

Most significantly, by the late 1990s the retail record-store business was concentrated in a few major chains. Over a twenty-year period, the ownership of about one-half of all record stores declined from 50 chains (1977) to 8 (1987) and finally 4 major firms (1997). Although this would still quality as effective competition as discussed in Chapter 6, there was clearly a trend toward a tight oligopoly in the record store business.

The trend continued through the end of the century and was even more significant than the 1997 data indicates. Mergers within the group of the five largest chains concentrated market share even more in the top four chains than the 47 percent indicated in Table 9.3. It all began in 1998 when

TABLE 9.3 Concentration Ratios of Largest Chains (percent of total record store sales)

Census Year	4 Largest Firms (%)	8 Largest Firms (%)	20 Largest Firms (%)	50 Largest Firms (%)
1977	20.4	28.9	39.0	49.5
1987	34.5	49.3	63.9	72.8
1992	40.9	57.8	70	76.2
1997	46.8	64.1	73.8	78.6

Source: U.S. Department of Commerce, Census of Retail Trade (1977–1997).

Wherehouse Entertainment became the third-largest chain with the purchase of Blockbuster from Viacom, increasing the number of Wherehouse stores to about 800.[12] Trans World purchased Camelot Music in 1999 after Camelot emerged from Chapter 11 reorganization a year earlier; that move doubled the number of Trans World's stores, bringing it up to about 1,000 locations by 2001.[13] In 2001 Best Buy, which had led the charge of recording sales through specialty electronics/appliance stores, purchased the then largest chain, Musicland; Best Buy's music-selling locations then numbered about 1,400.[14] However, by then the record market was beginning to decline; after two consecutive years of losses, Best Buy called the Musicland acquisition "a strategic mistake."[15] Within weeks Best Buy sold Musicland to an investment firm in exchange for Musicland's debts. The new owner indicated that it might to close as many as 200 or 300 Musicland locations as part of Musicland's Chapter 11 reorganization.[16]

The Weakest Link

All was well in the record retail chain business until the mid-1990s. At that time a combination of factors led to significant problems in chain management and profitability.

1. The overall growth of record sales leveled off in the mid-1990s and actually declined for several years in the early 2000s.
2. The chains became overextended.
3. Price competition became fierce.
4. Other places to buy records began to compete more effectively, including record clubs, rack jobbers, and other non-record store outlets.
5. Some consumer dollars were channeled off into the purchase of used CDs.

Overall Growth of Record Sales

From 1979 to the mid-1990s, the sales of records through stores had grown steadily and consistently. The stores had participated in this growth to the detriment of rack locations through the 1980s. Furthermore, this growth of overall sales and of the chain share of the sales was real. Until 1995 record-store sales grew even when accounting for inflation, but in 1995 when total unit sales dropped about 1.0 percent (down to 1,113,100,000 units from the 1,122,700,000 units of the previous year) the slight increase (2.1 percent) in dollar value of shipments was nullified by an approximate 3-percent inflation. As Table 9.4 indicates, the result was an actual decrease in retail store sales in constant dollars. The decrease of sales in constant dollars continued through the end of the twentieth century. By 2000, sales in constant dollars had declined to 1992 levels. In 2002

TABLE 9.4 Sales Growth of Record Stores (Adjusted for Inflation by Consumer Price Index, 1984 = 100*)

Year	CPI for Entertainment Commodities (1984 = 100)	Record Store Sales (Constant Dollars in Millions)
1977	69.0	1,775
1987	110.5	3,325
1992	131.3	4,123
1995	140	4,579
2000	147.2	4,126
2002	149.5	3,105

Source: U.S. Department of Labor, *Monthly Labor Review;* and Recording Industry Association of America. www.riaa.com/news/newsletter/pdf/yearend.pdf. Accessed 5 March 2004.
*In 1997 the Bureau of Labor Statistics stopped computing a general "Entertainment Commodities" CPI and converted to a more specific "Audio Discs, tapes and other media" CPI; 1997 = 100. This table converts that back to 1982–1984 dollars using the 1997 CPI for Entertainment Commodities = 144.2.

the decrease in overall sales of recordings combined with a decline in the share of sales through record stores, spelled double trouble for traditional record retailers (Table 9.4). Sales through record stores in constant, non-inflated, dollars had dropped to levels comparable to the early 1990s.

Overextended Chains

As the sales bloom faded, music retail chains discovered they were trying to run too many outlets in marginal locations, yet they continued to open or acquire new stores at a rapid rate. In 1993 Musicland opened 51 music stores, closed 35,[17] and announced it would open 30 Media Play super-stores (stores that operated with enormous inventories of recordings) in 1994. Also in 1993, Blockbuster Music acquired 270 music stores from the Super Club including Record Bar, Tracks, and Turtles stores.[18] Even small chains jumped in the act with Hear Music adding five stores to a seven-store chain in 1995.[19] By 1995 the five largest record store chains operated 2,854 record stores (see Table 9.5).

Problems were close at hand as growth turned into retrenchment for the chains. Camelot Music, the fourth largest retail chain, dropped below 400 stores, closed 18 early in 1996, and went into Chapter 11 reorganization later that year.[20] Musicland announced it would close at least 50 stores in 1996 and went into Chapter 11 reorganization.[21] Blockbuster Music closed thirty stores in 1995 and 1996.[22] Trans World closed 190 stores and also went into Chapter 11 reorganization.[23] Tower Records neared Chapter 11 by the end of 2002 but closed some stores, sold its international stores, and laid-off employees to try to remain afloat. Some smaller chains,

TABLE 9.5 Largest Retail Chains (1995)

Chain	Number of Stores	Stores Included
Musicland Group	861 stores	Musicland, Sam Goody, Discount Records
Trans World Entertainment	700 stores	Record Town, Tape World, Coconuts, Saturday Matinee, Abraham/Strauss
Blockbuster Music	540 stores	Blockbuster, Music Plus, Sound Warehouse, Turtles, Tracks, Record Bar
Camelot Music	405 stores	Camelot Music
Wherehouse Entertainment	348 stores	Wherehouse

Source: *Billboard 1995 Record Retailing Directory.* New York: Billboard Publications (1995).

TABLE 9.6 Largest Retail Chains, 2001

Chain	Number of Stores	Stores Included
Best Buy Group	1,750 stores (music)	Best Buy, Musicland, Sam Goody, Discount Records, Media Play
Trans World Entertainment	1,052 stores	Record Town, Tape World, Coconuts, Saturday Matinee, Abraham/Strauss, Camelot, Wax Works
Wherehouse Entertainment	540 stores	Wherehouse, Blockbuster, Music Plus, Sound Warehouse, Turtles, Tracks, Record Bar

Source: *Billboard 2001 Record Retailing Directory.* New York: BPI Communications (2001).

including National Record Mart and Harmony House, disappeared altogether.[24] Chapter 11 of the "bankruptcy" code[25] permits a debtor to go to court to ask for time to restructure its operations to allow it to pay off its debts. If the creditors and bankruptcy court approve the plan, any creditors are stayed from foreclosing on its debts pending the completion of the reorganization plan.

Competition to get into the shopping malls tended to bid up the rent paid by the mall music retailers. While they had been paying 9 to 12 percent of store revenue to the mall owners in the 1980s, the chains, in their desire to get the mall locations, had bid that up to 14 to 17 percent in the 1990s. As rents went up, profit margins went down. Declining profit margins and sales in general strained the chains' profit margins, but that was not the end of the record retailers' woes.

Price Competition Problems

In the early 1990s the mall record merchants had been getting a premium price for their CDs, as much as a dollar or two over list price. During the mid-1990s the concept of the megastore, featuring a huge selection of recordings along with videos and books and computer software, had emerged. The megastores were often located in vacant building-supply or grocery stores, keeping construction costs down. They would offer product at $10.99 or $11.99, not much margin on a new CD that would cost the retailer about $10.72 at that time. Other nonmusic merchants began using music as a loss leader to draw customers into the store. Circuit City, primarily an electronics and appliance retailer, often sold CDs below cost at $9.99. Wal-Mart offered CD titles as low as $8.88. One writer noted that the average price paid by the customer for a CD had fallen 63 cents since 1990, while the average wholesale price paid by the retailer had risen 43 cents since 1991. NARM reported in 1996 that of the 10 percent of music consumers who purchased recordings at the electronics store discounters (often known as "big box" stores) such as Best Buy, Circuit City, and Fry's Electronics, two-thirds said price was the primary reason.[26]

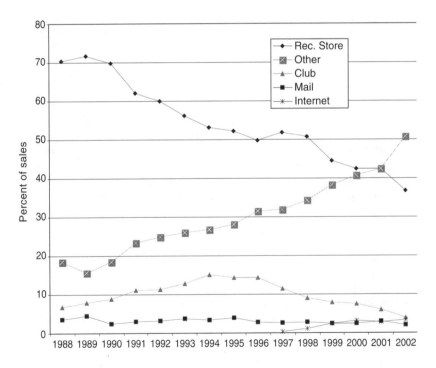

Fig. 9.1 The declining record store share. Recording Industry Association of America. www.riaa.com/news/marketingdata/pdf/2002consumerprofile.pdf. Accessed 6 March 2004.

Alternatives to Specialty Record Stores

As the old saying goes, you can't sell at a loss and make up the difference on volume. The music-only retailers had nowhere to make up the loss. They could not lose $20 on CD sales and make it up by selling a DVD player for $100. The competition offered lower price, often in locations surrounding malls, and in many instances a greater selection.[27] Figure 9.1 indicates the extent to which alternative outlets eroded the record stores' market share from 1988 to 2002. By the end of 2002 sales through alternative outlets had surpassed record specialty stores for the first time since the 1970s.

A *Rolling Stone* article hit on another not-so-obvious problem, calling many of the 6,000-plus record retail outlets a "huge bore." Commented the writer, "The hip, funky record stores of the Sixties gave way to the carnival like emporium stores of the Seventies, but with wide scale corporate consolidation of the music business during the last decade, retailers have decided to play it safe ... and boring."[28] Store atmosphere, one of the four significant factors that determined where consumers shopped (mentioned earlier), had declined. The article reported a NARM survey that showed that 34 percent of record buyers were not able to find what they wanted at record stores, and an earlier Warner Music Group survey that found that only 35 percent of buyers were "very satisfied" with their stores.

The chains were being effectively competed with on all four of the most important factors in choice of retail record store. The megastores and superstores had greater selection and the mom-and-pop specialty stores still catered to real specialty audiences. The electronics store discounters and some of the mass merchants were effectively competing on price. Mall locations are only convenient for mall shoppers. Freestanding stores are more convenient for shoppers just out to buy recordings. Finally, the mall locations had become bland, look-alikes—leaving store atmosphere to the mom-and-pop stores and the freestanding chain stores.

Used CDs

Although there had been limited resale of used recordings at backyard sales, flea markets, and some specialty used record stores catering to serious collectors, it was not until the advent of the compact disc that the used record business became widespread and of concern to the record labels and artists. In a compact disc, the sound quality of a used copy is usually the same as a new copy unless the disc has been so damaged as to be unplayable. While sales of new CDs soared from 22.6 million units in 1985 to more than 727 million units a decade later in 1995,[29] consumers and some mom-and-pop retailers discovered the value of used recordings. They could be purchased from consumers who were tired of them or in need of quick cash for anywhere from $3 to $5 apiece and resold for about twice that amount. With the price of new discs running in the $15 range (except for sale items), the sound of used discs being equal to the sound of new discs, and some items no longer being available, the used disc market grew rapidly.

From a strictly legal perspective, there is nothing in the copyright laws to prevent someone who owns a copy of a CD or other recording from selling it to someone else—either a store or another individual. The "first sale doctrine" allows "the owner of a particular copy or phonorecord lawfully made ..., or any person authorized by such owner, ... without the authority of the copyright owner, to sell or otherwise dispose of the possession of that copy or phonorecord."[30] Although sale of used recordings is legal, *rental* of sound recordings is specifically prohibited under the Record Rental Amendment of 1984.[31] The copyright laws now prohibit the owner of a copy of a sound recording from disposing of a particular copy for the purpose of direct or indirect commercial advantage by rental, lease, or lending, or "any other act or practice in the nature of rental lease or lending."[32]

Some industry spokesmen claimed that the sale of used recordings was just another way to rent the recordings, where the customer could buy the disc one day and return it a few days later for credit or cash.[33] However, a survey sponsored by the National Association of Recording Merchandisers (the record distributor and retailer trade organization) found that only 9 percent of the buyers of used CDs said they purchased the product to tape it and then sell it back.[34] As CD burning became more widespread, label executives continued to complain, saying things such as, "The used-CD business promotes CD burning. They can buy it, burn it, and then return it or sell it and get some of their money back and still have the music."[35] But there were no indications that any substantial numbers of consumers abused the market in that way. Similarly, the sale of used CDs was only a sideline for most recording retailers. Only 18 percent of stores surveyed had more than 50 percent of their inventory in used product. Sixty-four percent of the stores had 25 percent or less of their inventory in used recordings. One could reason that since the vast majority of the used CD sales would go to legitimate (nonrental) activities, then it would not be likely that the entire practice of selling used CDs could be stopped.[36] Even with the sales crunch in the late 1990s, the sale of used CDs seldom exceeded 5 to 10 percent of most retailers' business.[37]

Sharing the Blame for the Used CD Market

Retailers cited several reasons for the growth of the used CD market.

1. Customers purchase used CDs because the price of a new CD is too high.[38] That was borne out by the NARM survey that found that 82 percent of used CD buyers said that lower cost was their primary

reason for purchasing them.[39] Even some label executives acknowledge this. "There's a perception on the public's behalf that compact discs, particularly at traditional retail, are priced too high. The industry, I don't believe, has responded very favorably to that perspective and people want a bargain," said David Blane, Senior Vice President of PolyGram.[40] By 2002, prices of typical used CDs were around $5 to $9, compared with a typical $17 shelf price for a new front line release. In summer 2003, Universal Music addressed this problem by unilaterally dropping its prices for all new CDs, and suggesting a retail price of $12—a $5 decrease.

2. There is more profit (i.e., a higher margin) on the sale of used CDs than on new CDs.[41] A typical used CD is sold for at least twice the purchase price with a profit of anywhere from $3 to $6 dollars creating markups ranging from 83 percent to 177 percent and dollar margins as high as $6.65.[42] Retailers typically pay the labels about $11.00 to $12.00 for new CDs and sell them for prices in the neighborhood of $16.00 to $17.00 if they are not on any special sale—a markup of 45 percent and a margin of about $5.00. [43]

3. Labels set up tight return policies on opened CDs, usually only accepting a 1.0 or 2.0 percent return.[44] That makes it difficult for retailers to return product that has been opened for airplay in the stores, a particular problem because many stores now have a policy of allowing a customer to hear any product before buying. That led some large record retail chains to open up independent used CD stores to dispose of the opened product. They discovered the business to be profitable and began to consider selling used product in their main "name" stores.[45]

4. Some label promotion persons and radio station personnel sell promotional copies, which they obtain at no cost, to used CD outlets to make some quick cash. Label and radio people agree that such practices exist, but disagreed on the size of the practice.[46] A 1995 NARM survey found that 32 percent of all used titles purchased were promotional copies.[47]

Strictly speaking, the sale of promotional copies violates the copyright laws. Because the labels purport to have given the copies to the radio stations for promotional purposes only and to have retained title, they have not transferred ownership of the copy; thus those copies are not subject to the first sale doctrine. On the other hand, many promotional copies are given to the radio stations with the intention that they be given away to consumers. It would be difficult to argue that giving the recording to a consumer does not constitute transfer of

TABLE 9.7 What Used CD Sellers Do with the Money or Trade

Action	Percentage (%)
Take the cash	32
Buy more used CDs	35
Buy new CDs	30
Buy a new cassette	4

Source: SoundData survey reported in *Billboard*, 2 October 1993: 4, 112.

TABLE 9.8 Why People Sell Used CDs

Reason	Percentage (%)
Don't listen to them anymore	37
To generate cash	13
Don't like the disc anymore	27
To make room for new CDs	7
Tired of the same CDs	7
Received as gift	2
To tape, then sell back	9

Source: SoundData survey reported in *Billboard*, 2 October 1993: 4, 112.

ownership. One can reasonably argue that recordings are loaned to the radio stations so the station will play them on the air, but contending that they are being *loaned* to consumers who are contest winners at radio stations and whose identities are unknown to the labels is a difficult case to make.

Note that whether the artist is paid royalties on these copies (which they are not) is irrelevant to a discussion of whether it is legal for a store that has obtained a copy to sell it. The artists must take up their concerns with the labels because all they have is a contractual right to be paid by the label. An artist would have to show that the label knew its promotion staff was selling promotional copies and either participated in the process or did nothing to stop it.

5. Customers want used CDs because the quality of CDs does not deteriorate in used copies. The customer can feel confident that a used product will sound as good as a new copy of the same recording but cost less.[48] Many retailers feel that the high quality and lower price of used CDs encourage consumers to try artists and recordings that they would not otherwise buy.

Pressure Points

Prior to late 1992, when some major retail chains started to get into the used CD business, the labels had generally ignored it as a small percent of business, confined mostly to mom-and-pop stores.[49] But in December 1992, three major chain retailers—Wherehouse, Hastings, and LIVE

Specialty—announced plans to begin carrying used product in some or all of their stores.[50] By summer of 1993, four of the six major distributors (at that time), Sony, WEA (Warner, Elektra, Atlantic), CEMA (Capitol-EMI, later to become EMI Music Distribution or EMD), and Uni (MCA, Geffen, and GRP), announced that they would no longer provide co-op advertising money to chains or stores that sold used CDs. Sony said "The sale of used, bootleg or counterfeit product ... is detrimental to our industry, unfair to the artist, publisher and manufacturing company, and ultimately both your customer and ours, the consuming public." The WEA announcement stated that sale of used CDs diminished the perceived value of the new product.[51] PolyGram (PolyGram, Mercury) and BMG (RCA, Arista), the other two major distributors, did not participate in the co-op pullout.[52] Later CEMA began to refuse to take *any* returns of opened CDs.[53] Country superstar artist, Garth Brooks, got on the bandwagon, announcing that he did not want his new album sold to any store that sold used CDs.[54] Said Brooks, "I'm against anyone who sells used CDs and if I have my way, we won't send any product to them, not just CDs, until they find a way to compensate those writers and publishers and all involved with the record."[55]

The retailers fired the next round. In 1993 they formed an ad hoc trade group, the Independent Music Retailers Association (IMRA), to petition the FTC Federal Trade Commission) to investigate the withholding of co-op advertising money as a possible unfair trade practice. Then in July 1993, the 339-unit chain, Wherehouse Entertainment, and IMRA filed suits in Federal District Court against CEMA, WEA, Uni, and Sony Music distributors. The suit alleged that the distributors were violating antitrust laws by conspiring to withhold advertising dollars from stores that sold used CDs.[56] By September the air had cleared. The distributors agreed to reverse their policy of withholding advertising money, as long the money was not used to promote the sale of used CDs.[57] The IMRA suit was finally settled in 1994 for $2 million. That payment from the labels was to be distributed among the 300 retailers in the IMRA class action suit to make up for lost co-op advertising money. The labels also agreed to a payment of about $250,000 to cover the costs of the litigation. The terms of the Wherehouse suit settlement were not disclosed.[58]

For his part, Garth Brooks was still not happy. He recanted his statements as they applied to small stores selling used CDs of rare albums. "My bitch and gripe is when mass retail takes over used CDs," Brooks told a press conference, adding that the chains would kill the independents. Meanwhile a number of stores were boycotting Brooks's newest album, which arrived in the middle of the controversy. Remarked one small retailer, "Garth can't be the person to decide who can sell used and who cannot."[59]

The Federal Trade Commission was not happy, either. It launched a separate investigation into price fixing and the used CD problem against all six major distributors. One distributor executive was quoted as saying, "We thought they were satisfied … Now it looks like they'll be checking into the books. Nobody here wants that."[60] What began as the used CD investigation spilled over into the Minimum Advertised Price investigation discussed in Chapter 8. Because the FTC concluded that MAP policies were an unfair restraint of trade, it is likely that they would have concluded that the distributors' used CD policy restrictions were also an unfair restraint of trade.

Internationalization of Record Retailing

Just as the recording industry became more internationalized in the 1980s with the emergence of the then six multinational record/entertainment conglomerates, the record retail end of the industry internationalized in the 1990s. Large U.S. chains began to open stores outside of the United States, and large foreign chains, particularly from the United Kingdom, began to compete in the U.S. market. The downturn in recording sales in late 1990s and early 2000s, however, forced some of the retailers that had internationalized to pull back and focus on domestic survival.

U.S. Chains Abroad

In most foreign territories where U.S. chains have opened up stores, they are competing with HMV and Virgin from the United Kingdom as well as each other and, of course, the domestic independents and chains. Japan was a particularly favorite target of these retailers in the 1990s, partly due to the fact that 70 to 80 percent of retail record outlets in Japan were independent record shops at that time. That is similar to the situation that existed in the United States in the 1960s and invited the rapid growth of chains in the 1970s and 1980s. The most aggressive U.S. retailer in foreign markets was Tower Records. Tower had 33 stores in Japan, and one to three stores each in Taiwan, Hong Kong, Singapore, Thailand, and Korea.[61] Most were large stores in the 6,000 to 10,000 square foot range.[62] However, in 2002 Tower retrenched and sold its Japanese chain to Nikko Principal Investment.[63] In 2003 Tower closed down or sold its European operations as well.[64] The Musicland group, through its Sam Goody name, also competed in the Pacific Rim market as well as the United Kingdom. The Sam Goody name was licensed to retailers by the Japan Record Sales Network, Inc. (JARECS). JARECS is owned by a consortium of record labels in Japan.[65]

Foreign Chains in the United States

The most significant British invasion of the U.S. record industry since the Beatles was the expansion of two of the United Kingdom's largest record retailers onto American soil. The retail arm of EMI Music (HMV stores) and W. H. Smith (The Wall and Virgin Retail stores) both opened stores in the United States. HMV is a 330-store international chain that began in London in 1921. It now operates stores in the United Kingdom, Canada, Japan, Hong Kong, Australia, Germany, and the United States. Through 1996 HMV had focused its fourteen stores and new store openings on the eastern United States.[66] In 1998 EMI Music sold the HMV chain to HMV Group, which had been formed to purchase those stores and Dillon's (another record retailer) from EMI and Waterstone's stores from the W. H. Smith chain. In 2003 HVM operated more than 500 record/video retail stores in ten different countries, including 111 in the United States, but ceased its German operations that year.[67]

By the mid-1990s WHS Music, the wholly owned U.S. subsidiary of W. H. Smith, operated more than 167 outlets in the United States under the names of Our Price and The Wall. They were small- to medium-sized stores averaging about 3,500 square feet. Competing on the large-store end of the spectrum, W. H. Smith and Blockbuster Music operated Virgin Retail in the United Kingdom as a 50/50 joint venture.[68] But in 1997 W. H. Smith sold The Wall stores to Camelot Music, and in 1998 sold its interests in Virgin to the Virgin Retail Group.[69] In the United States and elsewhere Virgin Megastores are in the over-10,000-square-foot category. In fact, the Virgin Megastore that opened in Times Square in New York City in May of 1996 became the world's largest record store at 70,000 square feet, topping the prior Virgin and world-record 60,000 square footer in London. When it opened, the Times Square store, developed at a cost to Virgin of about $15 million, needed to generate $21 million of sales per year just to break even.[70] Virgin Entertainment operated 23 large music stores in the United States in 2003.

Indies: The Mom-and-Pop Stores

> There is no competing with the big guys ... You can only offer something different.
>
> —Mary Mancini, owner of Lucy's Record Shop, Nashville, Tennessee[71]

The independent, single, mom-and-pop store remains an important segment of the retail end of the recording industry. These stores provide entrepreneurs with entries into the industry. They operate in locations where the chains might not wish to build or might have overlooked. They are often niche stores catering to special catalogs or oldies. They frequently sell used CDs. They provide a means for local talent to distribute their recordings locally (although many chain managers also have the option of picking up a local album on consignment).

TABLE 9.9 Comparison of Chain and Mom-and-Pop Stores

Census Year	Sales Per Unit Mom-and-		Payroll (% of Sales) Mom-and-		Paid Employees Mom-and-	
	Pop	Chain	Pop	Chain	Pop	Chain
1977	$188,986	$437,246	11.1	10.0	3.3	7.1
1987	$308,376	$857,254	12.3	8.7	4.2	8.8
1992	$362,644	$959,852	13.4	9.4	4.1	9.7
1997	$404,201	$1,223,151	14.0	9.0	4.3	10.6
1987–1997 % change	+ 31.1	+42.7	+13.8	+3.4	+2.3	+20.5

Source: U.S. Department of Commerce, Census of Retail Trade, and Economic Census. Recording Industry Association of America.

The number of the indie stores barely grew at all while the chain explosion took place. Table 9.2 indicates a modest growth of about 39 percent for single-unit firms from 1977 to 1992. During that same period the total number of stores grew 117 percent. But the growth in independent stores appeared to be at a rather constant rate. From 1992 to 1995 the number of independent stores grew about 9 percent while the number of units in the larger chains (more than 25 units) leveled out with only a 2 percent growth.

Creating a Niche

Independent stores tend to be smaller than the chain locations; most are in the 2,000 to 4,000 square foot range, and some even smaller. Therefore they cannot stock the breadth of titles that the chains do. However, they frequently do stock a deep catalog in some specialty area such as jazz, country, rap, reggae, alternative, or imports. With a special inventory, they develop sales personnel that are particularly knowledgeable in that genre of music—a fact that many customers appreciate. The special inventory also enables them to create a store atmosphere that is geared to particular kinds of customers, not the generic mall browsers that chains cater to. As mentioned at the beginning of this chapter, these other kinds of image components are important to significant numbers of record buyers.[72]

Most of the independents do not compete on price. They feel that their deep inventory is worth a higher price. As one indie owner put it, "So, pay me for having it."[73] The possibility of selling used CDs is also important to independent stores. Many of them carry used CDs and the used business accounts for anywhere from 15 to 100 percent of their business.[74] Out of deference to the major distributors, many chains do not carry used CDs. The independent store, however, is much more likely to buy from a one-stop or independent distributor, and so is not as concerned with how the majors feel about their used CD business.

Table 9.9 indicates other important differences between the individual store units in chain operations and the typical independent record retailer. Chain stores average about 2.6 times the sales of the indies. Chain stores

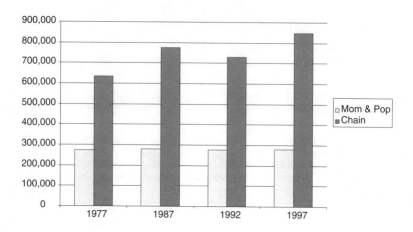

Fig. 9.2 Record store sales in constant dollars (1982–1984 = 100). U.S. Dept. of Commerce, Census Bureau, *Census of Retail Trade (1977–1992); Economic Census* (1997).

operate more efficiently as far as payroll is concerned, spending about 4 percent less of their sales on salaries than the indies do, even though they employ more people.

An examination of Figure 9.2 indicates just how little, in some respects, the mom-and-pop stores changed from 1977 to 1997. The nearly doubling of sales per unit indicated in Table 9.9 is virtually flat when adjusted for consumer price index changes between 1977 and 1997 into constant (1982 to 1984 = 100) dollars. On the other hand, the chains enjoyed real growth in sales per store until the early 1990s when price competition (and other factors discussed above) cut into chain store volume.

Retail Management Considerations

For the most part, record-store managers face the same problems as other retailers. However, there are some considerations particular to the recording industry that are worth mentioning because they create specific headaches for record retailers. Most of these would fall under the general heading of inventory management; including problem areas such as multiple configurations, packaging, shrinkage, and breadth of inventory.

Multiple Configurations

Multiple configurations have been a fact of life in record retail since the days of cylinders and discs. Later it was 78s, 45s, and LPs, with the latter being available in 10-inch and 12-inch formats. Often the same selection or album was available in multiple formats. Next it was 45s, LPs, and 8-tracks. There is wide speculation in the industry that one reason retailers were quick to delete 8-tracks from inventory in favor of the cassette was that they simply did not want to have to carry the same album in three formats. By the mid-1990s, most retailers found themselves carrying the same albums and singles in Compact Disc and cassette form. Retailers proved to be as lukewarm as consumers were to the mini-disc and Digital Compact Cassette (DCC) tapes of the early 1990s. Many retailers began to drop cassette inventories entirely in the twenty-first century as cassette sales dropped below 20 percent of the market in 2002. But as DVD became a hot product in 2002 and 2003, many more record stores contemplated dropping audiocassettes and carrying inventories of DVD movies as well as CD audio. In the first half of 2003, DVD shipments rose by more than 50 percent over the previous year, and reached a level of nearly half that of CD shipments for the same period. In addition, nearly half of all U.S. homes had DVD players.[75]

Packaging

Packaging is important to retailers for four reasons:

1. Packaging determines the size of the recording and therefore the amount of space that a unit takes up. The more space taken up by a package, the fewer units the retailer can fit into the store, and the smaller the inventory that can be carried.

2. Changes in packaging affect the way the store fixtures that hold the products have to be built. Often a change in packaging that affects the size of the product will result in an expensive re-fixturing of part of the store. For example, CDs were originally sold in large (12" x 6") cardboard packaging, requiring special racks to hold them. When retailers complained about the amount of space required to show CDs, the labels responded by eliminating the elaborate packaging—saving overall production costs as well.

3. Smaller packages such as cassettes and Compact Discs are less likely to make effective display items. The 12" x 12" LP cover was an effective package that could convey lots of information and make a visual impact because of its size. In fact, manufacturers often supplied retailers with blank album jackets or cardboard *flats* (which had only the album cover on one side) to use in creating store displays. With CDs, cassettes, and DVDs, the point-of-purchase display material provided by the labels must be a different size and shape from the product package. This makes it more difficult for the customer to link the display to the item.

4. CDs, cassettes, and DVDs without larger packaging are more easily shoplifted unless tagged with electronic inventory control devices.

Shrinkage

Among all retailers, audio and video stores have the third highest rate of shrinkage (merchandise that was supposedly purchased by the retailer, but that disappears from inventory), accounting for 2.73 percent of total sales. Shoplifting accounts for 45 percent of music and video shrinkage, while employee theft accounts for 40 percent, administrative and bookkeeping errors for 13 percent, and vendor fraud for 2 percent. That is why over 80 percent of music retailers use some form of inventory tagging theft-prevention system, and why they lobbied the manufacturers to tag items at the pressing plant.[76]

Breadth of Inventory

The 1990s development of the megastore that carries a large inventory of recordings, plus home video products, paper and audio books, and computer software and CD-ROM titles, forced record retailers to diversify their inventories. As the number of computer systems with CD-ROM capabilities pushed 20 million in the mid-1990s, record stores began to consider stocking CD-ROM music, education, and entertainment titles.[77] The presence of audiobooks in CD format and the presence of more audiobook labels with music-industry ties encouraged record retailers to begin carrying this line of merchandise.[78] The high-profit margins offered by sheet music and songbooks encouraged many record retailers to carry print music as well as recorded music. By 1994 music books (folios) sold for $17.00 to $25.00 with luxury editions, often containing CD-ROMs, priced as high as $60.00 and $75.00. Titles were usually not discounted and sold at a 40 to 50 percent profit margin. The lower margins on CDs made music books attractive to some retailers.[79] As mentioned above, more record stores also began handling DVDs. In deciding how much precious retail floor space to allocate to which kind of product, record retailers were becoming aware of what one audiobook executive noted: "People who buy records don't just buy records."[80]

Record Clubs

The record club is a method by which the label can sell direct, or almost direct, to the customer. As such, it is competing for consumers' record purchase dollars with other means of retail. Columbia started the first record club, Columbia House, in 1955. At that time there were not record-selling outlets everywhere and clubs represented a way to reach a customer directly, without having to sell to a middleman. Without a wholesaler between the label and the customer, the label could sell at list price and therefore at a higher profit margin. Capitol and RCA started their own clubs in 1958. By the end of 1959 clubs had nearly two million members, with Columbia at 1,300,000, RCA at 600,000, Capitol at 250,000, and Diners Club at 125,000.[81]

Columbia moved to distribute not only its own labels, but those of Warner Bros., A&M, Kapp, and Vanguard through exclusive club distribution licenses, meaning that those outside labels sold through Columbia House could not be distributed through other clubs. Former Columbia president, Clive Davis, noted: "The Record Club, in turn, was turning a nice profit and controlling something like 60 to 70 percent of the industry's mail order business."[82] The other clubs complained and the Federal Trade Commission launched an antitrust investigation in 1962. The investigation ended with Columbia agreeing not to use exclusive club licensing for outside labels. That meant that labels that did not have clubs could have their records distributed through any or all of the clubs. The record retail stores and rack jobbers also complained that the clubs were competing unfairly with dealer sales—a complaint that survived into 1996.[83] Club sales declined from nearly 15 percent of the total in the 1950s and 1960s to a low of 6.8 percent in 1988. They then proceeded to climb back up to a high of 15.1 percent in 1994 and 14.5 percent in 1995, and then dropped to less than 5 percent by 2002 (see Figure 9.1).

The price competition between retail stores, the general stagnation of sales in 1995, the decline of the chain retailers, and the frustration of the retailers and labels over the sale of used CDs sparked renewed controversy about the record clubs. By that time there were two clubs that controlled the majority of the direct sales business: Columbia House, which was jointly owned by Sony Music Entertainment (Columbia's parent) and Warner Music Group (a subsidiary of Time Warner); and BMG Music Service, owned by BMG Entertainment (RCA's parent). These two clubs shared about 64 percent of the club sales market, with Columbia House netting sales of about $615 million and BMG Music Service netting sales of about $500 million.

Both clubs ran incentive plans to entice members to join by giving them eight to as many as twelve CDs free if they agree to buy one to four at the regular club price. The clubs could do this for several reasons, all having to do with their cost of goods sold. First, manufacturing costs for CDs had fallen to about $1.00 per disc. Because the clubs actually manufacture their own copies of the discs under a license from the labels, their pressing costs are low. Second, the clubs do not pay royalties to the artists or labels on any of the "free" records. They do pay the music publishers on all product sold, but at a reduced rate of usually 75 percent of the statutory mechanical rate. When the clubs do pay the labels, it is usually a royalty of 10 to 25 percent of the suggested retail list price (SRLP). The labels then pay the artists out of what they receive from the club, usually half of the artist's royalty rate or a maximum of one-half of what the label receives from club sales.

The economics are simple. The direct cost to the club on a "free" incentive or bonus record is about $1.50 to $1.60 per disc. For a disc sold at full list, the club's direct costs are about $3.20 to $5.50 including label and mechanical royalties and manufacturing costs. Even if the club only sells one of every three discs distributed, there is a gross margin of at least

$10.50 (assuming a $15.98 list) on the sold copy, less costs of $3.20 for the free copies leaves a gross margin of $7.20 for each sold disc. A retail store has a maximum gross margin on the same disc of about $6.50 (wholesale of about $10.50 on a CD with a $15.98 SRLP) if it is sold at full list price—an occurrence that is not very common. If the retailer is trying to move the discs at a more common sale price of $11.99 or $12.99, the margin is reduced to $1.50 to $2.50. The clubs counter that they have heavy advertising costs, estimated to be as high as $150 million per year.[84]

Partially in response to the retailers' complaints, and to their own growing feelings that the clubs actually do take away more profitable sales at retail stores and rack locations, several labels (Disney, Virgin, MCA and Geffen) abandoned the clubs in 1995 and 1996. The clubs' parent labels often contend that the club sales are "extra," reaching people who would not otherwise buy records. However a 1995 NARM survey revealed that 72 percent of club members are heavy buyers—the same kind of people who frequent record stores. To make matters worse, another NARM survey found that club product accounted for about 11 percent of used CD sales, thus competing twice with the retail store—once as a club purchase and again as a used CD.[85]

By 2003 the club business had more competition from Internet sales from other sources such as CD Now and Amazon.com. Internet sales had risen to about 3.4 percent, almost equal to the clubs' 4-percent share for that same year. Unauthorized downloads hurt the clubs as well as the labels. Finally, in 2003, Sony Music Entertainment and Warner Music Group sold 85 percent of their interest in Columbia House to the Blackstone Group, an investment-banking firm.[86]

Future of Record Retailing

> No one can predict with any certainty the future of the media world.
>
> —John Pavlik, New Media and the Information Superhighway[87]

In 1996 there were at least five sites on the World Wide Web offering a computer-based shopping service for recordings. Most offered large catalogs, and catalog search by title, artist, or genre. Some even offered samples of the albums, artist biographies, and reviews.[88] In these instances, the "place" utility of the merchandiser becomes the computer user's home or office; that is a convenience that is hard to beat. However, early response to these sites was small. NARM reported that in 1995 only 1 percent of their Sound-Data panel had actually purchased recordings online.[89] By 2003 less than 4 percent of sales of hard copies was via the Internet. Unauthorized downloads of singles and entire albums had become a major problem for the industry even as it began to develop the means for a legitimate download market, albeit at a very slow pace. For a detailed discussion see Chapter 11.

TABLE 9.10 Record Store Hierarchy

Store Size	Size in Square Feet	Average Number of Employees	Average SKUs	Average Annual Sales ($)
Small	1,000–2,499	5.4	33,200	752,000
Medium	2,500–5,999	6.8	50,500	1.2 million
Large	6,000–11,999	11.1	78,500	1.96 million
Superstore	12,000–20,000	19.4	122,900	3.2 million
Megastore	over 20,000	36.6	281,500	6 million

Source: NARM data reported in "NARM Survey: Average Record Store Sale Dropped Almost $5 over Last Three Years," *Billboard*, 20 July 1996. 44.

The End of Record Stores?

The labels, record clubs, and Web services could all sell hard copies directly to the consumer, bypassing the retail store. They could even utilize digital delivery of the recording to the purchaser's computer or recorder. These methods of retailing recordings will probably develop parallel to the in-place retail system, just as the rack jobber and record club did earlier. As CD burners become standard on computers and consumers obtain more sophisticated printing capabilities to reproduce album artwork and inserts, it seems likely that the desire to own an object that contains the recording will increase download sales, piracy, or both.

One of the redeeming features of the cassette was its portability. Now consumers take their music everywhere and take portability of their music for granted. The CD has become just as portable as the cassette and almost as easy to reproduce. In 1995 audio hardware manufacturers began looking to a huge nearly untapped market for CD playback units in autos; by 2003 they were the standard in most models. The Compact Disc is still the format preferred by consumers. The questions are, who will manufacture the CD: the consumer or the label? Who will sell the CDs manufactured by the labels: record stores, mass merchants, big box electronics stores, Web sites, or clubs?

Conclusion

By 1995 record stores had evolved into a five-tiered structure based on size: small, medium, large, superstore, and megastore (see Table 9.10). By 2003 it was apparent that there would be fewer record stores of all sizes in the immediate future. There were simply too many alternative sources of recordings with price points everywhere from free for unauthorized downloads, to loss leader at the mass-merchants and big-box stores, to full SRLP at some retailers. There will continue to be independent record stores (usually small and medium sized) that cater to special niches in terms of location, inventory, and ambiance. The independent stores survived the onslaught of the mass merchants in the 1960s and 1970s, and the chains in the 1980s and 1990s. They can survive the onslaught of the e-tailers and big boxes as well.

10

The Recording Industry and Other Media

As mentioned in Chapter 1, the recording industry has become a major media player not only because of its own size, but also because it has a significant impact on and in other media. Most importantly, popular recordings are the dominant programming content of radio. Broadcasters rely on the popularity of recordings to attract a listening audience. The presence of that audience in turn helps the broadcaster sell advertising time to clients who want their message to reach those listeners. Recordings are also an important part of television programming with the presence of music video channels on cable and satellite, and the inclusion of significant amounts of popular music and recordings as background music in popular television programs. Those programmers and program creators rely on the popularity of recordings and music to attract television, cable, and satellite viewers in order to sell advertising or to sell access to the programs. Similar uses of popular recordings and music in film attract moviegoing audiences and help sell soundtrack and other recordings. Although not as significant as in the electronic media, the recording industry also has an important impact in the print media, especially magazines, with significant consumer and trade publications devoting either the entire publication or substantial content to popular recording artists, audio and recording, and the music business. This chapter details those relationships and their positive, and sometimes negative, effects on those media. The stormy relationship of the recording industry and the Internet is discussed at length in Chapter 11.

Recordings in Radio

Overview: A Love–Hate Relationship

It is no secret that radio stations and record companies do not sell the same thing. Get any label promotion people and radio programmers in the same room and the programmers will quickly remind the promotion people that radio programming is created to sell advertising, not records. None of the top twenty-five advertisers on radio (or even their conglomerate owners) are record labels; they are retail, business and consumer services, and automobiles and auto accessories. These advertisers account for one-third of radio advertising billings.[1] On the other hand, recorded music is the primary content of 70 to 80 percent of all radio stations (see Table 10.1); those stations rely mainly on the music they play to attract and hold listeners.

From the label perspective, radio airplay still accounts for a significant percentage of the exposure of record buyers to new music. 1995 market research revealed that 44 percent of music consumers made their last album purchase because of the influence of radio or television airplay of a record.[2] In the 1970s, radio had a stranglehold on the influence of record purchases. At the 1975 NARM Convention, Warner Brothers vice-president, Stan Cornyn, lamented the dependency of the recording industry on radio airplay with a speech, "The Day Radio Died." Said Cornyn, "There is more to promotion than disc jockeys. For promotion men, radio should not be the only game in town. Records should be."[3] A 1977 Warner Communications survey noted, "[T]he 43 percent of the total population who listen to music [on the radio] for at least 10 hours per week comprise 54 percent of all buyers and account for 62 percent of the total dollar market."[4] In 1979, CBS records reported to the NARM convention that 80 percent of singles buyers learned about the records they purchased from

TABLE 10.1 Growth of Radio Music Formats*

	1986	1995	2001
Stations with music formats+	9,055	11,101	11,970
Stations with nonmusic formats	2,681	4,709	6,455
Number of different music formats	12	23	38
Total station formats	11,736	15,810	18,425

*Only clearly music formats are counted. Thus, foreign language, ethnic, and Indian are not counted as music even though they may contain significant portions of music. The number of formats exceeds the number of stations because a station using a given format for a significant part of the day could report more than one format.

+ Music formats identified include Adult Contemporary, Country, Oldies, Christian, Gospel, Rock/AOR, Contemporary Hit/Top 40, Classic Rock, Classical, Jazz, Urban Contemporary, MOR, Alternative, Progressive, Big Band, Nostalgia, Black, Blues, Beautiful Music, Album-oriented Rock, Triple A, Easy Listening, Top-430, Light Rock, New Age, Tejano, Golden Oldies, Bluegrass, Folk, Soul, Polka, and Reggae.

Source: *Broadcasting and Cable Yearbook*, 1986, 1995, and 2001.

radio.[5] Researcher Paul Hirsch concluded that radio programmers were gatekeepers who preselected the music that listeners and potential buyers would hear.[6]

The Historical Context: 1920s through 1955

From the days of the first commercial radio broadcast in 1922, popular music began to have an impact on radio programming. By playing popular music, the stations and networks could attract listeners that the advertisers wanted to reach. Most of the programs were not locally produced but were supplied by the networks with which the local stations were affiliated. The programs were produced largely by either the advertising agency, the network (for the sponsor), or by the sponsor itself. Programs with musical content were the most popular. A 1929 survey of the ten most popular programs listed only two nonmusical or musical/variety programs, the comedy series *Amos 'n' Andy* and the dramatic series *True Story*, at numbers four and five, respectively.[7] The musical shows usually had live orchestras with guest and regular performers. These programs, together with classical music programs, amateur hours, and a small segment of popular singles programs (with only a 0.7 percent average rating), accounted for just over a 50-percent share of the nighttime radio audience in the late 1930s. The dramatic difference between nighttime and daytime programming is illustrated by the fact that during the daytime, adult serial drama, talk shows, and juvenile shows accounted for over 82 percent of listenership share.[8] Daytime radio programming in those days was strikingly similar to daytime television programming today.

During the Depression it became more of a common practice for local radio stations to fill their non-network time by playing recordings, especially when the quality of the recordings became better with the continued development of electrical recording. While the music publishers did not particularly care in what form a song was played (live or recorded), the record companies and the orchestras who recorded for them at first took a dim view of airplay of records. They attempted to stop radio stations from playing records by marking the labels "Not Licensed for Radio Broadcast" or "Licensed Only for Non-Commercial Use on Phonographs in Homes. Mfr. & Original Purchaser Have Agreed This Record Shall Not be Resold or Used for Any Other Purpose." Those attempts ended in a 1940 Federal Appeals Court case in New York.[9] Orchestra leader Paul Whiteman had complained of a radio station (W.B.O. Broadcasting) playing records of his musical performances. Whiteman's label, RCA, joined the suit against the radio station and Whiteman, saying that Whiteman had no interest left in the recordings that had not been contracted away to RCA. The court held that having fixed the recording of Whiteman's performance on records and distributed them to the public, neither the label nor Whiteman could complain if radio stations or others then performed the recordings for the public. At that time there were no statutory rights protecting sound recordings (see Chapter 3). Judge Learned Hand commented, "If the talents of conductors of orchestras are denied that compensation which is necessary to evoke their efforts because they get too little for phonographic records, we have no means of knowing it."[10]

With the legal path cleared to play more recordings, the radio stations of the early 1940s began to do so. The first disc jockeys were born. One of them, Martin Block, who aired a program called *Martin Block's Make Believe Ballroom*, realized the future importance of radio to the recording industry. Speaking of radio airplay in 1942 Block said, "If the platter is a good one, the most effective type of direct marketing has just taken place. And sales are sure to reflect the airing of the disk."[11] But it was not until the mid-1950s, when television threatened the death of radio, that records became the mainstay of radio programming. The dramatic, comedy, and variety shows that had been the bulwark of radio programming since the early days of the networks could not compete with the visual impact of the same kind of programs aired on television. Radio stations were going off the air and advertising revenues plunged. In 1955 *Billboard* reported that playing records was the clear trend for radio programming, noting that records comprised 53 percent of the programming of stations with power of less than 5,000 watts, and 42 percent of stations with greater than 5,000 watts power.[12] Even so, popular music was not the primary programming of those stations that did play music. Only 12 percent of the stations that did program popular music played it for 75 hours per week (half of the available air time). Twenty-three percent played classical music at least 10 hours per week and 16 percent played country music at least 20 hours per week.[13]

Radio Turns to Records

Three other events of the mid-1950s combined with the threat of television to transform radio into a predominantly music medium. The introduction of the 45-rpm single in 1949 by RCA Victor brought an easily handled, nearly unbreakable, inexpensive, high-fidelity recording into the market place. The 45 took less space than the 78 or the LP (introduced by Columbia the year before). The vinyl material was lightweight, especially in the seven-inch format chosen for the 45, compared to the ten- or twelve-inch format for the older 78s. Because the 45 used the same recorded material as the LP but ran at a nearly 50 percent greater speed, it had potentially higher fidelity than the LP. Finally, the 45 was less expensive to purchase than the LP and 45 players were less expensive, factors that would prove attractive to the teen market. Radio initially objected to the 45 single. Some stations were reluctant to switch to the 45-rpm format because they had built up libraries of 78 RPM ETs (electrical transcriptions), which included complete programs that they could easily slot into their schedules. The practice of sending radio stations transcriptions of programs had developed as a way to distribute high-quality recordings of programs and music to stations. Most stations paid for the ETs as part of a subscription service from the labels. Most complaints about the 45s died out when the labels began supplying the new 45s free of charge to all but the smallest stations.

Disc jockey Todd Storz was responsible for the second breakthrough that made radio broadcasters and record companies reluctant partners. In 1955 he introduced the Top 40 format on station WTIX in New Orleans.[14] The concept of Top 40 was more than just playing the 40 most popular records; that had been done for some time. What Storz noticed, allegedly at a bar one night as he observed customers playing a couple of songs over and over, was that listeners wanted to hear certain songs more often than others. He devised a closed play list with a limited number of selections and a rotation that played the most popular songs more often. Now virtually all commercial radio stations with a music format apply this formula in one way or another. Many stations have several rotations. How often a record gets played depends upon several factors, including such things as the current strength of the recording, whether it is waxing or waning in popularity, or whether it is a recent hit (a *recurrent*) or a hit from several years past. The result was a sound that attracted listeners and therefore advertisers. *Billboard* noted, "It was Storz who saved radio from death."[15]

Rock 'n' roll was the other "savior" of radio. From 1951 to 1955 sales of recorded music grew a modest 19 percent to about $230 million as reported by the RIAA. The 1956 through 1959 sales figures indicated a growth of more than 125 percent to almost $515 million—largely the result of rock. Rock also delivered a new radio audience that had not been listening to the predominantly middle-of-the-road formats of the early 1950s. It was an audience that had more money to spend and more leisure time than the youth audience had ever had before. Advertisers were attracted to the potential market that could be reached through rock radio and bought air time; rock radio prospered. By attracting listeners who were not part of the mainstream radio audience, the rock stations were able to succeed quickly in markets where it would have taken years to develop a sizable listenership by eating away at the audiences of several other stations. The existence of the rock format stations created a demand for more music to program. As more music was programmed, more was exposed to potential buyers who then made purchases that benefited the labels.

The availability of records made it possible to produce inexpensive programming and to sell advertising at the local level. Radio advertising revenues increased over 800 percent from 1940 to 1970 from about $157 million to about $1,257 million. During that same time period, the share of advertising revenues produced from local billings (as opposed to national or regional networks, or other national accounts) increased from a mere 28 percent in 1940 to 68 percent in 1970. It was no longer necessary to rely on a network that could afford to hire an orchestra and popular entertainers; those orchestras and entertainers were available on disc to perform at the spin of a platter. As a result the share of revenues from network billings dropped from 47 percent in 1940 to 4 percent in 1977.[16]

Diversity in Radio Brings Diversity in Music

Table 10.2 illustrates the rapid growth and proliferation of radio stations from a mere 30 in 1922 when the first National Radio Conference began licensing stations to more than 13,000 stations in 2001. In the 40 years between 1955 and 1995, the number of broadcast radio stations increased by 256 percent.

By 1995 radio reached 99 percent of U.S. homes. But not all of the people in the 98 million homes were listening to the same thing. The proliferation of stations brought with it a proliferation of formats. The more stations that existed in a radio market, the more they found that they had to have some way to divide the audience pie, and perhaps attract listeners who were not tuned in to the other stations. The stations began to divide the audience pie into smaller shares and look for programming niches. One way to achieve this was by playing different music from the competitors. The demand for different music led to airplay of a wider variety of music. The radio market has not become homogeneous as some had predicted in the early days of Top 40. In fact, the overall trend for a significant number of years has been to increase heterogeneity in music available to radio listeners. Even in the decade and a half from 1986 to 2001, the number of radio stations reporting predominantly music formats grew by nearly 3,000, and the number of different music formats reported tripled (see Table 10.1).

The trend toward increasing format diversity in radio is being driven in part by the increasing concentration of ownership in broadcast stations. In the early days of radio the Federal Communications Commission (FCC)

TABLE 10.2 Growth of Licensed Radio Stations in the United States

Year	AM Stations	FM Stations*	Total Stations
1922	30**	—	30
1935	585	—	585
1955	2,669	552	3,221
1975	4,432	3,353	7,785
1995	4,945	6,613	11,558
2001	4,864	8,575	13,439

*The first FM permits were granted in 1940.

**Numbers are of licensed, on-air stations (except in 1922 when stations were not licensed), not including those under construction.

Source: *Broadcasting and Cable Yearbook*, 1995: B653, B655; *Broadcasting and Cable Yearbook*, 2001: B639.

adopted the *duopoly* rule. The essence of the regulation was that the FCC would not grant a license to an applicant who already owned or controlled another broadcast outlet in the same area so that the two stations would have overlapping service areas. In the early days of FM radio, the FCC allowed ownership of AM-FM combinations on the theory that they were not competing services.[17] During the first half of the 1960s, many AM-FM combination stations had simply duplicated the AM programming on the FM station. But in 1966 the FCC ruled that jointly owned AM and FM stations had to provide separate programming. FM owners discovered progressive rock and music formats that reached audiences beyond the Top 40 and MOR programming common on the AM dial at that time.[18]

By the 1970s FM had become a significant competitor. The reasons were the development of stereo recordings, FM stereo broadcasting, and the widespread use of stereo receivers in homes and automobiles. The FCC first authorized FM *stereo* broadcasts in 1961. At that time the number of AM stations on the air (3,539) exceeded the number of FM stations (815) by more than a four-to-one margin. By 1971 that margin had shrunk to less than two-to-one as the number of FM stations increased to over 2,600 in ten years. By 1983 the number of *authorized* FM stations surpassed the number of *authorized* AM stations for the first time, and in 1985 the number of *on-the-air* FM stations surpassed the number of *on-the-air* AM stations with 4,888 and 4,754, respectively. (A station being developed would have a license and be authorized, but not yet on the air, as would a station that had "gone dark," but whose license still existed.) By 2001 the number of FM stations on the air exceeded the number of AM stations by over 35 percent (8,575 FM and 4,864 AM).[19] Although the FCC authorized stereo AM in 1982 and adopted a standard broadcasting system in 1993, it never caught on. Music programming in stereo had become the dominant content of FM radio. Although there was still significant music content on AM, by 1995 news, news/talk, talk, religious, and sports accounted for more than 35 percent of AM formats, and continued to increase; that same programming accounted for only about 16 percent of FM formats.[20] For all stations, by 2001, those formats reached a total audience share of nearly 17 percent.[21]

Less Diversity in Ownership and More Diversity in Programming?

Throughout the 1980s and 1990s, the FCC relaxed its rules regarding the number of broadcast outlets in a single market that could be owned by one entity, as well as the total number of broadcast outlets that could be owned by one entity nationwide. In 1988 the Commission began to allow greater overlap between commonly owned AM and FM stations. In 1992 the Commission changed its rules to allow the same owner to operate up to four stations in markets with more than fifteen stations and up to three stations in smaller markets, as long as they controlled less than half of the

TABLE 10.3 1996 Communications Act Radio Ownership Limits

Number of Radio Stations in Market	Maximum Total Stations Allowed to One Owner	AM/FM Limits
45 or more	8	5/5
30–44	7	4/4
15–29	6	4/4
14 or less	5	3/3

Source: *Communications Act of 1996*, Section 202(b)(1)(D). Pub. L. 104–104, 104th Cong.; 2nd Sess. Feb. 8, 1996.

stations in that market. Congress further relaxed the rules with passage of the Communications Act of 1996 (see Table 10.3), with a limit that no single party can own more than half of the stations in a given market. At the same time the national ownership restrictions were also being relaxed. Since 1953 the FCC rule had been total ownership limits of 7 AM, 7 FM, and 7 TV stations (the 7-7-7 rule). Beginning in 1984, the limits were expanded, first to 12-12-12, then in 1988 radio ownership limits moved to 18-18, and 20-20 in 1990.[22] Finally, the Communications Act of 1996 removed all limits on the total number of stations that could be owned by a single entity nationwide.

The relaxation of the ownership limits had a predictable effect. In the early 1990s the sale of radio station licenses reached a fever pitch. The reason was the consolidation of ownership into larger and larger chains. Growth-oriented broadcasting owners purchased everything from single stations to entire chains.[23] The removal of all limits by the Communications Act of 1996 led to megamergers. Westinghouse Electric purchased CBS, Inc. and Infinity Broadcasting, creating a chain of 83 stations. The Infinity deal cost Westinghouse $3.9 billion but raised its market shares in a number of major markets, including San Francisco (19 percent) and Philadelphia (44 percent).[24] In the first half of 1996, mergers totaled more than $5.2 billion.[25] By 2001 the number of different owners of radio stations had decreased from 5,100 in 1996 to 3,800, a 25-percent drop. In 1996 the average Arbitron metro market had 13.5 owners; by 2001 that had dropped 22 percent to 10.3 owners.[26] The rapid consolidation prompted the FCC to adopt a rule to look very closely at mergers where a single entity would control 50 percent, or where two entities could control 70 percent or more, of the advertising revenue in a single market. The Commission noted that "[I]t had an independent obligation to consider whether a proposed pattern of radio ownership that complies with the local ownership limits would otherwise have an adverse competitive effect in a particular local radio market, such that it would be inconsistent with the public interest."[27]

The trading, merging, and consolidating fever continued into the next century. By the end of 2002 the largest radio chain, Clear Channel Communications, owned 1,238 radio stations that generated $3.3 billion in revenue. That amounts to 10.8 percent of the commercial stations nationwide

TABLE 10.4 Radio Station Chain Ownership: Top Five Chains

Chain	Number of Radio Stations Owned	Annual Radio Revenue ($)
Clear Channel	1,238	3.2 billion
Infinity (Viacom)	183	2.1 billion
Cox Radio	79	431 million
Entercomm Communications	103	408 million
ABC Radio (Disney)	65	404 million

Source: *Broadcasting and Cable*, 9 September 2002, 32.

and 20.4 percent of the total radio revenue. As Table 10.4 indicates, what was a large chain of 80 or more stations in 1996 would barely make the top five in 2002 (compare to Table 10.3). Consolidation had reached the point where the top twenty-five chains controlled over 25 percent of all commercial radio stations and over 59 percent of all radio revenue.[28] Although not an oligopoly by the definition used in this book, the radio industry may be approaching such a state.

Radio executives predicted that the dual trends of format diversity and ownership concentration will continue. "As the market contracts in the number of owners there will be greater program diversity," said Randy Michaels of Jaycor Broadcasting. Another executive predicted that there would be a consolidation down to about fifteen large radio groups over a short period of time.[29] Those predictions are in contradiction to a study, completed before the 1996 Communications Act, which suggested that increasing the total number of stations in a market would have a small effect on the number of available formats for listeners, finding a 10 percent increase in the number of stations would lead to less than a 2-percent increase in the number of formats. The study concluded, "[R]elaxing ownership rules will generate only small program diversity benefits if only modest increases in either the number of stations or in the incentives to offer different formats or higher quality programming result."[30]

A counterargument was offered by the broadcasters. They contend that as more stations per market are owned by the same entity, that entity will choose not to compete with itself, but rather to be able to deliver to advertisers a larger share of the total market. Theoretical models of mass media, and broadcasting in particular, suggest that advertiser-supported media firms cater to delivering as large an audience as possible. That can be accomplished by programming different stations with noncompeting formats. The noncompeting formats can get a larger total share of the audience by appealing to a larger and more diverse group of listeners. The broadcasting owner can then sell a package deal to advertisers who will buy because they can reach a larger share of the total audience.

In 2002 the Future of Music Coalition (FMC) announced the results of a study that found that format diversity did not necessarily lead to diversity of music being programmed. The FMC study found considerable overlap in the playlists in various formats (76 percent in some instances), and found over five hundred instances in which a company that owned competing stations in the same market programmed the same format and *did* directly compete with themselves.[31] In 2003, the U.S. Senate held hearings on the state of radio consolidation, during which a variety of parties expressed concern that consolidation had led to a lack of local programming, a decrease in the number of gatekeepers, and overall loss to consumers.[32]

The View from the Charts

The growth in the number of music popularity charts in trade publications such as *Billboard* and *Radio and Records* (*R&R*) is another indicator of format proliferation and increased diversity. Table 10.5 indicates that each increased the number of radio airplay charts by over 100 percent from 1986 to 2003. Although there is a 50 percent overlap of artists and cuts on the various new rock formats, they still manage enough diversity to compete on an overall station sound and attract different audiences.[33] *Billboard* reported in 1996 that such niche formatting stations are "winning [the] battle against homogenization" in England.[34]

An increase in available information has contributed to the ability of local radio programmers to more accurately target their particular audiences in their own markets. Until the 1970s, the trade popularity charts tended to report only aggregate totals on popularity nationwide. In 1974 *R&R* began publication with a splash when it introduced a section reporting the actual playlists of the reporting stations. The radio programmers no longer had to rely on calling their friends at other stations in other cities or on possibly hyped reports from record company promotion persons to find out what was popular around the country. Beginning in 1994, local stations no longer had to rely on sales information provided through contacts at local record stores or the record company promotion personnel. SoundScan, the company that gathers point-of-sale bar code scanning information from thousands of record retail locations, made its reports available to ABC radio networks configured to show local sales.[35] BDS (Broadcast Data Service) began reporting actual counts of times recordings were played, by station, by market. (For a further discussion of the impact of actual airplay reports and piece-count sales reports on the labels' marketing plans, and for a discussion of the development of BDS and SoundScan, see Chapter 8.)

In 1995, *R&R* began doing call-out research on a regional basis, reporting to the stations what particular songs the public wanted to hear more of (favorability), what ones they had heard (familiarity), and what ones they were tired of hearing (burnout). While many stations do their own call-out research, the *R&R* research reached more listeners and gave a better picture of patterns so that a radio programmer could know how long it

TABLE 10.5 Radio Popularity Charts 1986–2003

Radio & Records, 1986	*Radio & Records,* 1996	*Radio & Records,* 2003
CHR	CHR/Pop	Spanish Contemporary
AOR Albums	Pop/Alternative	Regional Mexican
AOR Tracks	CHR/Rhythmic	Tropical
AC	Hip-Hop	Christian AC
Country	Urban	Christian Inspirational
Black/Urban	Urban AC	Christian Rock
	Country	Christian CHR
	AC	AC
	NAC Tracks	Hot AC
	NAC Albums	Alternative
	Active Rock	CHR/Pop
	Rock	CHR/Rhythmic
	Alternative	Country
	Adult Alternative	Rock
	Adult Alt. Album	Active Rock
		Triple A
		Urban
		Urban AC

Billboard, 1986	*Billboard,* 1996	*Billboard,* 2003
Album Rock Tracks	R and B Airplay	Hot 100
Adult Contemporary	Country Singles and Tracks	Country
Black Singles	Latin Tracks	Modern Rock
Black Singles Airplay	Mainstream Rock Tracks	Latin Tracks
Country Singles	Modern Rock Tracks	Adult Contemporary Tracks
Hot 100	Adult Contemporary	Christian A/C
Hot 100 Airplay	Adult Top 40	R&B/Hip Hop
	Hot 100 Airplay	Rap
		Mainstream Rock
		Hot Dance/Club
		Top 40
		Christian Singles
		Country Album
		Electronic Album
		Top Catalog Album
		Top Latin Album
		R & B/Hip Hop Album
		Heatseekers Album
		Indie Album

Source: Billboard, 7 June 1986; 8 June 1996; 8 August 2003.

would take the listeners to "burn out" on a particular record. This was particularly important information to stations in the CHR (Contemporary Hit Radio, the successor to Top 40) format because they tended to play fewer records for their listeners than many other formats. *R&R* compared the advantages of its call-out research to retail sales reports saying, "Less than 25 percent of young adults (CHR's target listeners) will visit a retail sales outlet in a given seven-day period." Listener requests are problematic because, "Less than 10 percent of a station's listeners will call a request line within a given year." Finally, radio airplay reports from other stations were useful, but tended to focus the programmer's attention inward and could be manipulated (presumably by record company promotion people).[36] To further combat that, *R&R* added actual BDS spin counts of recordings on reporting stations for the various charts. From a radio programming perspective it is important to know which recordings the listeners most want to hear, which are not necessarily the same recordings that are the bestsellers. In fact, it is possible to have a record that receives lots of airplay but does not sell well—what record promotion people call a turntable hit.

Radio Music Listenership

The music preference of radio listeners changed dramatically in the last half of the twentieth century. Several points need to be made about Figure 10.1. Some form of rock continues to be the most listened-to music on the radio. Country music's dramatic increase in popularity slipped back to even lower than previous levels by 2000. The "adult contemporary" of 2000 sounded more like rock than did its predecessor pop/adult in 1979. Finally, beautiful music, a format whose music accounted for virtually no sales of recordings, has all but disappeared. By 2000, news and talk formats had eroded the music share of the radio audience. Spanish-language stations, which feature predominantly Spanish-language music content, had mushroomed in

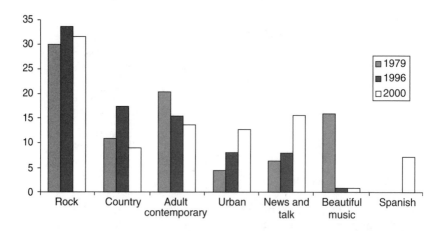

Fig. 10.1 Radio Audience Share by Format. *R&R Ratings Report* 1979 and 1996. "Rock, R&B, Country See New Life," *Billboard*, 2 September 2000, 87. Some editorial liberties had to be taken to equate 1979 format terminology with 1996 and 2000 format terminology. Rock includes Rock and Album-Oriented Rock in 1979; it includes Oldies/Classic Rock, Contemporary Hit Radio (CHR), Rock, and Alternative in 1996; it includes Top 40, AOR, Classic Rock, Modern Rock, and Oldies in 2000. Pop Adult in 1979 is equated to Adult Contemporary in 1996. Urban was called Black in 1979, and R&B in 2000.

number. As rap and dance-oriented music continued to grow in popularity, the format strength of the various musical styles began to level off. Even rock lost some audience share.

One might think that the record labels would be pleased with radio, but they are not. The fundamental problem is that the radio stations, using the Top 40 style format invented by Todd Storz, limit their playlists and only add about three to five new records per week to replace those that have dropped out of the rotation. Much to the frustration of the label promotion people, it is the radio station programmers and their consultants who choose which new records will be added each week. Even with the greater diversity of formats in the rock genre, there are still tight playlists.[37] Country formats were very homogenous until the mid-1990s, but even then were slow to move beyond a split between modern and traditional country. Programmers complained to the labels that the product they were given to play all sounded the same. The labels retorted that whenever they tried to get the stations to play something different, the stations complained that it was too different.[38]

Radio continues to be a significant source of exposure to recordings and an important marketing tool for the labels. But other significant promotion and marketing tools have emerged, especially television.

Music and Recordings in Television

Before Music Video

The first public broadcast of a television program was in 1936, but World War II stymied the development of stations, receiving sets, and production facilities. Only ten commercial stations were on the air by 1942 and only six of those made it through the war years. Television really took off during the 1950s. In 1950 there were only 5.9 million TV homes, compared with over 42 million radio homes. By 1960 the market penetration of television had almost equaled that of radio with 45.2 million homes compared to radio's 49.5 million.[39]

Until the mid-1950s, the popular music that was on television was primarily on variety shows like the Ed Sullivan and Milton Berle programs. The few music-specialty programs usually featured regular performers performing the hits of the day. *Your Hit Parade* was the most successful of these; it was patterned on the radio program of the same name and ran throughout the 1950s. It ultimately became the victim of rock and roll, when the middle-of-the-road vocalists could not adequately perform the new material. For the recording industry, the biggest music show of the 1950s was Dick Clark's *American Bandstand*. The show consisted of teen audience members dancing to the hits (and some that were not yet hits but whose labels had paid to get their recordings on the program) and a guest artist or two who lip-synched the vocals to their records. The success of Clark's show at selling records was legendary. Frankie Avalon attributed sales of nearly 1.5 million copies of "Venus" to exposure on *American Bandstand*. The sad truth was that most of the songs Clark played were not even on the *Billboard* charts at the time. He played them because he had some financial interest in the record company, publishing, or artist.[40]

Television programs had occasionally produced hit singles, usually their theme songs. The success of the themes from *Peter Gunn* (1955), *Dr. Kildare* (1962), *Charlie's Angels* (1977), *Hill Street Blues* (1981), and *Miami Vice* (1985) proved that popular television programs could generate hit recordings.[41]

By the 1980s the variety shows that had helped the music industry during the earlier decades were a dying breed. It was up to music video to show the labels how television again could be used to sell anybody's records, not just those of an artist who was a regular in the show or who had recorded the theme song for the show.

Music Television

The forerunners of the *concept music videos*, where the primary focus of the audience attention is not an artist performing the song but rather on other images or some story line, were contained in the TV show, *The Monkees*, in the late 1960s. Other 1960s music shows were generally limited to lip-synched performances by the artist in front of some kind of live audience. *Billboard* speculates that the music video had its main origin in the United States with label promotional films that were shot for annual sales meetings: "When the acts weren't available, the film crews would shoot extraneous footage they felt complemented the tune. Conceptual or atmospheric shots would often be intercut with the performance clips."[42]

In the middle and late 1970s the labels began to produce more and more music videos to use for promotion. They were distributed at little or no cost to any TV station that would program them. They mainly aired late at night on local television stations that were grateful to be able to get the free programming, and in dance clubs and restaurants. In 1981 Warner Cable started the "Pop Clips" program, the same year that Music Television (MTV) launched. MTV's historic first clip was the Buggles's "Video Killed the Radio Star." It took two years for MTV to reach a large enough cable audience that it could start showing a profit. By that time, video shows were popping up everywhere. "Video friendly" artists whose appearance or material was particularly suited to turn into *short form videos* became major acts. *Long form videos*, on the other hand, were concert-length performances. They were typically shot live over a series of two or more concerts and worked for established acts by providing a relatively inexpensive source of singles videos and a program that could then be sold separately to one of the cable channels such as HBO or Showtime.

The labels, however, did not make much money directly from any of the video programming. Although there was speculation in the early 2000s that DVD sales might spur sales of music videos, the primary focus of the music videos, both short and long form, remained the sale of the recordings, not the videos.[43] For some artists, sales of recordings started immediately after MTV airplay; for others MTV did nothing. Video production budgets began to soar from less than $10,000 per clip in the late 1970s to $30,000 to $70,000 per clip by the mid-1980s. The home video market was almost nonexistent at this time because the price of home video had not come down to less than $20.00 per cassette and because home VCR penetration had not risen enough.

Some artists who had been successful prior to the video binge discovered themselves displaced by the new video acts. Others found that that their own videos did not come out well. Recording artist Joe Jackson complained that music video devalued the musician and music: "[M]any artists lose their credibility and/or self respect by coming across as bad actors rather than as good musicians. One result of this is that artists are now being signed for their video potential rather than for their musical talent."[44] The labels that had been paying video production costs as promotional/marketing costs began to ask the artists to help them bear the expense. Music publishers often had to deliver free synchronization licenses for music videos and hope to make their money through the performance royalties generated by the airplay. By 1994 it was standard in recording artist contracts that video production costs were 100-percent recoupable from artist royalties, usually from a 50/50 combination of record and video royalties.

The labels, mindful of the difficulty of guaranteeing radio airplay and the problems with payola, sought to gain some control of the MTV rotations. In 1984 they signed deals with MTV where MTV paid the labels for providing the programming (i.e., video clips) with cash and advertising time, and guaranteed a certain number of exposures of clips that the labels picked. In return, MTV was guaranteed that it had exclusive rights to air the clips for up to 30 days in most cases.[45] The labels and video networks continued to negotiate into the 1990s, with the labels wanting either some form of guarantee of exposure or a payment for the use of the videos. New Country Network in Canada entered deals with the labels to play each video a guaranteed minimum of thirty performances, with a payment of $150 to the music video copyright owner each time it was performed.[46] The College Music Video channel, which had a monthly three-hour show, paid $550 to $650 per clip and guaranteed at least twenty plays per month. Some labels took the step of getting into ownership of video channels, with Sony owning a 19-percent share of the German Viva Music TV channel[47] and PolyGram buying a 50-percent share of MTV Asia.[48]

As the video industry evolved, more cable outlets began to program different genres of music. Country videos began to appear on CMT (Country Music Television) and TNN (The Nashville Network) in 1983. VH-1, originally another Warner-Amex cable channel like MTV, began to program videos aimed at an older demographic in 1985. MTV was accused of being racist, with Michael Jackson being nearly the only minority artist whose videos appeared on the network. In response, BET (Black Entertainment Television) began programming nearly all minority artists, targeting largely an African American audience. The 1990s saw even more diversification in music video programming. Cable channels for classical music, contemporary Christian music, jazz, and even a channel for the Austin, Texas, music scene developed.[49] Although there continued to be diversity in music video programming, by 2000 there was virtually no diversity in music video channel *ownership*. By that time, the radio/film/television conglomerate Viacom owned all four major music-video channels, MTV, VH1, BET, and CMT![50]

Meanwhile, the jury was still out on the direct effects of music video watching on music sales. While anecdotal evidence supported direct relationships between music video airplay and sales of a particular recording, the overall results proved mixed. Two surveys found no correlation between the number of music videos watched and number of recordings purchased. Studies of whether seeing a music video influenced a purchase of a particular recording are inconclusive; one study reported that only 6 percent of the respondents said music videos influenced their decision, while another found a much higher 25 percent claiming videos influenced their purchasing. Differences in the survey samples and precise wording of questions may account for some of the difference. However, it is clear that music video is still not as important as radio airplay overall in influencing the purchase of recordings. Forty percent of the respondents in those same surveys reported that radio airplay was "most always" or "frequently" the influence for a recording purchase.[51]

The development of the music video had an important related effect on the way music was used in television programs. In music video the recordings of the artist are often performed while visual images that are unrelated to the actual performance (and may not even feature the artist) appear on the screen. The images may be inspired by the song or may relate a story that the video director imagines the song could support. The success of music videos suggested that recordings by popular artists could serve as a soundtrack for a wide variety of scenes. The recordings were the sole or featured audio while some other sequence was happening on the screen. The mid-1980s series *Miami Vice* was one of the early programs to make extensive use of "music videos" woven into the plot. They proved to be an effective way of gaining attention from a younger audience and of promoting recordings. By the mid-1990s such uses were quite common in popular dramatic and comedy series. The labels had found another medium for reaching their potential audience. Although none of the major recording industry conglomerates own actual television stations in the United States, they all produce programming for television, film, or cable, and the tie-ins are natural.

Selling Music Video

During the 1990s music video sell-through at the retail level began to rise. List prices of music video titles dropped mainly into the $14.95 and $19.95 slots, making them competitive with CDs as a music purchase. That same period saw the rise of more home theater stereo VCRs and DVDs, stereo TV receivers, and speaker systems with TV that could reproduce high-quality sound. The RIAA sales data in Table 10.6 reflect the changes in the music video market through the 1990s. Sales more than doubled, but the dollar value of the sales only increased about 86 percent, reflecting the trend toward lower list prices. Not only did overall music video sales improve, but the top selling videos had stronger sales. The best selling music video charts in *Billboard* began to contain an increasing number of RIAA certified gold or platinum videos. The RIAA certification levels are considerably lower for music video than they are for recordings; a gold music video has sales of 50,000 units or $1 million at the SRLP, while a platinum music video certification is for sales of 100,000 units or $2 million at SRLP. By 1996 it was not unusual for the *Billboard* Top Music Video chart to show over half of its forty videos with at least gold certifications. Because the charts are based on SoundScan data reflecting actual sales by record retailers and record rack locations, they are a good representation of the growing strength of the music-video market. When *Billboard* began using the SoundScan data in 1993, it reported a marked increase in the number of country acts on the music video chart and in their chart position. The change was attributed to the fact that rack jobber locations in places like K-Mart, Wal-Mart, and other mass merchandiser chains were reported in the sales data used to compile the video popularity charts for the first time.[52]

Keeping music video sales in perspective with the total home video market, the music video share was only about 1.7 percent of the roughly 730 million home video units sold per year in the mid-1990s.[53] By 2002 the DVD had taken over nearly 73 percent of the sales volume of music video (Table 10.6). DVD players were in nearly 50 percent of U.S. homes.[54] DVD music videos began to take on more of a long form look. Most had

TABLE 10.6 Music Video Sales 1991–2002

	1991	1993	1995	1997	1999	2002
Total Units (millions)	6.1	11.0	12.6	18.6	19.8	14.7
Dollar Value at SRLP ($ in millions)	$118.1	$213.3	$220.3	$323.9	$376.7	$288.4
DVD Video Product (millions of units)	–	–	–	–	2.5	10.7

Source: RIAA 2002 Year-end Statistics. DVD audio sales are included in music video sales totals for 1999 and 2002. www.riaa.com/news/marketingdata/pdf/year_end_2002pdf. Accessed 8 March 2004.

behind-the-scenes footage or "the making of …" footage. In 2002 retailers noticed an upsurge in music video sales; a release by rapper 50 Cent sold nearly 250,000 copies in the first week.[55]

Still, the economic realities of even a gold music video are sobering. By way of example, wholesale on a $20 music video title runs about $12 ($9 on a $15 video).[56] Of that $12, artist royalties account for about $2 (they run 10 to 20 percent of wholesale price), manufacturing costs about $2, and distribution costs about another $2. That leaves about a $6 margin for the label. Out of that come any direct marketing expenses, which are usually not high for a music video because it is the video channel exposure and recording exposure that will help sell the video. Even if the entire $6 were available, the label's gross profit would be about $300,000. Production costs for five or six short form videos, or a concert-length long form video, could easily take 50 to 100 percent of that sum. Suppose production costs come up to $200,000. If half of the production costs ($100,000) are recoupable from artist royalties, the artist will receive no royalties from this video because 50,000 units @ $2 royalty generates only $100,000. Because the video has probably sold because the album has sold, it is likely that the label will be able to recoup the other half of its production costs from the recording royalties due to the artist—leaving it with the $300,000 gross profit. The reality, however, is that most music videos will not be sold to consumers at all and the label and artist will have to eat the production costs. That, of course, is why the label wants production expenses to be recoupable.

Recordings and Film

The recording and the motion picture industries have a symbiotic relationship that dates back to the first talkie, *The Jazz Singer*, in 1927. The next year Al Jolson's use of "Sonny Boy" and "Rainbow Round My Shoulder" in his second film generated sales of over a million copies of sheet music. The motion picture companies began to acquire music-publishing interests so they could control the music in their movies, making major acquisitions and mergers through the 1930s. Until the mid-1960s the only soundtrack albums that were significant sellers were film versions of Broadway plays that had already proven successful. In 1966 the RIAA certified as gold the soundtrack from *Dr. Zhivago*, the first film soundtrack that had not been a Broadway musical to achieve that status.

The first gold-selling soundtrack that featured significant amounts of pop music was the hit movie *The Graduate*, which featured songs from Simon and Garfunkel. Rock made it big in film in 1970 with the gold soundtracks for *Easy Rider* and *Midnight Cowboy*.[57] But the soundtrack that turned the labels' collective heads was *Saturday Night Fever* in 1977. The movie was made to feature music right from the start with a plot loosely woven around a lowly painter who became a disco star at night.

The soundtrack had as many as four singles in the charts at once and ultimately sold over 11 million copies in the United States and over 25 million copies worldwide—a number not surpassed by a soundtrack album until 1995 when *The Bodyguard* soundtrack of the Whitney Houston film was certified at over 14 million domestic sales.[58]

The notion of a movie that was little more than a vehicle for music was nothing new. The dance musicals of the 1930s, the crooner musicals of the 1940s, and the rock movies of the 1950s, such as *Rock Around the Clock* and *Blackboard Jungle*, and the Beatles movies of the 1960s such as *Hard Day's Night*, all drew an audience because they were full of music that the public wanted to hear. They also all helped sell records, especially once the nation had pulled out of the depression.

In the 1980s and 1990s, the marriage of recordings and movies continued but took on a different twist. The labels began viewing movies as sales and promotional vehicles to introduce singles and artists, and the moviemakers began using songs to help reach the movie's target audience. What both moviemakers and record labels realized is that the people who go to movies and the people who buy recordings are the same. Coordinated marketing campaigns are the key to the big hits. Singles are usually released four to six weeks ahead of the movie. If the single and music video for the single, (which often contains some film footage) are successful, there is a presold audience for the film. The album and movie are then usually released simultaneously to maximize cross-promotional benefits. For the biggest successes, the movie and the album are both hits. Sometimes the movie is a hit without the soundtrack selling well, and sometimes the soundtrack is a hit without the movie doing very well except in home video.

In addition, songs had moved into a different kind of use. In *Saturday Night Fever* and most other soundtracks, the songs were either totally background or featured a performance by somebody on screen. Music Television showed filmmakers that the songs could also be used as miniature music videos to help tell part of the story or emphasize some mood or theme. That is the way that music has always been used, but the use of orchestral scores began to be replaced by portions of popular recordings, even for action sequences.

The other thing that helped soundtracks in the 1980s and 1990s was the rapid diffusion of videocassette players and home video rentals. Soundtracks like *Dazed and Confused*, a box office also-ran, sold over 500,000 copies because, said an A&M Records executive, "People discovered it at the video store."[59] Quipped one writer in *Vogue*, "Years ago we bought sound tracks because we liked the music and wanted to be reminded of the movie. Today, we buy soundtracks because we like the music and want to be reminded to rent the movie."[60]

Typical soundtracks feature not one or two artists but more often nine or ten different artists. Some of the songs on a soundtrack album may not even be heard in the final version of the film at all, or be heard so briefly that no one can remember where or when the music appeared. Record companies use small independent moviemakers to help introduce their newer, cutting edge artists. The filmmaker gets a soundtrack, the likes of which they could not otherwise afford, and the artist gets exposure that just might launch a career. Even though those kinds of movies show mostly in large cities or on college campuses, the exposure can be significant. Major U.S. films also drive soundtrack sales in Europe. In Germany, for example, soundtrack sales account for 3 percent of record sales.[61] In 1996 *Billboard* launched a special soundtrack column, "Nothin' Like the Reel Thing."[62] Then Arista Records president Clive Davis summed up the movie-music marriage, "It's always been about the same thing: a merger of music within the context of a film. One drives the other. It's a marriage of mediums."[63] The marriage was strengthened with the development and rapid consumer acceptance of DVDs.

It is also a marriage of corporate profits. All of the major conglomerates that own record labels also own film production interests.[64] The exact nature of the working relationships between the various groups and profit centers within each of the conglomerates needs to be examined more closely. One might ask, for example, whether Sony Pictures and Columbia Pictures feature Sony Music artists or songs more than those of other labels or publishers.

Recordings and the Print Media

The impact of the recording industry on print media and vice versa has not been a subject of much study or debate. Music/entertainment magazines have been described as a "major niche" in the magazine industry,[65] but their influence on the sale of recordings is problematic. A *Billboard* article concluded, "While it's unlikely that there will ever be a fully quantifiable way to measure the impact that consumer music magazines have in selling records or influencing airplay, the one certainty is that no one wants to live without them."[66] Their direct influence on the purchase of recordings has been variously rated at 3 percent,[67] 3.7 percent,[68] and 7.4 percent[69] of respondents to various surveys who said they were motivated to purchase a recording by a print ad or review. When people are asked about how they first heard about a recording that they have purchased, one study indicated that 4.5 percent heard first from a review and 2.4 percent heard first from a print media advertisement.[70] Record reviewers do not have a very high opinion of their effects on the record-buying audience either. On a scale of 1 through 5 (with 5 being the highest degree of influence) the critics rate their influence as an average of 1.9 with almost 49 percent rating their influence in the lowest category, a 1.[71]

The effects on consumers are probably much more indirect. If magazines serve a function of correlation, bringing together sometimes-disparate parts of a news story or a culture, then reviews of performances or recordings, and articles about recording artists in publications, help readers place an artist within the context of the magazine's general editorial slant. The magazine itself is also situated within the context of either the entire culture or the particular subculture about which the magazine writes.[72] For example, an article or review in a hip-hop publication such as *The Source* serves to clearly identify the artist with that subculture and legitimize that artist to the readers. Many of the music publications, even specialty publications like *Mix*, have reviews of recordings or feature articles about how some artist made their latest recording, and are potential publicity sources.

Sizing Up Print[73]

Magazines are typically divided into two broad classes depending upon whom they serve, either consumers or businesses. The business publications are often referred to as *trades*. There are music and recording publications of both types. An additional useful split in the trade category for purposes of our understanding is that of music business and audio.

Trade Publications

Music Business Publications. The publications classified as *business* for music run a wide gamut. There are a half-dozen educators' publications like the *American Music Teacher*, another half-dozen specialist instrument publications like *Drum Business*, and approximately 17 publications in core recording industry/music business areas such as *Billboard, Variety, Amusement Business, Pollstar, Radio and Records,* and *DJ Times*. Putting this category into the context of total magazine sales, the top ten *Standard Rate and Data Service (SRDS)* trade publication categories (which do not include music and music trades) measured by total circulation have a combined circulation of about 26 million.[74] The combined circulation of the music-business publications is about 650,000, only about 2.5 percent of the total for the top ten groups.[75] Table 10.7 shows circulation figures for a variety of recording and music-related publications.

The leading recording industry publication is *Billboard*—sometimes referred to as the "Bible" of the recording industry. It began circulation in 1894 as *Billboard Advertising*, a trade publication covering the outdoor advertising and bill-posting business. Because many bills involved circus and other live performers, it naturally evolved into carrying news of those businesses as well. By 1900 the *Billboard* (as it was renamed) recast itself as covering "the Great Out-Door Amusement World." It moved indoors in the first decade of the twentieth century adding coverage of vaudeville, film, and theater. Gradually, coverage of the music business increased. Coverage of the outdoor fair and carnival business continued until 1961

TABLE 10.7 Circulation of Some Music-Related Publications (2002)

Publication	Total Circulation
Rolling Stone	1,267,000
Film Score Monthly	6,000
Bass Player	44,000
The Source	465,000
Blender	350,000
Stereophile	82,000
Spin	549,000
Billboard	33,000
Jazziz	170,000
Audio	115,000

Source: SRDS Consumer Magazine Advertising Source, July 2002; *SRDS Business Publication Advertising Source,* July 2002.

when the parent company split off *Amusement Business* for that purpose and focused *Billboard Music Week* entirely on the music business.[76] With an audited circulation of over 32,000, it has the largest readership of the music-business publications.

Billboard is a trade publication, providing news and features of interest to those on the inside of the business. Its editorial slant is generally positive. It is an important chronicler of news events and information about the industry. There is a section of reviews as well as the infamous charts (see earlier discussion in this chapter) that track the success of recordings in achieving airplay and sales. *Daily Variety* (usually just referred to as *Variety*) is broader in scope and covers the entertainment industry in general, including recordings, television, movies, and theater. Other significant music business publications are *Radio and Records, Pollstar, Music Trades Magazine,* and *Music and Sound Retailer.*

Audio Publications. Business publications about audio include those dealing with recording, sound reinforcement, audio/video applications, consumer audio trade publications, and even two scholarly journals from the Audio Engineering Society and the Society of Motion Picture and Television Engineers. *Mix* and *Audio Video International* have the largest circulations with about 51,000 and 30,000, respectively. Some of the publications, such as *Mix* and *Pro Sound News,* review artists' recordings, concerts, or video productions and can be sources of publicity within a segment of the industry.

Collectively the audio and music-business trade publications have a combined circulation of about 500,000. For the sake of putting things into perspective, *Folio Magazine's* (the trade publication for the magazine publishing industry) top ten categories of trade publications had a combined circulation of 26.1 million in 1995. The smallest category in the top ten, restaurant and food service trades, had a circulation of about 950,000.[77] Recording industry trade publications amounted to less than 2.2 percent of total trade publication circulation.

Consumer Publications

Recordings. *Rolling Stone* is the king of the music-related consumer publications with a circulation of nearly 1.3 million. National publications with large circulations, other than those inserted in Sunday newspapers such as *USA Weekend* and *Parade*, tend to have circulations in the 3 to 7 million range. (Notable exceptions are *TV Guide* and *Reader's Digest* with circulations over 9 million and 12 million, respectively.) *Rolling Stone*, with nearly 1.3 million in circulation, heads the category of music/lifestyle publications. Others with circulations of near or over 100,000 are *Spin* (progressive rock), *Blender* (contemporary), *Request* (all contemporary), *Vibe* (urban), *Jazziz* (jazz), *Hit Parader* (rock), *Pulse* (Tower Records/contemporary), *Rap Sheet* (rap), *The Source* (hip-hop), *XXL* (urban), and *Country Music* (country). Publications exist for all styles of music, from bluegrass to black gospel to opera to Christian to chamber music.

Audio. Consumer audio publications tend to combine coverage of audio equipment with audio/video or home theater. These publications are important because the main drive for consumer's interest in home and car audio is the availability of high-quality recordings. Two of the consumer publications are targeted at the semiprofessional home and project recording environment. *EQ* and *Recording* are closer to the recording industry core function of the creation of recordings. They encourage people without major recording contracts or the resources provided by the labels to create their own recording studios. By supplying the encouragement and some "how to" information, these publications contribute to a growing pool of recording talent at the margins of the industry. They are the new, specialty, and independent-label artists who can survive on selling 30,000 units or less of a CD release and playing club dates. It is from their ranks that many new sounds and future mainstream acts often emerge.

Collectively, the recording industry consumer publications have a total circulation of about 6.6 million. Putting this in perspective, the *SRDS* top ten consumer categories (which do not include music) have a combined circulation of about 301.3 million. The tenth-ranked category in consumer publications is business publications with a combined circulation of about 7.2 million.[78] So, recording industry magazines are probably less than 5 percent of total magazine circulation.

The conglomerates that own the major music labels lack a direct connection to recording-industry publications. Of the majors, only Time Warner and Bertelsmann had large magazine-publishing divisions, and neither published any recording industry magazines but focused instead primarily on larger circulation publications such as *People* and *Time* (Time Warner), and *Family Circle* and *Fast Company* (Bertelsmann). Time Warner was apparently interested in using the synergy that can develop with cross-promotion of its entertainment products. At least one study found Warner Music Group recordings were mentioned in disproportionate share in Time Warner magazines, although reviews or mentions of Warner Music Group products were no more likely to be positive or negative than those of other labels; just more frequent.[79]

Summary

From the perspective of the recording industry, the other media primarily provide promotional vehicles to help sell recordings. Because most people will not purchase a recording until they have heard it, or at least some of it, radio, television, and motion pictures are the most valuable. The print media command a distant fourth place in the promotional hierarchy, but the labels are reluctant to ignore them.

11
The Recording Industry and the Internet

There is no doubt that the Internet has changed and will change the recording industry for some time to come. It has opened new ways to promote, distribute, and sell recordings and songs—as well as to copy them illegally. It has offered artists fresh opportunities to reach fans and to promote live appearances. It is having a significant impact on all three income streams, publishing, live performance, and recording. There are three dimensions of Internet use to be explored for each income stream: the Internet as a *promotional tool* for artists, labels, and publishers; as a *distribution pipeline* for hard and digital copies; and the *legal battles* being fought over unauthorized distribution and downloading of copies. All of these dimensions offer both good news and bad news for the music industry.

The Internet as Promotional Tool

Although the Internet began as a defense network (ARPANET) in the late 1960s, and began to reach significant numbers of ordinary people in the 1980s, it was not until the development of the World Wide Web in 1991 that it became capable of being a mass medium. The Web languages of HTTP and HTML enabled the creation of programs that allowed any user to easily access and transmit information. The development of the first graphical browser in 1993 meant that everyone with a personal computer could easily locate information on the Internet and that every company could easily tell its story to every user. Internet and Web usage skyrocketed. In 2002, usage in the United States exceeded 50 percent of the population, representing a potential audience of 140 million people.[1] Consumer Internet use was pegged at 124 hours per person per year in 2000 and predicted to be nearly 194 hours in 2005.[2] Younger persons, precisely the market for many recordings, adopted the new technology sooner. Clearly, the Internet and the Web spelled opportunity for the promotion of recordings, artists, and music.

By the mid-1990s virtually all of the major record labels and most of the smaller labels were operating Web sites. Mostly, these were sites that promoted the artists and their new releases, often giving background on the artists, photos, and brief samples of video or audio clips. The fans developed unofficial sites of their own, much like the fanzines of the 1970s, and some artists developed their own sites. The labels and artists began to argue over who could control the Web sites. For example, in 1999 Sony Music began to insert clauses in their contracts giving them the rights to the artists' names as may be used in any URL or Web site and the right to run the artist's official Web site for perpetuity; artist's managers and attorneys vowed to fight and restrict the label's rights.[3] The labels hired Internet-savvy young folks to engage in Internet marketing in chat rooms, mail groups, and list serves. Meanwhile, Internet leaks of tracks and entire albums forced labels to move up release dates and alter marketing plans in an effort to combat the illegal downloads.

A good example of an Internet marketing campaign was that geared around the 2003 release of Madonna's *American Life* album. Warner Brothers, the distributing label for Madonna's Maverick label, made use of its corporate synergy with AOL. The first single was made available for streaming on March 25, the title track on April 18, and the entire album on a stream-only basis on April 21, all before the album's April 22 release date.[4] To combat peer-to-peer (P2P) piracy, users of such networks as KaZaA were bombarded with phony download cuts that featured Madonna saying "What the f*** do you think you are doing?"[5]

By the end of 2002 it was clear that the Internet was a big boon to the live entertainment business. Ticketmaster reported that 40 percent of its sales were online. Artist sites and venue sites began promoting shows before Ticketmaster even released the tickets to the general public, resulting in presales of thousands of tickets. Because the presales were so efficiently run through artist and venue sites, the promoters could save advertising money; one promoter estimated savings on advertising as high as 80 percent of what he had previously spent. Some artists charged fees to join their sites and get inside information, prerelease previews of recordings, and advance opportunities to buy concert tickets. The Internet closed in on radio as the way that concert goers heard about concerts, at 12 percent, approaching radio's 14 percent. Tickets could be printed at home on the user's computer. The 2002 Bonnaroo Festival sold over 75,000 tickets through its own Web site. Because a Web presence can be relatively inexpensive, an indie artist site can look almost as sophisticated as that of a multiplatinum act. The agent for indie artist Ani DiFranco was quoted by *Billboard* as saying that the independent artists' Web sites "put them on a level playing field. They may not be as sophisticated as others, but it gives out the info. It's empowering for indie artists."[6]

The music publishers also utilized the promotional aspects of the Web. They set up sites that allowed users to search catalogs and to access streaming samples of their songs. Most often the initial pages revealed current releases by writers/artists that were on the parent company's labels. However, there were often samples of songs recorded by artists on other labels as well. The ability to send MP3s of demos to producers, artists, and motion-picture music coordinators made it easier for music publishers to get demos to prospective clients.

The Internet as a Distribution Tool

There is not much doubt that peer-to-peer file sharing is the most efficient method of distribution of music and recordings ever used. There are literally millions of distribution points: any computer sharing files that is on the network. Once a file is in the network, the number of distribution points grows exponentially until all those interested in the file have it. It then remains on the computers for a long time. The only problem is how to make the Internet downloaders pay, instead of taking the recordings for free. Even as the industry began to sell or rent downloads in 2001, and as significant singles downloading sales began to develop in 2003, the labels still had not worked out how to harness the power of peer-to-peer sharing and sales. The legal battles of the industry are discussed later. What follows is a look at how the industry sought to make a legitimate business out of Internet distribution of files, as opposed to hard copy sales.

Internet distribution of recordings was not really practical until the Moving Picture Experts Group developed the MPEG-3 (MP3) protocol for compressing audio files into small-enough packets that they could be more readily transmitted via the Internet. For example, a normal-length CD single is a digital audio file of about 40 megabytes, which would take a couple of hours to download over a dial-up modem. An MP3 version of the same file is about one-tenth the size, and so could be downloaded in a matter of minutes. The program to convert CD audio to MP3 became available to the public in the mid-1990s and consumers began to *rip* CD audio files and convert them into MP3 files. They would then send the MP3 files to friends or share them with anyone who happened to be on a particular network. Coupled with that was the increased access of consumers, particularly college students, to high-speed Internet connections that could transfer files anywhere from five to one hundred times faster than the old 28.8 kbps dial-up modems. Soon *file swapping* of recordings was rampant.

One of the first attempts to utilize this technology on a widespread basis was MP3.com. What began in 1997 as a promotional tool for unsigned bands and artists soon turned to the larger market for MP3s of popular recordings. The service began promoting itself as a place where members could upload MP3s of recordings that they already owned and then download them anywhere. Ostensibly the user had to prove to MP3.com that they owned the recording, but all that was required was a snippet to see if it matched an MP3 on file. What MP3.com had really done was to purchase thousands of recordings, then rip the most popular tracks into MP3 files that it stored on its servers. However, Universal Music's UMG Recordings, Inc. sued for infringement and won in 2000.[7] MP3.com then agreed to pay $53.4 million to license the entire UMG catalog. The other majors and MP3.com soon came to terms as well.

Meantime, the majors finally decided that they should launch some digital distribution services of their own. In 2001 Universal purchased MP3.com, Emusic.com, and obtained 100 percent ownership of GetMusic (they previously owned it 50/50 with BMG).[8] It then partnered with Sony to start a subscription-based service called PressPlay. BMG, Warner Music Group, and EMI combined forces to launch a competing system, Music-Net. Both had monthly fees for which the subscriber could access a certain number of streams or limited downloads (i.e., downloads that would either time out after 30 days or that could not be copied from a computer to another device or burned on to a CD). Unfortunately, neither system would license its songs to the other. So, as in the old days of the record clubs, if you wanted a Warner product it could only be found on Music-Net; if you wanted a Universal product, it could only be on PressPlay. That difficulty was finally resolved by the end of 2002 when the two services agreed to cross-licensing. The cross-licensing deals inspired the Justice Department to probe into possible price-fixing violations, but did not bring out many consumers.[9] By mid-2002 the majors had dropped an estimated $2 billion into various digital media initiatives.[10] By mid-2003, the estimates were that both services had only in the neighborhood of 250,000 customers—a far cry from the millions of music lovers who were illegally downloading recordings.

The whole complexion of the legitimate download market changed in 2003 when Apple started its iTunes service. Apple impresario Steve Jobs negotiated licenses from all of the majors to allow his service to send unlimited 99-cent singles downloads to customers who had Apple iPod players. For those who wanted albums, the rates were simply multiplied by the number of songs on the album. The downloads were not limited, did not time out, and could be burned onto a CD.[11] During the first roughly two months of its existence, iTunes sold five million downloads. Forty-six percent of the purchases were as albums and 80 percent of the available 200,000 tracks had been downloaded at least once. A version for Windows computers was launched in late 2003.

Shortly after the iTunes launch, Sony and Universal sold PressPlay to Roxio, a company that sold CD burner and other software, for $39.5 million. In November 2000, Roxio had purchased all rights to the Napster brand at a bankruptcy sale for a reported $5 million. Roxio planned to launch a legitimate service using PressPlay's licenses and the Napster logo and name. In October 2003 the new Napster came online. It, too, offered unrestricted 99 cent downloads, along with radio service, streaming and *tethered* downloads, and more resembled iTunes than Napster's original peer-to-peer network setup.[12]

How Much Pie Does 99 Cents Buy?

The industry struggled to develop a workable business model for the download market. The apparent success of iTunes in early 2003 at selling 99-cent single downloads led to the following model. Because the amount of profit per download was expected to be very small, less than 50 cents for the label, most experts believed that the number of downloads would have to be quite large in order for it to be a profitable market—as many as 10 million per week. Table 11.1 reflects the basic split of profits and fees on a 99-cent downloaded single.

There are several assumptions in this table that may be at variance with any one, or even many, of the digital distribution deals. First, the assumed wholesale price of 65 cents is what Apple reportedly pays for its iTunes tracks; other licensing arrangements may vary. Also, if there is substantial success with this system, the labels may introduce some singles at a wholesale price higher than 65 cents, for example a new release by a hot act. Wholesale prices varied from 52 cents to as high as 80 cents per track in 2003. Credit card fees and service provider fees are per transaction and the average cost drops as a person orders more cuts in one transaction. The artist and producer royalty rates assume an album rate of 10 percent SRLP and no other deductions. However, labels typically deduct a packaging charge, 25 percent for CDs, even from digital files where there is no package. Labels also typically pay a rate on singles that is lower than the album base rate, often 75 to 80 percent of the album rate. Labels also pay a lower rate on "new technologies"; also often 75 to 80 percent of the base album rate. If all of those deductions were taken, the artist's and producer's combined royalty would shrink to about 4.2 cents per download. Some major

TABLE 11.1 Revenues from a 99-Cent Download

Participant	Revenue
Label	47 cents
Distribution affiliate	10 cents
Service provider	17 cents
Artist	7 cents
Producer	3 cents
Music publisher	8 cents
Credit card fees	5 cents
Bandwidth costs	2 cents

Source: Garrity, Brian. "Seeking Profits at 99 Cents," *Billboard*, 12 July 2003, 1.

artists objected to this small portion of the small pie. Linkin Park, Madonna, Radiohead, Jewel, and Green Day required that their recordings not be distributed as digital download singles.[13] On the other side of the battle, a nonscientific *Billboard* poll in 2003 indicated that many consumers thought even 99 cents was too high a price for a single download. Thirty-two percent said it was too much to pay, and 29 percent said they would rather download for free.[14]

The music publishers did not have nearly as much difficulty with the digital delivery of songs as did the labels, primarily because the publishers simply had to license the labels to distribute copies via the Internet, not actually come up with the methodology to distribute those copies. Recall from Chapter 2 that a digital delivery of a phonorecord is covered by the mechanical license. The most difficult issue the publishers faced was to come up with a way to license the thousands of songs represented by the Harry Fox Agency in some kind of efficient manner. In November 2001 the HFA began bulk licensing services to use any songs represented by the HFA. Rhapsody and Listen.com received the first licenses.[15] HFA had earlier reached agreements directly with the majors for distribution of their own recordings and MyMP3.com's listening service.[16]

For the live entertainment income stream, the Internet as a delivery system offered streaming (Webcasting) of concerts. The birth of netcasting concerts was in San Francisco in June 1993 by a group called Severe Tire Damage (some of whose members were technical staff of XeroxPARC, the company that developed the MBONE streaming technology). The honor of the first widely available Internet concert belonged to the Rolling Stones on November 18, 1994. As bandwidth and streaming technology improved, more artists began to stream concerts on a pay-per-view basis. Artists became interested in streaming concerts because, as one writer put it, "[N]etcasting is a way to make the experience of a concert accessible to the world in an interactive format."[17] By 1999, the Webcast of Woodstock '99 was able to claim over 400,000 listeners worldwide.[18]

Internet Radio

Within a year of the 1994 Rolling Stones's concert netcast, the technology for broadcasting over the Internet took on a new dimension. Progressive Networks unveiled its RealAudio streaming technology at the National Association of Broadcasters (NAB) convention in April of 1995. By compressing the audio, delivering it in small bits, and by synchronizing the rates of transmission between the sending and receiving computers, audio could be transmitted almost live. All the receiving computer had to do was to build up enough of a buffer of the audio file so that it would not produce its playback ahead of the incoming packets of audio.[19] Within a matter of months, there were over 20 sites streaming radio-style broadcasts on the Internet. Webcasters sprang up in South Korea, Canada, the United

States, and elsewhere. Although early sound quality was only slightly better than AM radio, enthusiasm was high.[20]

Even as the Webcasters were going online, Congress was working on the Digital Performance Right in Sound Recordings Act of 1995 (see Chapter 3). The initial version of the act was meant to cover only digital audio transmissions by background music services and so-called *celestial jukeboxes* (interactive digital audio services by satellite or Internet). Over-the-air broadcasters were specifically exempted from coverage by the act, even if they later began transmitting their over-the-air signals in digital form.[21]

By 1998, noninteractive streaming over the Internet had become quite common and Congress was asked to clarify how digital audio performances of sound recordings might be applied to such services. As part of the Digital Millennium Copyright Act, Congress amended the statute to apply it to noninteractive Internet "webcasting" services. The broadcasters felt that this did not apply to them if they simulcast their regular broadcast signals over the Internet because their over-the-air transmissions had been exempted by the original act; however, the record companies disagreed. The Copyright Office made a determination that such services were covered by the new law and that the record companies would be owed a royalty by broadcasters who simulcast their signals on the Web.[22] Clear Channel stations all ceased Webcasting, as did hundreds of other stations, rather than pay the royalty. By 2003 many stations were back on the Web, particularly noncommercial stations that had lower royalty rates and news/talk stations that did not play recordings. Internet Radio directories had sprung up to help Web users find their favorite music on the Internat. However, it was too early to tell whether the Webcasters would represent a significant source of revenues for the record companies.

Highway Robbery on the Information Superhighway

> There are just too many holes in the Internet. –
>
> Ed Murphy, president/CEO of National Music Publishers' Association.[23]

The Case of "Unchained Melody"

In late 1993 the recording industry became one of the first media to challenge copyright infringement on the information superhighway. It was the music publishers who started the litigation phase of this story. A class action lawsuit on behalf of 141 music publishers against CompuServe, then H&R Block's online service provider, raised the specter of an online service provider being liable for the infringing activities of its clients. Frank Music Group, one of the plaintiffs and owners of the copyright in the musical composition "Unchained Melody," which had become popular at the time because of its inclusion in the movie *Ghost*, said that electronic versions of the song were being created by users using MIDI equipment and sound cards in computers, and uploaded to a CompuServe music database. From there thousands of users could download a copy of the song to play or keep for use on their own computers. CompuServe had turned down a request to pay damages of $25 to $100 for each downloaded copy of the song. The National Music Publishers' Association and Frank Music claimed that CompuServe should be liable as a contributory infringer, even though the initial infringer was the person who made the unauthorized version and then attempted to distribute it to the public through the bulletin board.[24] CompuServe ultimately settled the dispute by agreeing to pay over $500,000 for the alleged infringements and to pay a license fee for each copy downloaded in the future. Whenever a CompuServe user wanted to download a MIDI file of a song, the service issued a mechanical license for the song to the user. CompuServe kept track of the licenses issued then paid the Harry Fox Agency royalties that were then distributed by the HFA to the copyright owners.[25]

Both ASCAP and BMI are involved in licensing music performances on the Internet and other online services. The first Internet performance license was issued by BMI to On Ramp, Inc. in April of 1995. Even before passage of the Digital Performance Rights Act in 1995, the Harry Fox Agency had licensed OmniBox, an interactive music provider, for digital delivery of copies of songs licensed by HFA.[26]

Who is Liable? Where there is an online provider like CompuServe providing a bulletin board or other means for files to be posted, there is a control point for the copyright owners to attack. However, when the access is via the Internet, who is responsible? In the litigation surrounding former Church of Scientology minister Dennis Erlich and the distribution of unpublished Scientology documents through online services, one court concluded that the service provider, in that case NetCom On-Line Communications Services, and the operator of the bulletin board where the documents were posted could be liable as contributory infringers. To be liable as a contributory infringer the operators must have knowledge of the infringing activity and induce, cause, or contribute to the infringement. Failure to act in the face of notice could constitute participation in the infringement. However, the court stopped short of making the provider responsible for screening all postings. The court further held that NetCom could not be liable as a contributory infringer because, even though it could control the conduct of subscribers, it did not receive any direct financial benefit from the infringement, only a monthly service charge for the service in general.[27]

In 1998 Congress acted to shield on-line service providers from liability in certain situations. The Digital Millennium Copyright Act contained a section that provided "safe harbors" from infringement claims for service providers in four situations: (1) "transitory digital communications" where the provider merely acted as a conduit for the infringing information; (2) system caching where the provider made temporary copies of possibly infringing files, but only for the sake of making the system operate more efficiently; (3) user-posted infringing material on Web pages, bulletin boards, and the like; and (4) for higher education facilities for infringements by faculty and graduate assistants. To qualify for the safe harbor the service providers had to have no knowledge of the infringing material, or upon being made aware of the infringements, take action to remove them, block access to infringing files, or disconnect service of repeat infringers.[28]

The Case of Napster

In August 1999 a file swapping service was launched that helped users locate files, particularly music files, available for uploading from other users. Napster software sorted files by type, artist, title, and speed of user connection. Users selected the file they wanted and the software would tell the two computers to connect to each other and begin the transfer of the designated file. Within months, transfers of music files using Napster reached into the millions per day.[29] The record labels and artists were most irate and sued to shut down Napster in December of 1999.

The record labels were largely victorious in their suit, *A & M Records, Inc. v. Napster, Inc.* Ultimately, a court of appeals ruled that it was likely that (1) Napster users were copyright infringers, engaging in unauthorized copying and distribution of recordings and songs; (2) Napster, Inc was liable for this infringement either as a vicarious or contributory infringer; (3) Napster, Inc. was not sheltered by the Digital Millennium Copyright Act because it was not a "service provider" as defined in the statute; and (4) that Napster must take positive steps to screen out infringing files and transfers.[30] By July 2001, BMG Music had bought a share of Napster to turn the service into a licensed digital music distribution company. That did not work and Napster was ultimately dissolved in a bankruptcy proceeding, only to be eventually purchased by Roxio with a relaunch as a legitimate service in late 2003.

The battle over P2P file sharing continued. In 2002 Audiogalaxy agreed to shut down its file sharing services and pay a "substantial sum" to publishers and labels. One Audiogalaxy user reportedly commented, "the free lunch is over. It was nice while it lasted."[31] However, no sooner were Napster and Audiogalaxy shut down than other networks developed variations on the same idea. Next the RIAA sued the Aimster Internet services. Aimster used AOL's instant-messaging service to allow users to locate "buddies" who had music files they were willing to share. All communications between users were encrypted so the Aimster owners could not know what was being transmitted. In upholding the preliminary injunction against Aimster, Judge Posner of the Seventh Circuit Court of Appeals said that Aimster could not hide behind the fact that the actual files being transferred were encrypted. "Deep [the Aimster owner] by using encryption software [cannot] prevent himself from learning what surely he strongly suspects to be the case: that the users of his service—maybe *all* the users of his service—are copyright infringers."[32]

The next two file swapping services to come under attack were Grokster and KaZaA. Grokster and KaZaA set up their systems so that there was no supervision or activation of the network by them, but an almost completely decentralized system of nodes that helped the users locate other potential file swappers. The node computers were not run by Grokster or KaZaA, and changed from time to time. Furthermore, KaZaA's owner, Sharman Networks, was located in Australia and incorporated in Vanuatu, a tiny nation composed of a group of small islands about 1,200 miles off the coast of Australia in the South Pacific. The court first held that the suit could continue, even though KaZaA was not a U.S. company.[33] Then, in 2003, the district court granted summary judgment for Grokster and Streamcast Networks saying that they were not liable as contributory or vicarious infringers even though thousands of their users were infringing.[34] The RIAA and other plaintiffs appealed the decision.[35] As part of the same suit, KaZaA countersued the RIAA and NMPA for antitrust violations, claiming that they were failing to work with Sharman Networks. That suit was quickly dismissed, but Sharman also promised to appeal.[36]

In 2003 the record labels, through the RIAA, started to take aim at a different target: the individual consumers who were doing the infringing. First, the RIAA won a case against Internet service provider Verizon, forcing them to disclose the name of a prolific file sharer.[37] Then they sued four college students who had set up their own peer-to-peer networks on their universities' computers. Faced with potentially enormous damage claims, the students settled with the RIAA for between $12,000 and $17,000 apiece.[38] Then the RIAA announced that it would target even individual users. In a campaign aimed at "egregious copyright infringers" the RIAA promised that it would file individual lawsuits during the latter half of 2003. There was no specific definition of what might constitute an "egregious infringer."[39] Grokster president Wayne Rosso said the RIAA's tactics would be unlikely to change any consumer behavior and that litigation was ultimately bound to fail as an antipiracy tactic.[40]

The live entertainment stream was also being impacted, primarily by the sharing of bootleg files and sale of bootleg recordings via the Internet. Recall from Chapter 3 that bootleg recordings are unauthorized recordings of live performances. In 2003, a simple Google search using the term "bootleg recordings" yielded 57,600 hits in 0.35 seconds. The RIAA reported that seizures of bootleg CD-Rs rose 114 percent to more than 200,000 units in 2002.[41] Seizures of all bootleg products nearly doubled from 2001 to 2002, up to 233,000 units.

The downloading was clearly hurting legitimate recording sales. By mid-2003 the RIAA estimated that 2.6 million copyrighted files were traded over P2P networks every month. KaZaA had more than doubled its number of users up to 230 million over the previous 12 months. One study, done for *Radio & Records*, revealed that the heaviest downloaders reported a 61-percent decrease in CD purchases. They frequently said they did not have to buy CDs because they "could download music for free over the Internet." Sixty-one percent of teen consumers surveyed,were burning copies of friends' CDs instead of buying.[42] Although the Audio Home Recording Act (see discussion in Chapter 3) allows individuals to make copies of CDs for their own use, the act does not protect copying made on a computer CD-R drive and, of course, no royalty at all is paid to the label, artist, producer, or songwriter. Ironically, that wonderful product, the compact disc, which spurred unparalleled growth of the recording industry in the 1980s and 1990s, was bringing it back to vinyl and cassette sales levels in 2003.

Is Copyright Passé?

While some may contend that these new delivery methods and difficulties portend the end of copyright as we know it, or that copyright is being taken over by commercial enterprises and no longer serves a general public interest,[43] it is well to remember two things. Copyright law has always had to change to cope with new technologies. From engraving, to the still photograph, to the motion picture; from sheet music, to phonorecords, to digital deliveries; copyright law has evolved over the course of more than 290 years. As the white paper on the National Information Infrastructure pointed out, there is no reason to expect copyright laws not to be able to evolve to cope with new technologies.[44] Second, a core purpose of copyright law in the United States has always been encouraging authors to create works that are for the general benefit of society, by making it possible for them to make a living from so doing; "by giving authors a means of securing the economic reward afforded by the market, copyright stimulates their creation and dissemination of intellectual works."[45]

If everything becomes free in some sort of Internet utopia, then the only ones creating new works will be hobbyists, not persons engaged full time in the creation of new works. While this might seem more democratic, we should ask ourselves would there be a Ninth Symphony if Beethoven had not had a patron? Would there be a *Madame Butterfly* if Puccini had not worked with G. Ricordi & Sons music publishing company? Would there be a "Yesterday" if the Beatles had to become dockworkers in Liverpool? Would we have heard Coolio's *Gangsta's Paradise* or

Alanis Morissette's *Jagged Little Pill* albums? How would we be aware of these works without record companies, music publishers, and performers who rely on copyrights to make their labors worthwhile financially? The three income streams need copyrights to exist in order to provide us with the recordings, songs, and performances we enjoy and appreciate. The consumers need the industry to stay afloat or there will be very few audio files to share, other than those from unknown artists of unknown quality.

Summary

The Internet has opened up new ways to market music on an instantaneous worldwide basis. It has made it easier for fans to connect with artists and each other. It may revive the single as a viable commercial product. It is also damaging the record companies, artists, music publishers, and songwriters because millions of users feel no compunction about making and distributing illegal copies of recordings in peer-to-peer networks. It will undoubtedly bring about significant changes in the ways the recording industry does its business. Major changes in technology have always had significant effects on this technologically grounded industry. The likelihood is that the industry will survive and there will continue to be new recordings by new artists to excite the public's interest and demand. After all, it is the cultural product that the consumer wants, not necessarily any particular plastic configuration of that product. Disks replaced cylinders, 45s and 33 $\frac{1}{3}$s replaced 78s, cassettes replaced vinyl, and CDs replaced cassettes. John Kennedy once said, "When written in Chinese, the word 'crisis' is composed of two characters—one represents danger and the other represents opportunity."[46]

Notes

Notes for Chapter One

1. Address in Frankfurt, Germany, June 25, 1963. From *The International Thesaurus of Quotations* (Harper and Row: New York, 1970), 74.
2. "NAMM Releases Music USA 2003," NAMM Website, www.namm.com/pressroom/pressreleases/2003July18a.html. Accessed 1 March 2004.
3. *Music U.S.A. 1996*, National Association of Music Merchandisers (1996), 48–49. Accessed 1 March 2004.
4. "Gallup Organization Reveals Findings of American Attitudes toward Making Music Survey," *NAMM Website*, www.namm.com/pressroom/pressreleases/2003Apr21.html.
5. "80th Annual Statistical Survey and Report," *Dealerscope*, August 2002, 14.
6. United States Department of Commerce, Bureau of Statistics (2002), 698.
7. Verna (2 March 1996), 3.
8. "Some Facts About Piracy," *RIAA Newsletter*, June 25, 2003, www.riaa.com/news/newsletter/062503_c.asp
9. Denisoff (1975), 33.
10. Hull (1977), 3.
11. NARM, *Consumer Research Study: The Growing Adult Market*, March 1976.
12. NPD Music, "The Music Customer Basic Profiles," May 2003. Retrieved from NARM subscription Website: www.narm.com/research/PDF/NPDJuneReport.pdf. This data was drawn from an online group of people who agreed to participate in the survey and may be somewhat biased because a much higher percentage of the young population is online than of the older population. Accessed 1 March 2004.
13. Burnett (1996), 1.
14. International Federation of Phonographic Industries (2002).
15. Ibid.
16. *Commercial Piracy Report 2003*, IFPI, www.ifpi.org/site-content/library/piracy2003.pdf. Accessed 1 March 2004.
17. *2001 IFPI Music Piracy Report*. www.ifpi.org/site-content/library/piracy2001.pdf. Accessed 1 March 2004.
18. International Federation of Phonographic Industries (2002).
19. See, *e.g.*, Daft (1988), 53–55; Mondy and Premeaux (1993), 36–38.
20. Alexander (1996): 171.
21. For this and other examples, see, Lewis (1990).
22. For one perspective see Gore (1987), Chapter 5.
23. See, *e.g.*, Schwichtenberg (1992), 116; Robinson, *et al.*, (1991), 1–31; Denisoff (1986), 1–35.
24. Lewis (1990).
25. Frith (1991), 287 (emphasis in original).

26. Recording Industry Association of America, "Recording Industry Releases 1995 Consumer Profile," press release 5 April 1996, 2.
27. Gore (1987).
28. Morris (2 May 1987), 1.
29. Camelot Music executive Jim Bonk quoted in Mayfield (2 May 1987), 87.
30. See, for example the NARM web site: http://www.narm.com/Content/NavigationMenu/Public_Affairs/Parental_Advisory2/Parental_Message/Parental_Message.htm. Accessed 1 March 2004.
31. "Censorship is Back ... But So Are We!" *NARM Sounding Board*, August 1995, online version.
32. "Band Is Held Not Liable in Suicides of Two Fans," *New York Times*, The Arts section, 25 August 1990.
33. DeFleur and Dennis (1991), 475.
34. National Music Publishers' Association (1991): 11. The NMPA points out that their first survey had a limited database of only eighteen nations and that the relationship was only significant at "reduced" level of statistical significance. Based on the available information the author estimates that reduced level to be 90 percent. The statistical analysis was not included in later editions of the report.
35. Drucker (1992), 8.
36. International Federation of Phonographic Industries (2002).
37. Vogel (1986), 149.
38. *Broadcasting and Cable Yearbook*, 1996, B-604; *Broadcasting and Cable Yearbook*, 2001, D-656.
39. McQuail (1994), 20.
40. Lull (1992), 1.
41. Campbell (2000), 66.
42. Severin and Tankard (1988), 43.
43. Hirsch (1969).
44. The story of Theresa Records, small jazz label, is eloquently told in Gray (1988).
45. Albarran (1996), 6.
46. Cusic, (1996), 25; Vogel (1986), 137.

Notes for Chapter Two

1. "IIPA Economic Study Reveals Copyright Industries Remain a Driving Force in the U.S. Economy." International Intellectual Property Alliance, retrieved from http://www.iipa.com/pressreleases/2002_Apr22_SIWEK.pdf. Accessed 1 March 2004.
2. *Mazer v. Stein*, 347 U.S. 201, 218 (1954).
3. 17 U.S.C. § 302(c).
4. Geoffrey Hull (March 1996). The Uruguay Round of the General Agreement on Tariffs and Trade, Trade Related Aspects of Intellectual Property Rights, Article 14 (1994). The Treaty of Rome (International Convention for the Protection of Performers, Producers of Phonograms and Broadcasting Organizations) only requires twenty-five years.
5. 17 U.S.C. § 304.
6. 17 U.S.C. § 305.
7. The International Convention for the Protection of Performers, Producers of Phonograms and Broadcasting Organizations, adopted at Rome on 26 October 1961. It is worth noting that the United States is unusual in that it protects sound recordings in fundamentally the same way as other literary or artistic works, whereas most nations treat rights in phonograms and rights for performers as *neighboring rights*.
8. *Copyright Act of 1909*, § 10.
9. 209 U.S. 1 (1908).
10. *Rosette v. Rainbo Record Manufacturing Corp.*, 345 F. Supp. 1183 (S.D.N.Y. 1973).
11. 44 F. 3d 813 (9th Cir. 1995).
12. 17 U.S.C. § 303 (b), Pub. L. No. 105–80 (1997).
13. 17 U.S.C. § 401(a).
14. 17 U.S.C. § 408(a).

15. 17 U.S.C. § 411.
16. 17 U.S.C. §410(c).
17. 17 U.S.C. § 412.
18. Register of Copyrights, Library of Congress, Washington, DC 20559-6000; forms hotline is (202) 707-9100; fax on demand (not forms but other information) (202) 707-2600; Internet address is http://www.copyright.gov
19. Holland (27 February 1993), 1.
20. H.R. Rep. No. 92–478, 92d Cong., 1st Sess. (1971), 9.
21. See, e.g., *Szabo v. Errisson*, 68 F.3d 940 (5th Cir. 1995).
22. 17 U.S.C. § 107.
23. 114 S.Ct. 1164 (1994).
24. 114 S.Ct. 1164 (1994), 1173.
25. 17 U.S.C. § 101.
26. 17 U.S.C. § 101.
27. 490 U.S. 730 (1989).
28. Ibid., 747–748.
29. Ibid., 751.
30. 490 U.S. at 751.
31. Ibid., 752.
32. 17 U.S.C. § 203.
33. "Sales of Beatles Set Give Retailers Hope," *Billboard*, 2 December 1995, 5, 106; Don Jeffrey, "Holidays Bring Retail Optimism," *Billboard*, 9 December 1995, 3, 93.
34. The Elvis album had sales of 500,000 units in the United States its first week and the Rolling Stones' had sales of 310,000 its first week. The October 19, 2002 Billboard 200 album chart had Elvis at number 1 and the Stones at number 2. Geoff Mayfield, "Over the Counter," *Billboard*, 12 October 2002, 51; Geoff Mayfield, "Over the Counter," *Billboard*, 19 October 2002, 69.
35. The 2003 date is because the termination provisions provide for a maximum of ten years notice to be sent to the copyright owner. Since the earliest termination cannot happen until 35 years after the transfer, and since termination rights did not exist until the 1976 Copyright Act took effect January 1, 1978, the earliest transfers that could be terminated would be those made in 1978. Thirty-five years after the transfer is 2013 for the effective date of termination, minus ten years notice, or 2003. 17 U.S.C. § 203.
36. H.R. Rep. No. 94-1476, 94th Cong., 1st Sess., 164–171 (1976).
37. David Nimmer & Melville Nimmer, 2 *Nimmer on Copyright* § 8.12[B][6] (2002).
38. Kozak (7 August 1982), 1.
39. 17 U.S.C. § 410.

Notes for Chapter Three

1. See, generally, Ringer (1960) and Henn (1960)
2. 209 U.S. 1 (1908).
3. "57th Statistical Issue and Marketing Report," *Merchandising*, March 1979, 31.
4. Recording Industry Association of America, *Inside the Recording Industry: A Statistical Overview 1987*, 4.
5. H.R. Rep. No. 92-487, 92nd Cong., 1st Sess. (1971).
6. *Capitol Records, Inc. v. Mercury Record Corp.*, 221 F.2d 657 (2nd Cir. 1955).
7. 1909 Copyright Act, Title 17 U.S. Code §1(e).
8. 17 U.S.C. § 301(c).
9. Embodied in the current Copyright Act as 17 U.S.C. § 109.
10. 17 U.S.C. § 106.
11. 17 U.S.C. § 114(a).
12. P.L. 98-450, 98 Stat. 1727 (1984).
13. Lichtman (16 May 1981), 1.
14. H.R. Rep. No. 98-987, 98th Cong., 2nd Sess., 2 (1984).

15. Uruguay Round Agreements Act, Statement of Administrative Action, P.L. 103–465, reprinted in 6 U.S. Code Congressional and Administrative News (108 Stat.) 4040, at 4281. The Agreement on Trade-Related Aspects of Intellectual Property Rights (TRIPS), Art. 14 prohibits commercial rental of phonograms.
16. Clark-Meads (29 April 1995), 5.
17. McClure (25 October 1997), 3.
18. Holland (7 November 1998), 8.
19. McClure (25 October 1997), 3.
20. 17 U.S.C. § 109(b).
21. Warner Communications, Inc. (1978), 78.
22. White (5 January 1980), 3.
23. Sutherland (3 April 1982), 1.
24. 464 U.S. 417 (1984).
25. H.R. Rep. No. 102-873(I), 102nd Cong., 2d Sess. 1992.
26. P.L. 102-563, 106 Stat. 4237 (October 28, 1992), codified in 17 U.S.C. §§ 1001 et seq..
27. Hull (Spring 2002), 76.
28. Holland (28 October 1995), 6.
29. H.R. 1506, P.L. 104-39, 109 Stat. 336, 104th Cong., 1st Sess. 1995.
30. Digital Millennium Copyright Act, 105th Cong. 2d Sess. 1998, §405.
31. 17 U.S.C. § 114(d).
32. *Bonneville International Corp. v. Peters*, 347 F. 3d 485 (3d Cir. 2003).
33. 67 F.R. 130, No. 130, 45236–45276, July 8, 2002; 37 C.F.R. 261.
34. SoundExchange, *An Introduction to SoundExchange*, (pamphlet) 2001.
35. 17 U.S.C. § 114(g).
36. 17 U.S.C. § 115 (a)(2).
37. *Tempo Music, Inc., v. Famous Music Corp.*, 838 F. Supp. 162 (S.D.N.Y. 1993).
38. *Woods v. Bourne Co.*, 841 F. Supp. 118, 121 (S.D.N.Y. 1994).
39. 17 U.S.C. §115 (c) 3 (A).
40. 17 U.S.C. § 115.
41. 37 C.F.R. § 201.19.
42. 29 Stat. 487 (1897).
43. *Herbert v. Shanley*, 242 U.S. 591, 592 (1917).
44. 17 U.S.C. § 101.
45. 17 U.S.C. § 110.
46. 17 U.S.C. § 110 (5)(B).
47. World Trade Organization, WT/DS160/R, 15 June 2000, 69.
48. World Trade Organization, WT/DS160/12, 15 January 2001.
49. *Grand Upright Music Limited v. Warner Brothers Records, Inc.*, 780 F. Supp. 182 (S.D.N.Y. 1991).
50. *Bridgeport Music, Inc. v. Dimension Films*, 230 F. Supp. 2d 830, 842 (M.D. Tenn. 2002).
51. *Elsemere Music , Inc. v. National Broadcasting Co.*, 482 F. Supp. 741 (S.D.N.Y. 1980).
52. *Selle v. Gibb*, 741 F.2d 896 (7th Cir. 1984).
53. *Bright Tunes Music Corp. v. Harrisongs Music, Ltd.*, 420 F. Supp. 177 (S.D.N.Y. 1976).
54. Nunziata (1 December 1990), 80.
55. Although there are claims to the Chinese invention of moveable type earlier, with all due respect to Chinese inventiveness, there was no interest in the mass reproduction and distribution of works in China, and hence no development of copyright law. In fact, there was no copyright law in China until a desire to participate more broadly in international trade in the early 1990s motivated the Chinese to pass a copyright law so they could join the Berne Convention for the Protection of Literary Property. At any rate, it was Gutenberg's press that was imported into England and that gave rise to the copyright laws we inherited from England.
56. Statute of Anne, 8 Anne C. 19 (1710), reprinted in, Robert A. Gorman and Jane C. Ginsburg, *Copyright Cases and Materials 6th ed*, (New York: Foundation Press, 2002), 2.
57. For an extended discussion of the history of copyright see Benjamin Kaplan, *An Unhurried View of Copyright* (New York: Columbia University Press, 1967).
58. Pavlik (1996), 125.

Notes for Chapter Four

1. An excellent long-term statistical compilation of publishing revenue data is in Ennis (1992), 100.
2. Ackerman (15 January 1955), 1.
3. Dranov (1980), 8.
4. Lichtman (20 July 1996), 34.
5. Lichtman (23 December 1995), 57, (17 June 1995), 14, and (17 April 1993), 1; Price (7 October 1995), 74; Edward Morris (5 February 1994), 9.
6. Clark-Meads (22 July 1995), 36.
7. Lichtman (4 May 1996), 39.
8. Lichtman (28 October 1995), 1 and (10 July 1993), 6.
9. Bennett (11 April 2003), 6.
10. ""WMG, BMG: A Struggle for Control," *Billboard*, 23 August, 2003; "Warner, BMG in Merger Talk; Giant Music Deal Would Face Anti-Trust Concerns," *Knight Ridder/Tribune Business News*, 13 May 2003, ITEM 03133026 <retrieved from InfoTrac>; Tim Burt, "Music Executives Set for Warner-BMG Talks Merger Negotiations," *The Financial Times*, 6 September 2003, 8.
11. "Details Prove Devilish for Sony, BMG Merger," *Billboard*, 22 November 2003.
12. "Cake, Candles Not Included," *Time*, 31 October 1988, 59.
13. *See, Mills Music, Inc. v. Snyder*, 496 U.S. 153, at 158 (1985).
14. Whitburn (1989).
15. Whitburn (1987).
16. Price (20 April 1996), 38.
17. Warner/Chappel Music creative vice president, John Titta, quoted in Newman (3 June 1995), 53.
18. Ennis, *supra* note 2, at 104.
19. See, *e.g.*, Newman (3 June 1995), 53; Flick (5 November 1994), 18.
20. Morris (18 May 1996), 12.
21. Rosen (28 October 1995), 46.
22. Lichtman (26 December 1992), 22.
23. For a more detailed discussion of single-song and exclusive songwriter terms of agreements see, for example, Kohn & Kohn (2002); Passman (2000); Shemel and Krasilovsky (2000); Halloran (2001); Practising Law Institute (2003); Farber (1989); and Lindey (1988). Farber and Lindey are loose-leaf publications that are updated annually.
24. Lichtman (25 December 1993), 24.
25. Kohn & Kohn (1996): 111.
26. Holland (5 April 2003), 1.
27. Kosser (January/February 1995), 34.
28. Brabec and Brabec (1994), 283.
29. Roland (5 January 1995), E1.
30. It was called "The Society of European Stage Authors and Composers" when it was founded in 1930, but later changed its name to just SESAC, Inc.
31. Kohn & Kohn (1996) distinguish between a performance of a composition or several compositions from a dramatico-musical work such as an opera or musical, and a performance which is dramatic in that it is used to tell all or part of a story line being portrayed in a dramatic fashion. Even this distinction would not require a dramatic license for a straight performance of a song that tells a story, such as "Ode to Billie Joe" or "The Wreck of the Edmund Fitzgerald," unless it was done in a dramatic fashion.
32. *Broadcast Music, Inc. v. Columbia Broadcasting System, Inc.*, 99 S. Ct. 1551, at 1562-1563 (1979).
33. Lichtman (4 February 1995), 1; Morris (26 February 1994), 13.
34. Lichtman (19 February 2000), 10.
35. "Music for Money," ASCAP pamphlet, 1996, 1.
36. The Web sites: ASCAP is www.ascap.org ; BMI is www.bmi.com ; SESAC is www.sesac.com.
37. Jeffrey (30 September 1995), 10.
38. "New ASCAP Venture Aims to Redefine Media Monitoring," *Communications Daily*, 18 September 2003. (Retrieved from Lexis–Nexis 9 March 2004.)

39. "SESAC, BDS to Monitor More Genres," *Billboard*, 24 February 1996, 12.
40. Kosser (January/February 1995), 34.
41. The HFA quit its general service in issuing and collecting for synchronization licenses in 2002. http://www.nmpa.org/hfa/licensing.html last visited June 3, 2003.
42. National Music Publisher's Association (1996). National Music Publisher's Association information.
43. http://www.nmpa.org.
44. The 1978 CPI was 65.2 (1982–1984 = 100) and the 2002 CPI was 179.9 (1982–1984 = 100). Data retrieved from www.bls.gov June, 2003.
45. Dranov (1980); National Music Publisher's Association (2002); U.S. Bureau of Labor Statistics, *Monthly Labor Review.*
46. DiConstanzo (24 September 1994), 64.
47. Based on a sample of *Billboard's* Hot 100 A–Z listings of the sheet music distributors of the Hot 100 singles chart songs in 1995, 1996, and 2003.
48. Lichtman (7 May 1994), 6.
49. See note 41.
50. See, *e.g.*, Kohn, supra note 22; Shemel and Krasilovsky (2000);Passman *(2000)*.
51. Bill Lowery is the owner of Lowery Music Group in Atlanta, GA and a past president of the National Academy of Recording Arts and Sciences. This is something that the author heard him say publicly on a number of occasions.
52. For example, Josefs (1996); Braheny (1988); Oland, (1989); Davis (1988).
53. Web sites are www.songwriters.org and www.nashvillesongwriters.com.
54. Quoted in Roland (5 January 1995), E1.
55. Mitchell (19 June 1999), 28.

Notes for Chapter Five

1. Quoted in Waddell (28 December 2002), YE-16.
2. Derr (29 December 1995), 9; Cohen & Grossweiner (29 December 1995), 8. The demise of *Performance* magazine in 2000 left *Billboard* and *Pollstar* as the two important trade publications tracking live performances of major artists. While *Billboard* and *Pollstar* report only musical/recording acts, *Performance's* list of the Top 50 grossing acts typically included five or fewer non-recording artists.
3. "2002 Top 100 Tours," *Pollstar*, 13 January 2003, 4.
4. Waddell (28 December 2002), YE-16.
5. "2002 Top 100 Tours," *Pollstar*, 13 January 2003, 13.
6. Good general sources for additional information on live performance, touring, and the relationships of the major players can be found in Boswell (1991; which also has good details on production), and in Stein & Zalkind (1979; although this book is becoming dated).
7. Personal manager Ed Bicknell, manager of Dire Straits, quoted in Flanagan (April 1991).
8. *Performance, 1996 Performance Guide: Talent/PM* (1996); *Pollstar, Pollstar Artist Management Rosters 1996* (Second Edition) (1996).
9. For additional information about personal managers and their functions, see Frascogna.& Hetherington (1997); Halloran (2001), 253; Brabec & Brabec (2000); Shemel and Krasilovsky, (2000), Chapter 32; Passman (2000), Chapter 3.
10. "1995 Top 50 Tours," *Pollstar*, 31 December 1995, 7.
11. "2002 Top 100 Tours," *Pollstar*, 13 January 2003, 4.
12. Quoted in Schoepe (1996), 6.
13. Newman (20 March 1993), 12.
14. Morris (3 February 1996), 13.
15. Nunziata (1 December 1990), 80.
16. For more detailed analysis of management agreements, see, e.g., Halloran (2001), 253; Brabec and Brabec (2000); Shemel and Krasilovsky (2000); Chapter 32; Passman (2000), Chapter 3.
17. Pollstar, *Booking Agency Directory,* (2003).
18. *Performance*, 29 December 1995, 12.

19. "2002 Top 100 Tours," *Pollstar*, 13 January 2003.
20. Sobel (1996).
21. For more detailed analysis of agency agreements, see, e.g., Halloran (2001), 253; Brabec and Brabec (2000); Shemel and Krasilovsky (2000); Chapter 32; Passman (2000), Chapter 3.
22. Regional promoter Philip Lashinsky, speaking in a concert promotion class at Middle Tennessee State University, 20 Sept. 1994.
23. Newman (14 August 1993), 10.
24. Gett (4 October 1986), 1.
25. "96 Tour Slate Is Heavy on Festivals, Classic Acts," *Billboard*, 13 April 1996, 97.
26. DeCurtis (11 September 1986), 15.
27. Zimmerman (5 August 1991), 56 and (6 January 1992), 89.
28. Boehlert (11 July 1996), 19.
29. Waddell (27 December 1997), 98 and (11 March 2000), 1.
30. House of Blues executive vice president, Alex Hodges, quoted in Waddell (11 March 2000), 1.
31. Waddell (21 December 2002), 7.
32. Bragg (3 February 2001).
33. A sample survey of concerts in venues of the 8,000 to 12,000 range in *Pollstar*, 26 August 1996 indicated that 13 of 35 shows reportedly sold less than 60 percent of available tickets. On the "manic" side of the business, 12 of the reported shows sold more than 90 percent of available tickets.
34. Duffy (8 August 1992), 10.
35. Stern (1994).
36. Boehlert (8 July 1995), 85.
37. "In Other On-line News," *Billboard*, 7 October 1995: 91; Matzer (8 July 1996), 20.
38. "Vivendi Makes Diller of a Deal," *Pollstar*, 7 January 2002, 52.
39. Reibman (3 February 1996), 6.
40. National Association of Recording Merchandisers, "Soundata Consumer Panel," *NARM Sounding Board* (online version), February 1996.
41. Newman and Duffy (6 October 1990), 1.
42. Verna (16 September 1995), 5.
43. See, e.g., "Ontario Place Corp.," *Billboard*, 4 June 1994, 77.
44. For a good biography/autobiography of Graham, read Greenfield and Graham (1992).
45. Corporate reports.
46. Spethmann (24 August 1994), 20.
47. Kafka (7 July 2003), 46; Paoletta (29 March 2003), 1.
48. Skinner (31 May 2003), 1.
49. American Federation of Musicians, Local 257, Nashville, TN.
50. "AFTRA Members Support Consolidation by 75.88%—SAG Vote Not Sufficient to Pass Referendum," AFTRA press release, 1 July 2003, retrieved from www.aftra.org.

Notes for Chapter Six

1. Caves (1987), 10.
2. See for example, Caves (1987), 10; Keat and Young (1992), 402.
3. R. Sanjek & D. Sanjek (1991).
4. "Top Pop Records, 1949" *Billboard*, 12 January 1950, 14.
5. Gehman (3 January 1953), 1.
6. Gehman (2 January 1954), 11.
7. Kramer (22 December 1956), 1.
8. Rolontz (5 January 1959), 3.
9. "LP Crown to Columbia, Victor Tops in Singles," *Billboard*, 5 January 1963, 4.
10. "Columbia and WEA Top Charts for 3rd Straight Year," *Billboard*, 17 February 1993, 1.
11. Christman (20 January 1996), 55 and (21 January 1995), 54); "SoundScan Releases 1996 Music Industry Figures," *Reuters Financial Service*, 6 January 1996 (Lexis).

12. Unless specifically noted, the information for this section comes from several sources including: Standard and Poor's *Stock Reports* and *Industry Surveys;* Marco (1993); R. Sanjek & D. Sanjek (1991).
13. Morris (2 March 1996), 13.
14. Garrity and White (26 August 2000), 1.
15. Teather (3 September 2002), *City Pages,* 19.
16. Neil Irwin, "Bronfman Builds His Very Next Empire," *The America's Intelligence Wire,* 25 November 2003.
17. "Warner Cos. Restructured as WEA Inc.," *Billboard,* 11 November 1995, 60.
18. Oppelaar (21 July 2003), 10.
19. http://www.sony.co.jp/en/SonyInfo/IR/Financial/AR/2001/pdf/ar2001e_10_04.pdf. (last visited 7/22/01).
20. Dezzani (20 August 1994), 38. Jeffrey (5 February 1994), 6.
21. Benz and Horwitz (7 December 2002), 3.
22. www.emigroup.com/financial/annrep2001/ (last visited 7/27/2001).
23. Boehm (12 August 1996), 7.
24. "EMI/Time Warner Merger Collapses," *Daily Music News,* 5 October 2000, www.billboard.com.
25. EMI, Bertelsmann Confirm Talk of Possible Merger," *Daily Music News,* 13 November 2000, www.billboard.com.
26. "Billboard Bits: EMI/WMG, Liza/VH1, 'Headbanger's Ball,'" *Daily Music News,* 22 September 2003, Billboard.com
27. See also Cusic (1996), 179.
28. Christman (28 April 2001), 66; Silverman (18 May 1996), 6.
29. "Indies Surprise Survival," Billboard, 3 December 1949, 1.
30. Christman (24 August 1996), 3, and (5 February 1994), 64; Bessman (20 May 1995), 47.
31. See, e.g., Garofalo (January 1987), 77.
32. A structure observed by Peterson and Berger (1996), 175.
33. An argument made in Stratton (1993), 183.
34. Burnett (December 1992), 749.
35. Alexander (1996), 171.

Notes for Chapter Seven

1. Thigpen (29 January 1996), 54.
2. Davis (1994).
3. Thigpen (29 January 1996), 54.
4. Melinda Newman, "Industry Analyzes Mariah Corey Deal," *Billboard,* 9 February 2002, 3.
5. "Warner Music Group and the Atlantic Group Expand Lava Records," *Business Wire,* 20 June 2002, 2269. Retrieved from InfoTrack.
6. For an interesting description of an A&R person's job, see, "A&R–A Week in the life," *Musician,* August 1994, 31.
7. Several excellent examples of books that explore in detail the ins and outs of recording artist agreements are: Passman (2000); Halloran (2001); Shemel and Krasilovsky (2000). More legalistic publications are, Farber (2002); Lindey (2002); Practising Law Institute (2002), annual seminar handbook. Farber and Lindey are loose-leaf publications updated regularly. All of these sources and personal experiences have been used in preparation of this chapter.
8. Daley (September 2001), 10; Oppelaar (18 June 2002), 6.
9. Leeds (11 April 2003) 1, Business, Part 3, 1.
10. R. Sanjek and D. Sanjek (1991), ix.
11. Rolontz (19 December 1960), 2.
12. Cooper (1978), 14.
13. Halloran (2001) and Passman (2000).
14. Hay (13 November 1999), 1.
15. Christman (28 April 2001), 66. 1995 data from SoundScan data through the Bluegrass Music Discussion Group on the Internet via Ken Irwin of Rounder Records.

16. Edward Morris (15 January 1994), 8.
17. Holland, (5 April 2003), 3.
18. Kipnis (19 April 2003), 36.
19. Frith (1992), 50.
20. Passman (2000), 135.
21. Marty (1981), 146.
22. "NOW That's What I Call Music, Vol. 12!" *Business Wire*, 4 March 2003, 5720.
23. Jones (1992).
24. "1995 Studio Business Operations Survey," *Pro Sound News*, September 1995, 20.
25. *Ibid.*
26. Daley (February 1996a), 98; Mandrell (1995), 4.
27. "1995 Studio Business Operations Survey," *Pro Sound News*, September 1995, 18.
28. *Ibid*, 19.
29. Mandrell (1995), 4.
30. "1994 *Pro Sound News* Recording Studio Operations Survey," *Pro Sound News*, September 1994, 28.
31. Steinwand (October 2001), 26.
32. World Studio Group and Record Plant founder, Chris Stone, quoted in Walsh, (15 February 2003), 1.
33. "1995 Studio Business Operations Survey," *Pro Sound News*, September 1995, 18–20.
34. Daley (February 1996b), 14.
35. Pete Moe, "Music Studios Face Challenges of the '90s," *Pro Sound News*, April 1996, 1.
36. "1995 Studio Business Operations Survey," *Pro Sound News*, September 1995, 18-20.
37. *The Mix 1996 Master Directory* listed 180 colleges and universities offering at least some course work in audio and 112 proprietary institutions offering some training in audio. The 1994 AES Directory of Educational Programs lists 49 providers of seminars and short courses, 25 programs leading to some form of certification of diploma, 40 leading to an associate's degree, 67 leading to a bachelor's degree, and 22 graduate level programs. The 2003 edition listed about 143 institutions offering such courses. The 2003 online version of the *Mix* directory lists 130 institutions. The AES Directory is available on the Internet at the AES home page at www.aes.org The *Mix* Directory is on-line at www.mixmag.com and the *Pro Sound News* directory is online at www.prosoundnews.com.
38. Hutchison and Progris (November 1996), 8.
39. See, for example, Cosola (December 1996), 52.
40. Marty (1981), 146.

Notes for Chapter Eight

1. American Marketing Association Board of Directors, 1985.
2. See, e.g., Willis and Willis, (1993), 299.
3. See, e.g., Lacy et al. (1993), 251; Peter and Donnelly (1986), 9.
4. "SoundData Consumer Panel," *NARM Sounding Board*, August 1996 (online version).
5. Cronin (29 April 1995), 1.
6. "SoundData Consumer Panel," *NARM Sounding Board*, September 1996 (online version).
7. Ibid.
8. Reunion Records president Terry Hemmings quoted in Price (13 January 1996), 1.
9. Cusic (1996), 127–128. For insight into the gospel and Christian music industry see Cusic (1990).
10. Macy (2002), 29–33; Carlozo (6 September 2002), pK4885.
11. RIAA, 2001 RIAA Year-end Statistics. Latin Music, www.riaa.com/pdf/2001_yearend_latin_2.pdf (last visited July 15, 2003).
12. The RIAA reported that more than 24 percent of pirate product seized in 2001 was Latin, compared to its roughly 4.5 percent of the market "Recording Industry Releases Year-end 2001 Latin Music Statistics," RIAA, retrieved from www.riaa.com/news/marketingdata/2001_latin_yearend.asp (last visited July 15, 2003).
13. National Association of Recording Merchandisers, *Annual Survey Results 1995* (1996), 6.

14. "SoundData Consumer Panel," *NARM Sounding Board*, September 1996 and June 1996 (online versions).
15. Ibid.
16. Rosen (30 March 1996), 5.
17. Transcript of preliminary injunction hearing, *A & M Records, Inc., v. Napster, Inc.*, (N.D. Cal.), July 26, 2000, at 6.
18. Leonard (12 May 2003), 52.
19. Harrison (25 June 2003).
20. Benz (12 July 2003), 5.
21. UMG Press Release, "Universal Music Group, World's Largest Music Company Dramatically Reduces CD Prices," UMG Web site new.umusic.com/News.aspx?News ID=182 (accessed 3 October 2003); Frank Aherns, "Universal Slashing CD Prices," *The America's Intelligence Wire*, 4 September 2003; Ed Christman, "Universal Sets $12.98 List, Eliminates Co-op Ad Funds, *Billboard Bulletin*, 4 September 2003, 1.
22. Christman, et al. (13 March 1993), 9.
23. Christman (23 December 1995), 5.
24. "Price List Reflects Firmer Structure in Cost of Disks," *Billboard*, 15 June 1955, 5.
25. "WEA Raises LP & Single Basic Prices," *Billboard*, 30 June 1979, 3.
26. Christman (20 February 1999), 6.
27. Steve Traiman, "Off-Price Millions: The Secret in the Vault," *Billboard*, 13 April 1996, 50.
28. As defined by Neilsen SoundScan, "Market Watch," *Billboard*, 2 August, 2003, 67.
29. Christman (13 April 1996), 5.
30. "Top Pop Catalog Albums" (chart), *Billboard*, 12 October 1996, 83.
31. Ibid.
32. Christman (23 December 1995), 5.
33. Belinfante and Davis (winter 1978–1979), 47, 51.
34. An unpublished report to the author from a graduate of the Recording Industry program at Middle Tennessee State University, who was one of the store managers involved. The name of the manager and chain are withheld by request.
35. Belinfante and Davis (winter 1978–1979), 47, 51.
36. "CD Prices Start to Tumble," *Billboard*, 7 July 1984, 1.
37. Nunziata (25 July 1992), 6.
38. "CD Prices: Why So High?" *Consumer Reports*, February 1996, 17.
39. Hinkley, David. "Suit Calls CD Prices a Steal—for Companies," *New York Daily News*, 11 July 1966, New York Now section: 2 (Lexis).
40. By late 2001 $18.98 was the most common SRLP of CDs in the Billboard Top 200 Album Chart (56 percent) with $17.98 being the second most common SRLP (32 percent). "Billboard Top 200," *Billboard*, 6 October 2001.
41. Strauss (5 July 1995), C-11.
42. Christman (30 March 1996), 59.
43. Christman (1 June 1996), 3.
44. "SoundData Consumer Panel," *NARM Sounding Board*, June 1996 (online version).
45. Christman, (23 October 1993), 43.
46. Christman (29 January 2000), 5.
47. Federal Trade Commission, "Record Companies Settle FTC Charges of Restraining Competition in CD Music Market," FTC Press Release, May 10, 2000, (www.ftc.gov/opa/2000/05/cdpres.htm).
48. Conniff (1 October 2002), 1; "Settlement OK'd in CD price-fixing suit," *Billboard Bulletin*, 17 June 2003, 1.
49. *United National Records, Inc. v. MCA, Inc.*, No. 82 C 7589 (N.D. Ill. 1985) (Notice of hearing on proposed additional settlements, proposed plan of distribution and allowance of expenses and attorneys' fees.)
50. Jeffrey (23 December 1995), 67.
51. Holland (2 March 1996), 1.
52. "NARM Withdraws Anti-Trust Suit vs. Sony Music," *Billboard Daily Music News*, Billboard.com, 4 December 2001.
53. Holland and Brandle (October 16, 2001).
54. "SoundData Consumer Panel," *NARM Sounding Board*, June 1996 (online version).

55. "SoundData Consumer Panel," *NARM Sounding Board*, March 1996 (online version).
56. Boehlert (22 August 1996), 34.
57. Ibid.
58. Quoted in "Payola 2003," *Online Reporter*, 15 March 2003.
59. For a detailed history of payola, see Segrave (1994).
60. R. Sanjek and D. Sanjek (1991), 74.
61. Segrave (1994), 16, 65.
62. Ibid., 173.
63. 47 U.S.C. §317(a)(1).
64. DiMartino (9 January 1988), 5. See also, J. Gregory Sidak and Kronemyer (summer 1987), 521.
65. Shemel and Krasilovsky (2000), 407–412.
66. Shields (August, 1990).
67. For example, Ennis (1992), 261.
68. Dannen (1990), 15.
69. Lichtman (15 March 1986), 1.
70. Philips (20 October 2000), C1.
71. Philips (March 2001), C1.
72. Philips (29 May 2001), AI1.
73. Rosenzweig, (24 July 2001), III6.
74. McConnell (14 April 2003), 3.
75. DiMartino (9 January 1988), 5.
76. Morris (13 April 1996), 96.
77. DiMartino (3 June 1989), 1.
78. Morris (8 September 1990), 1.
79. "SoundData Consumer Panel," *NARM Sounding Board*, December 1995 (online version).
80. "SoundData Consumer Panel," *NARM Sounding Board*, January 1996 (online version).
81. Jeffrey (8 June 1996), 1.
82. "SoundData Consumer Panel," *NARM Sounding Board*, August 1996 (online version).
83. "Victor's LP Offer Sets Trade Buzzing," *Billboard*, 30 December 1957, 11.
84. "SoundData Consumer Panel," *NARM Sounding Board*, January 1996 (online version).
85. Mayfield (23 December 1996), 106.
86. Ibid.
87. Denisoff (1975), 180.
88. Hull (1977), 3.
89. National Association of Recording Merchandisers, Inc. (1979), 20.
90. "Billboard Debuts Piece Counts on Two Music Charts," *Billboard*, 25 May 1991, 1.
91. Terry (1 June 1991), 1.
92. Quoted in McCormick (21 March 1992), I4.
93. Ibid.
94. Ibid.
95. SoundScan promotional materials (2003).
96. *Billboard's* Hot 100 Singles (11/30/91), Bubbling under the Hot 100 Singles (12/5/92), R&B Singles Sales (7/11/92), Hot R&B Singles and Bubbling under Hot R&B Singles (12/5/92), Top R&B Albums, Top Pop Catalog Albums (5/25/91), Top Reggae Albums (2/5/94), Top Jazz Albums (12/4/93), Top Contemporary Jazz Albums (12/4/93), Hot Dance Music (8/28/ 93), Billboard Latin 50 (7/10/93), Top Christmas Albums (12/7/91), Top Music Videos (4/ 24/93), Hot Rap Singles (12/4/93), and The Billboard Classical 50 (12/4/93) "Chart Histories," *Billboard 100th Anniversary Issue 1984–1994*, 1 November 1994, 262–273.
97. SoundScan promotional materials (2003).
98. SoundScan Data for end of year 1999; *Radio & Records* reports of SoundScan data for 21 February 2003.
99. "New Technology Will Strengthen Accuracy of BDS," *Billboard*, 1 July 1994, 1.
100. Ibid.
101. Fleming & Zimmerman (31 Dec. 1990), 1.

102. The Hot 100 (singles) 11/30/91, Bubbling under the Hot 100 (12/5/92), Top 40 Radio Monitor/Hot 100 Airplay (12/8/90), Top 40/Mainstream and Top 40/Rhythm Crossover (10/3/92), Hot R&B Singles and Bubbling under Hot 100 R&B Singles (12/5/92), R&B Radio Monitor (7/11/92), Hot Adult Contemporary (7/17/93), and Modern Rock Tracks (6/12/93). "Chart Histories," *Billboard 100th Anniversary Issue 1984–1994*, 1 November 1994, 262–273.
103. Boehlert (22 January 1994), 1.
104. "BDS, CMR to Merge Services," *Mediaweek*, 23 January 1995, 41.
105. "Dutch Conglomerate VNU to Purchase BPI Communications," *Billboard*, 22 January 1994, 3.
106. "SoundData Consumer Panel," *NARM Sounding Board*, March 1996 (online version).
107. Tom Hutchison quoted in Roland (5 June 1995), 1.
108. *Radio & Records*, 21 February 2003 (Various charts).

Notes for Chapter Nine

1. "State of the Industry," (NARM President Ann Leiff's remarks at the 1995–1996 NARM Convention) *NARM Sounding Board*, May 1995 (online version).
2. Geoffrey Hull, *Atlanta Record Buyers Survey*, (1976) Georgia State University. The survey did include rack locations, but was dominated by stores.
3. General sources are Sanjek and Sanjek (1991); Marco (1993).
4. Former NARM President Jules Malmud, quoted in Denisoff (1986) 212.
5. "SoundData Consumer Panel," *NARM Sounding Board*, December 1994, 10.
6. *National Association Recording Merchandisers Survey*, 1981.
7. "A Guide to Profitability," *Music Retailer*, July 1975, 34, 50.
8. Christman (16 October 1993), 5.
9. Handleman information from: *Moody's Handbook of Common Stocks*, winter 1995-1996; *Standard and Poor's Stock Reports*, February 1996; Gubernick (24 July 1989), 80; Christman (12 February 1994), 5; Goldstein (18 July 1992), 6.
10. "Handleman Company," *Hoover's Company Capsule Database–American Public Companies*, (Lexis-Nexis) 2001.
11. Christman and Goldstein (18 June 1994), 6.
12. Christman (27 December 1997), 63.
13. "Trans World Entertainment Corporation," *Hoover's Company Capsule Database–American Public Companies*, (Lexis-Nexis) 2001.
14. "Best Buy Company, Inc.," *Hoover's Company Capsule Database–American Public Companies*, (Lexis-Nexis) 2001.
15. Benz (19 June 2003), 2.
16. Christman (5 July 2003), 35
17. Jeffrey (12 February 1994), 85.
18. Christman (16 October 1993), 5.
19. Christman (4 March 1995), 64. (Hear Music was a Boston-based chain with stores spread across the country in a number of major markets, most recently opening stores in California.)
20. Christman (13 April 1996), 68.
21. Christman (20 April 1996), 72.
22. Christman (18 May 1996), 52.
23. Christman (3 February 1996), 62.
24. Christman (28 December 2002), 45.
25. *Bankruptcy* is no longer a term used in the code to describe a debtor.
26. "SoundData Consumer Panel," *NARM Sounding Board*, January 1996 (online version).
27. Webb-Pressler (29 April 1995), C1; Christman, (28 October 1995), 66 and (23 December 1995), 1.
28. Ressner (3 September 1992), 13, 80.
29. "1996 Yearend Market Report on U.S. Recorded Music Shipments." Retrieved from www.riaa.com/news/marketingdata/1996_US_yearend.asp (Accessed 6 March 2004).
30. 17 U.S.C. § 109.
31. P.L. 98-450, 98 Stat. 1727, 98th Cong., 2nd Sess. (1984).

32. 17 U.S.C. § 109(b)(1)(A).
33. See, e.g., Diamond (17 June 1993).
34. "Both Retailer, Label Claims Backed by Used-CD Survey," *Billboard*, 2 October 1993, 4, 112.
35. Garrity, Benz, Christman, and Holland (8 June 2002), 1.
36. That is the theory that the U.S. Supreme Court applied in declining to prohibit the copying of broadcast television programs on home VCRs in *Sony Corp. v. Universal City Studios, Inc.*, 464 U.S. 417 (1984). Considering the question of whether the manufacturers of VCRs could be liable as contributory infringers, the Court stated, "The sale of copying equipment, like the sale of other articles of commerce, does not constitute contributory infringement if the product is widely used for legitimate, unobjectionable purposes." Although the used CD retailer would be more directly liable under the specific terms of the statute, the overall logic applies."
37. Garrity, Benz, Christman, and Holland (8 June 2002), 1.
38. Hamlin (16 June 1993), D1; Wherehouse record store chain vice president for Marketing, Bruce Jesse cited in Kaberline (18 June 1993), I1; MacDougall (21 June 1993), I1.
39. "Both Retailer, Label Claims Backed by Used-CD Survey," *Billboard*, 2 October 1993, 4, 112.
40. Morning Edition, *National Public Radio*, 14 July 1993 (Transcript, Lexis).
41. Kaberline (18 June 1993), I1, estimating the profit on a used CD is twice that of a new product; MacDougall (21 June 1993), I1; Christman (5 December 1992), 1.
42. Based on purchasing a used product for $6.00 and selling it for $10.99, or purchasing for $3.60 and selling it for $10.95. Hamlin (16 June 1993), D1.
43. Strauss (5 June 1995), C11.
44. Christman (5 December 1992), 1; Rosen & Christman (7 December 1971), 1.
45. Christman (5 December 1992), 1.
46. "Radio, Promo People Said to Sell CDs," *Billboard*, 7 December 1995, 79.
47. "Both Retailer, Label Claims Backed by Used-CD Survey," *Billboard*, 2 October 1993, 4, 112.
48. Hamlin (16 June 1993), D1; Kaberline (18 June 1993), I1; Philips (29 June 1993), F3.
49. Rosen and Christman (7 December 1971), 1.
50. Christman (5 December 1992), 1.
51. Diamond (17 June 1993).
52. Hamlin (16 June 1993), D1; Jolson-Colburn (17 June 1993),14C; MacDougall (21 June 1993), I1.
53. Christman (5 December 1992), 1.
54. "Brooks Delivers Used-CD Ultimatum," *Billboard*, 10 July 1993, 6.
55. Ibid.
56. Rosen (31 July 1993), 8.
57. Rosen (11 September 1993), 1.
58. Greene (11 July 1994), I1; "Dispute between Music Companies and Record Store Owners Over Sale of Used CDs is Settled," 15 *Entertainment Law Reporter*, April 1994, 26 (Lexis).
59. Rosen (11 September 1993), 1.
60. Sandler (3 May 1994), 1.
61. Tower Records advertisement, *Billboard*, 18 May 1996, APQ-29.
62. McClure (9 July 1994), 39.
63. Christman (28 December 2002), 45.
64. Brandle and Ferguson (27 January 2003), 2.
65. McClure (2 July 1994), 80.
66. Clark-Meads (16 March 1996), 1, 116.
67. Corporate Web site: www.hmvgroup.com ; Brandle and Ferguson (27 January 2003), 2.
68. Pride (4 September 1993), 12.
69. W. H. Smith Web site: www.whsmithplc.com.
70. Christman (4 May 1996), 54.
71. Mary Mancini, Owner of Lucy's Record Shop, Nashville, TN, quoted in Borzillo (30 March 1996), 66.
72. The following articles describe typical examples of indie stores: Bessman (20 January 1996), 61; Hadler (7 January 1995), 78; Phalen (20 November 1993), 93; Jeffrey (17 July 1993), 93; Christman (5 June 1993), 73.
73. Borzillo (30 March 1996), 66.
74. Stander (14 August 1993), 4.

75. Mateja (30 July 2003).
76. Jeffrey (26 November 1994), 63.
77. Atwood (30 March 1996), 59; Traiman (25 February 1995), 76.
78. Rosenblum (15 July 1995), 61.
79. DeConstanzo (24 September 1994), 64.
80. Seth Gershel, vice president of Simon & Schuster Audio, quoted in Rosenblum (15 July 1995), 61.
81. Rolontz (5 October 1959), 1.
82. Davis (1974), 19.
83. General record club information sources: Denisoff (1986), 211, 212, 219; Shemel and Krasilovsky (2000), 383–387; Sanjek and Sanjek, (1991).
84. See generally Christman (3 February 1996); Christman and Jeffrey (23 March 1996), 1; and "Record Clubs: An Inside Look at an Evolving Enterprise," *Billboard*, 30 March 1996, 1.
85. "Both Retailer, Label Claims Backed by Used-CD Survey," *Billboard*, 2 October 1993, 4.
86. Christman (28 December 2002), 45.
87. Pavlik (1996), 394.
88. Ayre (28 May 1996), 56.
89. "SoundData Consumer Panel," *NARM Sounding Board*, January 1996 (online version).

Notes for Chapter Ten

1. See for example, "Study Reveals Top Advertisers," *Billboard*, 13 April 1996, 85; "Radio's Top Advertisers," *Brandweek*, 18 September 2000, 8.
2. "Soundata Consumer Panel," *NARM Sounding Board*, March 1996 (Retrieved from NARM's internet site, http://www.narm.com.).
3. Reprinted in *Music Retailer*, April 1975, 29.
4. Warner Communications, Inc. (1978), 77.
5. CBS Records, "Today's Singles Buyer," distributed at the NARM Convention.
6. Hirsch (1969).
7. Grunwald (1937).
8. Ibid.
9. *RCA Mfg. Co., Inc. v. Whiteman*, 144 F.2d 86 (2d Cir. 1940).
10. Ibid. at. 90.
11. "The Bionic Radio," *Billboard*, 21 May 1977, RS-71 (Century of Recorded Sound Special Issue).
12. *Ibid.*, at RS-96.
13. "Radio Meets the TV Challenge and Re-invents Itself," *Media Week, Radio 75th Anniversary Supplement*, 4 September 1995, Supp. Page 20.
14. Denisoff (1975) notes the 1955 date at 233. Sanjek and Sanjek (1991) notes it as KOWH, Omaha at 109.
15. "The Bionic Radio," *Billboard*, 21 May 1977, RS-71 (Century of Recorded Sound Special Issue).
16. Data from "Radio Billings 1935-1974," *Broadcasting Yearbook* (1976), C-298.
17. The rule was changed briefly in 1970 to prohibit AM-FM ownership, but within a year it was relaxed so that dual ownership was again allowed.
18. See generally, Denisoff (1986); Ennis (1992); Sanjek and Sanjek (1991).
19. "Record of Radio Station Growth since Television Began," *Broadcasting & Cable Yearbook* (1995), B-655; *Broadcasting & Cable Yearbook* (2001), B-639.
20. "U.S. and Canada Radio Programming Formats," *Broadcasting and Cable Yearbook* (1995), B-592.
21. "National Format Shares, Fall 2000," *R&R Directory*, Vol. 1 (2001), 5.
22. Carter, et al. (1994), 609-619.
23. See, e.g., "Sage Acquires Stations," *New York Times*, 26 June 1996, C3-national; "Chancellor Agrees to Buy 8 Radio Stations, *New York Times*, 16 May 1996, C4-national; "American Radio Merging with Henry Broadcasting," *Broadcasting and Cable*, 25 March 1996, 14; Heuton, (4 December 1995).
24. "The New Empire of the Air," *U.S. News and World Report*, 1 July 1996, 10.

25. Rathburn (1 July 1996), 6.
26. "FCC Launches Comprehensive Examination of Rules on Multiple Ownership of Local Market Radio Stations," FCC News Release, November 8, 2001, retrieved from http://ftp.fcc.gov/Bureaus/Mass_Media/News_Releases/2001/nrmm0115.html.
27. "Radio Mergers" retrieved from www.fcc.gov/mb/audio/includes/18-mergers.htm.
28. "Security in Numbers: The Top 25 Radio Groups Now Control Nearly One-quarter of All Stations," *Broadcasting and Cable*, 9 September 2002, 32.
29. Petrozzello (24 October 1994), 3.
30. Rogers and Woodbury (January 1996), 81.
31. Retrieved from www.futureofmusic.org/images/FMCradioexecsum.pdf.
32. Holland (8 February 2003), 2.
33. Jepsen (20 April 1996), 91.
34. "U.K.'s Niche Stations Willing Battle against Homogenization," *Billboard*, 13 April 1996, 85.
35. "ABC Radio, SoundScan to Feed Sales Info to Affiliates," *Billboard*, 16 April 1994, 85.
36. Novia (10 May 1996), 28.
37. Petrozzello (20 May 1996), 51.
38. Taylor (24 February 1996), 90.
39. *Broadcasting & Cable Yearbook 1986*, G-16.
40. See, e.g., Jackson, (1997); Denisoff (1986), 238; Sanjek and Sanjek (1991), 173–175.
41. Whitburn (1987).
42. Russell (1 November 1994), 196.
43. "Will DVD Be Music Video's Champion?" *DVD Report*, 28 April 2003. Retrieved from InfoTrac.
44. Jackson (16 June 1984), 10.
45. Seideman (23 June 1984), 1.
46. E. Morris (29 May 1995), 26.
47. Pride and Newman (12 November 1994), 5.
48. Levin (29 April 1995), 5.
49. Russell (11 June 1994), 56 and (7 May 1994), 44; Price (20 May 1995); Levenson (2 October 1993), 8.
50. "Top 25 Media Groups," *Broadcasting and Cable*, 28 August 2000, 38.
51. Recording Industry Marketing Research Class, Middle Tennessee State University, *Music Videos and Record Store Customers* (A 1995 study for the Music Video Association).
52. "Music Video Sales Chart Moves to SoundScan Data," *Billboard*, 24 April 1993, 6.
53. Goldstein (6 January 1996), 43.
54. "U.S. DVD Sales Rise," *The Americas Intelligence Wire*, 31 July 2003, retrieved from InfoTrac.
55. Desjardins (9 June 2003), 17.
56. Stewart (1 April 1989), 1.
57. Recording Industry Association of America (1984).
58. Nunziata (16 January 1993), 10; Top 200 Albums Chart, *Billboard*, 29 July 1995.
59. Atwood (8 October 1994), 8.
60. Kalogerakis (May 1996), 170.
61. Spahr (17 September 1994), 50.
62. "There's 'Nothin' Like the Reel Thing,'" *Billboard*, 18 May 1996, 4.
63. Quoted in Seay (3 April 1993), S3.
64. Time Warner owns Warner Brothers studios, Lorimar Television productions, and HBO. Universal owns Universal Pictures. Sony, where movie revenues were $3.1 billion and recording revenues were $5.6 billion in 1995, owns Sony Pictures and Columbia Pictures Entertainment. Prior to the merger with Universal, PolyGram sold its major film interest, MGM/United Artists in 1993, but still owned Interscope Communications, Island Pictures, and Working Title Films. In 1995 film revenues made up 14 percent PolyGram's sales. Bertelsmann, A.G. owns primarily European film, television, and radio interests. EMI purchased Filmtrax in 1990 and owns Thames Television. Sources: Sony Corporation, *1995 Annual Report*, online version, at http://www.sony.co.jp. And *Standard and Poor's Stock Reports* unless otherwise noted.
65. Daley, Henry, and Ryder (1997), 9.
66. Newman (23 December 1995), 1.

67. Newman (23 December 1995), 1, citing a 1994 study.
68. Hull (1977)).
69. R. Serge Denisoff, citing a 1984 study in *Tarnished Gold* (1986), 289.
70. Hull (1977).
71. Previously unpublished results from the survey discussed in Wyatt and Hull (1990), 38.
72. See, e.g., DeFleur and Dennis (1991), 127.
73. Unless otherwise noted, circulation figures for publications are obtained from Standard Rate and Data Service's (SRDS) *Business Publication Advertising Source*, July 1996 and *Consumer Magazine Advertising Source*, July 1996.
74. "The Folio 500," *Folio*, 1 July 1996, 53.
75. The figure was arrived at by adding all *SRDS Business Publications* category 99 (Music and Music Trades) for which circulation figures were given, plus *Variety* and *Radio and Records*, plus appropriate selections from category 122 (Radio, TV, Video).
76. Schlager (1994), 18.
77. "The Folio 500," *Folio*, 1 July 1996, 53.
78. "The Folio 500," *Folio*, 1 July 1996, 52.
79. Hull (August 2000)

Notes for Chapter Eleven

1. "America, Land of the Web Surfers," *Business Week*, 18 February 2002, 46.
2. "Media Usage and Consumer Spending: 1996 to 2005," *Statistical Abstract of the United States 2002*, U.S. Census Bureau, 2002, 698.
3. Lipton (15 September 1999).
4. Garrity (27 March 2003), 1.
5. Garrity (17 April 2003).
6. Ault (21 December 2002), 1, 72.
7. *UMG Recordings, Inc. v. MP3.com, Inc.*, 92 F. Supp. 2d 349 (S.D.N.Y. 2000).
8. Garrity (5 May 2002), 4.
9. "Sony Takes 4% Stake in MusicNet," *The Online Reporter*, 8 March 2003. Retrieved from InfoTrac.
10. The breakout was $789 million for UMG, $630 million for Warner Music Group, $366 million for BMG, $100 million for Sony, and $80 million for EMI. Benz (6 April 2002), 1.
11. Leonard (12 May 2003), 52.
12. Oppelaar (20 May 2003), 5; Marlowe (19 May 2003), 4; Garrity (10 October 2003).
13. Garrity (21 June 2003).
14. Cohen (19 August 2003).
15. "Music Publishers Support Landmark Accord with Record Industry Internet Subscription Services," Harry Fox Agency News Release, November 27, 2001, retrieved from www.harryfox.com/pressrelease.html?id=3.
16. Lichtman (21 October 2000), 4; "Music Publishers and MP3.com Reach Preliminary Landmark Agreement; Agreement Intended to Cover in Excess of One Million Songs Licensed Into the MyMP3.com Service," *Business Wire*, 18 October 2000: 2015.
17. Paulson (May 1996), C4.
18. "e-Media reports Woodstock '99 Streaming Media Results: Woodstock.com Is Largest Live Internet Music Event in History," *PR Newswire*, 3 August 1999: 4752.
19. Yoshida (10 April 1995), 1.
20. Atwood (10 June 1995), 6.
21. 17 U.S.C. § 114(d)(1). See also the Senate Report, S. Rep. No. 104-128, P.L. 104-39, 104th Cong. 1st Sess. 1995, 362.
22. 37 C.F.R. Part 201, December 11, 2000. 65 Fed. Reg. No. 238, 77292, December 11, 2000.
23. Traiman (10 June 1995), 39.
24. Woo (16 December 1993), B1, B16.
25. Frahn (1996), 3.
26. Traiman (10 June 1995), 39.
27. Rosenthal and Hamburg (12 February 1996), C4.
28. 17 U.S.C. § 512(c).

29. Greenfeld (27 March 2000), 82.
30. *A & M Records, Inc. v. Napster, Inc.*, 239 F. 3d. 1004 (9th Cir. 2001).
31. Cohen (18 June 2002).
32. In *Re: Aimster Copyright Litigation*, 2003 U.S. App. LEXIS 13229 (7th Cir. 2003): 7.
33. *Metro-Goldwyn-Mayer Studios, Inc. v. Grokster, Ltd.*, 243 F. Supp. 2d 1073; (C.D.Cal. 2003).
34. *Metro-Goldwyn-Mayer Studios, Inc. v. Grokster, Ltd.*, 259 F. Supp. 2d 1029 (C.D. Cal 2003).
35. "Entertainment Industry Appeals Court Decision on Peer-to-Peer systems," *States News Service*, August 20, 2003:1008232u7840.
36. *Metro-Goldwyn-Mayer Studios, Inc. v. Grokster, Ltd.*, 259 F. Supp. 2d 1029 (C.D. Cal. 2003); "KaZaA Owner Sharman Networks Has Vowed to Appeal after It Lost Its Bid to Countersue the RIAA," *Music Week*, 19 July 2003, 2.
37. In re: *Verizon Internet services, Inc.* 2003 U.S. Dist. LEXIS 681 (D.C. D.C 2003)
38. Cohen (2 May 2003).
39. Garrity (26 June 2003), 1.
40. Cohen (27 June 2003).
41. "2002 Yearend Anti-Piracy Statistics," RIAA. <Retrieved from RIAA.com>.
42. "Why Are Music Sales Falling? DOWNLOADING," *PR Newswire*, 18 June 2003, pLATU09118062003.
43. Nimmer (1995).
44. "Intellectual Property and the National Information Infrastructure: A Preliminary Draft of the Report of the Working Group on Intellectual Property Rights, Executive Summary," 13 *Cardozo Arts & Entertainment Law Journal* 275 (1994).
45. *Report of the Register of Copyrights on the General Revision of the U.S. Copyright Law* (1961). As pointed out in the legislative history of the 1909 Copyright Act, U.S. copyright law is not based on any natural right of the authors in their works, but is a means of benefiting the public. H. Rep. No. 2222, 60th Cong, 2d Sess. 1909.
46. Address to the United Negro College Fund Convocation, Indianapolis, IN, 12 April 1959. In *The International Thesaurus of Quotations*, (New York: Harper and Row) 1970.
47. Garrity (12 July 2003), 1.

Glossary

In the entries that follow, if the abbreviated form of a term is most commonly used, it is listed first.

A&R (Artist and Repertoire). — The department in a record company that is in charge of finding new artists to record. *A&R person* refers to persons who fulfill A&R functions by scouting new talent or listening to demos of artists and songs to decide who and what to record. Traditionally A&R people also found songs for their artists to record, and still do so where the artist is does not record only their own compositions.

AARC (Alliance of Artists and Recording Companies). — A nonprofit organization formed to distribute royalties collected by the U.S. Copyright Office under the Audio Home Recording Act.

add. — A record added to the playlist at a radio station or video channel.

Adult Contemporary. — A current radio format playing recordings by contemporary artists and primarily targeted at a listening audience that is over 24 years old. The overall sound tends to be softer than CHR (Contemporary Hit Radio) or the various rock formats.

advance. — A prepayment of royalties or other earnings. For example, a recording artist may be paid a flat sum upon delivery to the label of a finished master in advance of earning any royalties from the sale of copies of the recordings. Many items such as recording costs or promotion expenses may also be considered advances under the definitions in the agreement. Advances are used in many different agreements in the recording industry including label-artist agreements, songwriter agreements, and master licensing agreements.

AES (**Audio Engineering Society**). — A trade and educational organization for audio engineers. Founded in the 1950s, its members include recording engineers, equipment designers, and other professionals involved in audio engineering. It helps set technical standards and publishes a technical journal for members.

AFIM (**Association for Independent Music**). — Formerly NAIRD (National Association of Independent Record Distributors) in 1972, AFIM is a trade association for independent record labels, distributors, retailers, and those who work with independent labels and artists.

AFM (**American Federation of Musicians of the United States and Canada**). — The musicians' union.

AFTRA (**American Federation of Television and Radio Artists**). — The singers' and voice announcers' union.

AGVA (**American Guild of Variety Artists**). — The union for live entertainers who are not AFM or AFTRA members.

airplay. — Primarily refers to play of a recording on the radio, but may also refer to play in a record store, or of a music video on a television or video channel or in a club.

album. — A recording containing usually eight or more individual songs or *cuts*, totaling 30 or more minutes of playing time. CDs can contain up to 75 minutes of playing time. Vinyl albums usually contained no more than 45 minutes of playing time.

all-in royalty or deal. — A royalty rate designed to include royalties paid to an artist *and* any royalties paid to a producer. An all-in deal provides to the label the services of the recording artist and producer for a single royalty rate.

Alternative. — In radio, a format that does not play the mainstream hits in any particular genre, such as alternative rock or alternative country. May also refer to a genre of music that styles itself as alternative to the mainstream styles.

AMC (**American Music Conference**). — A nonprofit organization that promotes music and music education.

ancillary income. — In concert promotion, the term for revenues for the venue from parking or food sales that are not part of the gate and are not commissionable by the promoter or artist.

artist concessions. — In concert promotion, artist revenues from the sale of merchandise at the concert such as T-shirts, hats, nightgowns, that bear the artist's name and likeness. The venue may demand a percentage of artist concessions.

ASCAP (American Society of Composers, Authors and Publishers). — An organization that licenses music performance rights for songwriters and music publishers. It was the first performing rights organization in the United States, started in 1914.

Audio engineer. — A person who operates or designs equipment for recording and reproduction of sound. The term is broader than recording engineer and includes sound reinforcement and facilities sound. *See also* **recording engineer.**

Author. — In copyright law, a person who creates a work–a songwriter, recording artist, sculptor, poet, or novelist—is called an author.

bar code. — Generally taken to mean the Universal Product Code (UPC) appearing as a series of vertical black and white bars on a product, the bar code identifies the specific product and its manufacturer.

BDS (Broadcast Data Service). — The company (part of Nielsen Retail Entertainment) that monitors radio airplay with computers that identify what records are being played by comparing the broadcast to identifiable *signature* parts of the recording stored in the computer's memory. BDS can deliver the actual count of the number of times a particular record is played.

BET (Black Entertainment Television). — As its name implies, a cable television channel primarily targeting African Americans, and specializing in music videos and other entertainment programming.

blacklist. *See* defaulters

blanket license. — A term used mainly in performance rights licensing where a performing rights organization gives a licensee, such as a radio station or nightclub, the right to perform all of the songs in the PRO's repertoire as many times as the licensee wants. The "blanket" covers all of the songs as compared to a per-song or per-use license for one song at a time.

BMI (Broadcast Music, Inc.). — A performing rights organization started in 1940 and owned by broadcasters. BMI and ASCAP are the two largest performing rights organizations in the United States. BMI licenses radio and television stations, nightclubs, retail outlets, and others to publicly perform musical compositions.

boom box. — A small portable stereo system with attached speakers.

bootleg. — A recording not authorized by the artist's label (usually of a live performance or studio outtakes) that is manufactured and sold to the public outside of the normal channels of distribution. Beginning in 1995, such recordings violated the performers' rights in the copyright law to be the first to record or transmit their performances.

boxed set. — A special package containing usually three or more individual albums with special notes, photos, and other matter. The albums often contain previously unreleased cuts and alternative versions of recordings.

branch distributor. — A term still applied to a regional distributorship owned and maintained by one of the major conglomerates.

break. — To break an artist or recording is to have sufficient airplay or other national exposure that is beginning to translate into significant sales and additional airplay.

breakage allowance. — A deduction from a recording artist's royalties originally designed to account for the fact that lacquer and shellac recordings were brittle and easily broken. The label would deduct typically 10 percent of sales to account for broken records. The allowance still exists in some contracts even though cassettes and CDs rarely break.

breakeven point. — In concert promotion, the point at which the promoter's gross revenues equal the fixed expenses, including artist guarantees but not such things as any percentages for the artist or venue. In economics, the point at which total revenues have equaled total costs so the firm is showing neither a profit nor a loss.

broad inventory. — A selection of goods that crosses a number of different product lines, such as those that exist in department stores and mass merchandisers. Record stores typically have a narrow inventory.

budget line or price. — An album product line of a label that sells at a list price usually less than two-thirds of the current **front line** (new releases for established artists) album SRLP.

burnout. — As used in radio programming, a term indicating that the public is tired of hearing a particular recording.

business manager. — A person hired by an artist or the artist's personal manager to take care of managing the artist's money and business ventures.

buy-back. — In concert promotion, a deal between the promoter and the artist's agent to give the promoter the right to promote that artist the next time the artist plays in that promoter's area, city, or venue.

call-out research. — Radio research initiated by the station where someone calls random or selected listeners to ask their opinions on certain records or other programming that the station may be doing.

cassingle. — A cassette single, usually containing two or three cuts.

catalog. — Generally refers to all of the songs (actually the copyrights in those songs) owned by a music publisher. May also refer to all of a label's master recordings, or recordings that are not current hits, but are still available from the distributor and "in print."

census. — As used in performing rights, refers to a PRO's logging of every performance of every song by a certain broadcaster or other licensee. It is compared to a **sample**, in which only some licensees or some performances of the licensee are logged.

chain (retail). — A group of two or more stores that are owned by the same entity. Strictly speaking, even if a mom-and-pop opened a second store it would be called a chain, but most people would still call it a mom-and pop-store with two locations.

CHR (Contemporary Hit Radio). — The successor to the **Top 40** format, usually with fewer (20 to 25) current hits being played, instead of 40.

Clearance. — In rights generally, permission to use a particular song, recording, photo, or other work. In music publishing, the writer or publisher will clear a new song for licensing by listing it with the performing rights organization.

CMT (Country Music Television). — The cable channel devoted to programming country music videos and other programs featuring country artists and themes.

coin-op. — An early coin operated jukebox.

collective work. — A work (in copyright) formed by the assembly of a number of separate independent works into a collective whole, such as an anthology, periodical issue, or (perhaps) a record album.

commercially acceptable. — A standard by which labels judge masters submitted to them by recording artists. It means the recording must be technically and artistically good enough, in the opinion of the label executives, to enjoy to public sales and acceptance.

commission. — The percentage of the artist's income taken by the agent for arranging the performance or by the personal manager for being the artist's manager.

commissioned work. — In copyright, a work that is created at the behest of some party other than the author, usually for pay, and not as part of the author's job. *See also* **work made for hire.**

common law copyright. — Originally, the right of authors to be the first to publish their works as protected by common law and not the federal copyright statute. Since 1978, common law copyright only applies to works not fixed in a tangible medium of expression.

compulsory license. — Refers to a license that is granted by the copyright act to use a musical composition, sound recording or other copyrighted work. It is *compulsory* because the copyright owner must permit the use if the user conforms to the requirements of the statute regarding payment of royalties and so on. The term is often used in the music industry to refer to the compulsory mechanical license for phonorecords, but the term is really broader than that.

concept video. — A music video usually not much longer than a single song, which features visual images *other than* the artist performing the song. Usually these images tell a story or set a certain mood to accompany the song.

configuration. — The type of phonogram in which a recording is fixed, such as LP, cassette, compact disc, or even an electronic/digital file.

conglomerate. — A business corporation that is formed by the ownership of a number of other businesses or divisions operating in a wide variety of areas. For example, Sony Corp. owns record companies, music publishing companies, film production and distribution, and consumer electronics hardware manufacturing.

container charge. — A deduction from a recording artist's royalties to account for the fact that the label produces the package or container for the recording and claims it should not have to pay royalties on the part of the list price that covers the package. The reduction, typically 20 to 25 percent for CDs, is usually from the list price of the recording and typically amounts to much more than the actual cost of manufacturing the recording and its container.

contributory infringer. — One whose actions make an infringement possible, and who knows that the infringement is occurring.

controlled compositions. — Compositions (songs) written or owned in whole or part, or controlled in whole or part by the recording artist. The term usually appears in recording agreements between recording artists and record labels in a clause that attempts to get the artist to permit the label to use such compositions at a reduced rate.

co-op advertising. — Sometimes referred to as just *co-op money*, this is advertising money given to retailers or distributors by the labels to advertise the label's records in local media. Usually this ad must feature the label product with mention of the retail location. More often than not the co-op is not really split between the label and retailer, but is entirely paid for by the label.

copublishing. — An arrangement where two or more music publishers own the copyrights in a given song.

copyright. — A property right in a creative work that allows the author, and those who receive rights from the author, to control reproduction and other uses of the work. Copyrights are intangible personal property.

copyright administration. — A music publishing function concerning the registration of songs for copyright, the recordation of other documents pertaining to those songs with the Copyright Office, and the licensing of those songs for various uses. A small publishing company owned by a writer, artist, or producer may outsource this function to another publisher in exchange for a percentage fee.

Copyright Arbitration Royalty Panels (CARPs). — These are ad hoc panels set up through the Copyright Office that can adjust or set compulsory royalty rates for compulsory mechanical, cable television secondary transmission, noncommercial broadcasts for nondramatic musical works, digital performance of sound recordings, and digital delivery of phonorecords. CARPs are only appointed when there is some dispute over a royalty distribution or rate determination to be made.

corporate. — Often used as a derogatory term referring to recordings that sound like they were produced to fill a market niche rather than as inspired performances by writers and recording artists, as in *corporate rock.*

counterfeit recordings. — A form of record piracy in which the packaging and graphics as well as the recording is duplicated, so that the counterfeit not only sounds like, but looks like the original, legitimate recording. Counterfeit copies are sometimes so good that only someone working at the label can tell them from the legitimate copies. Sometimes they are so poorly done, with smudged ink, color registration errors, and things such as improperly printed or aligned UPC bar codes, that anyone could recognize them.

cover (band or versions). — Recordings or performances of a song by artists and performers other than the artist who originally recorded the song. A cover band does mostly cover versions of songs originally recorded and performed by other artists. Sometimes also used to refer to artists who do not write the compositions they record.

creative controls. — Authority to exercise control over the creative aspects of a recording, such as selection of material to be recorded, studios to use, producer, and side musicians. Artists and producers seek more creative controls from the labels.

cross-collateralization. — The practice (common in the recording industry) of using income from one source to recover advances made for a different source between the same two parties. For example, if an artist records an album that does not sell well, the recording advances for that album may be recovered out of royalties earned by a later album that does sell well.

deep inventory. — A selection of goods covering a lot of different varieties of the same basic good. Record stores typically have fairly deep inventories of recordings.

defaulters. — A union term for people who do not pay musicians or vocalists for their performances in clubs or on recordings. Union musicians will not perform for persons on a defaulters list.

demo. — A demonstration recording made to promote an artist, songwriter, or song to an agent, manager, music publisher, or record company.

derivative work. — In copyright law, a work that is based substantially on a preexisting work or works that edits, recasts, or changes the form of the prior work into a new copyrightable work.

development deal. — Usually a recording contract where a label gives an artist a small sum or perhaps annual amount to remain obligated to sign a full recording agreement with the label. The label may want to keep the option of signing the artist while the artist works on songwriting, performance, or some other aspect that the label feels is not quite ready for master recording. Music publishers may also offer similar deals to songwriters.

diamond. — A diamond album or single that the RIAA certifies has sold 10 million units at the wholesale level. There are no multiple diamond awards like there are multiplatinum awards.

digital performance of sound recordings. — Performance of a sound recording (as opposed to the song contained in the recording) by means of a digital audio transmission. This includes Internet streaming, satellite transmission, and background music services, but does not include transmission via the airways by regular licensed terrestrial broadcasters such as radio and TV stations, even though they may be broadcasting a digital signal.

digital sampling. — The electronic process where an audio signal is transformed into a numeric (digital) sequence that represents the level (amplitude) of the signal at various times during its duration. Those numbers are then stored in a digital form on some computer-readable device such as a computer disc, audio tape, or compact disc. If the sampling device measures (samples) the level of the signal often enough, it can then reproduce the level of the signal with the stored numbers that represent the amplitude at very close intervals of time. The closer the intervals of time (i.e., the higher the sampling frequency), the more accurate the picture of the complex audio signal can be. Compact discs, for example, have a sampling rate of 44.1 thousand times per second. The term *sample* comes from the fact that the digital representations are really only a sample of the entire signal. They are just so close together that when reproduced they sound so much like the original that the human ear cannot detect any difference. *See also* **sampling.**

disc jockey. — The person at a radio station who announces which recordings are being played. In the 1940s and 1950s these persons also tended to select which records were played, but those decisions are usually now in the hands of a music director or program director.

door. — The revenues made from admission fees, usually at a club. *See also* **gate.**

download. — An Internet or other digital transmission of a recording that enables the person receiving the download to retain a file copy of the recording.

dramatic performance. — A performance of a work that tells a story. Usually associated with musical theater or opera and multiple songs, but a single song may be a dramatic performance if accompanied by other action or visuals.

draw. — Another term for an advance. Most often heard in relation to exclusive songwriter agreements with music publishers or in live entertainment where musicians performing in clubs may get a draw after performing for a portion of their contracted term, say three days out of a six-day engagement.

dubbing. — In copyright law, literal duplication of a prior recording. In audio engineering, taking a recorded sound and editing it into or with a preexisting recording.

duopoly rule. — The FCC rule that prohibited the same company from owning two radio or TV stations in the same market. This rule was modified to allow ownership of AM and FM stations, then later abandoned completely.

effective competition. — A market condition in which it takes more than four firms to control 60 percent of the market.

8-track tape. — An audiotape with room to record eight separate tracks of information. Consumer 8-track tapes were endless loop tape cartridges, similar to those used in broadcasting, which contained four separate stereo programs. When the loop of tape had played all of two of the tracks (one program) a signal on the tape would cause the player to switch to playing back the next two tracks. On crudely recorded 8-tracks the program change would sometimes occur in the middle of a song.

elasticity of demand. — The percent change in quantity demanded (sold) that is brought about by a percent change in price. When the percent change in quantity demanded is greater than the percent change in price, then the demand is said to be *price elastic*. When a given percentage change in price results in a smaller percentage change in quantity demanded it is said to be *price inelastic*. The demand for current hit records is generally said to be price inelastic.

end caps. — The portions of record browsers (or other retail displays) located at the end of the aisles, facing the main aisles of the store.

established artist. — A recording artist who has had at least one (labels would say two) successful albums on a label of significant stature.

ET (electrical transcription). — A recording distributed to radio stations for the purpose of broadcast and not for sale to the public. National advertisements, syndicated programs, and musical recordings (into the 1950s) were distributed to radio this way. The ET had higher quality audio than was available on consumer records.

evergreen. — In music publishing, a song that is recorded by many artists and performed on a continuing basis for many years.

exclusive artist. — A recording artist under agreement to make recordings only for one record company.

exclusive contract. — Any arrangement where one party promises not to provide services or goods to any third party.

exclusive license. — Permission to use a song or some other right that is given only to one user and may not be given to any competing user.

exclusive songwriter. — A songwriter under agreement to write songs only for one publishing company.

fair use. — A provision of the copyright law allowing some limited uses of works where the use is particularly beneficial to the public and does not do much harm to the copyright owner.

first sale doctrine. — Part of the copyright law that allows the lawful owner of a copy of a work to dispose of possession of that copy in any way they wish. Copies may be resold, rented, leased, or given away. There is an exception to the doctrine that allows the owners of copyrights in sound recordings and computer programs to control rental of those works.

flown. — Term used for sound reinforcement, stage lighting, or other effects that are suspended from the rafters of a venue instead of being supported on the floor.

folios. — Songbooks containing multiple songs usually on a common theme or by the same artist or writer, as opposed to sheet music of single songs.

45. — The 45-rpm single with one song recorded on each side.

four walls. — In concert promotion a deal to rent a venue that includes only the right to use the facility with the venue providing nothing more than the four walls (i.e., no box office, no ticket takers, no ushers, no clean up, or other such service).

free goods. — In recording artist contracts and record marketing, a term of art meaning recordings given away to a distributor or retailer as a method of discount. For example, the retailer may get one free copy for each nine copies that are ordered. These are to be distinguished from promotional copies that are not meant for retail sale.

freestanding store. — A record store whose walls are not attached to other stores, compared to a strip center or mall.

front line. — The label's most recent releases from their top artists. These are usually the highest priced regular releases.

gate. — The admission revenues from a concert. Same as *door* but the latter is usually a club term.

gatekeeper. — In communication theory, a person who decides which messages will be communicated from one channel to another. Thus, radio music directors are gatekeepers, deciding which recordings will be communicated through radio.

GATT (General Agreement on Tariffs and Trade). — An international trade treaty that established the **World Trade Organization** and that provides for trade sanctions for member nations that do not properly protect copyrights.

gold. — A recording or music video that has wholesale sales of 500,000 units certified by the RIAA for an album or single or 50,000 for a music video. There are other gold standards for other kinds of video. *See also* **platinum** and **diamond.**

good ears. — A music industry term referring to the ability tell which artists and recordings will be successful. When used by audio engineers, it refers to the ability to distinguish technical and performance nuances in the recording and production process.

Grammy Awards. *See* NARAS.

grand rights. — Dramatic performance rights. *See* **dramatic performance.**

guarantee. — In concert promotion, the fixed amount that the artist will be paid, regardless of how many tickets are sold.

hard tickets. — Admission tickets preprinted and distributed for sale, as compared to **soft tickets**, which are only printed at the time of sale.

Harry Fox Agency (HFA). — A collection and licensing agency created and run by the National Music Publishers Association. It was designed to serve as a clearinghouse for mechanical and other licensing. The agency issues mechanical, synchronization, electrical transcription, and other licenses on behalf of its member publishing companies, collects licensing fees from the record companies and other users, and distributes those collections to the appropriate publishers.

hold. — In music publishing, a verbal agreement between a publisher and producer to not pitch the song to other producers until the first producer decides whether to record the song. In concert promotion, a verbal agreement between a promoter and a venue to keep a certain date open for that promoter and not to license the venue to another event for that date until the first promoter decides whether or not to use it.

horizontal integration. — An economic term describing the actions of a firm to buy out competing companies at the same level, such as one record store chain acquiring another record store chain.

hype. — Exaggerated claims as to the worth of a particular product or event. Short for hyperbole.

IATSE (International Association of Theatrical and Stage Employees). — A union for stagehands, lighting technicians, and other behind-the-scenes people who put on theatrical and concert events.

IFPI (International Federation of Phonographic Industries). — An international trade organization for record labels, composed of the trade associations from the individual countries, such as the *RIAA* in the United States.

IMRA (Independent Music Retailers Association). — An ad hoc group of record retailers who banded together to fight the labels' policies against stores selling used CDs.

independent distributor. — A record wholesaler who distributes records from **independent labels**.

independent label. — A record label not owned by one of the major conglomerates or their subsidiaries. Independent labels may have their recordings distributed by one of the majors and still be referred to as **indies**.

independent producer. — A record producer who is not on salary from a record label. Independent producers usually work on a royalty basis similar to recording artists, and may also be paid fees for each recording completed. *See also* **staff producer**.

independent record store. — A record store that is not part of a chain. A **mom-and-pop store**.

indie. — A term usually referring to an **independent label** or an **independent record store**.

in-house promotion. — A performance promoted by the venue itself, without any outside promoter.

initiation fee. — A one-time fee to join a union. Not to be confused with dues, which are paid on an ongoing basis.

joint work. — In copyright law, a work created by two or more people with the intention that their contributions be merged into an integrated whole.

jukebox. — The contemporary name for a coin operated record player.

Librarian of Congress. — The appointed head of the Library of Congress. This person has important administrative duties for a number of the compulsory licenses in the copyright law. The librarian is the ultimate overseer of the Copyright Office, which is part of the Library of Congress. The librarian distributes the royalties collected through the Copyright Office and is also responsible for convening Copyright Arbitration Royalty Panels for the settlement of distribution disputes and for the establishment of certain royalty rates.

license. — Permission to use something, such as a song or a recording, for some particular purpose.

lip-synch. — A performer pretends to be singing their song while a recording is being played, most often done in motion pictures or television, though sometimes done at concerts as well.

liquidate reserves. — A recording contract term meaning the label must pay out any **reserves for returns** that have not been accounted for with actual returns.

listening station. — A kiosk or manned listening area in a record store where consumers can hear samples or full of selections from albums or singles.

local (union). — The organizational unit of a labor union that covers a particular city or geographic area.

logging. — The practice of keeping track of individual songs or recordings played or performed, usually used in referring to the performing rights organizations.

long form video. — Usually a video recording of a concert that includes a significant number of songs.

loss leader. — Any product sold below cost in order to attract customers into a store.

LP. — The long-playing, 33 $1/3$-rpm, twelve-inch disc phonograph recording introduced in 1948. Usually contained eight to ten songs.

major label. — A term, probably somewhat out of date, used to refer to a label owned by one of the big four, which had its "own" distribution system. Now many small labels are owned by the big four and, therefore, technically have their own distribution because the same corporate parent owns the distribution system.

majors. — The "majors" refers to the four recording/entertainment conglomerates.

manufacturing clause. — A part of the copyright law that prohibits copies of recordings made outside of the United States for sale outside of the United States from being sold *in* the United States unless the U.S. copyright owner has given specific permission to import.

MAP (Minimum Advertised Price). — A price established by a label to discourage retailers from selling recordings below cost. The labels attempted to cut off some advertising funds for retailers that advertised albums below that label's MAP. The Federal Trade Commission found this to be an illegal restraint of trade and the labels entered into a consent decree to stop the practice.

margin. — The amount of revenue left from the sale of a product after deducting the cost of the item sold.

marketing concept. — The creation and delivery of a product or service that will satisfy consumer needs and allow a profit to be made.

masters. — The recordings from which other recordings are later going to be made or duplicated. May refer to a multitrack master, a stereo master, or a duplicating master.

mechanical license. — Permission from the copyright owner of a musical composition to manufacture and distribute copies of the composition embodied in phonorecords intended for sale to the public.

mechanical royalties. — Payments made from record labels to music publishers for the right to reproduce copies of songs (nondramatic musical compositions) in the recordings made by the labels. The term relates back to the 1909 Copyright Act, when Congress was creating a new right for music publishers that would give them the right to control recordings of their compositions in piano-roll or recorded form. Player pianos and talking machines (phonographs/gramophones) were primarily regarded as mechanical devices upon which the composition could be reproduced or performed. The term still applies to such rights, even though new devices may be less mechanical and more electronic in nature.

MEIEA (Music and Entertainment Industry Educators Association). — An organization of people who teach audio and music business courses, mostly at colleges and universities, but does include some trade school teachers and related professionals.

megastore. — A very large record store (typically over 20,000 square feet) that usually carries recordings, home video, computer software, and books.

MIDI (Musical Instrument Digital Interface). — A computer communications protocol designed to let synthesizers, controllers, and sequencers from different manufacturers communicate with each other. Now also used as a control language for lighting and other equipment as well.

mid-line. — A label's record albums that have an *SRLP* of 66⅔ to 75 or 85 percent of the SRLP of front line albums. *See also* **budget line.**

mom-and-pop store. — A single store (usually a sole proprietorship) that is not part of a chain.

MOR (Middle-of-the-Road). — Refers to pop music aimed at older audiences. May specifically refer to recording artists popular in the 1940s and 1950s, who were not rock, R&B, or country; or a radio format playing recordings by those performers.

MPA (Music Publishers' Association). — A trade organization for music publishers that primarily emphasizes issues relative to print music for education and concerts.

MSRP (Manufacturer's Suggested Retail Price). — A term often used in contracts where a recording artist's royalties are computed as a percentage of MSRP as opposed to wholesale price. Same as **SRLP**.

MTV (Music Television). — The music video cable television channel launched in 1981 by Warner Communications.

NAMM (National Association of Music Merchants). — The trade organization for music store owners. Music instrument manufacturers are associate members.

NARAS (National Academy of Recording Arts and Sciences). — Also known as the Recording Academy. The organization for creative people associated with the production of recordings, including performers, engineers, producers, graphic designers, and more. NARAS gives the annual **Grammy Awards** to recognize excellence in creative achievement in recordings.

NARM (National Association of Recording Merchandisers). — The trade association for all record retailers and distributors. The labels are associate members.

niche marketing. — Finding a small group of people who will purchase the product you are selling rather than trying to sell to a mass market (significant percentage of all consumers). For example, a record store selling only jazz recordings is engaged in niche marketing.

NMPA (National Music Publishers' Association). — A trade organization for music publishers. Formerly known as the Music Publishers' Protective Association.

nondramatic performance. — Performance of a single song in such a way that it does not tell any particular story. Usually any performance of a single song that is not part of an opera or musical is nondramatic unless it tells a story accompanied by action or visuals. Nondramatic performances are the only kind licensed by the performing rights organizations (**ASCAP**, **BMI**, and **SESAC**).

nonexclusive license. — Permission to use a work, such as a song or recording, where that same permission may also be given to other users. Performance licenses and mechanical licenses are nonexclusive.

nonreturnable. — A term usually applied to an advance, meaning the advance does not have to be given back to the provider, even if no royalties are ever earned. The advance is therefore not a debt. Advances are usually recoupable but nonreturnable.

notice. — In copyright law, the copyright notice placed on published copies of works.

oligopoly. — A market condition in which there are only a few firms competing in the market. A few could be anywhere from 2 to 20.

one-nighter. — A performance engagement for only one night. Also known as a *one-night stand*.

one-stop. — A distributor that sells all records from all labels to retailers.

out-of-the-box. — A radio term for adding a record to a playlist as soon as it is received; usually reserved for new releases by hot artists.

overdub. — An audio engineering term meaning to record an additional part along with a previously recorded part.

packaging deduction. *See* **container charge.**

parallel imports. — Copies of works lawfully made outside of a country for distribution outside of that country, but then imported back into the country of origin and sold alongside copies manufactured in the country of origin.

pay-for-play. — Refers to the practice of some popular clubs, particularly in Los Angeles, of having the performer pay to use the facility. The performer hopes to attract attention from labels and other music industry professionals.

payola. — The practice of paying someone to perform a particular song or recording. Historically, music publishers paid performers to sing their songs. More recently it refers to attempts by labels to make undisclosed payments to radio stations or disc jockeys to play their recordings. The latter practice is illegal.

perform publicly. — A term of art in the Copyright Act meaning to perform a work at a place open to the public, or at a place where a substantial number of people outside the normal circle of a family and its circle of social acquaintances is gathered, or to broadcast a performance of a work for public reception.

performance right. — The right to perform a work publicly. Usually the right to perform a song, but the term can also apply to limited situations in which sound recordings are digitally transmitted via the Internet, satellite, or by background music services. *See* **Digital performance of sound recordings.**

performance royalty. — The royalty paid to songwriters and music publishers for public performance rights. May also apply in limited situations to royalties paid to record companies for the public performance of sound recordings by digital audio transmission. *See* **Digital performance of sound recordings.**

per-program use (or license). — Permission to use a single recording or song on a one-time basis, as compared to a **blanket license.**

personal manager. — An artist's representative who works closely with the artist at all stages and usually for all purposes to develop the artist's career.

personality folio. — A songbook featuring songs as recorded by a particular artist or writer.

phonogram. — The term most often used internationally for **sound recordings.**

phonorecords. — Tangible objects such as tapes, compact discs, or vinyl discs in/on which a sound recording is embodied. The term also applies to a digital file containing a recording.

piracy. — Unauthorized duplications of sound recordings where the person or organization literally dubs a copy of the recording and sells a copy with identical sounds on it. Piracy is usually distinguished from **counterfeiting,** although the latter is a form of piracy.

pitch. — To promote a song to a music publisher or producer, or an artist to a label.

platinum. — The RIAA certification of sales of 1,000,000 copies of a recording at the wholesale level, or sales of 100,000 units or $2,000,000 at SRLP of music videos, and for each equal amount after that. Thus an album selling more than 2 million copies is *multiplatinum* or *double platinum.*

play or pay (also, pay or play). — A clause in a recording artist's contract meaning the label can either have the artist *play* for a recording session, or simply *pay* them scale wages as if a session were held and fulfill their entire obligation to the artist. Not to be confused with **pay-for-play.**

point-of-purchase materials (POP materials). — Advertising and display materials intended to be used/displayed in a retail location that sells the merchandise advertised. A poster for a record album is POP material distributed to record stores.

point-of-sale (POS). — Literally the cash register or other device where the sale of an item is recorded and the payment made.

power of attorney. — A contractual right to act on someone's behalf in a way that legally binds that person to obligations entered into by the attorney on behalf of the person represented.

prima facie evidence. — A legal term meaning evidence that is sufficient on its face to make a case or prove a point. A copyright registration is prima facie evidence of the validity of the copyright and other information on the registration form. It would then be up to the other party to prove otherwise.

PRO (performing rights organization). — A generic term used to denote any performing pights organization. Not a formal term, but one used for convenience in discussing any or all such organizations that license performance rights and pay performance royalties to songwriters and music publishers.

producer. — In recording, the person in charge of all aspects of the recording process.

professional manager. — The person at a music publishing company who is in charge of finding new songs and songwriters. They may also negotiate special uses of songs such as commercials or motion pictures.

progressive. — A radio format (initially rock) playing longer versions of records and other records and artists not usually heard on Top 40 formats. Now more likely known as **alternative**.

project studio. — A recording studio, usually owned by an artist or producer, which is used mainly to make recordings for that particular artist or producer and is not rented out to outsiders.

promotion person. — Term applied to a record label person or independent contractor whose job it is to get radio stations to play records released by the label.

promotional copies. — Copies of a recording given away to radio stations for the purpose of airplay or for giveaways to listeners, or given to album reviewers to expose the record to the public.

public domain (PD). — A term of art regarding the status of works whose copyrights have expired or that were not subject to copyright protection. Public domain works may be used by anyone without obtaining licenses or clearances because PD works have no copyrights.

public performance. *See* perform publicly.

publishing administration. — A deal in which one music publisher (usually a small artist or producer owned company) has a larger music publisher issue licenses and collect royalties in exchange for a percentage of the money collected.

rack jobber. — A distributor who buys records from branches or independent distributors and services the record departments in mass merchandiser stores or other non-record stores.

rack locations. — Those stores that have **rack jobber**–serviced record departments.

rating. — A radio station's percentage of the total available listeners at any given time or over a given time span (cf. **share**).

Recording Academy. *See* NARAS.

recording artist. — A person who makes phonograph recordings under a contractual arrangement with a record label whereby the label pays the performer a percentage royalty based on sales of the recordings; to be distinguished from a side musician or background vocalist who does not receive a royalty.

Recording Artists' Coalition (RAC). — A nonprofit organization that represents the interests of recording artists in legislative and public policy questions when the artists' interests conflict with those of the record labels.

recording engineer. — A type of **audio engineer** whose job it is to operate equipment in a recording studio to capture and reproduce sounds being made for a recording.

recording fund. — A kind of advance where the record label designates a fixed amount of money available to produce a master recording. Usually the artist and producer are allowed to keep any money that has not been used to create the finished master.

Recording Trust Fund. — Also called the Music Performance Trust Fund, this fund was established by the AFM. The labels pay a small percentage of the list price of all recordings sold into the fund. The fund is then used to pay musicians who perform in free concerts for the general public. The idea of the fund is to make more live music available to more people.

recoupable. — Money recoverable out of royalties actually earned or otherwise due. Advances are usually recoupable but **nonreturnable**, meaning that they are *not a debt* that would have to be repaid.

recurrent. — Radio programming term for a recent current hit. A recurrent is not a hit at the present time, but is still popular enough to play fairly regularly, compared to a current hit, or an oldie.

release. — A recording made available to the public, or to make a recording available to the public.

release date. — The day designated by the record label when a recording is available to the public.

renegotiate. — A term used in the recording industry to refer to the practice of artists who are under recording agreements to redefine the terms of the agreement before it would otherwise end by using their substantial success as leverage.

reserve for returns. — An amount of royalties, or the royalties that would be paid for a certain amount of sales, that are not paid to a recording artist because records are shipped to retailers and wholesalers subject to being returned at a later date. Artists are not paid for recordings that are returned. *See also* **liquidate reserves.**

returns. — Records sent back to the distributor or label because they have not been sold at the retail level. Returns may include defective merchandise as well as simple overstock.

reversion. — A term usually seen in songwriter-publisher agreements referring to the writer's right to recapture the copyrights in the songs. There is a statutory reversion right called the **termination right** in the Copyright Act. The reversion may also be strictly contractual.

RIAA (Recording Industry Association of America). — The trade association for record labels and manufacturers.

rider. — An attachment to an agreement. In concert promotion, the rider is where the artist spells out specific requirements for the performance, such as sound, lights, size of stage, power requirements, kind and amount of food, and other considerations. There may be a technical rider and a separate food rider with requirements that the promoter is expected to meet.

right to work. — A provision of the laws of some states, particularly in the South, that prohibits unions from requiring that all employees of a particular firm belong to that union.

rotation. — Radio programming term referring to a group of records that is played through in a certain period of time. A station may have several rotations, such as a *power rotation* that is played through entirely every couple of hours, and an oldies rotation that is played through every few days.

royalties. — Payments to writers or performers due from the sale of copies, performances, or other uses of their works.

sampling. — Commonly understood as the process of capturing a portion of a recording via a digital recorder so that the sound from the previous recording can be used to create part of a new recording. The sampled signal is manipulated through signal processing or computer sequencing to form an integral part of the rhythm, melody, lyrics, or overall production of the new recording. The process of sampling is important because the digital sounds can be manipulated much more than an analog recording. *See also* **Digital sampling.**

scale wages. — Payments to musicians or vocalists for live or recorded performances at the amount (scale) required by the union.

self-contained. — Usually refers to performing artists who write their own material, but may also refer to a band that does not require any additional musicians for their performances.

78. — The 78-rpm record, usually with one song recorded on each side, which was the standard record from its introduction until the 1950s, when the 45 and LP formats became dominant.

SESAC. — SESAC, Inc. is the smallest of the three main performing rights organizations in the United States. SESAC used to stand for Society of European Stage Authors and Composers, but now does not have any particular meaning beyond its letters as the name of the organization.

share. — The percentage of people actually listening to *any* radio station that are listening to a particular station. Thus, if a station has a 15-percent share, 15 percent of the people listening to radio at that time are listening to that station. The other 85 percent are listening to other radio stations.

shed. — Another term for an outdoor amphitheater.

shelf price. — The usual price at which comparable albums are sold in a given store. This is usually not the SRLP, but is typically below that; to be distinguished from a sale price.

short form video. — A music video, usually containing just one song.

shortfall. — A kind of *tour support* with the label making up any difference between an agreed-upon amount per performance and the amount the artist actually makes per performance.

showcase. — A performance, usually in a small club, designed to promote a performer to radio programmers, label A&R people, music publishing people, or some other industry audience, as opposed to the general public.

shrinkage. — Loss of inventory due to factors not accounted for, such as theft, damage, or accounting errors.

side. — A term in recording contracts referring to a recording of a single song. It may also be used in a nonlegal sense to refer to all of the songs on one side of an LP, cassette, or single.

single. — A recording of a single composition released by itself or with only one other composition. CD-5 or maxi singles usually have four or five cuts on them.

small rights. — Nondramatic public performance rights (i.e., the kind licensed by ASCAP, BMI, and SESAC).

SMPTE (Society of Motion Picture and Television Engineers). — An organization for the technical people associated with the production of television programs and motion pictures. It includes people in multimedia productions. Audio engineers often belong to this and **AES**.

soft tickets. — Tickets for an event that are not printed in advance of sale, but are printed by a computer at the time of sale.

song plugger. — A person who works for a music publishing company whose job it is to get the song recorded, performed, and used in other ways.

soundalike. — A recording made to sound as much like the one by the original artists as possible. It is a new recording, but the musicians and singers imitate the sounds on the previous recording.

SoundExchange. — The organization formed by the **RIAA** that is in charge of distribution of royalties collected for the digital performance of sound recordings. It also negotiates royalty rates for **Webcasters** and others not subject to the compulsory license for digital audio performance of sound recordings.

sound recording. — A kind of copyrightable work in which sounds created by various sources are captured or fixed in some tangible medium such as tape or disk. These works are to be distinguished from the underlying works such as musical compositions or dramatic works that are recorded, and the material objects or phonorecords in/on which the recordings are fixed. Sound recordings do not include sound accompanying motion pictures; those recordings are part of the motion picture copyright.

SoundScan. — The company that collects point-of-sale information from the UPC bar code scanners at a variety of record retail outlets and sells sales pattern information to the labels or other parties; now actually Nielsen SoundScan, a division of Nielsen Retail Information.

soundtrack. — The audio accompaniment to a motion picture or television program.

soundtrack album. — An album consisting of a collection of the musical works (and sometimes other sounds) in a motion picture or television program.

SPARS (Society of Professional Recording Services). — A trade organization for recording studio owners, and tape and CD replicators.

special payments fund. — A fund administered by the AFM composed of payments from record labels based on a small percentage of the price of recordings sold. The fund is distributed to musicians on an annual basis based on the amount of master recording sessions on which the musician had played over the previous year.

spin count. — Also called simply *spins*. The number of times a particular recording has been played over the radio, as recorded by **BDS**.

sponsored tour. — A live appearance tour where part of the costs and probably some advertising is underwritten by a third party who uses the appearances of the artist to promote and sell non-artist-related merchandise, such as soft drinks or clothing.

SRDS (Standard Rate and Data Service). — A series of publications that lists media outlets, their facilities, policies, and advertising rates.

SRLP. *See* MSRP.

staff producer. — A producer who works on a salaried basis for the label (and probably a small royalty, too). Currently such persons are likely to be label executives who also happen to be producers. Most producers are now **independent producers**.

staff writer. — A songwriter who works under an exclusive agreement with a music publisher, usually on a weekly or monthly advance.

statutory rate. — A term usually applied to the compulsory mechanical royalty rate. Originally the rate was set by Congress in the 1909 Copyright Act and later the 1976 Copyright Act, hence the term *statutory*. Later, when the rate was set by the Copyright Royalty Tribunal, and later still by Copyright Arbitration Royalty Panels, it was still referred to as a statutory rate.

stiff. — A record that does not sell well at all or that does not get much radio airplay.

strip center. — A shopping center with stores spread out in a row, usually along a main road, with common walls and no enclosed pedestrian area.

superstore. — A very large record store, typically 12,000 to 20,000 square feet.

synchronization right. — The right of the owner of a musical composition copyright to use the composition in time relation to visual images, such as in movies or television shows, or perhaps in multimedia.

take. — A recorded attempt by the recording artists or musicians at a complete performance of a song.

technically acceptable. — In recording contracts, this means that a master is of high enough quality to be suitable for release to the public. This is distinguished from **commercially acceptable**, which implies a higher standard, and the label's judgment as to whether a particular recording will be successful commercially as opposed to artistically.

termination rights. — Statutory rights of authors (or certain of their heirs) to end transfers of copyrights and nonexclusive licenses during a 5-year period beginning after 35 years from the date of transfer and running through the 40th year. (If the transfer includes the right to publish, then the 5-year period starts 40 years after the date of transfer or 35 years after the date of first publication, whichever is earlier.) Thus, the author can recapture the transferred copyrights.

tight oligopoly. — An **oligopoly** where four firms control 60 percent or more of the market.

TNN (The Nashville Network). — Originally a cable television network devoted to country music and other country lifestyle programming. In 2003 it changed to Spike TV and changed its programming to appeal to 18- to 24-year-old males.

Top 40. — The radio format that plays the 40 most popular recordings in the broadcaster's market. Used generically to refer to any format that plays the most popular recordings, including **CHR**.

tour support. — Usually monetary support for new recording artists to help them make personal appearance performances. Tour support is often given when the label believes that live appearances will help sell recordings. It is usually a **recoupable** advance. *See also* **shortfall**.

track. — A recording of one particular instrument or vocalist that is separate from the other performances on the session for that song, or the process of recording such tracks. Also refers to a segment of a recording medium that can be recorded and played back separately from the others for that song. Also refers to keeping track of radio airplay.

trades. — The magazines devoted to a particular business. *Billboard*, *Radio & Records*, *Pollstar*, *Broadcasting and Cable*, and *Variety* are among the important trade publications in the recording industry.

transcription license. — Permission to make a recording of a song where copies of the recording are not intended for distribution to the public. Radio stations frequently receive transcription recordings for broadcast purposes of advertisements or programs.

triple A format. — A radio format (Adult Album Alternative) that plays hits, but also includes other album cuts of alternative music, mainly targeted to an audience over twenty-four years of age.

turntable hit. — A recording that receives lots of radio airplay but does not generate many sales.

UPC (Universal Product Code). *See* bar code.

venue. — The place where a live performance happens. It could be a club, a theater, an auditorium, a stadium, or an open field.

vertical integration. — A market condition in which a firm owns more than one portion of the total distribution chain from manufacturer to consumer. A record label that owns a pressing plant is an example of vertical integration, as is a distributor that owns record stores.

VH-1. — The cable television channel programmed for viewers who prefer a wider range of music and softer music than programmed by the rock/urban-oriented *MTV.*

vicarious infringer. — A party who benefits financially from an infringement, and who could control whether the infringement occurred. They do not have to have knowledge of the infringement (c.f., **contributory infringer**).

videogram. — A video recording of a motion picture, music video, or other visual work. Usually the term refers to videograms that are manufactured and distributed for consumer purchase.

Webcasting. — Transmitting a performance of songs, recordings, or videos by streaming the performance over the World Wide Web. Known originally as Netcasting.

work dues. — Dues paid to the union by performers based on their earnings from live appearances.

work made for hire. — In copyright law, a work made by an employee within the scope of employment, or a commissioned work of certain kinds if the parties agree in writing that the work is to be considered for hire. The employer or commissioning party owns the copyrights in works made for hire.

World Trade Organization (WTO). — The international trade organization created in 1995 by the General Agreement on Tariffs and Trade (**GATT**) treaty of 1994. WTO members promise to provide "Berne Level" protection to copyrights and may be subject to trade sanctions from the organization and other members for failure to do so. Major disputes between the United States and China over China's lack of copyright protection for recordings, motion pictures, and computer software prevented China from joining the organization until 2001.

Internet Appendix

The Recording Industry on the Internet

Listed below are some of the many World Wide Web sites that provide valuable information and insight into the recording industry—and some that are just plain fun. Anyone who tries to publish an Internet list on anything but the Internet and who updates it less than weekly is likely to be left in the silicon dust of this rapidly changing medium. Record labels, music publications, organizations, and others are adding and changing Web pages and sites at a feverish rate. I am sure that by the time this is published some of these sites will have disappeared, and others will form to take their places. Many of these sites contain listings and links to other good, new sites. Surf's up!

Labels

A&M Records: www.amrecords.com
American Recordings: www.americanrecordings.com
AOL Time Warner: www.aoltimewarner.com
Arista Records: www.aristarec.com/
Bembe Records: www.bembe.com/
Bertelsmann A.G.: www.bertelsmann.com
BMG Records: www.bmg.de
Capitol Records: www.hollywoodandvine.com
Columbia Records: www.columbiarecords.com
Curb Records: www.curb.com
Decca Records: www.decca.com/
Earache Records: www.earache.com/
EMI Group: www.emigroup.com
EMI Music Publishing: www.emimusicpub.com
Geffen Records: www.geffen.com/

Hollywood Records: www.hollywoodrec.com/
Interscope Records: www.interscope.com
Island Records: www.islandrecords.com/
Jive Records and Zomba Records: www.jiverecords.com
LaFace Records: www.laface.com/
Mammoth Records: www.mammoth.com/
Margaritaville Records: www.margaritaville.com
MCA Records: www.mcarecords.com
Metalblade Records: www.metalblade.com
Rhino Records: www.rhino.com
Sony Corp. (Japan): www.sony.co.jp
Sony Music: www.sonymusic.com/
Universal Music Group: www.umg.com
Virgin Records U.S.A.: www.virginrecords.com/
Vivendi Universal: www.vivendiuniversal.com
Warner Music Group: www.wmg.com/
Windham Hill Records: www.windham.com/

Record Clubs

BMG Music Service: www.bmgmusic.com
CD Now: www.cdnow.com
Columbia House: www.columbiahouse.com
MP3.com: www.mp3.com
Musical Heritage Society: www.musicalheritage.com

Periodicals

Access Online Magazine: www.accessmag.com/
Acoustic Guitar: www.shentel.net/acousticmusician
Acoustic Musician: www.netshop.net/acoustic
Billboard: www.billboard.com/
Blues Access: www.he.net/~blues/ba_home.html
Broadcasting and Cable: www.broadcastigandcable.com
Buzz: www.thebuzz.nireland.com/
Contempory Christian Music: www.ccm.com
Creative Loafing: www.cln.com/
Dealerscope Merchandising: www.dealerscope.com
Electronic Urban Report: www.eurweb.com
Keyboard Central: www.keyboardmag.com/
LCD or Lowest Common Denominator: wfmu.org/LCD/
Mix(online): www.mixmag.com/
Music Network U.S.A.: www.mnusa.com/
Music Trades: www.musictrades.com/

Music Universe: www.musicuniverse.com/
Music Week: www.musicweek.com/
Nashville Scene: www.nashscene.com/
Pollstar: www.pollstar.com
ProSound News: www.prosoundnews.com
Radio and Records: www.radioandrecords.com
Rock and Roll Reporter: www.rocknrollreporter.com
Songtalk: www.songtalk.com/
Spin: www.spin.com
Vibe: www.vibe.com

music publishers

BMG Music Publishing: www.bmgmusicsearch.com
Cherry Lane Music: www.cherrylane.com
EMI Music Publishing: emimusicpub.com/
Hal Leonard Music: www.halleonard.com
Lowery Music: www.lowerymusic.com
Music Sales Group: www.musicsales.com
Sony/ATV Music Publishing: www.sonyatv.com
Warner/Chappell Music: www.warnerchappell.com

performing rights organizations

ASCAP: www.ascap.com
APRA (Australia): www.apra.com.au
BMI: www.bmi.com
BUMA (Netherlands): www.buma.nl/
GEMA (Germany): www.gema.de
International Conference of Societies of Authors and Composers
    (CISAC): www.cisac.org
PRS (United Kingdom): www.prs.co.uk/
SABAM (Belgium): www.sabam.be/
SESAC: www.sesac.com

Miscellaneous

Bluebird Café: www.bluebirdcafe.com
Broadcast Data Service: www.bdsonline.com
CMT: www.cmt.com
Country Crossroads: www.countrycrossroads.org/
Country Music Hall of Fame: www.halloffame.org
EMusic.com: www.emusic.com
Great American Country: www.countrystars.com

HMV Group (Record Stores): www.hmvgroup.com
MTV: www.mtv.com
Neilsen SoundScan: www.soundscan.com
Network Music: www.networkmusic.com
Rock and Roll Hall of Fame: www.rockhall.com
Roland Corporation U.S.: www.rolandus.com
Signature Sound: www.signaturetech.com
Sweetwater: www.sweetwater.com
Tascam: www.tascam.com
VH-1: vh1.com
VNU Media: www.vnu.com
Yamaha: www.yamaha.com

Organizations

Acoustical Society of America: asa.aip.org
Alliance of Artists and Record Companies: www.aarcroyalties.com
American Federation of Musicians: www.afm.org
American Federation of Television and Radio Artists: www.aftra.org
American Music Conference: www.amc-music.com
Association for Independent Music: www.afim.org
Audio Engineering Society: www.aes.org
Austin Music Server: www.txmusic.com
Australian Recording Industry Association: www.aria.com.au
Backstage World: www.stagelight.se/backstage/index.html
Black Gospel Experience: www.yesonline.com/gospel
Canadian Country Music Awards: www.ccma.org/awards
Canadian Music Trade: nor.canadianmusictrade.com
Copyright Agency Limited (Australia): www.copyright.com.au
U.S. Copyright Office: www.copyright.gov
Copyright Society of the U.S.A.: www.csusa.org
Federal Communications Commission: www.fcc.gov
Future of Music Coalition: www.futureofmusic.org
Global Alliance of Performers: www.gap.org
Grammy Awards: www.grammy.com
Home Recording Rights Coalition: www.hhrc.org
International Alliance for Women in Music: music.acu.edu/www/iawm
International Association of Theatrical and Stage Employees: www.iatse.org
International Bluegrass Music Association: www.imba.org
International Federation of Phonographic Industries: www.ifpi.org
International Intellectual Property Alliance: www.iipa.com
Irish Music Rights Organization: www.imro.ie
IRMA: www.recordingmedia.com
Mechanical Copyright and Protection Society: www.mcps.co.uk

Music and Entertainment Industry Educators Association:
www.meiea.org
Music Managers Forum: www.mmf-us.org
Music Network USA: www.mnusa.com
Music Publishers Association (MPA): host.mpa.org/
Nashville Entertainment Association: www.nea.net
National Association of Broadcasters: www.nab.org/
National Association of Recording Merchandisers: www.narm.com
National Music Foundation: www.nmc.org
National Music Publishers' Association: www.nmpa.org
Nashville Songwriter's Organization International: www.nashvillesong-
writers.org
North by Northeast Conference: www.nxne.com
Patent and Trademark Office: www.uspto.gov/
Professional Lighting and Sound Association: www.plasa.org
The Recording Academy (NARAS): www.grammy.com
RIAA (Recording Industry Association of America): www.riaa.com
Society of Motion Picture and Television Engineers: www/smpte.org/
Society of Professional Audio Recording Services: www.spars.com/
Songwriters Guild of America: www.songwriters.org
SoundExchange: www.soundexchange.com
South by Southwest Conference: www.sxsw.com/sxsw/directory.html
Texas Music Association: www.txma.com
World Forum on Music and Censorship: www.freemus.org

Reference
Bibliography

Ackerman, Paul. "New Income Studies Face Publishers as Sheet Music Income Drops." *Billboard*, 15 January 1955, 1.

Albarran, Alan B. *Media Economics*. Ames: Iowa State University Press, 1996.

Alexander, Peter J. "Entropy and Popular Culture: Product Diversity in the Popular Music Recording Industry." *American Sociological Review* 61 (1996): 171.

Atwood, Brett. "Indie Film Soundtracks Help Expose Modern Rock Acts," *Billboard*, 8 October 1994, 8.

Atwood, Brett. "Global 'Desktop Bcasting Catches On," *Billboard*, 10 June 1995, 6.

Atwood, Brett. "Multimedia in Stores," *Billboard*, 30 March 1996, 59

Ault, Susanne. "Web Is a Windfall for Touring Biz," *Billboard*, 21 December 2002, 1, 72.

Ayre, Rick. "Five Virtual Record Stores," *PC Magazine*, 28 May 1996, 56.

Belinfante, Alexander and Reuben R. Davis Jr., "Estimating the Demand for Record Albums," *Review of Business and Economic Research*, (winter 1978–1979), 47, 51.

Bennett, Ray. "EMI Picks up Another 30% of Jobette for $110 Million: Publisher Owns 80% of That Gordy Firm," *Hollywood Reporter*, 11 April 2003, 6.

Benz, Matthew. "Losses Mount for Music Industrys Digital Services," *Billboard*, 6 April 2002, 1.

Benz, Matthew and Carolyn Horwitz, "Best Buy Blames Musicland for $25mil Quarterly Loss," *Billboard Bulletin*, 19 June 2003, 2.

Benz, Matthew and Carolyn Horwitz, "SoundScan Adds Download Data," *Billboard*, 12 July 2003, 5.

Benz, Matthew and Carolyn Horwitz, "BMG's New Task: Maintaining Zomba's Culture, Creativity" *Billboard*, 7 December 2002, 3.

Bessman, Jim. "Indie Distributor Changes More Than Name," *Billboard*, 20 May 1995, 47.

Bessman, Jim. "At the Heart of Cajun Country, Floyds Record Shop Has Finger on Regions Pulse," *Billboard*, 20 January 1996, 61

Boehlert, Eric. "Labels Put New Spin on Indie Promo; Many Eye BDS Data for Payment Plans," *Billboard*, 22 January 1994, 1.

Boehlert, Eric. "Play-by-Play Account of Pearl Jam Saga," *Billboard*, 8 July 1995, 85.

Boehlert, Eric. "Is Moshing Murder," *Rolling Stone*, 11 July 1996, 19.

Boehlert, Eric. "Pay to Play," *Rolling Stone*, 22 August 1996, 34.

Boehm, Eric. "For Those with Cash EMI Has the Flash," *Variety*, 12 August 1996, 7.

Borzillo, Carrie. "Unable to Compete with Chains, Indies Offer Alternatives," *Billboard*, 30 March 1996, 66.

Boswell, William R. *Life on the Road*. Needham Heights, MA: Ginn Press, 1991.

Broadcasting Yearbook 1986. New Providence, NJ: R.R. Bowker (1986).

Broadcasting & Cable Yearbook 1996; 2001. New Providence, NJ: R.R. Bowker (1996, 2001).

Brabec, Jeffrey and Todd Brabec. *Music, Money, and Success.* 2d ed. New York: Schirmer Books, 2000.

Bragg, Roy. "Denver Promoter Accuses Concert Behemoth Clear Channel of Not Playing Fair," *Knight Ridder/Tribune Business News,* 3 February 2001 (InfoTrack).

Braheny, John. *The Craft and Business of Song Writing.* Cincinnati, OH: Writers Digest Books, 1988.

Brandle, Lars and Tom Ferguson, "Tower Pulling out of UK; HMV Closing in Germany," *Billboard Bulletin,* 27 January 2003, 2

Burnett, Robert. "The Implications of Ownership Changes on Concentration and Diversity in the Phonogram Industry." *Communication Research* (December 1992): 749.

Burnett, Robert. *The Global Jukebox.* New York: Routledge, 1996.

Campbell, Richard. *Media and Culture.* 2d ed. Boston, MA: Bedford/St.Martins, 2000.

Carlozo, Lou. "In Christian Music, Sales Are up—and so Is the Confusion," *Knight Ridder/Tribune News Service,* 6 September 2002, pK4885 (Chicago Tribune).

Carter, T. Barton et al. *The First Amendment and The Fourth Estate.* 6th ed. Westbury, NY: Foundation Press, 1994.

Caves, Richard. *American Industry: Structure, Conduct and Performance.* 6th ed. Englewood Cliffs, NJ: Prentice Hall, 1987.

Christman, Ed. 3 Big Chains Test Used-CD Waters," *Billboard,* 5 December 1992, 1.

Christman, Ed. "D.C.-Area Indie-Intensive Record Shop Is Ready to GO!" *Billboard,* 5 June 1993, 73.

Christman, Ed. "Blockbuster to Add Super Club to Expanding Retail Portfolio," *Billboard,* 16 October 1993, 5.

Christman, Ed. "FTC Broadens Its Biz Inquiry into Majors Ad Policies," *Billboard,* 23 October 1993, 43.

Christman, Ed. "Alliance Shifts Distrib Gears: Trans World Fills No. 2 Slot," *Billboard,* 5 February 1994, 64.

Christman, Ed. "2 Deals Alter Rackjobbing Landscape," *Billboard,* 12 February 1994.

Christman, Ed. "WEAs94 Market Share Dips Slightly, But Still Top U.S. Distributor with 21.1%," *Billboard,* 21 Jan.1995, 54;

Christman, Ed. "The Positive Sounds of Hear Musics Expansion," *Billboard,* 4 March 1995, 64.

Christman, Ed. "Closings Reveal Chinks in Chains Long-Term Strategies," *Billboard,* 28 October 1995, 66.

Christman, Ed. "Can Retails Shaky Health Be Cured?" *Billboard,* 23 December 1995, 1.

Christman, Ed. "PGD Reduces Boxlot Prices, Boosting Retain Profit Margins," *Billboard,* 23 December 1995, 5.

Christman, Ed. "WEA Remains Top U.S. Music Distributor in95," *Billboard,* 20 January 1996, 55.

Christman, Ed. "The Brass Tacks of Camelot Musics Financial Restructuring," *Billboard,* 3 February 1996, 62.

Christman, Ed. "Disney Records Pulls Out of Record Clubs," *Billboard,* 3 February 1996.

Christman, Ed. "MAPing the Route to Consistent Pricing," *Billboard,* 30 March 1996, 59.

Christman, Ed. "EMI-Capitol Creates Marketing Arm," *Billboard,* 13 April 1996, 5.

Christman, Ed. "More Downsizing at Camelot," *Billboard,* 13 April 1996, 68.

Christman, Ed. "Musicland to Shutter More Stores," *Billboard,* 20 April 1996, 72.

Christman, Ed. "Million-Dollar Times Square Gamble by Virgin Megastore," *Billboard,* 4 May 1996, 54.

Christman, Ed. "Alliance Breathing Easy after Failed Metromedia Merger," *Billboard,* 18 May 1996, 52.

Christman, Ed. "MAP Policies Bring Price War Cease-Fire," *Billboard,* 1 June 1996, 3.

Christman, Ed. "Alliance to Acquire Red Ant Entertainment," *Billboard,* 24 August 1996, 3.

Christman, Ed. "Retail Sees Turnaround in the Midst of Reorganizations," *Billboard,* 27 December 1997, 63.

Christman, Ed. "Sony to Raise CD Prices," *Billboard,* 20 February 1999, 6.

Christman, Ed. "FTC Tips Hand on Its MAP Ruling," *Billboard,* 29 January 2000, 5.

Christman, Ed. "Sound Scan Numbers Show. 35 % of Albums Account for More Than Half of All Units Sold," *Billboard,* 28 April 2001, 66.

Christman, Ed. "Tower Records Struggles Reflected Industrys Turmoil," *Billboard*, 28 December 2002, 45.

Christman, Ed. "Suns Shine on Musicland Still Clouded by Finances," *Billboard*, 5 July 2003, 35

Christman, Ed and Seth Goldstein, "Book Distrib Turns Music Racker; also, Handleman Set to Buy Starmaker," *Billboard*, 18 June 1994, 6.

Christman, Ed and Don Jeffrey, "Record Clubs Focus of Closed-Door Meeting," *Billboard*, 23 March 1996, 1.

Christman, Ed et al. "WEA Reduces Wholesale Prices on CDs," *Billboard*, 13 March 1993, 9.

Clark-Meads, Jeff. "10-Year Dispute over Japanese Record Rental Business Settled," *Billboard*, 29 April 1995, 5.

Clark-Meads, Jeff. "PolyGram Takes Globe via London," *Billboard*, 22 July 1995, 36.

Clark-Meads, Jeff. "HMVs 75th Year Marked by Celebration, Expansion," *Billboard*, 16 March 1996, 1, 116.

Cohen, Jane and Bob Grossweiner, "1995 Year End Analysis," *Performance*, 29 December 1995, 8.

Cohen, Jonathan. "Audiogalaxy Ordered to Block Copyrighted Songs," *Billboard Daily Music News*, 18 June 2002. <retrieved from *Billboard.com*>.

Cohen, Jonathan. "RIAA Settles with Students," *Billboard Daily Music News*, 2 May 2003.

Cohen, Jonathan. "Grokster Blasts RIAA Anti-Piracy Tactics," *Billboard Daily Music News*, 27 June 2003. <Retrieved from Billboard.com>.

Cohen, Jonathan. "99 Cents Too Expensive for Downloads," *Billboard Daily Music News*, August 19, 2003. Retrieved from Billboard.com.

Conniff, Tamara. "CD Price-Fixing Suit Settled: Labels, Chains to Compensate States to Tune of $143 Mil," *Hollywood Reporter*, 1 October 2002, 1.

Cooper, Jay L. "Current Trends in Recording Contract Negotiations." *NARAS Institute Journal* 2, no. 1 (1978): 14.

Cosola, Mary. "Going Global," *Electronic Musician*, December 1996, 52.

Cronin, Peter. "Country Labels, Radio Adjust to Reality of Boom," *Billboard*, 29 April 1995, 1.

Cusic, Don. *The Sound of Light: A History of Gospel Music*. Bowling Green, OH: Popular Press, 1990.

Cusic, Don. *Music in the Market*. Bowling Green, OH: Popular Press, 1996.

Daft, Richard L. *Management*. New York: Dryden Press, 1988.

Daley, Charles P., Patrick Henry, and Ellen Ryder. *The Magazine Publishing Industry*. Needham Heights, MA: Allyn & Bacon, 1997.

Daley, Dan. "The Big Shift: When Personal Studios Go Public, *Mix*, February 1996a, 98.

Daley, Dan. "Studios Develop Coping Skills as Margins Shrink," *Pro Sound News*, February 1996b, 14.

Daley, Dan. "One Door Closes, Another One Opens," *Tape-Disk Business*, September 2001, 10.

Dannen, Fredric. *Hit Men*. New York: Vintage Books, 1990.

Davis, Clive. *Clive: Inside the Record Business*. New York: Ballantine Books, 1974.

Davis, Sheila. *Successful Lyric Writing*. Cincinnati, OH: Writers Digest Books, 1988.

DeConstanzo, Frank. "Print Music Strikes Profitable Chord," *Billboard*, 24 September 1994, 64.

DeCurtis, Anthony. "Concert Insurance Crisis," *Rolling Stone*, 11 September 1986, 15.

DeFleur, Melvin L. and Everette E. Dennis. *Understanding Mass Communication*. 4th ed. Boston, MA: Houghton Mifflin, 1991.

Denisoff, R. Serge. *Solid Gold*. New Brunswick, NJ: Transaction Books, 1975.

Denisoff, R. *Tarnished Gold*. New Brunswick, NJ: Transaction Books, 1986.

Derr, Joshua. "Year End Charts," *Performance*, 29 December 1995, 9.

Desjardins, Doug. "Sales of DVD Music Videos Hit Crescendo," *DSN Retailing Today*, 9 June 2003, 17.

Dezzani, Mark. "BMG Buys Europes Last 'Major Indie'," *Billboard*, 20 August 1994, 38.

Diamond, Michael. "Music Companies Try to Crack Down on Sales of Used CDs," *Gannett News Service*, 17 June 1993 (Lexis).

DiConstanzo, Frank. "Print Strikes Profitable Chord," *Billboard*, 24 September 1994, 64.

DiMartino, Dave. "Lawyers Mull 'Legal Payola'," *Billboard*, 9 January 1988, 5.

DiMartino, Dave. "Tashjian Pleads Guilty to Payola," *Billboard*, 3 June 1989, 1.

Dranov, Paula. *Inside the Music Publishing Industry*. White Plains, NY: Knowledge Industry Publications, 1980.

Drucker, Peter F. *Managing for the Future*. New York: Truman Talley Books, 1992.

Duffy, Thom. "N.Y. Says Concert Ads Deceived Public on Tix Pricing," *Billboard*, 8 August 1992, 10.

Ennis, Philip H. *The Seventh Stream: The Emergence of Rock 'n' Roll in American Popular Music.* Hanover, NH: Wesleyan University Press, 1992.

Farber, Donald S. (ed.). *Entertainment Industry Contracts: Negotiating and Drafting Guide.* New York: Matthew Bender, 2002.

Flanagan, Bill. "We Three Kings," *Musician*, April 1991, 52, 59.

Fleming, Charles and Kevin Zimmerman, "Charts Off Course," *Daily Variety*, 31 December 1990, 1.

Flick, Larry. "A&R Role Expanding for Publishers," *Billboard*, 5 November 1994, 18.

Frahn, Harrison. "CompuServe Settles Infringement Charges and Agrees to New Electronic Licensing," *Exclusive Right* 1, no. 1 (1996):3.

Frascogna, Xavier M., Jr. and H. Lee Hetherington. *The Business of Artist Management.* 3d ed. New York: Billboard Books, 1997.

Frith, Simon. "Critical Response." In Deanna Campbell Robinson, et al. *Music at the Margins*, Newbury Park, CA: Sage Publications, 1991, 287.

Frith, Simon. "The Industrialization of Popular Music." In *Popular Music and Communication*, 2d ed., edited by James Lull. Newbury Park, CA: Sage Publications, 1992.

Garofalo, Reebee. "How Autonomous Is Relative: Popular Music, the Social Formation and Cultural Struggle," *Popular Music*, January 1987, 77.

Garrity, Brian. "Universal Acquires the Remaining 50% Share of GetMusic from BMG," *Billboard*, 5 May 2002, 4.

Garrity, Brian. "Warner Bros., AOL plan Madonna Blitz," *Billboard Bulletin*, 27 March 2003, 1.

Garrity, Brian. "Madonna Has Choice Words for Music Pirates," *Billboard Daily Music News*, 17 April 2003. Retrieved from Billboard.com.

Garrity, Brian. "Top Artists Balking at A La Carte Downloads," *Billboard Daily Music News*, 21 June 2003. Retrieved from Billboard.com.

Garrity, Brian. "Piracy Battle Gets Personal as RIAA Targets Consumers," *Billboard Bulletin*, 26 June 2003: 1.

Garrity, Brian. "Seeking Profits at 99¢," *Billboard*, 12 July 2003; 1.

Garrity, Brian. "Roxio Reveals Details of Retooled Napster, *Billboard Daily Music Index*, 10 October 2003. Retrieved from Billboard.com.

Garrity, Brian and Adam White, "UMG Profit Tops $1 Bil," *Billboard*, 26 August 2000, 1.

Garrity, Brian, Matthew Benz, Ed Christman, and Bill Holland, "CD Pricing, Used Sales Debated: Concerns Rise Over High Retail Profile of Used CDs," *Billboard*, 8 June 2002, 1.

Gehman, Nev. "Poll Clocks 35 Also-Rans for Every Solid-Selling Disk Hit," *Billboard*, 3 January 1953, 1.

Gehman, Nev. "The Years Music Roundup," *Billboard*, 2 January 1954, 11.

Gett, Steve. "Promoters Balk at Flat Fees," *Billboard*, 4 October 1986, 1.

Goldstein, Seth. "Direct Moves Pinch Levy Home Ent.," *Billboard*, 18 July 1992, 6.

Goldstein, Seth. "Managing Ever-Changing Sell-Thru," *Billboard*, 6 January 1996, 43.

Gore, Tipper. *Raising PG Children in an X-Rated Society.* Nashville, TN: Abingdon Press, 1987.

Gray, Herman. *Producing Jazz.* Philadelphia, PA: Temple University Press, 1988.

Greene, Kelly. "Local Retailers Win Settlement in Battle Over Used CDs," *Business Journal-Charlotte*, 11 July 1994, I1 (Lexis).

Greenfeld, Karl Taro. "The Free Juke Box: College Kids Are Using New, Simple Software Like Napster to Help Themselves to Pirated Music," *Time*, 27 March 2000, 82.

Greenfield, Robert and Bill Graham. *Bill Graham Presents.* New York: Doubleday, 1992.

Grunwald, Edgar A. "Program Production History 1927 and 1937." In *Variety 1937–1938 Radio Directory* (1937).

Gubernick, Lisa. "We Are a Society of Collectors," *Forbes*, 24 July 1989.

Hadler, Pat. "Rap, Vinyl Fans Boogie to Columbus Groove Shack," *Billboard*, 7 January 1995, 78.

Halloran, Mark. *The Musicians Business & Legal Guide.* Upper Saddle River, NJ: Prentice Hall, 2001.

Hamlin, Jesse. "Big Labels Declare War on Used CDs," *San Francisco Chronicle*, 16 June 1993, D1 (Lexis).

Harrison, Crayton. "Apple iTUnes Service Sells Over Five Mil Songs," *Americas Intelligence Wire*, 25 June 2003.

Hay, Carla. "Music Video: Trying to Envision the Future: Rock Acts Weigh Costs/Benefits of Vids," *Billboard*, 13 November 1999, 1.

Henn, Harry G. "The Compulsory License Provision of the U.S. Copyright Law," *Study No. 5 for the Senate Committee on the Judiciary, Copyright Law Revision, Studies Prepared for the Subcommittee on Patents, Trademarks, and Copyrights*, 86th Cong., 2d Sess., 1960.

Heuton, Cheryl. "The Large Get Larger: SFX Purchase of Liberty Continues Run on Stations in Big Markets," *Mediaweek*, 4 December 1995.

Hinkley, David. "Suit Calls CD Prices a Steal — for Companies," *New York Daily News*, 11 July 1966, New York Now section, 2 (Lexis).

Hirsch, Paul. *The Structure of the Popular Music Industry*. Ann Arbor, MI: Institute for Social Research, University of Michigan, 1969.

Holland, Bill. "Labels Lose Legal Ground Over Lax Library of Congress Filings," *Billboard*, 27 February 1993, 1.

Holland, Bill. "Perf. Right Bill on Way to White House," *Billboard*, 28 October 1995, 6.

Holland, Bill. "Justice Dept Investigating Music-Video Fee Collusion," *Billboard*, 2 March 1996, 1.

Holland, Bill. "U.S. Artists Receive First Japanese Rental Royalties," *Billboard*, 7 November 1998, 8.

Holland, Bill. "Foes Swap Barbs Ad Radio Ownership Hearings," *Billboard*, 8 February 2003, 2.

Holland, Bill. "Big Publishing Advances Dry Up for Most New Acts, " *Billboard*, 5 April 2003, 1.

Holland, Bill. "WMG Revises Artist Contracts," *Billboard*, 5 April 2003, 3.

Holland, Bill and Lars Brandle, "Justice Dept Steps Up MusicNet, PressPlay Probe," *Billboard Daily Music News*, Billboard.com, 16 October 2001.

Hull, Geoffrey P. "The Aging of America: The Recording and Broadcasting Industries Awareness of Shifting Demographic Patterns." *NARAS Institute Journal* 1, no. 1 (1977): 3.

Hull, Geoffrey P. "The GATT and the Media: How the Uruguay Round of the General Agreement on Tariffs and Trade Affects Media in the United States." Paper presented at the Southeast Colloquium, Association of Educators in Journalism and Mass Communiation, Law Division, March 1996, Roanoke, VA.

Hull, Geoffrey P. AOL Time Warners Magazine and Music Interests: Good Business Makes Poor Journalism," Paper presented at the Association of Educators in Journalism and Mass Communication Annual Conference, August 2000, Phoenix, AZ.

Hull, Geoffrey P. "The Audio Home Recording Act of 1992: A Digital Dead Duck, or Finally Coming Home to Roost?" *Journal of the Music & Entertainment Industry Educators Association* (spring 2002): 76.

Hutchison, Thomas W. and James A. Progris, "Study Shows Music Biz Graduates Are Given Top Priority," *NARM Sounding Board*, November 1996, 8.

"Intellectual Property and the National Information Infrastructure: A Preliminary Draft of the Report of the Working Group on Intellectual Property Rights, Executive Summary." *Cardozo Arts & Entertainment Law Journal* 13 (1994): 275.

International Federation of Phonographic Industries, *The Recording Industry in Numbers 2002*, London: International Federation of Phonographic Industries, 2002.

Jackson, Joe. "Video Clips: A Personal View," *Billboard*, 16 June 1984, 10.

Jackson, John A. *American Bandstand: Dick Clark and the Making of a Rock 'n' Roll Empire*. New York: Oxford University Press (1997).

Jeffrey, Don. "Atlantas Wax 'n Facts is Hip_and Hot," *Billboard*, 17 July 1993, 93.

Jeffrey, Don. "Acquired by BMG, Private Music Begins a New Age," *Billboard*, 5 February 1994, 6.

Jeffrey, Don. "Musicland Reports Double-Digit Profit Hike in '93," *Billboard*, 12 February 1994, 85.

Jeffrey, Don. "Shrinkage Ebbs at Music/Vid Stores," *Billboard*, 26 November 1994, 63.

Jeffrey, Don. "ASCAP Revamps Live Show System," *Billboard*, 30 September 1995, 10.

Jeffrey, Don. "Embattled Majors Act to Protect Music Stores," *Billboard*, 23 December 1995, 67.

Jeffrey, Don. "Survey, Listening Posts 'Important to Customers," *Billboard*, 8 June 1996, 1.

Jepsen, Cara. "Mainstream Rock Updates Itself," *Billboard*, 20 April 1996, 91.

Jolson-Colburn, Jeffrey. "Merchandisers Call for Study on Used CDs," Dallas Morning News, Thursday, 17 June 1993, 14C.

Jones, Steve. *Rock Formation*. Newbury Park, CA: Sage Publications, 1992.

Josefs, Jai. *Writing Music for Hit Songs*. 2d ed. New York: Schirmer Books, 1996.

Kaberline, Brian. "Used CDs Are Good and Cheap—Unless You Manufacture New Ones," *Kansas City Business Journal*, 18 June 1993, I1 (Lexis).

Kafka, Peter. "The Road to Riches," *Forbes Global*, 7 July 2003, 46.

Kalogerakis, George. "Keeping Score," *Vogue*, May 1996, 170.

Kaplan, Benjamin. *An Unhurried View of Copyright.* New York: Columbia University Press, 1967.

Keat, Paul and Philip K.Y. Young. *Managerial Economics: Economic Tools for Todays Decision Makers.* New York: Macmillan, 1992.

Kipnis, Jill. "Global Music Video Shipments Up 33%," *Billboard*, 19 April 2003, 36.

Knoedelseder, William. *Stiffed: A True Story of MCA, the Music Business and the Mafia.* New York: HarperCollins, 1993.

Kohn, Al and Bob Kohn. *Kohn on Music Licensing.* 3d ed. New York: Aspen Law & Business, 2002.

Kosser, Michael. "Big Hits Mean Big Money," *American Songwriter*, January/February 1995, 34.

Kozak, Roman. "Court Ruling Hits U.S. Importers," *Billboard*, 7 August 1982, 1.

Kramer, Gary. "Record Firm Rule of Thumb Slips from Fickle Public Pulse," *Billboard*, 22 December 1956, 1.

Kronemyer, David E. "The New Payola and the American Record Industry," *Harvard Journal of Law and Public Policy* (summer 1987): 521.

Lacy, Stephen et al. *Media Management.* Hillsdale, NJ: Lawrence Erlbaum, 1993.

Leeds, Jeff. "Sony and Incubus Reach New Agreement," *Los Angeles Times*, 11 April 2003, Business, Part 3, 1.

Leonard, Devin. "Songs in the Key of Steve: Steve Jobs May Have Just Created the First Great Legal Online Music Service. Thats Got the Record Biz Singing His Praises," *Fortune*, 12 May 2003, 52.

Levenson, Jeff. "BET to Bow Jazz Network," *Billboard*, 2 October 1993, 8.

Levin, Mike. "PolyGram NV Buys 50% of MTV Asia," *Billboard*, 29 April 1995, 5.

Lewis, Lisa A. *Gender Politics and MTV.* Philadelphia, PA: Temple University Press, 1990.

Lichtman, Irv. "King Karol Tests Disk Rental Idea," *Billboard*, 16 May 1981, 1.

Lichtman, Irv. "More Key Labels Sever Indie Ties," *Billboard*, 15 March 1986, 1.

Lichtman, Irv. "War Waged on Words: Pubs Expand A&R Role," *Billboard*, 26 December 1992, 22.

Lichtman, Irv. "Sony Establishes New Vigor in Market Share," *Billboard*, 17 April 1993, 1.

Lichtman, Irv. "Firth Says BMG Publishing Can Double Biz in 5 Years," *Billboard*, 10 July 1993, 6.

Lichtman, Irv. "Strong NMPA Stats in Past Indicate Happy Times Now," *Billboard*, 25 December 1993, 24.

Lichtman, Irv. "WB Publications Agrees to Buy C.P.P./Belwin," *Billboard*, 7 May 1994, 6.

Lichtman, Irv. "SESAC Boosts Profile with Dylan, Diamond Signings," *Billboard*, 4 February 1995.

Lichtman, Irv. "Sony Pub Adds Nile Rogers, Fisher Catalogs," *Billboard*, 17 June 1995, 14.

Lichtman, Irv. "Famous to BMG in Global Shift," *Billboard*, 28 October 1995, 1.

Lichtman, Irv. "1995 a Year of Deals, Court Action, and Legislation," *Billboard*, 23 December 1995, 57.

Lichtman, Irv. "MCA Music Eyes 'Mid-Size' Power," *Billboard*, 4 May 1996, 39.

Lichtman, Irv. "Japan Hops to 2nd in NMPA Survey," *Billboard*, 20 July 1996, 34.

Lichtman, Irv. "ASCAP Marks 10% Growth in 1999 Revenue," *Billboard*, 19 February 2000, 10.

Lichtman, Irv. "RIAA, HFA Set Digital Licensing Procedures," *Billboard*, 21 October 2000, 4.

Lindey, Alexander. *Lindey on Entertainment, Publishing, and the Arts: Agreements and the Law.* Deerfield, IL : Clark Boardman Callaghan, 2002.

Lipton, Beth. "Sony Seeks Musician Domain Names for Life," *CNET*, 15 September 1999. Retrieved from home.cnet.com/category/0-1005-200-120262.html

Lull, James. "Popular Music and Communication," in *Popular Music and Communication.* 2d ed. Newbury, CA: Sage Publications, 1992.

MacDougall, John. "Small Record Stores Feud with Big Distributors Over Used CDs," *Houston Business Journal*, 21 June 1993, I1 (Lexis).

Macy, Amy Sue. "Country and Christian Music Sales Shine in the Wake of the Terrorist Attacks," *Tennessees Business* 11, no. 2 (2002): 29–33.

Malueg, David A. and Marius Schwartz. "Parallel Imports, Demand Dispersion, and International Price Discrimination." *Journal of International Economics* 37 (1994): 167.

Mandrell, Jim. *The Studio Business Book.* 2d ed. Los Angeles, CA: First House Press, 1995.

Marco, Guy A. *Encyclopedia of Recorded Sound in the United States.* New York: Garland Publishing, 1993.

Marlowe, Chris. "Roxio Tunes into PressPlay: $30 Mil to Buy Sony-UMC Service," *Hollywood Reporter*, 19 May 2003, 4.

Marty, Daniel. *The Illustrated History of Talking Machines.* Lausanne, Switzerland: Edita, 1981.

Mateja, Jim. "U.S. DVD Sales Rise," *Americas Intelligence Wire,* 30 July 2003.

Matzer, Marla. "Ticket to Ride," *Brandweek,* 8 July 1996, 20.

Mayfield, Geoff. "Camelot Pulls Live Crew," *Billboard,* 2 May 1987, 87.

Mayfield, Geoff. "Between the Bullets," *Billboard,* 23 December 1996, 106.

McClure, Steve. "Sam Goody Joins Japans Retail Wars," *Billboard,* 2 July 1994, 80.

McClure, Steve. "Tower Records to Open in Seoul," *Billboard,* 9 July 1994, 39.

McClure, Steve. "U.S. Product Rental in Japan to Bring $2.3 Mil. in Royalties," *Billboard,* 25 October 1997, 3.

McConnell, Bill. "Clear Channel Drops Pay-for-Play Deals," *Broadcasting & Cable,* 14 April 2003, 3.

McCormick, Moira. "SoundScan: Boon or Bane for Indies," *Billboard,* 21 March 1992, 14.

McQuail, Dennis. *Mass Communication Theory.* 3d ed. Thousand Oaks, CA: Sage Publications, Inc., 1994.

Mitchell, Gail. "They Write the Songs," *Billboard,* 19 June 1999, 28.

Mondy, R. Wayne and Shane R. Premeaux. *Management Concepts Practices and Skills.* 6th ed. Needham Heights, MA: Allyn & Bacon, 1993.

Moody's Handbook of Common Stocks, Winter 1995. New York: Moody's Inventors Services, Inc. (1996).

Morris, Chris. "FL Clerk Faces Obscenity Charge for Cassette Sale," *Billboard,* 2 May 1987, 1.

Morris, Chris. "Isgro Trial Testimony Bares Payoffs," *Billboard,* 8 September 1990, 1.

Morris, Chris. "George Harrison Wins $11.6 Mill. in Suit vs. Ex-partner," *Billboard,* 3 February 1996, 13.

Morris, Chris. "MCA Purchases 50% of Interscope," *Billboard,* 2 March 1996, 13.

Morris, Chris. "Federal Judge Dismisses Joe Isgro Case," *Billboard,* 13 April 1996, 96.

Morris, Chris. "April Sets Mark Milestones for Alanis, Beatles," *Billboard,* 18 May 1996, 12.

Morris, Edward. "NSAI Blasts Controlled Composition Clause," *Billboard,* 15 January 1994, 8.

Morris, Edward. "Hilley Named President/CEO at Sony Tree," *Billboard,* 5 February 1994, 9.

Morris, Edward. "SESAC Puts out Its Welcome Mat," *Billboard,* 26 February 1994, 13.

Morris, Edward. "NCN Cites $1.1 Mil Paid for Use of Music Videos," *Billboard,* 29 May 1995, 26.

National Association of Recording Merchandisers, Inc. *What UPC Means to the Recording Industry,* 1979.

National Music Publishers Association. *International Survey of Music Publishing Revenues.* New York: National Music Publishers Association, 1991.

Newman, Melinda. "Joel Wins Another Round in Suit vs. Ex-manager," *Billboard,* 20 March 1993, 12.

Newman, Melinda. "Colleagues Recall Huletts Cutting-Edge Tour Biz Work," *Billboard,* 14 August 1993, 10.

Newman, Melinda. "The A&R Angle," *Billboard,* 3 June 1995, 53.

Newman, Melinda. "Consumer Music Mags Win Clout," *Billboard,* 23 December 1995, 1, at 105.

Newman, Melinda and Thom Duffy, "PolyGram Enters Concert Biz With Scher," *Billboard,* 6 October 1990, 1.

Nimmer, David. "The End of Copyright." *Vanderbilt Law Review* 48 (1995): 1385.

Nimmer, David and Melville Nimmer. *Nimmer on Copyright.* New York: Matthew Bender, 2002.

Novia, Tony. "Is CHR an Endangered Species?" *R&R,* 10 May 1996, 28.

Nunziata, Susan. "Harrison, ABKCO Suit 'Fineally Ending After 20 Years," *Billboard,* 1 December 1990, 80.

Nunziata, Susan. "CD Plants Expand in Anticipation of Business Boom," *Billboard,* 25 July 1992, 6.

Nunziata, Susan. "Bodyguard Album, Single Soar at Sales Counters," *Billboard,* 16 January 1993, 10.

Oland, Pamela Phillips. *You Can Write Great Lyrics.* Cincinnati, OH: Writers Digest Books, 1989.

Oppelaar, Justin. "Chicks, Sony Hatch Deal, End Lawsuits," *Daily Variety,* 18 June 2002, 6.

Oppelaar, Justin. "Napster Goes Legit: Roxio Buys Pressplay for Legal File Sharing," *Daily Variety,* 20 May 2003, 5.

Oppelaar, Justin. "WMG Slips Disc Ops: AOL TW Sells DVD, CD Unit to Canuck Firm Cinram," *Daily Variety,* 21 July 2003, 10.

Paoletta, Michael. "Williams Seeks to Break in the U.S." *Billboard,* 29 March 2003, 1.

Passman, Donald S. *All You Need to Know About the Music Business.* New York: Simon & Schuster, 2000.

Paulson, Daily. "Live on the Internet: The Interactive Music Scene," *Computer Shopper,* May 1996, C4.

Pavlik, John V. *New Media and the Information Superhighway.* Needham Heights, MA: Allyn and Bacon, 1996.

Peter, J. Paul and James H. Donnelly, Jr., *Marketing Management: Knowledge and Skills.* Plano, TX: Business Publications, Inc., 1986.

Peterson, Richard A. and David G. Berger. "Measuring Industry Concentration, Diversity, and Innovation in Popular Music." *American Sociological Review* 61 (1996): 175.

Petrozzello, Donna. "Radio Group Heads Foresee Consolidation, Format Diversity," *Broadcasting & Cable,* 24 October 1994, 3.

Petrozzello, Donna. "Alternative Rock in the Mainstream," *Broadcasting & Cable,* 20 May 1996, 51.

Phalen, Tom. "Easy Street Stores a Family Affair," *Billboard,* 20 November 1993, 93.

Philips, Chuck. "Wherehouse Ups Ante in Used CDs," *Los Angeles Times,* 29 June 1993, F3 (Lexis).

Philips, Chuck. "Clear Channel Fined Just $8,000 by FCC for Payola Violation," *Los Angeles Times,* 20 October 2000, C1.

Philips, Chuck. "Clear Channel Seeks Direct Connection to Record Labels," *Los Angeles Times,* 9 March 2001, C1.

Philips, Chuck. "Logs Link Payments with Radio Airplay," *Los Angeles Times,* 29 May 2001, Tuesday Home Edition, A11.

Practising Law Institute. *Counseling Clients in the Entertainment Industry.* New York: PLI, 1994; 2003.

Price, Deborah Evans. "Benson, Z Musics Retail Team Up," *Billboard,* 20 May 1995.

Price, Deborah Evans. "Sony Adds to Country Music," *Billboard,* 7 October 1995, 74.

Price, Deborah Evans. "Christian Music Searches for Sales Strength for its Journey," *Billboard,* 13 January 1996, 1.

Price, Deborah Evans. "Writer-Producers Churn Out Hits in Music City," *Billboard,* 20 April 1996, 38.

Pride, Dominic. "W. H. Smith Plans to Add More Bricks to the Wall," *Billboard,* 4 September 1993, 12.

Pride, Dominic and Melinda Newman, "MTV Deal Marks Strategy Shift for Sony," *Billboard,* 12 November 1994, 5.

Rathburn, Elizabeth H. "The Reordering of Radio," *Broadcasting & Cable,* 1 July 1996, 6.

Recording Industry Association of America, *Gold and Platinum Record Awards.* New York: RIAA (1984).

Reibman, Greg. "Bostons Don Law Launches Ticketing Firm," *Billboard,* 3 February 1996, 6.

Ressner, Jeffrey. "You Cant Always Get What You Want," *Rolling Stone,* 3 September 1992, 13, 80.

Ringer, Barbara. "The Unauthorized Duplication of Sound Recordings" (1957). *Study No. 26 for the Senate Committee on the Judiciary, Copyright Law Revision, Studies Prepared for the Subcommittee on Patents, Trademarks, and Copyrights,* 86th Cong., 2d Sess., 1960.

Robinson, Deanna Campbell et al. *Music at the Margins.* Newbury Park, CA: Sage Publications, 1991.

Rogers, Robert P. and John R. Woodbury. "Market Structure, Program Diversity, and Radio Audience Size," *Contemporary Economic Policy* (January 1996): 81.

Roland, Tom. "Not an Easy Way to Make a Buck," *The Tennessean,* 5 January 1995, E1.

Roland, Tom. "Record Labels Debate Research," *The Tennessean,* 5 June 1995, Business Section, 1.

Rolontz, Bob. "72 Labels Landed on Charts in '58—a Feverish Year," *Billboard,* 5 January 1959, 3.

Rolontz, Bob. "Disk Clubs Zoom to 2 Mil Subscribers," *Billboard,* 5 October 1959, 1.

Rolontz, Bob. "Artist Pressure Liberalizing Standard Record Contracts," *Billboard,* 19 December 1960, 2.

Rosen, Craig. "Wherehouse Suit Hits Used CD Policies," *Billboard,* 31 July 1993, 8.

Rosen, Craig. "Used CD Rivals Near Truce," *Billboard,* 11 September 1993, 1.

Rosen, Craig. "MCA Publishing Lands New Talent," *Billboard,* 28 October 1995, 46.

Rosen, Craig. "CD Singles Spurred by Addition of Non-Album Cuts," *Billboard,* 30 March 1996, 5.

Rosen, Craig and Ed Christman, "Retailers Sound Used CD Alarm," *Billboard,* 7 December 1971, 1.

Rosenblum, Trudi Miller. "Audiobooks Aimed at Record Stores," *Billboard,* 15 July 1995, 61.

Rosenthal, Edward and Jeanne Hamburg. "Are 'Net Providers Liable for Users Infringement?" *National Law Journal* (12 February 1996): C4.

Rosenzweig, David. "Executive Fined in Fonovisa Payola Case." *Los Angeles Times,* 24 July 2001, III6.

Russell, Deborah. "Austin Scene Spawns Vid Network," *Billboard,* 7 May 1994, 44.

Russell, Deborah. "No Art to Making Vid a Class Act," *Billboard,* 11 June 1994, 56.

Russell, Deborah. "Video Kills the Radio Star," *Billboard 100th Anniversary Issue 1894–1994,* 1 November 1994, 196.

Sandler, Adam. "FTC Subpoenas Record Distribs in Used CD Case," *Daily Variety,* 3 May 1994, 1.

Sanjek, Russell and David Sanjek. *American Popular Music Business in the 20th Century.* New York: Oxford University Press, 1991.

Schlager, Ken. "On The Boards, 1894–1920," *Billboard 100th Anniversary Issue,* 1994, 18.

Schoepe, Zenon. "Management Maven," *1996 Performance Guide: Talent/PM,* 1996, 6.

Schwichtenberg, Cathy. "Music Video: The Popular Pleasures of Visual Music," in Lull, James. *Popular Music in Mass Communication,* 2d ed. Newbury, CA: Sage Publications, 1992.

Seay, David. "The Sound of Movie Music," *Billboard,* 3 April 1993, S3.

Segrave, Kerry. *Payola in the Music Business: A History 1880—1991.* Jefferson, NC: McFarland, 1994.

Seideman, Tony. "Four Labels Ink Vidclip Deals with MTV," *Billboard,* 23 June 1984, 1.

Severin, Werner J. and James W. Tankard, Jr. *Communication Theories: Origins, Methods and Used in the Mass Media.* 3d ed. White Plains, NY: Longman, 1988.

Shields, Steven O. *"Creativity and Creative Control in the Work of American Radio Announcers."* Paper presented to the Association for Education in Journalism and Mass Communication annual meeting, Minneapolis, MN, August 1990.

Shemel, Sidney and M. Willliam Krasilovsky. *This Business of Music.* 8th ed. New York: Billboard Publications, 2000.

Sidak, J. Gregory and David E. Kronemyer. "The New Payola and the American Record Industry," *Harvard Journal of Law and Public Policy* (summer 1987): 521.

Silverman, Tom. "Preserving Diversity in the Music Biz," *Billboard,* 18 May 1996, 6.

Skinner, Liz. "Bling! Bling! Ka-Ching! Products Get Play for Love and Money," *Billboard,* 31 May 2003, 1.

Sobel, Lionel S. "Regulation of Talent Agents and Managers: Registration and Licensing Requirements for Those Who Seek Employment for Entertainment Industry Talent" In *American Bar Association Forum on the Entertainment and Sports Industries 1996 Annual Meeting, Vol II.,* 1996.

Spahr, Wolfgang. "Movie Soundtracks Start Moving Units in Germany," *Billboard,* 17 September 1994, 50.

Spethmann, Betsy. "Sponsors Sing a Profitable Tune with Event Promos," *Brandweek,* 24 August 1994, 20.

Standard & Poor's Stock Reports, February 1996 (vol. D–K) New York: McGraw-Hill (1996).

Stander, Kevin. "Used CDs Integral to Industry," *Billboard,* 14 August 1993, 4.

Stein, Howard and Ronald Zalkind. *Promoting Rock Concerts.* New York: Schirmer Books, 1979.

Steinwand, Chris. "An Industry in Transition, Part I," *Pro Sound News,* October 2001, 26.

Stern, Kevin E. "The High Cost of Convenience: Antitrust Law Violations in the Computerized Ticketing Services Industry," *Hastings Comm/Ent Law Journal* 16 (1994): 349.

Stewart, Al. "Suppliers Weigh $14.95 Vid Prices," *Billboard,* 1 April 1989, 1.

Stratton, Jon. "Capitalism and Romantic Ideology in the Record Business," *Popular Music* 3 (1993): 183.

Strauss, Neil. "Pennies That Add Up to $16.98: Why CDs Cost So Much," *New York Times,* 5 July 1995, Final edition, C11 (Lexis).

Sutherland, Sam. "Taping Losses Near $3 Billion," *Billboard,* 3 April 1982, 1.

Taylor, Chuck. "Format Issues Tackled at Gavin Seminar, " *Billboard,* 24 February 1996, 90.

Teather, David. "Birth of a New Media Monster: Vivendi and GE in Exclusive Talks on Dollars 13 bn Merger ," *The Guardian,* 3 September 2002, City Pages, 19.

Terry, Ken."Labels to Billboard: Balance New POS Charting System," *Billboard,* 1 June 1991, 1.

Thigpen, David. "Are They Worth All That Cash?" *Time,* 29 January 1996, 54.

Traiman, Steve. "Finally, Retailers Get Smitten by 'CD ROMance," *Billboard,* 25 February 1995, 76.

Traiman, Steve. "Publishers, Music Licensing Groups Seek Rights on Info Superhighway," *Billboard*, 10 June 1995, 39.

United States Code, Title 17 § 101, *et seq.* (Copyright).

United States Department of Commerce, Bureau of Statistics. *Statistical Abstract of the United States, 2002.* Washington, DC: U.S. Department of Commerce, Bureau of the Census, 2002.

Verna, Paul. "Ogden Acquires 50% of Metropolitan," *Billboard*, 16 September 1995, 5.

Verna, Paul. "RIAA Report Shows Stagnant '95 Shipments for Music, Video," *Billboard*, 2 March 1996, 3.

Vogel, Harold L. *Entertainment Industry Economics.* New York: Cambridge University Press, 1986.

Waddell, Ray. "SFX Buys Three Concert Promoters," *Billboard*, 27 December 1997, 98.

Waddell, Ray. "Concert Outlook Bright as Biz Weighs Mega-Merger," *Billboard*, 11 March 2000, 1.

Waddell, Ray. "Slater Sells Metropolitan to Clear Channel Entertainment," *Billboard*, 21 December 2002, 7.

Waddell, Ray. "The Top Tours of 2002," *Billboard*, 28 December 2002, YE-16.

Walsh, Christopher. "Recording Studios Squeezed as Labels Tighten Budgets," *Billboard*, 15 February 2003, 1.

Warner Communications, Inc. "The Prerecorded Music Market: An Industry Survey." *NARAS Institute Journal* 2, no. 1 (1978): 78.

Webb-Pressler, Margaret. "The Unsound of Music," *Washington Post*, 29 April 1995, C1.

Whitburn, Joel. *Joel Whitburns Pop Singles Annual 1955–1986.* Menomee Falls, WI: Record Research, Inc., 1987.

Whitburn, Joel. *Top Country Singles 1944–1988*, Menomonee Falls, WI: Record Research, Inc., 1989.

White, Adam. "Villain: Home Taping," *Billboard*, 5 January 1980, 3.

Willis, Jim and Diane B. Willis. *New Directions in Media Management.* Needham Heights, MA: Allyn & Bacon, 1993.

Woo, Junda. "Publisher Sues CompuServe Over a Song," *Wall Street Journal*, 16 December 1993, B1, B16.

Wyatt, Robert O. and Geoffrey P Hull. "The Music Critic in the American Press: A Nationwide Survey of Newspapers and Magazines." *Mass Comm Review* 17, no. 3 (1990): 38.

Yoshida, Junko. "Startup Turns Up Its Online Radio; Progressive Nets Plays Real-Time Audio," *Electronic Engineering Times*, 10 April 1995, 1.

Zimmerman, Kevin. "Security in the Eye of Summer Storms," *Variety*, 5 August 1991, 56.

Zimmerman, Kevin. "Rap Braces for Big Chill," *Variety*, 6 January 1992, 89.

Index